SPIRIT OF
TIME AND PLACE

Books by HORACE GREGORY

POETRY

Chelsea Rooming House
A Wreath for Margery
No Retreat
Chorus for Survival
Poems 1930–1940
Selected Poems
Medusa in Gramercy Park
Alphabet for Joanna
Collected Poems

PROSE

Pilgrim of the Apocalypse: A STUDY OF D. H. LAWRENCE
The Shield of Achilles: ESSAYS ON BELIEFS IN POETRY
A History of American Poetry 1900–1940 (in collaboration with Marya Zaturenska)
Amy Lowell: PORTRAIT OF THE POET IN HER TIME
The World of James McNeill Whistler
The Dying Gladiators and Other Essays
Dorothy Richardson: AN ADVENTURE IN SELF-DISCOVERY
The House on Jefferson Street: A CYCLE OF MEMORIES

Translations

The Poems of Catullus
Ovid's Metamorphoses
Love Poems of Ovid

Editor

New Letters in America
The Triumph of Life: AN ANTHOLOGY OF DEVOTIONAL AND ELEGIAC VERSE
The Portable Sherwood Anderson
The Snake Lady and Other Stories of Vernon Lee
Selected Poems of Robert Browning (Rinehart Editions)
Evangeline and Other Poems by Henry Wadsworth Longfellow
Selected Poems of E. E. Cummings
The Mentor Book of Religious Verse (in collaboration with Marya Zaturenska)
The Crystal Cabinet: AN INVITATION TO POETRY (in collaboration with Marya Zaturenska)
The Silver Swan: POEMS OF ROMANCE AND MYSTERY (in collaboration with Marya Zaturenska)
Selected Poems of George Gordon, Lord Byron

SPIRIT OF TIME AND PLACE

Collected Essays of

Horace Gregory

W · W · NORTON & COMPANY · INC ·

NEW YORK

First Edition

Library of Congress Cataloging in Publication Data

Gregory, Horace, 1898–
Spirit of time and place.

Includes most writings from The shield of Achilles (1944) and The dying gladiators (1961) in revised form.
1. English literature—Addresses, essays, lectures.
I. Title.
PR99.G6854 820'.9 72-10090
ISBN 0-393-04265-0

Published simultaneously in Canada
by George J. McLeod Limited, Toronto

PRINTED IN THE UNITED STATES OF AMERICA

1 2 3 4 5 6 7 8 9 0

For

Samuel Beckett

IN GRATITUDE FOR HIS WRITINGS

AND HIS EXAMPLE

CONTENTS

PREFACE

The present collection of essays, not unlike certain books of collected poems, has been in the making for more than several years. It covers a period of writing from the mid-1930s to 1971, years of many startling revivals and changes in feeling and thinking. In the writing and revision of the essays, I like to think that the Muse of History guided my hand, a muse closely related to memory and poetic perception. Whatever insights I may lay claim to have their sources in those beginnings. Thus the revisions are substantive, rather than a matter of "updating"; references to time reflect literary tastes, fashions, or currents, as well as speculations about the future at the period when each essay was written—which is made clear by the date following each piece.

This collection includes most of the writings of two earlier books. *The Shield of Achilles* (1944) and *The Dying Gladiators* (1961). And what did the title of the first book mean?

Since the shield has been best described by Homer, and since poetry carries with it certain ambiguities, I can not be too ruthlessly dogmatic in speaking of its meaning. I select the following associations that the shield brings to mind. Hephaestus, artist and ironmonger like so many modern sculptors, was the maker of the shield, and his work of art was a gift to Achilles. It was made to be useful as well as beautiful, and there is nothing obscure about the use that Achilles made of it. The true question arises when we consider the care with which Homer described it. It is then that we begin to perceive the many images, the many details of active life reflected on the surface of the shield: there one looks upward to huge Orion and the Bear and below them to the scenes of war and peace on earth. As in an epiphany the entire universe is revealed. Shall we say that the description of the shield and its creation provides an analogy to and a criterion for the writing of poetry? I would say it does. Perhaps the story of the shield was in fact the statement—so far as he cared to make it—of Homer's esthetic, which contained a large measure of morality and showed the relationship between men and gods. However that may be, the legend of the shield remains a valid criterion for the writing and the criticism of poetry in any age; and today its associations of war and peace in respect to human activity are of greater importance than they were before two great world wars. It is probable that the period beginning in 1914 marks the presence of another Hundred Years' War and that future ages will call it "The Decline of the British Empire"; a period, which at its end, shored up its ruins, leaving England as the new Athens—much reduced in material power in a semibarbaric world. But to return to the shield as it shows forth the creative act: I wish to make it clear that I do not believe "art is a weapon," but I do believe that a weapon, if finely tempered and accurate can resemble in the seriousness of its purpose a work of art. All the writers I have mentioned in this book have created with variable success an Achilles' shield with which to face the world.

The title of the second book of essays, *The Dying Gladiators*, refers to an early appreciation I wrote of the *dramatis personae* of Samuel Beckett. It is the best that I can do, yet I wish it were far better, for Beckett is, I believe, a dramatic poet of the first order, living through an age when the writing of actual poetry has become increasingly rare.

The essays I have assembled here have their own points of interrelationship—even those as far apart as the note on Edwin Muir and "Guns of the Roaring West," which is a commentary on American subculture: the point in common is the heritage come down to us from the ballads of the Scottish border. In Muir's case the result was poetry of quiet simplicity and power. And in the case of its transoceanic-transcontinental mutations, far west, indeed, of Saturn, the result was an inflated TV vision of the cowboy with his guitar. The reader will find, I think, other interrelationships within the book that I hope will reilluminate its principal figures and ideas. And now, since I have described the intentions of the book this far, perhaps a few words should be said about critics and criticism.

For my part, I believe the responsible critic should attempt to establish a parity between whatever he thinks is good and the very manner in which he voices his opinion. So far, at least, his position becomes that of the artist. He should not allow his writings to drop into the clichés of his own day. Following this line, one of his most important services is to guide his readers away from "the beaten track." He should encourage rediscoveries in reading. He should not be intimidated by the past nor fearful of new ideas. It should be taken for granted that he is well-informed enough not to spread misinformation through ignorance.

I hope I have not made my idea of a responsible critic too unearthly to be believed—or too ideal for myself to emulate. As a last touch to his portrait, he should have the courage of his own—not other men's—convictions.

1 January 1972
Palisades, New York

HORACE GREGORY

Acknowledgments

Earlier versions of these essays have appeared in a variety of periodicals and collections. Although many of the pieces have been considerably rewritten, I will owe special debts to the editors who encouraged me to write them and, in particular, I want to thank Mrs. Arabel Porter of *New World Writing*, Philip Rahv of *Modern Writing*, Francis Brown of *The New York Times Book Review*, the late Morton Dauwen Zabel of *Poetry* and to The English Institute for the opportunity to lecture on Wordsworth, Alice and her White Knight at Columbia University, New York City, during September 1941. I owe a debt of gratitude to Barney Rosset for suggesting that I make a collection of my essays; and I want to thank Diana Pollack and Marilynn Meeker for help in preparation of this book.

SPIRIT OF
TIME AND PLACE

THE SHIELD OF ACHILLES

ON SAMUEL JOHNSON IN THE TWENTIETH CENTURY

A new edition of Samuel Johnson's *Poems*[1] is on the library table, its pages freshly cut, its magnificent typeface visible to all who enjoy the reading of a well-printed and sensibly bound book. The book is an expensive luxury, and being what it is, a book of poems, and many of them in Latin, it is quite impossible to think of it being loaned from the stationery shop, "Where fiction flourishes," one almost says, "and arts decay." The book has been the patient, brilliant, cautious labor of almost twenty years in research by two editors, a work of collaboration which bridges the Atlantic westward, using the resources of the Huntington and Yale libraries, and publishing for the first time in a complete collection of Johnson's verse some half a hundred pieces, including translations into English of the Latin and Greek mottoes and quotations in *The Rambler*. The result is, I repeat, a beautiful book—and a luxury—and I am reminded, perhaps irreverently, of the protest that Samuel Johnson wrote to the printers at Oxford concerning the high prices of their fine books. That was almost two hundred years ago, and I am reassured that human nature as well as its learning process, even in universities, may change with time for better or for worse, but the progress, whenever it moves, is very, very slow.

As one turns the pages of Johnson's *Poems* in their new dress, many questions are opened to the mind, and the first of these is a test of our general interest in the eighteenth century. Why is Johnson's verse revived today, and why is it that both his verse and prose awaken respect as well as curiosity? Two generations ago quotations from Boswell's *Life of Johnson* occasioned more amusement than enjoyment or a serious regard, and the occasion (inspired perhaps by readings of Macaulay, Thackeray, and Taine) was a signal for hilarity rather than serious regard. But to continue with our question: Is the revival of Johnson a mere turning of the wheel that raises the fame of one writer and his age and obscures the others, a recurrent movement accompanied by the cries of "Down with Shelley, up with Pope; it is growing far too late for Donne and

[1] *The Poems of Samuel Johnson*, edited by David Nichol Smith and Edward L. McAdam. Oxford: The Clarendon Press, 1941. (Originally priced at $7.50, this book would be considered inexpensive today, 1971.)

Crashaw, therefore, up with Johnson—and do not forget that excellent though neglected poet, Christopher Smart"? Is our interest in Johnson's major writings, his "Lives" of Milton, Savage, and Pope, *The Vanity of Human Wishes* and his *London* a subconscious desire to unsay Wordsworth's *Preface* to the second edition of the *Lyrical Ballads*—that preface which was written in the wraithlike but resounding presence of Johnson's authority and which dispelled that shadow for a hundred years to come? I think not. Nor is our general curiosity concerning an age that was devout, and yet followed the lights of reason, a complete rejection of all nineteenth-century notions of progress in the worship of scientific skills and innovations. This general question, no matter how briefly answered, and in which I may have seemed to persist at length, supplies a key and perhaps unlocks a door to a few of the multiple reasons why Johnson's stature has not decreased during a generation that has felt the earth shake with the impact of two world wars. In times such as our own, all serious writing reflects the strength of radical conviction (and Johnson was decidedly radical in his expression of conservative beliefs), all scenes that mirror the origin of our institutions as they are today attain the power and vividness of a renewed perception into the heart of human activity. In England—and I am thinking of the island and not the near and far reaches of the British Empire—the appeal of an eighteenth-century formality in literary diction, wit, and manner has its own elegiac, and one might say, "romantic" air. It is of the same heightened mood that a young man or woman achieves in a last look about the house before leaving home for foreign lands; the look embraces all things with an unconscious lift of being: chairs, tables, doors, and windows take on the quality of animate life and seem to speak; and for the first time, each in its proper place acquires meanings that hitherto had been left in darkness, and until this moment had been unfelt, unknown. Something of that sensibility, which one hesitates to call "emotion," has been conveyed by Edith Sitwell's book on Bath and in her *Alexander Pope;* and one finds that in her literary essays Virginia Woolf is at her happiest when she brings to mind Dr. Burney's evening parties in Poland Street, or the masks that Horace Walpole wore to face the world. These are tributes written to a past which has an imaginative being within the present, but is perceived in years of crisis as though it were seen for the last time. On our side of the Atlantic—and may we take it as a symbol that the senior editor of Johnson's *Poems* is David Nichol Smith and that his collaborator, Edward McAdam, is an American—on our side of the water? The memory of eighteenth-century imagination and its initiative revives the day that saw the birth of our governmental institutions; and remembering them, we accept the contradictions of our national heroes, Washington, Adams, Hamilton, Marshall, and Jefferson, as a peculiarly American complex whose continuity remains unbroken and today reasserts its claim to an enduring life.

We can then agree, I think, that with all the visible changes which have taken place in the last two hundred years, differences in dress, in architecture, in social habit, in modes of speech and of travel, our general outlook toward the eighteenth century is neither disinterested, nor unreasonably cold. But in speaking of so broad a view and looking into the new edition of Johnson's *Poems,* another question rises: What of Johnson's view, how far did it go, was it clear or clouded; did it run farther than that queer distance he described "from China to Peru," by air or land or sea, and did it in a final glance embrace the world? That is a pertinent question in a day when world views are extremely popular and the names of many places ring in our ears. We wait for news from foreign correspondents, we rely on photographs of distant towns and cities, and some of us have perfected the art of tuning in casually on the short-wave of the bright-dialed radio; the view is globular and swift, but not, I fear, completely translatable to sight and feeling on the written page. In articles and even in books of considerable bulk written by experts, so I have heard, of world affairs, the *Weltanschauung* grows thin with the blue of empyrean distances: whole nations, plateaus, valleys, mountain ranges, and even continents are bombed off the earth, replanned, and perhaps repopulated within a single paragraph; the world view, since we must have it, is still there, but its skirts (if I may change the figure) are of sheerest organdy, and the lady looks shameless, anemic, and about to perish in a winter storm. A world view of this sort, I must confess, does not appear in Johnson's prose or verse, nor does a world view of another kind, and of a sort expressed by the deliberate philosopher, a Thomas Hobbes, a Bishop Berkeley, or a Professor Whitehead, enter the central stream of Johnson's morality. Despite the strength of Johnson's will and mind, it would be possible to argue that he was not an intellectual at all, and if we insist upon reading a world view into the content of Johnson's verse we must speak in terms of a theology nourished by the Anglican Church, and then agree that it was of a different order than that which possessed the imagination of his peers.

It is of some significance to know that in conversation Johnson's vowels were spoken with the same accent which marked the speech of his fellow countrymen at Lichfield, and that many years of living in the city of London could not alter them. David Garrick, mimicking his old schoolmaster's voice, rolling head and heaving shoulders, once shouted, "Who's for *poonsh?*" to the great joy of the assembled company. One need not labor the point that Johnson was firmly of his time and place, and more than that, was at least two decades behind the moment at which his influence was most deeply felt. If it can be said that one drop of provincialism in a man's blood makes all mankind his kin, then Johnson's heavy frame and swelling veins contained a full pint of that heady liquor. At the moment of his celebrity in London he moved as an ancient Titan in the company of a highly self-conscious and sophisticated group of young and active men; he was the father of their "Literary Club," voicing taboos and parental discriminations among its members; his corpulent figure was the totem of their belief, and his contrasting fits of kindness, or anger, or of despair were the signs of his all-too-human relationship to earth. He entered the latter and declining years of the Augustan Age with the conventions of Queen Anne's day unflawed, untarnished: From the sources of Juvenal, Horace, Dryden, and Pope he drew sustenance for the external forms of his literary style, and it should be added that however well he knew his Greek, his skills were Latin, corresponding to the usefulness, the spans, and masses of the Roman aqueduct. But the melancholy strains within the forms, transfiguring the style and making it his own, were not of the European continent nor of its southern peninsulas:

> Year chases year, decay pursues decay,
> Still drops some joy from with'ring life away.

These strains are of a northern heritage, sounded in the epic of *Beowulf* and heard within the soliloquies of *Hamlet* and *Macbeth,* and their last echoes are resumed beyond Johnson's century in the dramatic verse of Henrik Ibsen. Perhaps it could be said that something which resembles or runs parallel to a *Weltanschauung* has been conveyed within the measures that define the melancholy temper, but we can say that all poetry worthy of our admiration enjoys a happy paradox of seeming most universal when it is most at home, voiced in a language that intones a familiar tongue and is sheltered by the protection of its own rooftree. In this sense Johnson's major verse as it is represented by *The Vanity of Human Wishes* has elements of greatness that place it within comparable reaches of Gray's *Elegy Written in a Country Churchyard* and Wordsworth's *Resolution and Independence.* It was Johnson's profound look inward to the passion of life beyond youth and its felicity that endowed his *Human Wishes* with a somber heat, and this perception, however else we may define it, is what we mean when we speak of a writer who possesses "a tragic sense of life."

Of Johnson the moralist—and his morality was of the same root from which his melancholy sprang—it can be said that one finds him less oppressive and certainly less static than he seemed a generation or two ago. His texts for sermons, for the language that he wrote closely resembled the idiom of the pulpit in his day, were drawn from lively observations of the scene around him, a habit which he may have learned from an attentive reading of Dryden and Juvenal, but which, I think, owes a slighter debt to literary influence than to the enforced leisure of his unconquered indolence, to his love of walking through crowded city streets, to his need for company in coffeehouses and to the slow growth of his own literary fame. As indolence increased his sense of guilt, the more urgent was his demand to break its spell, and in that conflict his will was often put to a test of strength between the prospect of lonely hours at his desk or an evening's talk over several bottles of wine. His imitation of Juvenal's *Third Satire*, his *London*, the verses of which Pope had praised and predicted future celebrity for their author, were constantly refreshed and kept in motion by commentary that sharply reflected the diversions of life at the nation's capital. The poem's wealth of contemporary reference was so complete, so vivid in its detail that it has been all too easy for studious readers of it to repeat and to half-accept Sir John Hawkins' claim that "injur'd THALES," who "bids the town farewell," was in fact a portrait of Johnson's old friend, Richard Savage. It seems strange that the editors, neither Smith nor McAdam, sought for a fresh interpretation of the line. For Thales, as we all know, was a wandering Greek philosopher of the seventh century B.C., who left no writings for posterity. It was he who believed that the single imperishable element of worldly life was water, and the Thales of the poem awaits a boat to take him out to sea; the classical reference ignites the wit that follows after, and we who read the poem today had better forget Sir John's attempt at scholarship and take our stand with Boswell who cheerfully denied THALES's identity with Savage, and who knew his Johnson literally like a book.

In reading Johnson's moral verses we must grant that the very terms of his theology have a further reach toward Heaven and a greater depth than any Thales-like spread through flux and motion; and in reading Johnson generally we should be aware of the penetration, the delicate niceties with which he viewed the weaknesses and merits of his fellow men. The motives behind his observations were avowedly critical, but the results as they appear in his verse and prose place Johnson among the more profound psychologists of his age. The moralist who shouted warnings in Mrs. Thrale's drawing room, and in one instance replied to her nephew's question as to whether or not the young man should marry by saying, "I would advise no man to marry, sir, who is not likely to propagate understanding," was at the very least a lexicographer well-schooled in the flaws of human character. The young man happened to be Sir John

Lade, and Johnson afterward commemorated the occasion of his asking an unfortunate question by writing the famous lines of *A Short Song of Congratulation* which appear in Sir Arthur Quiller-Couch's *Oxford Book of English Verse* under the less ironic title of *One-and-Twenty*. But the fine balance with which Johnson weighed and sustained his judgments of human flaws and virtues was never better exemplified than in the concluding paragraphs of his *Life of Richard Savage*. The sermon was graced by an extraordinarily vital text, and I think I may be pardoned for quoting this particular passage at length, for the delicacy with which Johnson set his scales cannot be shown by citing isolated phrases:

> He appeared to think himself born to be supported by others, and dispensed from all necessity for providing for himself; he therefore never prosecuted any scheme of advantage, nor endeavored even to secure the profits which his writings might have afforded him. His temper was, in consequence of the dominion of his passions, uncertain and capricious; he was easily engaged and easily disgusted; but he is accused of retaining his hatred more tenaciously than his benevolence.
>
> He was compassionate both by nature and principle, and was always ready to perform offices of humanity; but when he was provoked (and very small offenses were sufficient to provoke him) he would prosecute his revenge with the utmost acrimony till his passion had subsided.
>
> His friendship was therefore of little value; for though he was zealous in the support or vindication of those whom he loved, yet it was always dangerous to trust him, because he considered himself as discharged by the first quarrel from all ties of honor and gratitude, and would betray those secrets which in the warmth of confidence had been imparted to him. This practice drew upon him an universal accusation of ingratitude; nor can it be denied that he was very ready to set himself free from the load of an obligation; for he could not bear to convince himself in a state of dependence, his pride being equally powerful with his other passions, and appearing in the form of insolence at one time and of vanity at another. Vanity, the most innocent species of pride, was most frequently predominant: he could not easily leave off when he had once begun to mention himself or his works; nor ever read his verses without stealing his eyes from the page, to discover in the faces of the audience how they were affected with any favorite passage.

It is here that we recognize in Richard Savage the character of men who are alive today; the individual and the type have by no means vanished from earth, and we know them with the same familiarity that we rediscover Iago, Uncle Toby, Emma Bovary, or Cousin Pons among the faces of our contemporaries. In *Richard*

Savage Johnson revealed the springs of human failure, and his creation walks upon a stage where curtains part and footlights gleam beyond the moment of a merely literary being.

Since we are on the subject of Johnson's *Lives of the Poets*, the occasion presents itself for a glance, however brief at his generally underrated essay on Swift. It is true that Johnson's attitude toward Swift could not be described in terms of unprejudiced affection, for the difference in temperament between the celebrated lexicographer and the late Dean of St. Patrick's would scarcely permit the semblance of a natural rapport. The character of Swift's education whose actual progress took place in Sir William Temple's library was of a seventeenth-century order, and in contrast to his tastes and discriminations, the literary preferences of both Pope and Johnson represented the learning of a new generation in English letters. If Johnson leaned backward in time to the conventions of Queen Anne's day, their limitations were fixed by the new order of an Augustan Age which took pride in acknowledging Dryden as its predecessor. The true gulf between Swift and Pope was of a far greater span than Swift's admiration of Pope's genius indicated, so great indeed that an appreciation of the gifts of one is almost certain to obscure the other's. An intelligent comparison of the *Verses on the Death of Dr. Swift* with Pope's *Epistle to Dr. Arbuthnot* is a near impossibility, and the contrast is all the more obvious because the two poems bear a superficial likeness to each other; both delight the reader by a display of self-knowledge beyond all ordinary wit, yet the moment that delight is gratified, the distinctly separate merits of the two poems assert their individuality; as Swift moves backward to Butler's *Hudibras* and ultimately to the rough pleasantries of Skelton, Pope moves forward from Dryden to anticipate the sensibility of William Collins, and from this point onward all comparison becomes irrelevant. Another illustration of the impassable gulf between the imaginations of Pope and Swift is shown in verse written from a common source of literary inspiration. Both poets had read Ovid with unusual insight, but it is significant that Pope chose *The Heroides* on which to model his *Eloisa to Abelard,* while Swift turned to the *Metamorphoses* for the inspiration of his *Baucis and Philemon.* In his *Baucis* Swift ran closer to the effects produced by the graphic art of Hieronymus Bosch, and incidentally to the twentieth century of Max Ernst and Ives Tanguy than to the world of Pope's *Eloisa* and his *Elegy to the Memory of an Unfortunate Lady.* A quotation from the transformation sense in *Baucis* clearly shows the trend of Swift's direction:

> The Groaning Chair began to crawl
> Like an huge Snail along the Wall;

There stuck aloft, in Publick View,
And with small Change, a Pulpit grew.

The Porringers, that in a Row
Hung high and made a glitt'ring Show,
To a less Noble Substance chang'd,
Were now but Leathern Buckets rang'd.

The Ballads pasted on the Wall
Of *Joan* of *France*, and *English Moll*,
Fair *Rosamond*, and *Robin Hood*,
The *Little Children in the Wood:*
Now seemed to look abundance better,
Improv'd in Picture, Size, and Letter;
And high in Order plac'd, describe
The Heraldry of ev'ry Tribe.

A bedstead of the Antique Mode,
Compact of Timber many a Load,
Such as our Ancestors did use,
Was Metamorphos'd into Pews;
Which still their ancient Nature keep;
By lodging Folks dispos'd to sleep.

The Cottage by such Feats as these,
Grown to a Church by just degrees,
The Hermits then desir'd their Host
To ask for what he fancy'd most:
Philemon, having paus'd a while,
Return'd them Thanks in Homely Stile;
Then said; my House is grown so Fine,
Methinks, I still wou'd call it mine:
I'm Old, and fain wou'd live at Ease,
Make me the *Parson*, if you please.

I can think of no further reach away from the scene of magic which took place in Philemon's cottage than the following lines from *Eloisa to Abelard*, which are as distant, let us say, as the sight of earth from Eloisa's Heaven:

Grace shines around her with serenest beams,
And whisp'ring angels prompt her golden dreams.
For her th' unfading rose of Eden blooms,
And wings of seraphs shed divine perfumes;
For her the spouse prepares the bridal ring;
For her white virgins hymeneals sing;
To sounds of heavenly harps she dies away,
And melts in visions of eternal day.

It is plain enough (as I have more than hinted in the contrasts of Swift's verse with Pope's) that the *Life of Swift* reflects the same cast of mind which steered Johnson's hand as he wrote his famous remarks on the metaphysical poets of the seventeenth century, but the essay, more than all else, is refined and tempered by the need to present the case of Swift with decent clarity and justice; it would be difficult to unsay Johnson's tributes to Swift's originality, or to quarrel with his apt and highly complimentary report of Swift's character from the confidences of Dr. Delany to Lord Orrery. The point is that even here where Johnson's heart was not warmed by his subject, his scale of values was as delicately set as in his *Life of Richard Savage*, and from that balance we find a definition of Swift's style which has not been improved upon since the day that it was written:

> His delight was in simplicity. That he has in his works no metaphor, as has been said, is not true; but his few metaphors seem to be received rather by necessity than choice. . . . His sentences are never too much dilated or contracted; and it will not be easy to find any embarrassment in the complication of his clauses, any inconsequence in his connections, or abruptness in his transitions.

But Johnson's moral instrument, however finely tempered it came to be, was uncommonly slow in taking its proper shape, and surely in the writing of his own verse, Johnson cannot be credited with the brilliance nor accused of the sins of an unlearned precocity. His mistaken venture into poetic drama, his *Irene*, was an early work over which he labored intermittently for ten years. Its production by David Garrick at the Theatre Royal in 1749 crowned its failure, and in the present edition of Johnson's *Poems*, Messrs. Smith and McAdams have erected a veritable Gothic monument of notes over its fallen ruins—a monument, by the way, so attractively placed and garnished that it would have delighted the eye and wit of Horace Walpole. The entire story of the play is told at length, including a memorable quotation from Richard Knolles's *The Generall Historie of the Turkes* from which Johnson received his inspiration, his plot, and the not unseductive figure of his heroine, the beautiful Greek captive, Irene, who had become chief concubine in the household of Sultan Mahomet II. The Sultan's sacrifice of, his murder in fact, of Irene—and this was to appease the critics of his inactivity in war—was neither a happy subject for Johnson's speculations on moral conduct nor was it convincing proof of his heroine's virtues. Nor were Johnson's abilities as a dramatic poet of sufficient energy to convert his lengthy and (it must be admitted) awkward phrasing of moral dialogues into scenes of action. His fortunate choice of epithet in writing verse was of a late maturity and one finds its best examples in the poems written some thirty odd years after the evening which made public *Irene*'s disaster in Drury Lane.

We reread Johnson for his last words rather than his first; and among them his *Irene* and *The Vanity of Human Wishes,* which were presented to public view in the same year, may be looked upon today as signs of a turning point in his literary development. The melancholy strains so distinctly overheard throughout the measures of *The Vanity of Human Wishes* continue their progress in the themes of his shorter verses. As Johnson passed the meridian of middle age, his temperament was emphatically less humanitarian than it was humane, and in this distinction we rediscover the high values that he found in masculine courage, individual integrity, and a devotion to the Christian faith. In his later verse it can be said that he practiced what he preached, and indeed the writing of his verses seemed to improve as the slowly growing volume of his prose enlarged from *An Account of the Life of Mr. Richard Savage* in 1744, through *Rasselas* in 1759, to the *Lives of the Poets* in 1779. Even if we remained unaided by Boswell's biography, the course of Johnson's mature development in verse could be traced in parallel lines to the greater exercise of his critical gifts in prose. It would seem that the authority of one proceeds from the other, until at last we are rewarded by *A Short Song of Congratulation* and his verses *On the Death of Dr. Robert Levet.*

Today we reread them in a friendly spirit, for since the passage of the last two decades, even the unwary reader of verse is considerably less frightened by the presence of a critical attitude as it reveals itself in poetry; and I would say that the discovery of moral aphorisms concealed in verse is far less distressing today than it was before the arrival of poetry written by—to name three dissimilar poets—Thomas Hardy, E. A. Robinson, and T. S. Eliot. Despite Johnson's positive mistrust of metaphysical poets, the revival of their work which caused voluble excitement in literary circles twenty-five years ago, actually paved the road for a renewed awareness of his own merits. The step between a poetry that admits the existence of metaphysical realities and the poetry that expresses the need for religious devotion has always been a short one: in both the presence of a matured poetic intelligence is often happily fused with the creative heat of poetic imagination. It is that intelligence which we rediscover in the following stanzas from Johnson's elegy on Dr. Levet, and in finding it, we are led to appreciate its manly attitudes of religious devotion as well as its sensibility which links the moment of its composition to the poetic imagination of our own day:

Well tried through many a varying year,
See Levet to the grave descend;
Officious, innocent, sincere,
Of ev'ry friendless name the friend.

. . . .

When fainting nature call'd for aid,
And hov'ring death prepar'd the blow,
His vig'rous remedy display'd
The power of art without the show.

. . . .

His virtues walk'd their narrow round,
Nor made a pause, nor left a void;
And sure th' Eternal Master found
The single talent well employ'd.

After reading these lines it is not too much to say that the profound depth of Johnson's piety found its most felicitous expression in a last tribute to the friend who once shared his apartments in Bolt Court—the chaste, industrious, and almost anonymous London physician whose round of practice remained among the poor and was circumscribed by poverty.

Of the many adaptations from Horace that Johnson wrote, none has greater claim to merit than the one which is said to have been written within the last month of his life, on 16 November 1784; and since Johnson's imitations of Horace are not generally known, it seems appropriate to make a full quotation of it here. The fifteenth and sixteenth lines as well as the last two couplets are among the best examples of imitation from the Latin that the eighteenth century has produced, and these were written in an age that regarded Horace as its master and imitation of his work as a fine art:

The snow dissolv'd no more is seen,
The fields, and woods, behold, are green,
The changing year renews the plain,
The rivers know their banks again,
The spritely Nymph and naked Grace
The mazy dance together trace.
The changing year's successive plan
Proclaims mortality to Man.
Rough Winter's blasts to Spring give way,
Spring yields to summer's sovereign ray,
Then Summer sinks in Autumn's reign,
And Winter chills the World again.
Her losses soon the Moon supplies,
But wretched Man, when once he lies
Where Priam and his sons are laid,

Is naught but Ashes and a Shade.
Who knows if Jove who counts our score
Will toss us in a morning more?
What with your friend you nobly share
At least you rescue from your heir.
Not you, Torquatus, boast of Rome,
When Minos once has fix'd your doom,
Or Eloquence, or splendid birth,
Or Virtue shall replace on earth.

Hippolytus unjustly slain
Diana calls to life in vain,
Nor can the might of Theseus rend
The chains of hell that hold his friend.

To read the verse of Johnson's declining years is to hear the voice of a singularly compact and unified literary personality, and I need not, I hope, insist that even in a literature and language which carry within them many diverse figures of a vital and enduring individuality, the phenomenon of a Samuel Johnson is extremely rare. Few writers have achieved his "integration of personality" (the phrase belongs to C. G. Jung, but his figure remains the corpulent lexicographer who received an honorary LL.D. from Oxford); and that state of being is perhaps the most frequently cherished hope of the individual of the present age. In England of the eighteenth century Johnson shared with Fielding and Smollett and even Laurence Sterne the will and authority, the patriarchal strength and tenderness of a wholly masculine genius that has not made its reappearance in British literature of the first order since the death of Thomas Hardy. The vigor of an indigenous wit that Boswell heard when Johnson remarked, "The Irish are a FAIR people, they never speak well of one another," has no voice among living Englishmen today; and since the present edition of his *Poems* has received high praise and affectionate regard in the British press, we can be assured that the voice is not forgotten among a people who have outfaced the terrors of a total war.

1941, 1944

THE DOUBLE VISION IN POPE'S POETRY

To some readers of poetry it may seem extraordinary that Alexander Pope is again reread for pleasure—and not merely for the further search of learning.[1] In universities, in survey courses of English literature, in research studies of eighteenth-century life and manners, Pope has always held his place, a place insured by Matthew Arnold's lecture on translating Homer. Yet the respect he earned came from the lips of middle-aged instructors and lecturers, and not from students. Even as recently as 1916 George Saintsbury with a show of boldness announced "to deny poetry to Pope is absurd," and a few years later, Lytton Strachey attempted what proved to be an artificial defense of Pope's artificiality. At the present hour, particularly among poets as critics, a defense of Pope is gratuitous: his lines are quoted as the title of a book by a popular novelist, and the wheel of fortune, carrying with it the changes of taste and fashion, has restored Pope to his eminence. In the present revivals he has again become the poet's poet, and since such revivals often help to define the temper of the time in which we live, it is a matter of some importance to find out why. I suspect that the present generation has turned from a rediscovery of Donne to a reawakening of Pope.

To reread Pope is to admit some of his failure to command attention from those who lived beyond the age for which he wrote. He was and still remains a topical poet, the acknowledged spokesman of London's brief Augustan Age. In his time, and for a period of nearly thirty years, everything that Pope wrote was in the highest fashion, so much so that no writer of the first half of the eighteenth century in London could claim to be more fashionable than he; and since nothing passes out of fashion more quickly than a highly modish dress in poetry, it is easy to see why the Victorians regarded Pope's poetry as scarcely more than the antiquarian's delight. To the Victorian reader, Pope's wit and polish had the same air of quaintness that today attends Broadway's productions of early plays by Bernard Shaw and Wilde's *Lady Windermere's Fan;* and what once shocked a wary audience of intellectuals and conservatives now holds its attraction as disenchanted costume drama. The serious reader of Pope's

[1] *The Pleasures of Pope,* edited with a foreword by Peter Quennell. New York: Pantheon, 1950.

satire, the *Dunciad,* is still forced to become a student of London's Grub Street as it existed between the years of 1727–43. Ezra Pound, many of whose cantos offer the same difficulties as Pope's great satire, justly complained that the *Dunciad* "needs footnotes longer than the text itself. . . . Such reading is not given for writers. It is a specialized form of archaeology."

Even in his own day adverse criticism of Pope contained charges of too much bookishness, of too many references in his verses that reflected, polished as they were, long labors pursued with the help of coffee and candlelight; and a number of these charges are still pertinent today. Pope's famous abstractions in verse which seemed to carry so much weight and said so little aroused the impatience of so friendly (to Pope at least) a critic as Dr. Johnson. It is still true that Pope was no orderly philosopher in verse, that his industrious essays on man and on criticism were as handsome, as curious, and were derived from as many sources as patchwork quilts contrived by the busy hands of New England spinsters and grandmothers. All this is obvious enough to readers of Pope's verse and these limitations and defects are not likely to be removed by time.

It is natural enough, I think, that the most prominent of Pope's twentieth-century admirers is a woman, and the particular admirer, whose life of Pope was originally published in 1930, is Edith Sitwell, and certainly she is a poet whose work cannot be charged with leaning too heavily in favor of neoclassicism. The legend of Pope's precocity, his deformed and childlike body, the brilliance of the gaze from his large eyes, seldom fails to inspire a maternal, if not matronly, affection. Behind, beyond the legend and within Pope's poetry itself lies a more profound reason for his appeal to feminine and twentieth-century sensibility. Pope's adaptation of a line from one of the Countess of Winchilsea's poems shows an understanding of and an affinity with feminine sensibility that is not accidental; his insights with respect to feminine emotion and intelligence are among the signs of his genius that have so long distinguished him from others who have chosen women as the subject of their verse. His *Eloisa to Abelard* with its seemingly unconscious revelations of sexual imagery, in the confessions of a modest, saintly, half-innocent girl, has in it one of the triumphs of feminine character portrayal in literature. One must turn to Shakespeare's Juliet, to the fiction of Henry James and Proust, to the plays of Euripides to find its equal. Nor is his penetration less revealing in *Elegy to the Memory of an Unfortunate Lady;* and the large success of *The Rape of the Lock* owes much of its imaginative reality to the same source. Pope possessed the rare quality (which in our time was one of the gifts cherished by Virginia Woolf) of seeming to speak *for* women, of seeming to be their partisan whenever he was not their foe; and whenever the occasion of his poetry required it, he proved that he knew women slightly better than they would care to know themselves.

It is no secret that among the preoccupations of the twentieth century, clinical psychology has held and still continues to hold a highly admired place in literature. And feminine psychology as it affects and enters into the emotions of the opposite sex is among the popular themes for speculation upon the contemporary stage. At no time since the Augustan Age itself has there been so marked an interest in the niceties and details of feminine behavior as it appears in the actions of both men and women, and in that sense the present age is more than well prepared to appreciate Pope's remarkable penetration into the hidden recesses of the feminine psyche.

In his own day, Pope's understanding of feminine motives and intellect was unusual enough: Prior, Swift, Johnson, Addison, and Gay, civilized as they were, were content to express with famous bluntness distinctly masculine opinions and attitudes toward women. Compared with their less delicate perception of womankind, Pope's insights often create the illusion of his being wholly possessed by feminine discriminations and responses to the world around him. The truth is that he was not; and we need go no further than his *Epistle to Dr. Arbuthnot* and his verses to Martha Blount to prove that however far his deformity removed him from normal masculine behavior, he was not unsexed. The very circumstances of Pope's life, unhappy as they sometimes were, led to his singular creation of a double vision of nearly everything he saw and felt, overheard and thought.

Pope's deformity reserved for him a place outside the usual ambitions and pursuits of eighteenth-century London's men and women. His "long disease, my life" would not permit indulgence in the excesses of the Augustan Age, excesses in eating, in drinking, in making love, pleasures in which so many of his contemporaries took delight. His father's conversion to the Roman Church cut short all prospects of the son's political ambitions, should he have had them—and in return for these losses, came a double vision of the world which passed before his eyes. By temperament and training Pope was scarcely one to claim the poet's prerogative as seer, yet his peculiar relationship to the world around him—the state of being of the world, and yet out of it (a position not unlike that of the majority of twentieth-century poets)—helped to sustain the double vision he enjoyed and therefore shielded the gifts which gave him insights reaching beyond the limitations of place and time.

Though Pope, like all "Papists," was disenfranchised, he was welcomed in coffeehouses and in Tory circles where he was usually accompanied by middle-aged friends, such as Sir William Trumbull, an ex-cabinet minister and Wycherley, the dramatist. From here, it was but a step to the fringes of the Court, and his social range was soon extended from the respectable Roman Catholic Blounts who lived near Windsor Forest to worldly London ladies who frequented the anterooms of St. James's—and one of these, whom Pope witnessed in a fit of "spleen," probably inspired the following passage in *The Rape of the Lock.*

> Here living Tea-pots stand, one Arm held out,
> One bent; the Handle this, and that the spout:
> A Pipkin there, like Homer's Tripod walks;
> Here sighs a Jar, and there a Goose-pye talks.
> Men prove with Child, as pow'rful Fancy works,
> And Maids turned Bottels, call aloud for Corks.

In these startling lines Pope's imagery—again his double vision—seems to carry us back to Brueghel and to anticipate Freud. It is, however, more likely that Pope's vision simply applied its own gifts of psychological insight.

And if one looks for lyrical imagery in Pope, there is another passage in *The Rape of the Lock* that demands attention:

> A sudden Star, it shot through liquid Air,
> And drew behind a radiant Trail of Hair.
> Not Berenice's Locks first rose so bright,
> The Heav'ns bespangling with dishevel'd Light.

One also sees a reflection of the last image in W. B. Yeats's line:

> And all disheveled, wandering stars.

Perhaps there is no better illustration of Pope's success in piercing the walls of masculine prejudice and to move at ease behind the masks of human sentiment than that which enters the descriptive passages of his epistle to Martha Blount; he speaks for her as well as for himself; and all she has to say is in her actions, not her words:

> She went, to plain-work, and to purling brooks,
> Old fashion'd halls, dull Aunts, and croaking rooks;
> She went from Op'ra, Park, Assembly, Play,
> To morning-walks, and pray'rs three hours a day;
> To pass her time 'twixt reading and bohea;
> To muse and spill her solitary tea;
> Or o'er cold coffee trifle with her spoon,
> Count the slow clock, and dine exact at noon;
> Divert her eyes with pictures in the fire,
> Hum half a tune, tell stories to the Squire;

As in the best of all Pope's writings, there is no mistaking the surface meaning of these lines; it is an excellent description of boredom at a country seat, and that is the general intention of this passage in the poem. Yet as one rereads it the subtle portrait of a particular bored lady enters the scene; decorum covers her inward restlessness; she spills her tea, she trifles with her spoon, counts the slow clock—and the portrait takes on all the finer shadings of repressed emotion. Later on in the poem we learn that she is not attracted by the Squire who "Makes love with nods and knees between a table,—" and the implication is that she has become used to, has formed a taste for, talk in urban and witty company and has the brains to share it. The poem is, of course, a love letter in verse, and Pope, unlike many a writer before and after him, does not neglect (within the poem itself) the object of his affections. If he does not tell us the color of the lady's hair and eyes, nor speak precisely of her voice and figure, he leaves no doubt as to what her actions are, and how she thought and felt—and this is the greatest compliment of all possible tributes to her character.

In the creation of Pope's particular gift of a double vision some acknowledgment is due to the household in which the poet spent his childhood. The elder Alexander Pope was a retired linen merchant of comfortable means, and after his conversion to the Roman Church, he married within the small circle that held to "the old religion," which included then as it does today, descendants of the elder British gentry. The Pope household thrived decorously within a group that had learned to give up political ambitions and civil privileges; it consciously avoided persecution and make the most of British tolerance that showed a smiling aspect to successful and respectable members of the merchant class. Even among the smaller landed gentry, doors were left slightly ajar to modest, respectable merchants like the older Pope who had the means to buy a little estate on the edge of Windsor Forest.

The true concern of the Pope household revolved around the education of the precocious and sickly boy; barred from public schools and universities because of the elder Pope's religious faith, barred from regular attendance at Catholic schools because of his own ill health, the poet was fortunate to find in his sympathetic father a first critic of his verse. Pope learned the rudiments (but scarcely more) of Greek and Latin at home, and though he maintained a love of books and an outward show of learning, he had little enough of the academic temperament acquired later in his century by Thomas Gray. What scholarship Pope possessed remained untouched by the vice of pedantry, and fortunately his gifts were free of recurrent premonitions of sterility which so often attend the fears of those who write within the uncharmed circles of academic life.

Like many who are forced by ill health to be a spectator of the world, Pope's curiosity seldom failed to be aroused by active scenes of urban life, and another aspect of his double vision is distinctly visual and shuttles between the library indoors, suburban woods and meadows, and the interior of houses in the town.

Pope's world moved readily from views of Windsor Forest to London's coffeehouses, and the contemplative child, fresh from his imitations of Chaucer and Spenser and exercises in translating Ovid, read both with precocious brilliance. Many years later in writing lines to his friend John Gay from Twickenham, the all-seeing child-like eye fixes its long gaze upon a pastoral detail of a hunting park or forest:

> So the struck deer in some sequestered part
> Lies down to die, the arrow in his heart;
> There stretched unseen in coverts hid from day,
> Bleeds drop by drop; and pants his life away.

And from another poem one finds these lines:

> More subtle web Arachne cannot spin,
> Nor the fine nets, which oft we woven see
> Of scorched dew, do not th'air more lightly flee.

The poet who cannot ride to hunt discovers his sentiment on the side of the struck deer; and the bright, sharp, nearsighted gaze selects an image, which is almost invisible, of scorched dew. Neither view is one that a countryman (and certainly not a hard-riding country squire) is likely to carry in his mind, and one need not press the point that both reflect an urban sensibility. Pope's town scenes are of rooms and halls, of which major examples may be drawn from *The Rape of the Lock*, and beyond these the double vision shifts from eye to ear; one overhears talk crowded with activity, gossip through which names float, and words pour from the coffeehouse, boudoir, council chamber, and narrow street: the sounds are often vigorous and sometimes shrill and loud; they are of the double vision speaking in the voice of the snake with a forked or double tongue:

> Know, there are Words, and Spells, which can control
> Between the fits this Fever of the soul:
> Know, there are Rhymes, which fresh and fresh apply'd
> Will cure the arrant'st Puppy of his Pride.
> Be furious, envious, slothful, mad, or drunk,
> Slave to a Wife, or Vassal to a Punk,
> A Switz, a High-dutch, or a Low-Dutch Bear;
> All that we ask is but a patient Ear.

In his *Moral Essays* there is still another kind of portrait of those who walk the town:

Boastful and rough, your first Son is a Squire
The next a Tradesman, meek, and much a liar;
Tom struts a Soldier, open, bold and brave;
Will sneaks a Scriv'ner, an exceeding knave:
Is he a Churchman? then he's fond of pow'r:
A quaker? sly: A Presbyterian? sour:
A smart Free-thinker? all things in an hour.
  Ask men's Opinions: Scoto now shall tell
How Trade increases, and the World goes well;
Strike off his Pension, by the setting sun,
And Britain, if not Europe, is undone.
  That gay Free-thinker, a fine talker once,
What turns him now a stupid silent dunce?
Some God or Spirit he has lately found:
Or chanc'd to meet a Minister that frown'd.

The passage brings to light some speculation as to the nature of Pope's Catholic faith: and was the double vision there? Since his father was a convert to that faith, Pope had no need to make religious vows in print. His religion was the private conviction of his household and it also included that of Martha Blount's. His position upheld and not without the use of reason, a conservative Christian standard of behavior, and what he gathered from his faith was an air of strict detachment in looking at the follies of British Protestant mankind. His opinions of the Quaker, Presbyterian, and freethinker were those that could be accepted and shared by any worldly Londoner of the day, yet it is perhaps a matter of interest to discover that members of his own faith were excluded in his list. In general Pope was content to say: "presume not God to scan;/The proper study of Mankind is Man," and this statement probably expresses all that he wished the world to know of his religious faith. In worldly matters his double vision permitted rays of skepticism to illuminate everything that was not reserved for the working of God's will.

Of all his writings the twentieth-century reader of Pope's verse is best prepared to understand the technical force and skill of the *Epistle to Dr. Arbuthnot,* and familiar as the piece may be, it still yields fresh claims upon our attention. During the present century there have been many successful innovations in writing conversational verse, and the range extends from many sources and in great variety from Frost, Pound, and Eliot to William Carlos Williams, E. E. Cummings, and Robinson Jeffers. To the contemporary eye and ear, Pope's famous *Epistle* is closer to our taste than passages of equal length from Tennyson and Longfellow—which is to say we feel the presence of poetry in Pope's *Epistle* with the same conviction that Victorian readers were certain that the *Epistle* was no more than admirably brilliant verse.

In modern reading of the *Epistle*, the piece becomes Pope's autobiography, his *ars poetica* and epitaph—and more than that, the "rocking horses" of his couplets, if not entirely stilled, have given way to the sound of human voices, Pope's and Arbuthnot's within a room. It is always the kind of poetry that is not declaimed, and to be heard correctly and understood, should be spoken without too many stresses upon its rhymes.

Pope's biographers and commentators have long discarded the literal truthfulness of what he had to say in his *Epistle* and they have been wary of assuming that unguarded confessions poured from his lips. But the occasion of writing a prologue to his satires from Horace was one that allowed him to tell essential truths about himself; he was at the height of his fame and had under his control the full resources of his skill, his art, his genius; he could well afford to permit the world to see the conflicts of his mind and heart. The *Epistle* was his proof that he had put into practice his instruction, "Know thyself," and that he also possessed the wit and strength of mind to purge self-pity from his lines. After his confession that his life was a "long disease," he pointed to his notoriety, his fame, and then permitted himself the luxury (which is not less revealing) of releasing the bitterest and most artful of his libels upon Lord Hervey. Anyone who reads his lines on Sporus cannot waste tears of pity over Pope; his success is far too evident, the triumph of his art and will are both too overwhelming and assured.

In his excursion into autobiography was it Pope who paved the way for Wordsworth's great poem, *The Prelude*, as well as Byron's *Don Juan*? There is, I think, the sight of truth in what may seem to be a "far-out" speculation. We know how much Byron owed to Pope and how readily he acknowledged his debt to him; and we know that Wordsworth's blank verse in *The Prelude* bears an honest kinship to the paragraphs of verse in Milton's *Paradise Lost*. We know that Wordsworth's conception of writing conversational verse was of a very different mind, temperament, accent and rhythm than any rules that Pope had held to in making his voice heard. In fact almost any meeting of Pope and Wordsworth on common ground is like the meeting of opposites where both extremes incontinently meet. Yet it is likely that we have forgotten that Wordsworth read Pope with care enough to oppose him with great success, and that most of the Romantics paid tribute to Pope's presence on the horizon that they had left behind them. Among these Robert Burns may seem to be a strange example, all the more so because his *Cotter's Saturday Night* illustrates how dull a merely correct imitation of Pope's couplets can be. Yet Burns's emulation of Pope (and Burns turned to Pope with all the humility of going to a master) had extremely fortunate results; Pope's *The Challenge, A Court Ballad,* points the way:

> To one fair lady out of Court,
> And two fair ladies in,
> Who think the Turk and Pope a sport,
> And wit and love no sin!
> Come, these soft lines, with nothing stiff in,
> To Bellenden, Lepell and Griffin.
>
> . . . .
>
> But should you catch the prudish itch,
> And each became a coward,
> Bring sometimes with you lady Rich,
> And sometimes mistress Howard;
> For virgins, to keep chaste, must go
> Abroad with such as are not so.
> With a fa, la, la.

The ease and lightness of these lines is a step in the direction of Burns's *The Jolly Beggars;* and in his own way Burns emulated the conversational vigor of the *Epistle to Dr. Arbuthnot* in his own epistles and satires. But to return to Wordsworth's masterpiece, *The Prelude*, and its probable, though well concealed, relationship to Pope's *Epistle*. If we admit that the *Epistle* is a poet's testament, written at the height of his powers, and is so balanced in its structure that all its parts combine to show the growth of a poet's mind, we have an excellent precedent for Wordsworth's major poem. There can be little doubt that the *Epistle*, at the very least, was intended to be and become a backward-looking survey of Pope's life and work; if not, why did he take the trouble to mention his earlier writings within it, why did he dwell on Lord Hervey who was so intimately associated with Pope's long-lived quarrel with Lady Mary Wortley Montague? It was not Pope's habit to write poems without a well deliberated purpose in his mind.

Although it may seem strange to credit a conscious neoclassicist like Pope with certain qualities that create a precedent for well-known elements in romantic poetry (and the personal testament in verse is one), a rereading of Pope's *Pastorals* brings us to the obvious conclusion that if a poet actually writes poetry, the naming of schools and movements becomes irrelevant; only the lesser and half-gifted poets are sustained by the naming of groups and classroom definitions. Pope, who seldom saw a classroom in his life, tends to escape the formulas of usual definitions for neoclassical verse. Like the romantics who came after him Pope in his youth read Edmund Spenser, and learned from him the finest, the most delicately written and heard lyric strains in English poetry; Pope made his own adaptation of Spenser's music (with unclaimed, unsuspected originality) to his chosen form of the heroic couplet. His pastoral *Autumn* has two refrains, "Go, gentle gales," and "Resound, ye hills;" the exercise is admittedly youthful and experimental, yet how fresh, how nearly "romantic" its images and music are today:

> Go, gentle gales, and bear my sighs away!
> Curs'd be the fields that cause my Delia stay!
> Fade ev'ry blossom, wither ev'ry tree,
> Die ev'ry flower, and perish all but she!
> What have I said? Where'er my Delia flies,
> Let Spring attend, and sudden flowers arise!
> Let op'ning roses knotted oaks adorn,
> And liquid amber drop from ev'ry thorn.

Even in these lines the curious insight of a double vision are in evidence; probably the inspiration behind them was no more than the delight of metrical invention and exercise; his Delia is unreal enough and has no relation to his Eloïsa and the fears and distractions of his "Unfortunate Lady," yet images of life, perhaps subconsciously conceived and drawn from an exact observation of natural forms close the passage just before the refrain begins again.

One of the survivals of Pope's legend in contemporary literature occurs in the last of Dylan Thomas's sketches in *The Portrait of the Artist as a Young Dog*. The scene is at a seaside resort, and "Come into the garden" from Tennyson's *Maud* has just been read. Someone remarks in the dialogue which follows:

'My Grandfather remembers seeing Lord Tennyson, he was a little man with a hump.'
'No, he was tall and he had long hair and a beard.'
'Did you ever see him?'
'I wasn't born then.'
'My grandfather saw him. He had a hump.'
'Not Alfred Tennyson.'
'Lord Alfred Tennyson was a little man with a hump.'
'It couldn't have been the same Tennyson.'
'You've got the wrong Tennyson, this was the famous poet with the hump.'

Needless to say, Thomas's setting of Pope among drinking men and girls is shamelessly romantic; it is a queer place to find him; but the sight of his figure and the sound of his voice, whenever we choose to rediscover them within his poetry, are as much alive today as they were in England's Augustan Age.

1950, 1971

THE SIGHT OF NATURE IN THE POETRY OF JOHN CLARE

It has taken a hundred years to rediscover John Clare.[1] He himself had lost his name and drifted into madness: was he a poet or merely the son of an impoverished Northamptonshire tenant farmer, or both or neither? There was a time in London, when no one could afford to say he had not read the *Poems Descriptive of Rural Life and Scenery*, but that was in the spring of 1820, and the season of celebrity was often quite as short then as it is today. Seventeen years later he was to deny his identity, and after that denial, he refused to recognize his wife and children. He was to say that he had been married in spirit to another woman, now long dead: and was he Lord Byron or John Clare?

We must return again to the spring of 1820. There, in the same room that shelters the death mask of John Keats, that moment is restored on canvas in the National Portrait Gallery of London. The portrait is by W. Hilton, R.A. (and he, too, is forgotten) and there we see a young man with sun-bleached golden hair, pale blue eyes, the thin nostril and slightly parted lips, each feature delicately and sharply turned. He had come up to London in late winter, up to the noisy city of new faces, up from the village of Helpstone in Northamptonshire. A local bookseller, Edward Drury, had advanced him money in payment for the right to publish all his poems and then resold the copyright to prosperous John Taylor, the London publisher.

The advantages of having Taylor for publisher were obvious: Taylor had befriended Keats and had a quick eye for merit in poetry. The disadvantages were far less discernible. Taylor saw in Clare a chance for immediate return upon a small investment and therefore publicized the poet and his book as a literary curiosity. Perhaps Taylor took his cue from the spectacular success of Burns in Edinburgh: here was another peasant with a book of poems, an exotic, handsome figure in a homespun smock under an ill-fitting greatcoat to be made the sensation of a London season. It was evident that Clare was fixed in Taylor's mind as so much commercial property and the first reviews encouraged sales which extended rapidly into a

[1] *The Poems of John Clare*. Edited and with an introduction by J. W. Tibble. 2 vols. London: J. M. Dent & Sons, 1935.

third edition. This premature success was to work against Clare's subsequent reputation, for Clare as the object of literary curiosity was to deflect attention from the true merit of his poetry.

For a few months Clare enjoyed the surprise of being famous:

> To think that I in humble dress
> Might have a right to happiness
> And sing as well as greater men;
> And then I strung the lyre again
> And heartened up o'er toil and fear
> And lived with rapture everywhere,
> Till dayshine to my themes did come.

Yet, for all the promise of success in London he became uneasy in city lodgings. Charles Lamb was cheerful company and kind; even the remote Lake poets, Coleridge, Southey, Wordsworth, even Byron, sent him their latest books, "bound for the author" and autographed in welcome to the farmer poet. Patrons were eager for nomination in his honor, yet Clare was impatient to be home again, back at Helpstone to the place he knew and cherished. He was to leave London suddenly, breaking an appointment with Taylor to meet Keats: the reason, so he said, was the climax of his determination to marry "Patty" Turner of Walkherd Lodge, nearby his father's farm in Northamptonshire.

At this moment, Clare's future seemed assured: Lord Radstock had invested capital on which the poet was to draw an annual income; another patron, a Mrs. Emmerson, was to watch over him, to send him gifts, to send him friendly letters, to give him, in short, that surplus of benevolence that a kindly English gentry, moved by eccentricity or whim, so often bestows upon the "worthy poor," with the understanding that such beings are admittedly inferior. I doubt if anyone could have foreseen the events which were to follow, could have known that Lord Radstock's investment was to yield but a few pounds a year, the interest steadily declining. Few, if any, could have read those warnings of disaster which attended the early stages of Clare's career: the roots of madness were well concealed, and Clare's bright moment of hopefulness outshone all premonitions of destined failure and obscurity.

It would be mere sentimentality to say that Clare's childhood was unhappy; he was frail but active—yet such happiness must be measured only in terms of the physical beauty of Helpstone. His father's farm, like many another in that neighborhood, had made futile effort toward survival under the shadow of the Enclosure Acts. There, in the calm expanse of the English countryside, relative independence was changed to actual slavery; the farmer was forced to carry an intolerable burden of debt, leaving his heirs a heritage of poverty. The unseen blight was on every blade of grass and in the swelling heart of every grain of corn.

Under this shadow, one incident in Clare's later boyhood was to leave its mark. One day at haying time, the boy saw a farm hand killed by a sharp fall from his wagon. Clare became distraught and fell ill, and for some years following, in spring and autumn, the vivid scene of death in the haying field would float before his eyes: work became impossible, and suddenly sick, faint, defeated, he would leave the plow or scythe until his head cleared and the fit was over. The accurate (and in this instance, painful) memory of realistic detail which was to shape the character of his poetry demanded its toll here; and emotional sensitivity, so valuable in his development as a poet, was to impede his efficiency in manual labor. Judging from his record of many small jobs held and lost, we may conclude that Clare was an inept farmer; he was too easily distracted by contemplation of a field or flower or by the reading of highly treasured books, among which he listed Thomson's *The Seasons,* Goldsmith's *The Deserted Village,* Milton's *Paradise Lost* and a translation into English of Aristotle.

Even at this time some hint of what was to become a divided personality might well have dropped into his mind. It was to rise to the surface of his journal on his first trip to London: there, "lolling in a coach," he was to see himself as another person, more talented than honest farmer John, and immeasurable degrees more fortunate. Clearly he saw the relative position of his class in English society, so clearly that Lord Radstock caused ten lines of an attack upon the gentry to be deleted from Clare's early poem, *Helpstone.* But the personal problem (the penumbra in which the farmer left off and the poet began) was a matter of inward confusion and a source of speculation. It was a problem that gave birth to what might well have seemed a contradiction: though dependent upon patronage and the continued good will of his publisher, the poet, Clare, gained an easy promise of material livelihood; the farmer, Clare, who had retained the sturdiness of the Anglo-Saxon freedmen, also retained the memory of complete independence which was the ambition of his ancestors, and supported "the radical slang" that Lord Radstock discovered in his poetry. Yet it was plain that Clare, the man, was to share (with other tenant farmers) the unequal burden of economic maladjustment. As peasant he was to observe that inequality, and with other Romantic poets of his time, to assert his independence as an Englishman by writing his convictions into poetry. He was to go mad before a solution of this seeming paradox appeared.

After the London visit of 1820, city patrons would come down to Helpstone to see how a peasant worked and wrote his poetry. Clare was genuinely shy of such patronage and sometimes openly resentful. Like many another self-educated man, he had penetrated to certain unexpected depths of learning and was impatient with a patronage that took for granted a fact that he was no more than a public curiosity. Fearful of those who came to see merely a Helpstone wonder, he would vanish quickly from the small cottage to get outdoors.

On subsequent short, infrequent trips to London to visit Lamb, or Hood, or his publisher, he would be silent, sitting in a corner, worrying about money for his wife and children, while in his brain would reappear the scenes of Helpstone: minute images of flowers, insects, birds, the clear sky over them and underfoot thick grass and through the fields small rivers flowing.

In ten years his London celebrity was gone and there was great delay in publishing his books. The British public, that had read the new poetry of the time and had welcomed Clare, now swung its mind to other things: to romances by the author of *Waverley*, then to Bulwer-Lytton, to economics, to Carlyle, and last to the novels of Charles Dickens. Meanwhile, Clare had come into his heritage as tenant farmer, and as his family grew, debts closed around him, and the shadow of poverty over Helpstone loomed deep and wide. At a final moment (then too late) a patron intervened; Clare and his wife and children were removed from the cottage at Helpstone to more comfortable quarters at Northborough. The move, though well intentioned, contributed further to growing symptoms of insanity; Clare was not "at home"; even this short removal from the place where he knew every foot of ground, seemed to increase his terror, seemed to hasten the birth of another John Clare who transfigured the memory of an adolescent love affair into a present state of being, and who denied the existence of his wife and children.

In 1837 the forgotten poet was committed to a private asylum from which he escaped to Northborough, through Epping Forest on foot for three days and nights of continuous walking, with no stop for food and no time for rest. His condition was hopeless; the image of Mary Joyce, a friend of his early manhood, grew stronger than ever, and against the will of his courageous wife, he was finally committed to the charity asylum of Northampton.

The rest of Clare's life is a history of literary discovery. In 1920 Edmund Blunden and Alan Porter edited, chiefly from manuscript, a selection of poems by John Clare. This selection, admittedly inadequate, was an effort to put Clare's best foot forward; more than all else, its purpose was to call attention to the poems, to overbalance the weight of legend and sentimentality set in motion by Frederick Martin's *Life* of 1865. The early Georgian poets, principally Edward Thomas, knew of Clare and set him up as a local deity; he was to aid them in their rediscovery of English countryside as a subject for poetry; his realism, his "botanizing," gained favor with young poets who had rejected the late Victorian interiors of Stephen Phillips and the backward-glancing imagination of the Pre-Raphaelites. But the great bulk of Clare's poetry remained in manuscript, in archives at Peterborough and Northborough, and it has taken fifteen years of research started by Edmund Blunden and completed by J. W. Tibble to arrange and publish some eight hundred poems in logical order.

In learning John Clare's language some patience is required. To judge Clare by a Wordsworthian scale of values, it would seem that he had no philosophy; compare him with Byron and he would be found lacking in brilliance and personality; contrast him with Keats and he seems provincial and (as Keats himself remarked) "Description too much prevails over the sentiment." In other words, Clare founded his esthetic upon a premise that refuted the work of his contemporaries. He was to write his own answer to Keats by saying:

Keats keeps up a constant allusion (or illusion) to the Grecian mythology, and there I cannot follow . . . where behind every rose bush he looks for a Venus and under every laurel a thrumming Apollo . . . he often described Nature as she appeared to his fancies, and not as he would have described her had he witnessed the things he described.

The positive statement of this same esthetic is made in his *Pastoral Poesy:*

True poesy is not in words,
  But images that thoughts express. . . .
A language that is ever green,
  That feelings unto all impart
As hawthorne blossoms, soon as seen,
  Give May to every heart.

Clare's earliest poetry was a direct outgrowth from eighteenth-century models: Thomson's *The Seasons* and Goldsmith's *The Deserted Village* were rewritten in a new setting, and the unwary reader is inclined to agree with Keats, for many of Clare's poems open with a sentiment proper to eighteenth-century verse and then wheel precipitously into factual description. After thirty lines are accomplished, almost without warning the poem becomes Clare's own: "description" becomes the "sentiment," both are closely interlaced and the visual image is registered upon the reader's brain before there is any consciousness of "meaning."

Snows on snows in heaps combine,
Hillocks, rais'd as mountains, shine,
And at distance rising proud,
Each appears a fleecy cloud.

So much for the winter scene; then this for a *Summer Evening:*

> Flowers now sleep within their hoods,
> Daisies button into buds;
> From soiling dew the buttercup
> Shuts his golden jewels up;
> And the rose and woodbine they
> Wait again the smiles of day.

In these poems Clare's world of natural objects becomes a world seen under a magnifying glass; at first each object seems minute, then quickly, growing, flowers open and close again and small birds suddenly alive and clear, break into song. Clare's flaw, of course, is rapid composition; in the earlier poems tens of lines are wasted; he was prodigal of both subject matter and vocabulary. However, his use of plain language, the very diction of the countryside in which he lived, preserves for us the vividness of a first impression. Clare's early period closes with a group of lyric narratives which contain *My Mary* (not to be confused with later "Marys") and *Dolly's Mistake*, two poems which not unlike *The Jolly Beggars* of Robert Burns and John Skelton's *The Tunnynge of Elynour Rummynge* owe their vitality, both in language and choice of subject, to strict representation of the lowest levels of society. The drawing is coarse and the humor broad, but the characters live by their own volition, and though they pretend to be no more than creatures of a specific time and locality, they are always contemporaneous; in them a universal law of human mortality is always reenacted.

Perhaps one word should be said of Clare's satire, *The Parish.* Briefly, Clare had little gift for satire, but he saw, not without terror, not without blunt-edged bitterness, the topheavy structure of a society above him. Among the shorter rural narratives there is a lively recitation of a brawl between recruiting sergeants and the Helpstone peasantry. Again his love of exact detail seems to guide his hand, and the description of an alehouse brawl has something of the same memorable quality (sentimentality and all) which distinguishes Hogarth's *March to Finchley.*

The pre-asylum poetry was to reach its climax in *Summer Images;* here was a poem that surpassed the observation of a Wordsworth and even outglanced the perceptive eye of Wordsworth's sister, Dorothy. It is one of the few poems that Clare is known to have rewritten thoroughly, and between the writing of the first and second versions, his art matured. From this time onward, he knew what his poetic intentions were, and I believe that his subsequent insanity was, in a measure, a means of protecting his right to continue his career as a poet. If we remember that Coleridge relieved the strain of domestic responsibility and checked the pain of neuralgia by generous doses of laudanum, and then assumed what T. S. Eliot has called the "vocation of a failure," we may grant that Clare, under equal pressure, tended to withdraw from a world that deflected the authority of his poetic vision. Meanwhile he rewrote his *Summer Images:*

> I love at early morn, from new-mown swath,
> To see the startled frog his route pursue,
> And mark while, leaping o'er the dripping path,
> His bright sides scatter dew;
> And early lark that from its bustle flies
> To hail his matin new;
> And watch him to the skies:
>
> And note on hedgerow haulks, in moisture sprent,
> The jetty snail creep from the mossy thorn,
> With earnest head and tremulous intent,
> Frail brother of the morn,
> That from the tiny bents and misted leaves
> Withdraws his timid horn,
> And fearful vision weaves.

Clare was to continue writing at this level beyond the publication of his last book, *The Rural Muse*, which was issued and rapidly forgotten in the year 1835.

Clare's loss of identity necessitated a change in his literary personality, and how much of his madness was willed in self-defense may be gathered from these lines:

> Free from the world I would a prisoner be
> And my own shadow all my company:
>
> And lonely see the shooting stars appear,
> Worlds rushing into judgement all the year.

A new John Clare was in the making, another poet who built the symbol of existence in a madhouse around the image of his singular madonna, Mary. In the first stages of his madness, his choice of Mary contained the same defiant guilt consciousness of Byron's *Manfred*. It was some time before he was to realize his new personality in terms of poetry above the level of mere violence, for the Byronic attitude had led him into a world of false emotions, into histrionic mannerisms and the darkness of self-pity.

Clare's countryside had changed into "this Hell and French Bastille of English Liberty," which were the asylum walls, but there, in that small world, he was to regain his peculiar intensity of vision:

> Say, wilt thou go with me, sweet maid,
> Say, maiden, wilt thou go with me

Through the valley-depths of shade,
Of night and dark obscurity;
Where the path has lost its way,
Where the sun forgets the day,
Where there's nor light nor life to see,
Sweet maiden, wilt thou go with me?
Where stones will turn to flooding streams,
Where plains will rise like ocean's waves,
Where life will fade like visioned dreams
And mountains darken into caves,
Say, maiden, wilt thou go with me
Through this sad non-identity,
Where parents live and are forgot,
And sisters live and know us not?

Then note:

Say, maiden, can thy life be led
To join the living and the dead?
Then trace thy footsteps on with me;
We are wed to one eternity.

In these last poems which he was to write until his death in the Northampton asylum in 1864, there is a purity of diction that recalls the early Blake. His affinity to William Cowper was expressed in one of the finest elegies of the day :

Cowper, the poet of the fields
  Who found the muse on common ground—
The homesteads that each cottage shields
  He loved—and made them classic ground.

. . . .

Who travels o'er those sweet fields now
  And brings not Cowper to his mind?
Birds sing his name in every bough,
  Nature repeats it in the wind.

And every place the poet trod
  And every place the poet sung
Are like the Holy Land of God,
  In every mouth, on every tongue.

And, like Cowper, he had become the "self-consumer of his woes"; his haven had become, in fact, the madhouse, which was for him, even to the last, the "Ivory Tower," the abiding refuge of the poor.

1935, 1944

LORD BYRON: THE POET AS LETTER-WRITER

It may seem gratuitous to remark that a critical enjoyment of Byron's work necessitates the reading of his letters as well as an appreciation of *Don Juan*, but the fact remains that for the past thirty years few people have actually read Byron or know him at first hand.[1] I say "few people"—and here I cheerfully exempt all those who read selections from his verse in junior colleges and in universities, and with them I exempt their lecturers and teachers who reread and reinterpret Byron because of his position in Romantic literature. Most of us have been content to read the growing literature surrounding Byron's name: Lord Lovelace's *Astarte*, Ethel Colburne Mayne's definitive biography, or more recently, Peter Quennell's enlivening commentary on the Byronic legend, *Byron: The Years of Fame* and *Byron in Italy* in which the charm that Byron exerted over his contemporaries is revived and presented to us in the light of twentieth-century sensibility. If anything, we know the details of Byron's physical appearance, his private maladjustments, and his dramatic entrances into and exits out of public favor a shade too well.[2] True as it may be that Byron lived literature as well as wrote it, it is a salutary exercise to rediscover what he wrote, to reread his prose as well as his best verse, and to recalculate the distance at which he stood from Keats and Shelley, Beddoes and Wordsworth, Coleridge and Southey.

With the notable exceptions of Poe, Emerson, and Coleridge, the poets of the early nineteenth century are scarcely remembered for distinction to be found within their prose. We have nothing here to compare with the richness and dramatic intensity of the prose in Shakespeare's later plays, or with the seasoned wit of Ben Jonson's

[1] *The Letters of Lord Byron*, selected by R. G. Howarth. With an introduction by André Maurois. New York: E. P. Dutton and Company, 1933.

[2] When I wrote this note on Byron's letters, I was too young to realize that writing a "definitive" biography of Byron is a near impossibility. Every few years another biography of the poet appears, and perhaps the most reliable of these is the massive three-volume work by Leslie A. Marchand. Professor Marchand makes clear that the immediate cause of Byron's death was uremia; and in this there is a hint that Byron's efforts to keep himself from growing fat—his self-imposed diet of vinegar and mashed potatoes—probably contributed to the nature of his fatal illness. What a nauseous way to guide oneself toward death!

Discoveries. Despite the wealth of commentary on Shakespeare, perhaps too little notice has yet been given to the prose which endowed Iago with a set of nerves and Pandarus with harsh, if not endearing, wit. We also know that little prose writing among poets of Byron's newly arrived nineteenth century could equal the quality and texture of Sir Phillip Sidney's *Arcadia* or of John Donne's sermons. Shelley's prose is thin, boyish, shrill, and stiff as though it had inherited the rhetorical flourishes of the century preceding it without bodily force or character; Wordsworth's prose, aside from the famous *Preface* over which he labored and almost fell ill with the effort to sustain his own eloquence, is all too frequently weighted with the sense of its author's importance among the Lake Poets of his generation.

In general, the prose of poets who lived through the period of Britain's Napoleonic Wars suffered the casualties of a transition from an Augustan Age to the Romantic; the balanced periods of Burke, Gibbon, and Samuel Johnson fell out of joint, but the sound of its rocking-horse overtones persisted, and in particular, Shelley's prose carried within it many of the disasters that marked the writing of the time. Perhaps some allowances should be made for Shelley's youth (for there are moments when we are likely to forget how immature the young Wordsworth and Keats and Shelley were) but it is more important to remember the kind of youth that Shelley was. His *Hymn to Intellectual Beauty* was rightly named because its author was a young intellectual of the most enthusiastic sort; he was less learned than swift and eager in his reading, always comprehending the naked scaffolding of an idea rather than its architectural fulfillment. His letters, journals, and footnotes sketch the scene, and the reader must apply his own imagination so as to fill the picture; meanwhile, the writer had left earth behind him to ride the light beams, winds, and clouds of a new theory.

Within the brief era that embraced the active lives of both young poets, no greater contrast can be found than that which distinguishes Shelley's prose from Byron's. Even a temporal distance seems to intervene between them, for among the contrasts, we are overly conscious of the dates which fix the moment of Shelley's letters, while Byron's are as fresh as though they were posted yesterday. Introspective as Byron may have been in *Manfred,* as he wrote his letters he stood with both feet on an earth that was known by its physical realities, its painted Turkish boys with "large black eyes," its exchanges in money equal to the British guinea, its swimming time—an hour and ten minutes—across the Hellespont, and its eternal presence in the life of literary men. "London," he wrote, "and the world is the only place to take the conceit out of a man—" and then went on to say:

Scott . . . is gone to the Orkneys in a gale of wind;—during which wind, he affirms, the said Scott, "he is sure, is not at his ease,—to say the best of it." Lord, Lord, if these homekeeping minstrels had crossed your Atlantic or my Mediterranean, and tasted a little open boating in a white squall—or a gale in "the Gut"—or the "Bay of Biscay" with no gale at all—how it would enliven and introduce them to a few of the sensations!—to say nothing of an illicit amour or two upon shore, in the way of essay upon the Passions, beginning with simple adultery, and compounding it as they went along.

This is the Byron that Matthew Arnold saw when he spoke of "that true and puissant personality, with its direct strokes, its ever-welling force, its satire, its energy." It was also the Byron whom Goethe recognized, was refreshed by the encounter, and of whom was impelled to say, no other poet "*der ihm zu vergleichen wäre.*" The singularity which Goethe was so happy to acknowledge lies at the heart of some two hundred and eighty letters selected from complete editions of Byron's prose.

Byron's energy, even in its surplus, was unique; it forced his growth from a bright and restless schoolboy at Harrow and Trinity College at Cambridge, into a citizen of the world who knew the Near East with the same glancing familiarity which accompanied his arrival in a drawing room at Holland House; its electric stream overflowed the pages of *Childe Harold*, the *Hebrew Melodies*, the *Oriental Tales* into a daylight world of action, into his letters, into grandiose schemes of travel, and last to a road which led to the battlefield at Missolonghi. Many of the letters were written, like the rapid cantos of *Don Juan*, because he could not stop the flow. At home he wrote and spoke openly of the boredom, the confusion, the excitements into which his domestic life had fallen; abroad, a like impulse caused him to record his entrances into each foreign setting, noting events and details of scenery, of habits and dress of men and women as he rode by. With rather more than a shrewd guess at the proportions of the world within his glance, he measured all against himself. This world, of course, was the very map of Europe which had been so recently traversed by dreams of Napoleonic conquest, and was now entered, scrawled with the percentage marks of loss and profit on its margins, within the balance sheets of the House of Rothschild.

Byronic legend had acquired an aura of sin, love-making, and guilt which strongly resembled the atmosphere and plot of Mozart's *Don Giovanni*. It was appropriate that Byron's mock epic and semi-autobiography should have been titled *Don Juan*. His image was that of the Demon Lover who was also the Doomed Hero, and it would seem that there is also a Faustian aspect to the story of Don Juan. No wonder Goethe at Weimar, with his own *Faust* in mind, had been fascinated by rumors of the young English poet's adventures! Yet Byron's position was not quite that of the poet poised against society—it was that of one who because of his wealth, his inherited title, his clearly cut profile, his auburn hyacinthine hair, as well as his gift for writing poetry, placed him above rules that had been made for ordinary men. He was notoriously "different." And his stance was complicated by a Calvinistic sense of sin that had been instilled during his early boyhood by a dark-minded, strong-willed Scottish governess, and Byron, through his mother, shared a turbulent measure of Scottish blood. In *Don Juan* he confessed:

> But I am half a Scot by birth, and bred
> A whole one, and my heart flies to my head.
>
> As 'Auld Lang Syne' brings Scotland, one and all,
> Scotch plaids, Scotch snoods, the blue hills and clear streams,
> The Dee, the Don, Balgounie's brig's *black wall*,
> All my boy feelings, all my gentler dreams
> Of what I *then dreamt*, clothed in their own pall,
> Like Banquo's offspring—floating past me seems
> My childhood in this childishness of mine:
> I care not— 'tis a glimpse of '*Auld Lang Syne*.'
>
> (canto 10, stanzas 17–18)

His birth had also been attended by superstitious awe, for he was born with a caul and a right clubfoot which handicap he surmounted by a show of exaggerated masculinity. In male company he often assumed the manners of a Regency buck and boasted of his skill in swimming. Though as Lord Byron he briefly visited his seat in the House of Lords, politics for the sake of politics bored him; though some of his friends were Whigs—and he joined them in ridicule of the house of Hanover and the Tories—in political company he chose to be known as the poet who stood out against all tyrannies.

In poetry his tastes were far more conservative. He had been the author of two facile, brilliantly precocious books of verse. Their models were clear enough: his catchy, tuneful lyrics stemmed from Thomas Moore's melodies; his heroic couplets and his turns of satire imitated the skills of Alexander Pope as well as those of a once popular, but now forgotten poet, William Gifford.

The sometimes flashing, sometimes grandiloquent rhetoric of Byron's *Childe Harold* which enchanted his contemporaries no longer dazzles us. His hero's journeys through Europe had been anticipated by other poets, particularly his friends, Thomas Campbell, and Samuel Rogers, the banker, who held literary salons at his breakfast table, loved to write travelogues in verse. On the authority of a fashionable poet of the day, a Dr. Beattie, Byron chose the Spenserian stanza for his recital of recent travel—and to this he added the manner of Ariosto's and James Thomson's descriptive sketches. On a tour of the Continent, his hero was scarcely more than still another sentimental traveler, another "man of feeling" who loved to rest his thoughts (and a weary elbow) upon a mass of historic ruins.

Yet before he published the last canto of *Childe Harold,* he grew critical of the very rhetoric that does not charm us today. He believed that poets like himself (and these included Keats and Shelley) had taken a wrong turning. To John Murray he wrote: "I am the more confirmed in this by having lately gone over some of our classics, particularly, *Pope* . . . and I was really astonished . . . at the ineffable distance in point of sense, harmony, effect, and even *Imagination,* passion, and *Invention,* between the little Queen Anne's man and us of the Lower Empire." In his tribute to Pope, he showed himself ready for swift changes in his own style of verse.

The tragic Byron of *Manfred* now seems an overweighted writer; as with other poets of his day, including Shelley, Byron's efforts to emulate Elizabethan dramatic verse were deadly. The living Byron is elsewhere. One has a glimpse of him in the lyric, *So, We'll Go No More A-Roving,* and in his positive genius for writing inextinguishable light verse, one overhears the accents of his true voice speaking the cantos of *Don Juan.* In Venice, in 1817, he read John Hookman Frere's *Whistlecraft,* a satire in imitation of Luigi Pulci's ottava rima.[3] Frere's plea was for the use of conversational diction in writing verse, and Byron, who had written so many engaging, freely spoken letters to his friends, promptly adapted Frere's suggestion and the ottava rima to his own voice and style. He now prepared to write his *Beppo* and *Don Juan.* To Murray he wrote, "Since you want *length,* you shall have enough of *Juan,* for I'll make 50 cantos."

As if to balance the recurrent fits of self-castigation, of torpor, and then renewed restlessness in Italy, stood the security of his own bank account and the fact that he had inherited a title. These last were

[3] Because *Don Juan* is a poem of the first order it is important to make clear John Hookham Frere's relationship to Byron and the poem. Byron first met John Hookham Frere (1769–1846) as early as 1809 in Spain, when Frere was serving as British Ambassador at Seville and Byron was on his Childe Harold tour of the Continent. A few years later he ran into Frere at Holland House. One can assume that the two men got on well together, for the diplomat, who obviously enjoyed reading and writing light verse, was also a friend of Byron's elderly friend, Samuel Rogers. So far as influences on his own writings were concerned, Byron's first impulse was to turn toward his friends—and a characteristic example was the relationship between his lyrics and those of Thomas Moore's *Melodies.* He was always frank in acknowledging his literary debts, and very clear in stating that *Beppo* and *Don Juan* had their "*model*" (his italics) in *Whistlecraft.* For this information I am indebted to Leslie A. Marchand's *Byron.*

of the material world that he knew so well and judged so brilliantly; these he remembered to feed his pride, nor did he forget them in viewing his less tangible reputation as a poet. It was in the person of Lord Byron that he wrote to Tom Moore, his friend, and to John Murray, his publisher; and in writing to them it was always clear enough that his fame was something which could be taken for granted, if not ignored. To Moore he stressed his conviction that he was far removed from literary rivalry: "Surely the field of fame is wide enough for all; and if it were not, I would not willingly rob my neighbor of a rood of it." His dislike of Southey was based upon a natural rejection of the gooseberry-tart–home-and-fireside character of Southey's verse, but as for the man himself, Byron was not ungenerous, and in his remarks to Moore one understands why Southey impressed his contemporaries and why his thoroughly mediocre gifts were rewarded by the Laureateship:

> Yesterday, at Holland House, I was introduced to Southey—the best-looking bard I have seen in some time. To have that poet's head and shoulders, I would almost have written his Sapphics. He is certainly a prepossessing person to look on, and a man of talent, and all that, and—*there* is his eulogy.

His distrust of Wordsworth also sprang from a difference in intellectual temper; as for the rest, he was willing to praise, and the measure of that praise may be noted in his early recognition of Coleridge, Shelley, and Keats. He urged Murray to publish an anonymous "Anti-Byron"; ". . . there is no earthly reason why you should *not,* on the contrary, I should receive it as the fairest compliment *you* could pay my candor." Many of Byron's best letters were addressed to Murray, for the publisher represented the world outside the dark, confused, semi-Faustian facets of Byron's character; to Byron, Murray's world was one of daylight and sanity and the relationship between the two men was kept alive through mutual—and material—profit.

We are not aware of how bad a correspondent Byron could be until we come upon the small cycle of letters to Anne Isabella Milbank. The courtship letters are stiff and dull; and the familiar stream of gossip, incident, and literary opinion seems to have been abruptly checked. One wonders if his role of the reformed rake had not been played a shade too well: objectively, Miss Milbank would have made the perfect Lady Byron; she possessed a fortune greater than his, she was by no means unintelligent, and had sufficient social poise to carry his title with ease and youthful dignity. For once, I think, his strong sense of external reality was to defeat its purpose. Because he had made up his mind to neglect the intangibilities of human emotion, both in himself and in his young wife, he was driven back into the mirrored, nightmare world of *Manfred*, and there was faced by his violent and helpless ego. He had seen that very danger in rejecting the advances of Lady Caroline Lamb, but she, of course, had been his female counterpart, a seductive, childish, almost ridiculous copy of himself. The famous Easter Sunday letter addressed to Lady Byron which was written immediately following his break with her shows how far he had miscalculated in reading her character; despair and broken pride punctuated the rapid sentences and phrases, and these were the warnings of a psychic instability that all women fear. The image of *Manfred* rose out of darkness to haunt young Lady Byron, and with him, his mistress and half-sister, the pliable Augusta, but it was a *Manfred* stripped of all power except that which carries wives and daughters down with him.

It is only in the letters to his wife that one reads how closely Byron steered toward the personal disintegration that marked the careers of Baudelaire and Poe; but it would be dangerous, I think, to speculate too freely on the incident which inspired them, or to overdramatize the process by which he righted himself; yet right himself he did as he left England to resume his travels on the Continent. The last grand tour of eight years had begun: by 17 September 1816, he was already writing to Augusta, "What a fool was I to marry—and *you* not very wise. . . . Had you been a Nun—and I a Monk—that we might have talked through a grate instead of across the sea—no matter —my voice and heart are ever thine—" He was of one piece again, and wrote to Murray of the guillotine in Rome and how he used opera glasses to see three thieves beheaded.

It was not until 1823 that signs of weariness and nervous irritation began to cloud his outward glancing eye: "I have not been so robustious as formerly," he wrote, "ever since the last summer, when I fell ill after a long swim in the Mediterranean," but to this he added a note of relief from his worry and fear of growing fat, "I am thin—perhaps thinner than when you saw me when I was nearly transparent, in 1812." He was about to shake himself free of the soft arms of the Guiccioli; with Shelley's death one chapter of his Italian holiday closed; the Leigh Hunts and their children ("They are dirtier and more mischievous than Yahoos," he wrote to Mary Shelley) had been packed up and sent back home to England. The prospect of an adventurous campaign in Greece became more attractive hourly and a newly shifting map of Europe was underfoot. He perceived that the end of kings and empires was near, and in looking toward that end his vision cleared again: "Give me a republic . . ." he wrote, "there will be blood shed like water and tears like mist, but the peoples will conquer."

There was less of wishful thinking in Byron's prophecy than one might suppose, and I believe that his view was that of the seasoned traveler who for some years had been quick to read the political equation concealed behind the passage of events; eighty years after Byron's death, Wilfrid Scawen Blunt possessed the same qualities of specific and realistic insight, and if he lacked the dramatic gifts of personality as well as the poetic talents that Byron so successfully employed, he was no less proficient in discerning the meaning of action behind the smoke screens of European diplomacy. Byron had little enough respect for the intelligence of a social order that had produced him; and though he showed no contempt for the British guineas that had made him wealthy, he had no intention of leaning backward among the ruins of an old order. Even the phrasing of his prophecy intones the eloquence that is sometimes heard in the phrasing of a military dispatch, as though he had been composing a message to be carried by a telegraph system that was as yet unknown. His executive ability which had hitherto been directed toward the management of a caravan winding its way across Italy, now leaped to generalship; the gesture was toward pure action, action that hoped to leave the ghost of *Manfred* asleep in London, and was to outdistance, if possible, the incompleted career of *Don Juan.* Perhaps this effort sought out the creation of a "pure" Byron, as though it were the last and logical refinement of his energy. Actually, he neared exhaustion and was ill, but the prospect of crowded duties beyond his physical strength effected temporary relief. The tempo of his last letters is of the pace that he had set himself to follow; to those who read them, they seemed mobile and alert, as though the writer had reawakened from a long sleep. In a last note to Murray dated 25 February 1824, he described the illness that had overtaken him at Missolonghi: ". . . but whether it was epilepsy, catalepsy, cachexy, or apoplexy, or what other *exy* or *epsy,* the doctors have not decided . . . but it was very unpleasant and nearly carried me off and all that." If *Don Juan* is the last and far-reaching illumination of Byron's genius, what of *Manfred,* which despite its attractions as one of the most enduring expressions of the "Romantic Agony," is seldom reread today?

It must be confessed that *Manfred,* measured by the depths of its penetration into the human soul, is a failure. Its flaws embody the flaws of Byron's art and character; the great release of energy that made its conception possible grew impatient, characteristically enough, of a choice of language and intensity of speech that the play demanded. Compared with Milton's *Samson Agonistes* or Baudelaire's *Fleurs du Mal,* or even Rainer Maria Rilke's *Duino Elegies, Manfred*'s reaches into the heart of human guilt seem superficial. But in the light of *Don Juan* and in reconsideration of Byron's Oriental romances, *Manfred* assumes a far more fortunate aspect; it is then and only then that *Manfred* takes a position of contrapuntal importance of which *Juan*'s career and Byron's letters were the true catharsis and critical resolution.

1933, 1971

THE SURVIVAL OF THOMAS LOVELL BEDDOES

If the temptation exists to place Beddoes in biographical proximity to Byron, an even greater temptation to view him as a belated Elizabethan has not been resisted. If we could be content with a second glance at Beddoes's works in the huge, eight-hundred-page volume, so devotedly, almost devoutly edited by Dr. H. W. Donner,[1] we would agree with the reiterated opinions of Lytton Strachey, which were dutifully followed by F. L. Lucas, and George Saintsbury. All opinions chimed to the belated Elizabethan character of Beddoes's poetry —nor was the epithet entirely without foundation. Beddoes's literary indebtedness to Marlowe, Marston, Webster, and Tourneur was of no inconsiderable weight; he read them with the fascination and joy that Keats described at his discovering Chapman's *Homer*. In reading for ourselves the shadowed pages and the luminous passages of Beddoes's Gothic mystery play, *Death's Jest-Book*, we are in little danger of forgetting the impress that Marlowe and Webster had left upon them—that is all too obvious, and to deny it would be as futile as denying Wordsworth's debt to Milton. Granting all this, the best of Beddoes's poetry merits a third reading, and in a final consideration a balance may be struck between a Victorian neglect of Beddoes's virtues and the excitement of their rediscovery in the twentieth century.

The story of Beddoes's extraordinary, brief, ineffectual, and obscure career has been told at length in H. W. Donner's biography.[2] Like many a patient, pure-minded labor of love, Donner's book has earned respect, if not reciprocal enthusiasm, and its sheets have not been imported to this side of the Atlantic. Beddoes's personality was formed by the same psychic disorder, maladjustment, and homosexual pattern that shaped the behavior of Rimbaud in the nineteenth century and Hart Crane in the twentieth, yet the environment of his early youth was far more fortunate than theirs; he was the son of the prosperous and notoriously eccentric Dr. Thomas Beddoes and a nephew of the witty and famous Maria Edgeworth. At the age of

[1] *The Works of Thomas Lovell Beddoes*, edited with an introduction by H. W. Donner. London: Oxford University Press, 1935.

[2] *Thomas Lovell Beddoes: The Making of a Poet*, by H. W. Donner. Oxford: Basil Blackwell, 1935.

nineteen and while still an undergraduate at Pembroke College, Oxford, the younger Thomas Beddoes achieved celebrity through the publication of his play in verse, *The Bride's Tragedy*—and in the second year after Keats's death in 1823, Beddoes received more spontaneous and authoritative praise than any young poet of his generation. Two years later, he had left Pembroke for the University of Göttingen, leaving England, and his "ambition to become poetically distinguished" behind him. Yet, as his friend Thomas Forbes Kelsall knew, Beddoes had already started work on the dramatic poem, *Death's Jest-Book,* which was to become the true object of his ambitions and to haunt his imagination for the next twenty years. Kelsall, and another friend, James Dykes Campbell, saw how persistently the growth of *Death's Jest-Book* broke through and was nourished by Beddoes's studies in medicine, and they were also in a position to know, through correspondence, the restless, guilt-haunted temper of Beddoes's intelligence, its release of energy in political oratory at Würzburg, its violence, its ardors, and the reaches of its last expression at its deathbed, "I am food for *what I am good for*—worms."

But even death itself and probable suicide in 1849 (which Donner establishes as a near certainty) did not check the pursuit of Nemesis which shadowed Beddoes's fame. Beddoes's misplaced confidence in the critical advice of Bryan Waller Procter ("Barry Cornwall"), which had smoothly glanced across the surfaces of fragmentary pieces from Beddoes's pen with an impartial lack of understanding, repeated its cycle in 1883 when Robert Browning, who had promised Kelsall that he would edit and publish Beddoes's manuscripts, called in the assistance of Sir Edmund Gosse. Both Sir Edmund and Browning were shocked at what they found within the box that Kelsall left them, and for the moment the incident served only to permit Dykes Campbell to make a transcript of everything the box contained.[3] We shall never be quite clear as to exactly what horrified the sensibilities of Gosse, but we do know that the box and its contents were handed over to the care of Browning's son, and were, thereafter, irrevocably lost. Gosse, with his adroit and habitual negligence, issued an edition of Beddoes's poetry in 1890, and in 1928 another edition appeared, prepared by Gosse and published in a manner that is usually reserved—including an evasive introduction and a garish typeface—for pornography. Aside from a few scraps of actual manuscript, and a pamphlet of verse in German, what we read today in Donner's excellent edition of *The Works of Thomas Lovell Beddoes* are the copies made of Beddoes's poems in Dykes Campbell's hand.

[3] They probably found evidence of Beddoes's homosexuality.

Because of the ill-luck which attended the posthumous publication of Beddoes's poetry, it would seem that we approach it with the utmost difficulty—and so we do. Sir Arthur Quiller-Couch's reprinting of a mutilated version of Beddoes's *Dream-Pedlary* in *The Oxford Book of English Verse* increased rather than diminished the general air of confusion which has so persuasively followed mention of Beddoes's name, and the question arises as to where and how the confusion originated. Were Procter, Browning, Gosse, and Sir Arthur wholly responsible for the obscurity of Beddoes's fame? It must be confessed that they materially aided its long career of darkness, but its true source lies in the uneasy relationship which existed between Beddoes and his work; self-knowledge was of slow and fatal growth within him, and when it came, it came too late. There was more of self-realization than of true humility or of pathos in Beddoes's last note to Revell Phillips: "I ought to have been among other things a good poet." It is not enough to say with Donner that Beddoes lacked self-confidence; the psychic split which marred his character and brought his private life within the area that we reserve for Rimbaud and Hart Crane, ran deeper than any loss of confidence in what he wrote. The attitude that he adopted toward his poetry swung between and often touched the two extremes of desiring an absolute perfection in its expression and the impulse to destroy it utterly, yet the ambition to write voluminously, to be heard, to speak aloud remained. His miscalculation in measuring the quality of Procter's literary friendship could almost be described as an act of literary suicide; it was his sin against the mark of his own genius, which had left its impress upon every brilliant passage that comes to light in the tortured progress of writing *Death's Jest-Book*.

Beyond the sources of literary stimulation which Beddoes received from a reading of the lesser Elizabethan dramatists, was his greater effort to clothe and vitalize the spirit and temper of the Gothic myth, the genius that had created the gargoyles on the towers of Notre Dame, the giantchild Gargantua, the merry voyages of Pantagruel, the fiery journey of Mad Meg across Flanders, the Dance of Death itself (which actually enters a scene of *Death's Jest-Book*), the very genius that had found its revival in Matthias Claudius's brief and exquisite lyric, *Der Tod und das Mädchen*. Beddoes's prose version of death and the maiden appears in semiclassical disguise in *The Tale of the Lover to his Mistress:*

After the fall of Jupiter came Love one night to Psyche: it was dark in her cottage and she began to strike a light. "Have done," said he, in a low whispering tone—in which the hinge of some dreadful dark truth out of another world seemed to turn. "Youth, power, and heaven have passed away from the gods: the curse of age has changed their shapes:—then seek not to look on me, Psyche; but if thou art faithful, kiss me, and we will then go into the darkness for ever."—"How art thou changed?" asked she; "methinks you do but try me, jestingly, for thou canst only have grown more beautiful. That thou art more powerful I hear, for the night air is full of rushing arrows, and many are struck and sigh. Hast thou lost thy wings that were so glorious?"—"Aye, but I am swifter than of old."—"Thy youth?"—"Aye, but I am stronger: all must fall before me."—"Thy charms and wiles?"—"Aye, but he whom I have once stricken, is mine for ever and ever."—"Why should I not see thee then? Art thou Love no more?"—"Aye, but not fleeting, earthly; eternal, heavenly Love."—Just then the moon rose, and Psyche saw beside her a gaunt anatomy, through which the blue o' th' sky shone and the stars twinkled, gold promises beaming through Death, armed with arrows, bearing an hour-glass. He stepped with her to the sea-side, and they sank where Venus rose.

The attraction that the Gothic imagination held for Beddoes may be sought for well outside the boundaries of his great admiration for Webster, Marston, and Marlowe, and the forces that drew him toward it were as strong as the impulse which Coleridge felt in the writing of *The Rime of the Ancient Mariner:*

> Are those her *ribs* through which the Sun
> Did peer, as through a grate?
> And is that Woman all her crew?
> Is that a Death? and are there two?
> Is death that woman's mate?
>
> *Her* lips were red, *her* looks were free,
> Her locks were yellow as gold:
> Her skin was as white as leprosy,
> The Nightmare Life-in-Death was she,
> Who thicks man's blood with cold.

The genius toward which Beddoes moved was of an older heritage and of the same, yet deeper root than any reading of the Elizabethan dramatists would disclose; the power of attraction had its true origins behind the façades of Renaissance literature at their noontide; Beddoes's effort to re-create a truly Gothic metaphysic from the slowly increasing manuscript of *Death's Jest-Book* was, if anything, kept alive and nurtured by his residence on central European soil, and the impulse which lay behind the creation of his incompleted masterpiece was as clear a symptom of his day as Coleridge's *Ancient Mariner* or Sir Walter Scott's translation of Goethe's remarkable *Erlkönig*. Truly enough *Death's Jest-Book* restrung and hinged together the common properties of Renaissance poetic drama, and among them the network of double plots and motives inspired by revenge, but what is important for us to rediscover is Beddoes's persistent stress upon those elements in Webster and in Marlowe in which the sources ran backward to the Middle Ages; and there it was that Beddoes had made his choice. Like Poe, Beddoes was a late arrival on the Romantic scene, and like the American poet, his lyricism expressed a last if fragmentary refinement of a first phase in Romantic emotion that had traced its conscious origins to the *Lyrical Ballads* of 1798. His fantastically late resurrection has blurred, almost beyond recognition, his true position within the literature of his day. No echoes of his voice were heard within it beyond the strains of that eminently precocious venture, *The Bride's Tragedy;* and Procter's friendly indifference had closed the door to those in England who might have heard him with a reawakened ear.

Since I have viewed at length the unfortunate aspects of Beddoes's career and its subsequent miscarriages of fame, one should modify that unequitable balance by saying that Donner's edition of *Works* appeared at a particularly happy moment for their twentieth-century revival. If Beddoes's relationship to his creative gifts and their fulfillment was, to put it mildly, sporadic and uncertain, their radical nature was remarkably consistent. In that respect alone, his life, his work, his political convictions, and the quality of his imagination resemble what we have read in the poems, the letters and notebooks of Gerard Manley Hopkins. Because of the singular likeness in radical temper, it can be said with certain obvious reservations that the discovery of Hopkins's poems immediately following the First World War prepared the critics for a favorable reception of Donner's edition of Beddoes's *Works.* In the mid-1930s and on both sides of the Atlantic, writers of conservative beliefs as well as left, sought out their origins of a radical heritage, and in this sense the revival of Beddoes's name carried with it associations of particular significance; and Beddoes's participation in revolutionary activity was of a nature that paralleled the activity of young British writers in the recent Spanish Civil War.

Beddoes's career in Germany and Switzerland had been punctuated by the writing of political satires, and the most successful of these were written in his adopted German, a language which he spoke with rapidly increasing facility. They were done as though the shift in language were a release from the demands of seeking the perfected line, the absolute phrase, the final word. Quite as *The Bride's Tragedy* had achieved distinction in the revival of Elizabethan dramatic verse, Beddoes's brilliantly turned political satires served a lively purpose in expressing the radical spirit of his time; among these, there are speeches and verses which were in effect a triple-edged attack on the forces that sanctioned the Holy Alliance, the Church itself, and reactionary Germany poetry. Quickened by Beddoes's wit and energy the German language was transformed into parody of itself, and what Beddoes had learned from reading Rabelais came to light in his pamphlet which contained verses *On the Enemies of David Friedrich Strauss*, his *Antistraussianischer Gruss*. To find their equal one must turn to John Skelton's satire *Why Come Ye Not to Court* or to certain passages of James Joyce's *Finnegans Wake;* and it is also of historical interest to remember that David Strauss and the incident which inspired the verses left an impression on the early education of Karl Marx. The pamphlet found an appreciative audience among Swiss and German revolutionaries, and its distribution warned educational authorities in central Europe of a certain medical student, Herr Beddoes, a little Englishman, who on one occasion at least had roused fellow students to revolt by reciting a mock tribute to the dying Wellington, "Prussia's one Field Marshal."

How deeply these activities affected the revised versions of *Death's Jest-Book*, we shall never know, but in the play of plot and counterplot of Beddoes's Gothic melodrama, the forces of established power, of revolution and of counterrevolution run their bloody courses, motivated by revenge. The two Fools in the play (and originally it was subtitled, *The Fool's Tragedy*) seem to speak in Beddoes's voice and certainly they recite a number of his finest lyrics, but what of Mario, a character who seeks a leader and who speaks with memorable eloquence?

A Roman am I;
A Roman in unroman times: I've slept
At midnight in our Capitolian ruins,
And breathed the ghost of our great ancient world,
Which there doth walk: and among glorious visions,
That the unquiet tomb sent forth to me,
Learned I the love of Freedom. Scipio saw I
Washing the stains of Carthage from his sword,
And his freed poet, playing on his lyre
A melody men's souls replied unto:
Oak-bound and laurelled heads, each man a country;
And in the midst, like a sun o'er the sea
(Each helm in the crowd gilt by a ray from him),
Bald Julius sitting lonely in his car,
Within the circle of whose laurel wreath
All spirits of the earth and sea were spell-bound.
Down with him to the grave! Down with the god!
Stab, Cassius; Brutus, through him; through him, all!
Dead.—As he fell there was a tearing sigh:
Earth stood on him; her roots were in his heart;
They fell together. Caesar and his world
Lie in the Capitol; and Jove lies there,
With all the gods of Rome and of Olympus; . . .

Despite the weight of inversions in Mario's speech, despite the rhetorical extravagance of "Down with him to the grave! Down with the god!" which show the marks of Schiller's influence as well as the intonations of a distinctly unmodulated school of German acting, the speech reveals a clear and vivid strength of movement that distinguishes the best of Beddoes's poetry from the work of his better known contemporaries. The historical imagination which finds its voice within the speech displays an insight of remarkable force and energy, and is of that quality which we associate with the utterance of prophetic truth.

Perhaps *Death's Jest-Book* by the very weight of its intentions was foredoomed to remain imperfect and unfinished; perhaps there is prophetic significance in the shift of its subtitle from *The Fool's Tragedy* to *The Day Will Come*, that is, the day of its completion placed forever in the future. Quite as D. H. Lawrence was never to complete the larger plan of *The Rainbow*, or as Keats's *Hyperion* remains a fragment, or as Hart Crane's *The Bridge* could not attain the elaborated structure of its early inspiration, so *Death's Jest-Book* falls short of its original design. The desire to create a work of all-embracing stature and dimensions is one of the deepest and most frequently noted pitfalls of the Romantic imagination; surely its shadows haunted Coleridge's *Kubla Khan* and his ode *Dejection*, and from then onward the path went downward into the darkness of being unable to write poetry at all. The last days of Beddoes's life were spent in that same darkness, yet before his work can be dismissed as one who "had made failure his vocation," some attention must be given to two short poems, which are, to my knowledge, among the best examples of lyric verse written in Beddoes's generation.

Since the complete version of *Dream-Pedlary* still lacks the public it deserves, and since the quality of its imagination merits its rediscovery in all discussions of nineteenth-century poetry, I need not apologize for including an entire quotation of it here:

I

If there were dreams to sell,
  What would you buy?
Some cost a passing bell;
  Some a light sigh,
That shakes from Life's fresh crown
Only a roseleaf down.
If there were dreams to sell,
Merry and sad to tell,
And the crier rung the bell,
  What would you buy?

II

A cottage lone and still,
  With bowers nigh,
Shadowy, my woes to still,
  Until I die.
Such pearl from Life's fresh crown
Fain would I shake me down.
Were dreams to have at will,
This would best heal my ill,
  This would I buy.

III

But there were dreams to sell,
  Ill didst thou buy;
Life is a dream, they tell,
  Waking, to die.
Dreaming a dream to prize,
Is wishing ghosts to rise;
  And, if I had the spell
  To call the buried, well,
    Which one would I?

IV

If there are ghosts to raise,
  What shall I call,
Out of hell's murky haze,
  Heaven's blue hall?
Raise my loved longlost boy
To lead me to his joy.
  There are no ghosts to raise;
  Out of death lead no ways;
    Vain is the call.

V

Know'st thou not ghosts to sue?
  No love thou hast.
Else lie, as I will do,
  And breathe thy last.
So out of Life's fresh crown
Fall like a roseleaf down.
  Thus are the ghosts to woo;
  Thus are all dreams made true,
    Ever to last!

Not even the sensitively gifted Tennsyson of *The Lady of Shalott* or of the lyrical interludes in *Maud* quite equal the play of sound and echo, of sight and recall of image that weave and finally complete the garland so gracefully thrown across death's shoulders in *Dream-Pedlary*. One would probably have a better chance of finding an equal among Hölderlin's lyrical remains, rather than in any selection of English poetry, but even there, only the like quality of spirit may be sought and not the melodic variations of Beddoes's lines. In contemporary literature, the nearest approach to Beddoes's lyric imagery may be found in the following lines from Walter de la Mare; the spirit has thinned and grown remote, but its shadow lingers:

> Not toward Death, who, stranger, fairer,
> Than any siren turns his head—
> Than sea-couched siren, arched with rainbows,
> Where knell the waves of her ocean bed.
> Alas, that beauty hangs her flowers
> For lure of his demoniac powers:
> Alas, that from these eyes should dart
> Such piercing summons to thy heart;
> That mine in frenzy of longing beats,
> Still lusting for these gross deceits.
> Not that way!

As one reads through the prose and verse fragments of *The Ivory Gate*, supposedly written by Beddoes between the years 1833 to 1838, the likeness of his verse and its imagery turns in the direction of his distant, and almost certainly unknown to him, American contemporary, Edgar Allan Poe; unfinished manuscripts bearing the title *The City of the Sea* appear, and the best (and apparently completed) union of prose and verse among the scattered papers is *Thanatos to Kenelm:*

"I have no feeling for the monuments of human labour," she would say, "the wood and the desert are more peopled with my household gods than the city or the cultivated country. Even with the living animals and the prevailing vegetation of the forest in this hemisphere, I have little sympathy. I know not the meaning of a daisy, nor what nature has symbolized by the light bird and the butterfly. But the sight of a palm with its lofty stem and tuft of long grassy leaves, high in the blue air, or even such a branch as this (breaking off a large fern leaf) awake in me a feeling, a sort of nostalgy and longing for ages long past. When my ancient sire used to sit with me under the old dragon tree of Dracaena, I was as happy as the ephemeral fly balanced on his wing in the sun, whose setting will be his death-warrant. But why do I speak to you so? You cannot understand me."—And then she would sing whisperingly to herself:

> The mighty thoughts of an old world
> Fan, like a dragon's wing unfurled,
> The surface of my yearnings deep;
> And solemn shadows then awake,

Like the fish-lizard in the lake,
  Troubling a planet's morning sleep.

My waking is a Titan's dream,
Where a strange sun, long set, doth beam
  Through Montezuma's cypress bough:
Through the fern wilderness forlorn
Glisten the giant hart's great horn
  And serpents vast with helmed brow.

The measureless from caverns rise
With steps of earthquake, thunderous cries,
  And graze upon the lofty wood;
The palmy grove, through which doth gleam
Such antediluvian ocean's stream,
  Haunts shadowy my domestic mood.

It is highly probable that the speech and its song were originally spoken by Sibylla, one of the heroines of *Death's Jest-Book,* that the song appeared in an early draft of the play's first act, and was later discarded from the revised versions. Like many passages within the play, the speech and the song circumscribe a completed unit of emotion and the forms which embody it, and as such it is one of the purest expressions of the Romantic genius in nineteenth-century literature. The first line of the song's last stanza recalls, of course, Coleridge's famous "caverns measureless to man," but on reading the entire passage, the impulse is to remark how Poesque it is, how gently it enters and then deeply penetrates the world that lives behind the conscious mind and eye; there it discloses as the song is sung the center of the world so persistently sought by the Romantic imagination, the heart of reality within the dream.

Beddoes's power to reawaken the images of Gothic heritage has its own force today; and in Poe's words, the death that looks gigantically down, stares with peculiar intensity upon the map of twentieth-century Europe. Now covered with the pall of rearmored warfare, one may perceive in the center of that map, the diminished figure of Beddoes's great Fool, Mandrake, and if one listens one may hear a few lines from a stanza of his song; the scene is lit only by flares dropped from the sky; death's triumph lingers there through broken streets and hallways, and human terror resumes its mask of Gothic irony:

Folly hath now turned out of door
Mankind and Fate, who were before
  Jove's Harlequin and Clown.
The world's no stage, no tavern more,
  Its sign, the Fool's ta'en down.

1935, 1944

THE GOTHIC IMAGINATION OF EDGAR ALLAN POE

First of all, so far as the public is concerned, Edgar Allan Poe is in no need of discovery or revival; [1] anthologists of American literature devote a considerable allotment of their treasured "space" to an adequate representation of his prose or verse. And as if to justify the anthologist's concern for Poe's general reputation, four generations of thoroughly respectable Americans have read his *Tales of Mystery and Imagination* with undiminishing, and perhaps (to judge by the number of popular reprint libraries that list among their titles one or another of his books)—no, certainly, increasing enthusiasm. It can be safely said that the works of Poe are better known (in the wholly selfish sense of being read for pleasure) than the poetry of Longfellow or of Whitman or the novels of Hawthorne, Melville, and Henry James. In contrast to this picture, only the critical attitude seems ill at ease, and of recent years it has been insisting, though almost in a voiceless gesture, that Poe is not to be considered a true poet, that by some sleight of hand or eye or psychic deformity he had tricked us into believing that he was something other that he was.

It is not without reason that critical opinion regards Poe warily, because, as all of us know well—and some of us within the past two decades have learned with grief—that matters of taste, esthetics, morality, religion, and politics cannot come to rest, and indeed, remain unsettled by measuring the fluctuations of popular response. In the case of Poe, critical objection carries with it a number of highly unpleasant names and it is well to consider a few of them before we go much further. Even the most casual reader of Poe's tales and verse has a word to offer here, and Poe's writings are frequently described as "morbid," "unreal," "unhealthy," or "fanciful." Once the spell of Poe's charm is broken, the more attentive and sophisticated reader offers similar objections, and phrases like those of "Romantic Decadence" and "a will toward death" are spoken and repeated. If we ignore the centrifugal powers of Poe's attraction, surely enough *The Fall of the House of Usher* can be made to fit neatly within the bounds of a decidedly unhealthy set of terms—and here even the word "morbid" would seem to understate the emotions roused by the

[1] *The Works of Edgar Allan Poe*. London: Oxford University Press, 1927.

presence of the lady Madeline of Usher entering the room with blood upon her shroud.

As we reread Poe at his second and third best—and here I am thinking of his vastly overrated poems, *The Raven* and *The Bells,* as well as such pieces in prose as *The Balloon Hoax,* his critical essay *The Rationale of Verse,* and his burlesques *The Business Man* and *Diddling Considered as One of the Exact Sciences*—criticism becomes progressively more serious and valid. We should confess that Poe dissipated the atmosphere of what he conceived to be his major poem by an attempt at a grim joke, a very parody of the emotion that shocked his readers into attention of all he had to say:

> Then this ebony bird beguiling my sad fancy into smiling,
> By the grave and stern decorum of the countenance it wore,
> "Though thy crest be shorn and shaven, thou," I said, "art
> sure no craven,
> Ghastly grim and ancient Raven wandering from the Nightly
> shore—
> Tell me what thy lordly name is on the Night's Plutonian
> shore!
> Quoth the Raven, "Nevermore."

This was the Poe whom Emerson once dismissed as "the jingle man," the same Poe who defended his skills and paraded his learning in *The Rationale of Verse.* In his essay he attempted to disarm his enemies, the schoolmasters, by a superior show of pedantry—and this effort, as we know too well, was unsuccessful. On this level he contrived *The Bells* and the sensational report, brilliantly written for the New York *Sun,* of a balloon that had crossed the Atlantic westward in three days and landed on the shores of Charleston, South Carolina. This was by no means a disgraceful second best; and if it was admittedly shallow, and often meretricious as it entered the field of critical journalism, it was lively and sharp, intelligent and clear.

As one descends through all the phases of Poe's writing that were less than his best (and these include the complimentary pieces, his valentines, his *An Enigma,* his second poem addressed *To Helen,* who this time was the fashionable poetess, Mrs. Whitman), it should be said plainly that Poe was more frequently the master of artifice than of art. His conscious skills are all too self-evident and are as strained as though they were making a desperate reach toward a world of daylight and of sanity. There were moments when he could and did write badly, but in these instances it is as difficult to charge Poe of mediocrity as it is to defend his exhibitions of childishly defective morality and taste. At the very heart of his defects, the preternaturally clear view of childhood fears remains one proof of the "genius" he undoubtedly possessed.

But before we find true glimpses of the genius which Poe claimed as his own, some attention should be given to the histrionic ability with which he presented his more felicitous ventures into literary criticism. There is an air of neatness, of shabby gentility, conscious of its white collar and clean cuffs, surrounding Poe (a fact which his biographers never fail to notice) and which makes its presence felt in his lecture on *The Poetic Principle*. It can be said that the lecture itself resembled a series of delicately timed dramatic entrances and scenes, each bringing to a close its moment of suspense by the recitation of an unfamiliar piece of verse. The small anthology within the lecture was one (so Poe admitted) that suited his own taste and with this preliminary hint of something about to happen, Poe contrived to make the lyrical verses of Shelley, Willis, Longfellow, Bryant, Pinkney, Moore, Hood, Byron, Tennyson, and Motherwell sound very like his own. Between the silent pause of surprise—and perhaps an approving handclap from his audience—one almost hears Poe's *apologie pour ma vie:* one listens to his remarks on the critics of the *North American Review*, that "magnanimous cabal" which encircled Boston, "the little Athens" of the mid-nineteenth century, one waits to hear the next entry in the charge of dullness against them and when suddenly one catches the name of Coleridge, it is remembered that Poe was among the first in America to read the *Biographia Literaria* with conscious respect. From then onward, the lecturer speaks of the "elevation of soul" and the "excitement of the heart" through the reading of lyric poetry, and though I suspect that Poe's eloquent use of such passionately abstract terms bewildered the ladies and their gentlemen who heard them, I am nearly certain that his utterance flattered their ability to understand and to applaud him. He had charmed them at the opening of his lecture by the promise that he had no design to be either thorough or profound, but before he stepped down from the platform he had pursued an able course against "size" and "bulk" in poetry, and in general, against "the curse of bigness," which even today—and many times within the past twenty years—has found its echoes in criticism of American life.

Though it may seem a willful paradox to read any moral implications whatsoever in Poe's critical commentaries, yet something that has the sound and color of literary morality has a voice among them—and it is heard even as he satirizes moral judgment of poetic merit in *The Poetic Principle*. In speaking for himself and for the position of the poet in a world where commercial enterprise received an overwhelming share of its own approval and material goods which was the very world of Philadelphia and New York, the slight, yet piercing moral overtone is felt; and like the shrill cry of a bat, it is all too clear once it has been discerned. Poe's list of mock virtues for the scarcely human creatures who practice diddling in *Diddling Considered as One of the Exact Sciences* includes Interest, Perseverance, Ingenuity, Audacity, Nonchalance, Impertinence, and Grin; and these virtues are so defined as to clothe some few of the literary figures of Poe's day as well as "the banker *in petto*" or the small merchant. The essay itself is far too highly pitched, too nervous, too grotesque to be entirely convincing, and in reading it one suffers the same chill of rejection that one experiences in viewing the habits of Dean Swift's Yahoos. Yet the mock virtues as Poe stated them reveal an important aspect of his critical intelligence; one begins to share the sight of evil which Baudelaire perceived at the very center of Poe's active imagination, and we quickly recognize that the same intelligence which Poe employed in his burlesques of *The Business Man*'s morality appears in all his comments relating his adventures among the New York literati to his own standards of literary excellence. In *The Mystery of Marie Roget* his experiences in journalism found their reflection in the following passage, which even today requires no further elaboration:

> We should bear in mind that, in general, it is the object of our newspapers rather to create a sensation—to make a point—than to further the cause of truth. The latter end is only pursued when it seems coincident with the former.

And in *The Purloined Letter* it is certainly plain that one object of Poe's satire within the story was and still is human stupidity in the person of the Prefect of Police; one sees the satire rise to a small climax as the Prefect betrays his own mental inactivity by ridiculing poetic insight and intelligence, and if one were to translate the Prefect's indolence into moral terms one would find him the very image of sloth and groundless pride.

One need not labor the point that Poe's critical position was heretical, or that in writing his prose narratives and verse, he never failed to follow his own advice. His failures may be obvious enough, failures of taste, proportion, and adult responsibility, but with the possible exception of his essay on *The Rationale of Verse*, he is never dull—and it would be a rare phenomenon indeed to find a reader who had fallen asleep in the progress of following the plot of one of Poe's tales.

It may be said that many of Poe's objects of satire were unworthy of his skill—but so were Alexander Pope's (and we may quote *The Dunciad* to prove it)—yet how cleverly and with sound judgment he discriminated in separating literary sheep from goats, herding the first, his "magnanimous cabal" of the *North American Review* into one field, and the latter, those who were subtly influenced by the mock virtues of diddling into the others:

> The most "popular," the most "successful" writers among us (for a brief period, at least) are ninety-nine times out of a hundred, persons of mere address, perseverance, effrontery—in a word, busy-bodies, toadies, quacks. These people easily succeed in *boring* editors (whose attention is too often entirely engrossed in politics or other "business" matter) into the admission of favorable notices written or caused to be written by interested parties—or, at least, into the admission of *some* notice where, under ordinary circumstances, *no* notice would be given at all. In this way ephemeral "reputations" are manufactured which, for the most part, serve all the purposes designated—that is to say, the putting of money into the purse of the quack and the quack's publisher; for there never was a quack who could be brought to comprehend the value of mere fame. Now, men of genius will not resort to these manoeuvers. . . .

The paradox of Poe's morality as he applied it to the writers of his time may be reread today with little loss of pertinancy or freshness; and it is only when we hear him bringing charges of plagiarism against Longfellow that we reencounter the darkened atmosphere in which the figure of Poe is the injured and yet petted child of an indulgent foster mother.

As we return to the prospect of a world that Poe saw in his childhood we rediscover the vividness of his attraction for the common reader. Poe's appeal is to the private world that exists in all of us, the world that E. M. Forster has so aptly described as the true "Ivory Tower," and which has always been the necessary and common refuge of the social human being whenever he seeks self-knowledge and wishes to be alone. Poe intensified the realization of that necessary refuge by the detailed descriptions of "being cast adrift" in *The Narrative of A. Gordon Pym* and throughout the course of telling that remarkable story, Poe touches depths of psychological reality that have been distorted or ignored by those who have attempted to explain his character by a facile use of Freudian analysis. The same penetration into the private world of human experience may be discerned in the following lines which were posthumously printed in 1875 and have not received the attention they deserve:

> From childhood's hour I have not been
> As others were; I have not seen
> As others saw; I could not bring
> My passions from a common spring.
> From the same source I have not taken
> My sorrow; I could not awaken

My heart to joy at the same tone;
And all I loved, *I* loved alone.
Then—in my childhood, in the dawn
Of a most stormy life—was drawn
From every depth of good and ill
The mystery which binds me still:
From the torrent, or the fountain,
From the red cliff of the monutain,
From the sun that round me rolled
In its autumn tint of gold,
From the lightning in the sky
As it passed me flying by,
From the thunder and the storm,
And the cloud that took the form
(And the rest of Heaven was blue)
Of a demon in my view.

Aside from the autobiographical nature of the poem what it has to say touches upon an experience common to self-identity in adolescence, the secret confession that the individual stands alone, victorious perhaps, in feeling himself distinct from all other creatures of God's making, but burdened with the self-love and self-pity of Narcissus. From this last extremity Poe frees himself (and the impressionable reader) by the image of a "demon" in his view; and the "demon" in its excellent ambiguity may be a figure of genius or a sight of evil, but probably signifies the two-in-one in a single look directed up toward Heaven.

The "demon" is, of course, Poe's close familiar, and its appearance in the poem describes the shifting of the newly awakened ego from the pride of seeming singular and distinct to pride of being among the fallen and outcast angels. This salvation from the fate of the too beautiful Narcissus is not merely the mutation of a sensibility in Romantic literature, but it exists and endures within all poetry that expresses the fullness and release of youthful emotion; it is the obverse side of the same coin which presents its self-identity to God, or to Nature, or to an amorphous vision of mankind, or to a concept (as Shelley saw it) of Platonic love.

Surely the circumstances of Poe's life nourished and enlarged the internal conviction that he occupied a unique position in the world. One might almost say that his marriage to Virginia Clemm (including his adoption of Virginia's mother as his own) was a decision which carried childhood with him into middle age, and indeed, within two years of his own death. In reading Poe, the childhood visit to England with its sight of Gothic towers and its glimpse of the sea's terrors during the long Atlantic voyage should not be ignored; here one restores fragments of Poe's memory which seem to float irresistibly to the surfaces of his shorter poems. One sees them in his "ultimate dim Thule," his "bottomless vales and boundless floods," his "Time-eaten towers that tremble not," his "o'er the Past (Dim gulf!) my spirit hovering," and brilliantly, his "one bright island smile." If these memories were brought to consciousness through his readings in the poetry of his day, or reinspired through his experiments in taking drugs, their actual sources and their "sepulchre by the sea" are definitely circumscribed by the first fourteen years of his life.

No poet (and indeed Wordsworth's recollections of childhood seem positively remote compared to these) has expressed the scenes of terror within childhood's fears with more enduring vividness than Poe; Rainer Maria Rilke's *Kindheit* with its "*. . . kleine bleiche Gesicht, das sinkend aus dem Teiche schien*" has, I admit, far more delicacy of perception into the same complex of youthful desires and an adult sense of loss, but Poe holds his own by associating a lack of security (which is so often felt and realized by the sensitive and unhappy child) with the conviction of being prematurely doomed, of being predestined for madness or for Hell.

In this sense, Poe's position in American literature during the first half of the nineteenth century is one that seems to stand alone; and if as critic he performed the same services in opposing dull-witted authority in the United States that Lewis Carroll voiced through Alice's lips during her adventures through wonderland and the looking-glass in Victorian England, his situation as a poet was no less critical, and in the worldly gaze of rival critics no less untenable. Poe, like the then unknown Thomas Lovell Beddoes and not unlike the youthful Longfellow and Tennyson, was a belated arrival on the Romantic scene. In America, Longfellow's relationship to his European contemporaries seemed more tangible, and even more "official" than any claim that Poe might have had to offer. While Longfellow traveled through Germany, Italy, and Spain in search of a soul that came to rest at Harvard and received the Smith professorship in comparative literatures, Poe's contact with the Europe of that day was limited to the reading of British periodicals that drifted through John Allan's commercial importing house in Richmond. As Longfellow's travels increased his reputation as an interpreter of modern Europe to Harvard undergraduates, Poe's readings in European letters—however intensive they were or seemed to be—were broadened only by his duties in editorial offices or by the writing of book reviews. Probably the fact that the latter half of his education was conducted in public tended to diminish what little respect he might have earned among the leaders of Boston's intellectual elite; certainly his disastrous experiences at the University of Virginia and at West Point were not of a nature to excite sympathy or understanding in the benign circle of gifted men who had confessed their allegiance to New England soil and were never weary of acknowledging the debt of their educational heritage to Harvard. Viewed in their perspective the singularity of Poe's poetry was heightened by its infrequency of classical image and reference; and today as then, his glory that was Greece and the grandeur that was Rome must be perceived through colors that are stained by the green tides of "the city in the sea" or the Gothic fire of the "Palace Metzengerstein." If at extremely infrequent intervals his classical images seem to shed or to reflect a purer light, it is of Psyche who is out of favor with her lover, or of the sexless, sky-wandering Aphrodite. We may, I think, allow a moment of speculation to enter here, and admit that a probable origin of Poe's angels and feminine deities floated in his imagination against the painted and domed ceiling of a church which he visited in early childhood in Richmond, safely escorted by his foster parents. But for us, it is perhaps more important to realize that his imagination had created its world at an immeasurable distance from the Colonial classicism of Jefferson and of New England. In this particular, Poe's relationship to an American culture will always seem extraordinary; and in general, our literary and historical imagination looks backward through the neoclassic eighteenth century to an Athens that never existed on our soil, and when it attempts to gaze into the future, it dimly discerns with growing optimism, the seemingly endless cycles of rebirth. In this climate, or atmosphere, or whatever name we wish to call it, the phenomenon of Edgar Allan Poe is all too likely to appear as an anomaly—and so it does until we remember that its emotional associations are of the secret places of the heart, and that they touch the springs of human failure. In this latter view it is significant that Paul Elmer More perceived a relationship that existed between Poe and Hawthorne, and here Poe's lonely figure stands at a not too distant call from the Herman Melville who wrote *Pierre* and the unread *Poems*, and in our day, it is not impossibly remote from the E. A. Robinson who conceived the spiritual isolation of *The Man Who Died Twice*. And perhaps—although it is still too soon to say that a similar critical uneasiness will result—we may yet discover that the exile of Poe in Baltimore, Philadelphia, or in New York was a shadowy premonition of Ezra Pound's exile in Italy.

In America no poet so widely read as Poe has left behind him so small a number of poems on which to rest the usual vicissitudes of fame. By a generous count and including the fragmentary *Politian*, the youthful and experimental *Al Aaraaf* and *Tamerlane*, the number rises to a scant half-hundred. After his second and third best poems have been dismissed, the number that remain are incredibly small, but among these few, Poe's imagination illuminates a world that has enduring relationship to the myths and *Popular Stories* of MM. Grimm (which, by the way, had been translated into English with revelatory notes and commentaries in 1823 and in 1826). In *The Sleeper*, and in *Romance*, and in *Lenore*, it is as though Poe had reached the same depths of delight and of terror that are perceived where the sun and moon and the night wind speak their warnings, where Rose-Bud sleeps her many years (is it sleep or death?) within an enchanted forest. In Poe's verses, no Prince escapes the spell, and the rescuing figure is powerless to disenchant the scene:

Far in the forest, dim and old,
For her may some tall vault unfold—
Against whose sounding door she hath thrown
In childhood, many an idle stone—
Some tomb, which oft hath flung its black
And vampire-winged panels back,
Flutt'ring triumphant o'er the palls
Of her old family funerals.[2]

Poe's spell-encircled Princesses are of the same ancient lineage that speaks in "*Van den Machandel-Boom*":

Min Moder de mi slacht't
Min Vader de mi att,
Min Swester de Marleeniken
Socht alle mine Beeniken,
Un bindt se in een syden Dook,
Legts unner den Machandel-boom.
Kywitt! Kywitt! ach watt een schon Vagel bin ick!

It is when one is certain that Poe freed himself from the conscious skills that he practiced so diligently in *The Raven* and in *The Bells* that one hears the accents that have assured him of an immortality; in *To One in Paradise*, the vision is restored of what Grimm's soldier saw as he witnessed, wrapped in his cloak of invisibility, the secret places where the twelve dancing Princesses held midnight festival:

And all my days are trances,
And all my nightly dreams
Are where thy grey eye glances,
And where thy footstep gleams—
In what ethereal dances,
By what eternal streams.

To this order of Poe's imagination I also attribute the first of his poems bearing the title *To Helen* and *The City in the Sea;* they are of a quality that one discovers in an imagination that glances the

[2] This is from the second version of *The Sleeper* (*Irene, 1831*).

roots of human evil and superhuman joy, and reveals their existence among the fears and desires of childhood origin. The "truth" of which Poe spoke so often in his critical asides was a truth that illuminated the hidden chambers of the human psyche, and among his fellows whom he saw on the streets of Philadelphia and of New York, his discovery, as he looked inward to the sources of his own spirit, was of the darkened, private aspect of the multitudinous cheerful face that met its clients and its creditors, its friends at a card table or at a game of draughts. Within that multitude of faces, hardened by what he called the "Grin," his personal appearance was obviously singular, and for a brief time he exerted the full dexterity of his intelligence to take advantage of what seemed to be a singular position in the world about him.

Perhaps Poe will always remain an embarrassment in critical discussions of American literature; and, of course, the final word that reilluminates completely the world of his imagination cannot and will never be written by a hand other than his own. For my part, I would repeat his warning which should be remembered as his epitaph: "The terror of which I write is not of Germany but of the soul."

1943, 1971

THE ELEGIAC ART OF WALTER SAVAGE LANDOR

I know what wages beauty gives,
How hard a life her servant lives,
Yet praise the winters gone:
There is not a fool can call me friend,
And I may dine at journey's end
With Landor and with Donne.
—Yeats, *To a Young Beauty*

As one rereads the last line of Yeats's poem which appears so archly placed under the title *To a Young Beauty*, it is natural to ask why Landor's name is there.[1] We should agree that Yeats wished to be seated in the rarest company, and in keeping with twentieth-century taste, it is signified by the presence of John Donne, but Landor is so clearly unlike Donne that the choice makes for strange companionship at dinner. I am not prepared to think of what Donne and Landor would have to say to one another; that is a problem that Yeats, having passed his journey's end, must solve; yet in one respect, Yeats was intuitively right: Landor's poetry at its best is among the rarities of our present heritage, and it enjoys, even today, an almost esoteric fame.

The poetry of Walter Savage Landor has the dubious distinction of being known chiefly through the helpful inventions of those who

[1] This poem of Yeats's has been subject to many critical distortions. One critic read its first two lines "Dear fellow-artist, why so free / With every sort of company," literally, and from them tried to erect a scaffold of a Yeatsian esthetic. The plain facts motivating the poem are these: Yeats had been making overtures to a very pretty young girl who had pretensions toward being an artist, and who turned down the attentions of the middle-aged Yeats to favor those of an ungifted young man who Yeats hints is a fool. The poet is telling "a young beauty" to keep better company —to pay attention to *him*.

Another critic insisted that Yeats wrote "Dante" not "Landor" in the last line of the poem—which, of course, is nonsense. Yeats is reminding us that Landor was an aristocrat of difficult temperament, who even in old age had an eye for pretty girls; that Donne, an aristocrat of another kind, chose friends carefully and was "passionate"—and both poets in middle age were handsome men. Yeats, not without wit, is giving his "young beauty" a proper scolding. The girl showed a lack of discrimination. In notes on the origins of his poems, Yeats is often candid enough in admitting their relevance to his personal life.

compile anthologies of English verse, and through their offices, its album pieces and scattered epigrams have suffered tedious repetition. It is not that the selections to which I refer have preserved Landor for us at his worst, but that repetition through the wear of time has made the few choice quotations seem thin and bodiless. In that light one thinks of it as possessing the qualities of finely tempered and beautifully wrought costume jewelry, and in reading it, an impression is left of graceful compliments being paid to ladies and of the author's readiness to depart from the sinking fire of life. These qualities, which include the merits of seeming cool and chaste and firm are deceptively easy to admire and then to set aside: "I strove with none," "the fire sinks," and that (it is very easy to conclude) is all that Landor had to say.

The many years of Landor's life, from 1775 to 1864, endowed him with an unusual richness of contemporaries. In Landor's youth, George Crabbe was vigorously alive (with Jane Austen among his most discriminating admirers) and the Pre-Raphaelites never forgot Swinburne's greetings to Landor as "England's eldest singer." Yet Landor's position had the superficial character of seeming to fall outside the literary movements of his day. His radical Toryism was, of course, enough to disenchant him in the eyes of Leigh Hunt's circle; Landor had seen Napoleon in the flesh at arm's length and did not share Byron's disillusion in hero worship; he was as far removed from Wordsworth as from the youthful eloquence of Keats—and in his poetry it can be said that he lived through his age without falling to rest within it.

In his personal conduct (which has been the concern of his biographers from John Foster to Malcolm Elwin) his eccentricities, his years of self-imposed exile in Italy, his restlessness, his mismanagement of even the most casual of his domestic affairs, follow the general pattern of misfortunes which attended the careers of Coleridge, Shelley, and Byron; in his narratives and dramatic sketches not a few of his subjects and scenes are as "Romantic" as anyone could well desire; in these he enjoyed the same interests that were shared by such temperamental opposites as Southey and Byron, but his occupation with classical themes and his sustained respect for traditional verse forms make it extremely difficult to speak too seriously of his "Romantic behavior" and its consequences.

In contrast to a number of young men who wrote poetry in his day, Landor was not precocious. His early writings contained little of the youthful brilliance that won partisans for the authors of *The Lyrical Ballads*, *Childe Harold*, *The Bride's Tragedy*, *Endymion*, and *Adonais;* Southey admired Landor's *Gebir*, but it must be confessed that *Gebir*, as well as the majority of his *Heroic Idylls*, belongs to that unhappy company of highly praised and industrious works of literature which include at one end of the spectrum Moore's *Lalla Rookh,* and at the other, Matthew Arnold's *Sohrab and Rustum.* Briefly, they are dull, and it requires greater industry to reread them than the effort that had been spent in creating their histrionic episodes and gestures.

There has been a tradition (which still exists in English literature) to measure a poet's stature by his ability to write a long narrative poem, rhymed or unrhymed, a poem, which as time goes on, has less resemblance to the ancient epic than to something described in publisher's announcements as "a novel in verse." Since Milton's day the successful composition of a narrative poem which runs beyond six hundred lines has become increasingly rare. Pope's translation of Homer may be counted an exception, and so may the realistic chronicles of George Crabbe; Byron's mock epic, *Don Juan,* is still another, and Longfellow's *Tales of a Wayside Inn* remain as lively as on the first day of their publication. Since 1900, E. A. Robinson's narratives may be looked upon as further exceptions to the rule—but are they? They are both more meditative and more dramatic in character than what is usually accepted when we think of narrative verse; their closest parallels are to be found in Crabbe's chronicles of the Borough and the Parish Register and of Robinson Jeffers's tales in verse (in which another exception can be brought up for the sake of argument) the best of them, *The Tower Beyond Tragedy,* closely approximates dramatic form.

However popular they may have been, however impressive they may have seemed at the moment of their arrival, narratives in verse resemble the character of fool's gold, and almost without exception they suffer the tarnish and destruction that time bestows upon a work whose ambitious intentions outride the excellence of its performance. Even as one generation of readers buys the latest attempt to emulate Homer, or Alexander Pope, or Milton, it yawns and falls asleep over an effort of the same kind which had the temerity to be written twenty-five or fifty years ago. At best, the modern narrative in verse yields a number of briefly inspired and isolated passages which may be quoted to prove the existence of a gifted writer, and it is charitable to view them in the same light that one finds interest in the studio paintings (many of which have been discarded by their maker) of a famous artist.

It is for this last reason only that Landor's narratives in verse deserve attention—and I must confess that the interest is more necrological, and perhaps more academic, than it is inspiring. Through reading them one seems to enter into the secrets of his writing table: one learns of his experiments in blank verse, of his writing some passages in Latin before presenting them in English, of his wide familiarity with the literature of Plutarch, Gibbon, Virgil, Dante, and Tasso, of his habits of hasty reading and rapid composition—but the poems are less poems in themselves than they are the fruit of Landor's enthusiasms in making literary discoveries, and of his speculating with heated vehemence upon them.

In the majority of his historical romances in verse and in his plays, Landor seems to impose his willful fancies upon his characters; his *Gebir*, his *Count Julian*, his elderly *Ulysses* are all presented without the benefit of psychological motivation. All are larger than life-size and are as wooden, though by no means as impressive, as the Etruscan gods and heroes who stand guard within the walls of the Metropolitan Museum [2]—and by comparison, even the Etruscan warriors seem to possess an image of life held within an eternal stillness that Landor's heroes lack. By their very nature the Etruscan gods inspire awe through silence, while Landor's heroes deliver their opinions in the language of poetic discourse, speaking what could have been better and more tersely said within the pages of a book of critical essays.

But perhaps the greatest barrier, the thickest walls of print, that stand between the world and the best of Landor's poetry are his own words in prose, the *Imaginary Conversations*, which so completely overshadowed his reputation as a poet, and so hugely instructed and entertained their readers in those moments which were reserved for leisure by our grandfathers. Landor was equally delighted by their success, for praise and fame were brought to his doors through publication of a novelty in English letters. The novelty was something that gave the illusion of being both a one-act play and a short story, and yet was neither—nor was it quite a Platonic dialogue or a literary essay; but it seemed to combine the merits of all four media, and the little sketches could be read aloud in the drawing room as though the speaker were reciting the most intimate of closet dramas for the entertainment of his wife, or son, or daughter. Great names and characters made rhetorical entrances and exits from the page—one had the pleasure of hearing that one was face to face with Oliver Cromwell, or Catherine of Russia, or Hannibal, or Diogenes, or Plato, or Marcellus. In effect, the appeal (and unreality) of their appearance was not at all unlike many of the present experiments in radio drama,[3] and Landor welcomed the task of writing his *Imaginary Conversations* with a nearly professional eye; he had conceived a means of expressing his political ideas, his concepts of history, his literary opinions

[2] Some of which were later to be discovered forgeries.
[3] Those current in 1944.

to the British public—did it matter that his fanciful conversation between Horace and Virgil was actually lifeless and devoid of wit? Not in the least; it had the air of conveying information, and the best-known facts were seldom violated. His characters possessed everything but an enduring vitality: they were capable of thought and violent action; they pleaded and declaimed; they declared undying love or hatred for one another—yet the flexible rhetoric in which they spoke weaves and rambles monotonously up and down and across the page. Did the classical dialogues of the *Imaginary Conversations* anticipate the prose which later ripened into the sinuous withdrawals and embraces of Walter Pater's *Marius the Epicurean?* I suspect they did, and despite their tendency to ramble from whatever had been chosen as the subject of a prolonged discussion, Landor's speech flows from a source of greater purity and firmness of expression than can be found in any comparable passage of Pater's prose. Landor's biographers accent, justly enough, the consistent and deeply unfortunate nature of his unworldliness, of his unhappy fortunes in dealing with his wife and children, of his misadventures in his attempts to be a landlord—the same lack of insight pervades the atmosphere of his *Imaginary Conversations.* They provided relaxation for the eager-to-be-well-read Victorian; all the delights of historical fancy and memory were rediscovered in their pages, but the breath of life was noted only by its absence.

If Landor lacked the knowledge of human character other than his own, what he did possess was an inspired appreciation of a Greco-Roman heritage in literature, but the true expression of its spirit in his own verse waited upon the arrival of his maturity. It can be said fairly that he did not begin to write poetry until he was past fifty, and then how brilliant, how clear, how firm are his *Hellenics*! And if one contrasts them with the lines of Keats's *Hyperion,* one reads the difference between the patient, conscious artistry of youthful talent and the easy strength of a mature poet who had found his tongue and could speak aloud without the merest sign of effort.

It can be said that the *Hellenics* introduce the reader to the hundred poems and more which comprise the rarities of Landor's gifts and from which the anthologists have made their selection. In the *Hellenics* (and I refer particularly to *The Hamadryad* and *Iphigeneia and Agamemnon*) the figures of youthful love and sacrifice are graced with a purity of color and movement that is seldom equaled and almost never surpassed in English poetry. In these brief narratives one does not ask for, nor does one feel the lack of psychological subtlety and conflict, and an illustration of what I mean is presented in the closing lines of *Iphigeneia:*

She lookt up and saw
The fillet of the priest and calm cold eyes.
Then turn'd she where her parent stood, and cried,
"O father! grieve no more: the ships can sail." [4]

It is here that the purity of Landor's speech is clearly heard, but in saying so I realize that as one speaks of purity in poetry, a word of explanation is required.

The search for whatever is called "pure" in poetry usually defeats its purpose in the rediscovery of minor lyric verse; and, because of this, we had best, I think, confine our attention to that quality of expression which is found in the writings of Ben Johnson, but is absent from Chapman's *Homer*—that quality which makes its presence known in the verses of John Wilmot, Earl of Rochester—and which must be sought for with only the briefest intervals of reward in the poetry of the seventeenth-century "metaphysicals." It is readily discoverable in Dryden's prose and almost totally absent from the pages of Sir Thomas Browne's *Urn Burial.* Its expression, when we find it, is a first cousin of what Shakespeare named as "simple truth" and which was so unhappily miscalled "simplicity."

The simple truth, so hard to come by anywhere, implies, of course, a lucid statement of it, and however unforced its accomplishment may be, it is almost never as simple as it seems. Wordsworth, I fear, often confused it with the unbrilliant simplicity that Shakespeare so rightly and so cleverly rejected. I believe that in poetry the presence of simple truth and the pure expression of it, cannot be called into being by anything less than art, nor can it be conjured out of a vacuum by an act of will.

In his later poems Landor relinquished the power of conscious will and the poetic ambitions of his early narratives in verse. The public success of his *Imaginary Conversations* had released him from the bitterness and the internal distractions of seeming to be forgotten while younger men received the highest praise. As he wrote to Robert Browning in 1831, the *Conversations* were his "business"; and like Byron, he preferred to think of himself as an English gentleman, freed from the necessity of ever writing a line of poetry at all—except when the internal, impulsive moment of necessity arrived. Perhaps this attitude was no more than a restatement of Congreve's desire to be known as a gentleman rather than the author of *The Way of the World;* but in Landor one perceives it as an admirable defense of

[4] *The Poetical Works of Walter Savage Landor*, edited by Stephen Wheeler. Oxford; The Clarendon Press, 1937. (Subsequent quotations are also from this edition.)

his easily wounded and abrasive ego. It was an attitude that Yeats sought in part to emulate and to revive—which was to be a poet only through the demands of an inner being and compulsion, and not through the external circumstances of good fortune or bad, or to be dependent upon the mutations of poetic fame.

It was the Landor of the love lyrics, the brief elegies, the poet who had outlived deservedly famous and younger men, and it was he with whom Yeats wished to dine at journey's end. For twenty years Landor wrote each poem as though it were his last, and as their number increases, their scope and variety almost equals the multitudinous, bell-tolling stanzas of Tennyson's *In Memoriam.* If it is possible to say that almost every poem, every translation that Samuel Johnson wrote was devotional in spirit, in the same fashion almost every lyric that Landor set down on paper, irrespective of whether or not it was addressed to Rose Aylmer or to Lady Blessington or to "Ianthe," was a revival of the elegiac note in English poetry. Here, Landor's mastery is unmistakably complete, and here, it is true enough that he "strove with none." Perhaps the best example of his uniqueness can be found in his lines *On the Dead*, his elegy written on a child who died at the age of six:

Thou in this wide cold church art laid,
Close to the wall, my little maid!
My little Fanny Verchild! thou
Sole idol of an infant vow!
My playmate in life's break of day,
When all we had to do was play!
Even then, if any girl
To kiss my forehead seiz'd a curl,
Thou wouldst with sad dismay run in,
And stamp and call it shame and sin.
And should some rough, intrusive boy
Bring thee an orange, flower, or toy,
My tiny fist was at his frill,
I bore my jealousy so ill,
And felt my bosom beat so bold,
Altho' he might be six years old.
Against the marble slab mine eyes
Dwell fixt; and from below arise
Thoughts, not yet cold nor mute, of thee
It was their earliest joy to see.
One who had marcht o'er Minden's plain
In thy young smile grew young again.
That stern man melted into love,
That father traced the lines above.
His Roman soul used Roman speech,
And taught (ah, thou too, didst teach!)

How, soon as in our course we start,
Death follows with uplifted dart.

Francis Verchild, "that stern man," the girl's father, veteran of Minden, fought in 1759 on the frontier of Prussia; he had caused *In cursu vitae mors nobis instat* to be written on the marble slab, a touch of Latinity that Landor admired—the tablet was in St. Mary's Church, Warwick. Within such elegies Landor spoke the language of "simple truth" which Yeats in his middle years consciously emulated. The mastery of such an art is very like the discovery of finding "freedom within form," which should always be the last reward of a lifetime spent in the writing of poetry. One hears its accents with its elegiac undertones in:

Rose Aylmer, whom these wakeful eyes
  May weep, but never see,
A night of memories and of sighs
I consecrate to thee.

And in Yeats, and in, of course, his own emotional environment, the same spirit is revived, the same notes are struck:

When day begins to break
I count my good and bad,
Being wakeful for her sake,
Remembering what she had,
What eagle look still shows,
While up from my heart's root
So great a sweetness flows
I shake from head to foot.

As one reads further into Landor's shorter poems, the distance between his time and ours seems to diminish, and that happy illusion is of the same character that makes certain passages of Dryden's *All for Love*, and a half-dozen of Rochester's lyrics seem as fresh as though they were written yesterday. Admitting that we are living in an age that is highly appreciative of an elegiac spirit in poetry, and that young men and their elders have been saying farewell repeatedly to the generation which preceded theirs, it is not this sentiment alone that endows the large majority of Landor's shorter pieces with a quality which remains unaffected by the distance in time between our day and his. We are refreshed by a language which seems "modern" in a sense that the poetry of many of Landor's contemporaries does not—the speech is direct and less consciously poetic (to the reader's ear at least) than, let us say, the language of *Adonis* or of *Endymion.* In his remarks on "age," does Landor's speech seem more remote than that of Yeats or of Housman?

Death, tho I see him not, is near
And grudges me my eightieth year.
Now, I would give him all these last
For one that fifty have run past.
Ah! he strikes all things, all alike,
But bargains: those he will not strike.

But for the exception of the presence of "beauteous" the following lines under the uninviting title *On Hair Falling Off After an Illness*, might well have been written during the last twenty years:

Conon was he whose piercing eyes
Saw Berenice's hair surmount the skies,
Saw Venus spring away from Mars
And twirl it round and fix it 'mid the stars.
Then every poet who had seen
The glorious sight sang to the youthful queen,
Until the many tears were dried,
Shed for that hair by that most lovely bride.
Hair far more beauteous be it mine
Not to behold amid the lights divine,
But gracing, as it graced before,
A brow serene which happier men adore.

The same quality of freshness, and I suspect, the same evidence of poetic maturity, is readily perceived in this brief passage among the many written to "Ianthe":

The torch of Love dispels the gloom
Of life, and animates the tomb;
But never let it idly flare
On gazers in the open air,
Nor turn it quite away from one
To whom it serves for moon and sun,
And who alike in night or day
Without it could not find his way.

If the *Conversations* were Landor's "business," the writing of his shorter poems filled the moments of his leisure, and he continued to write them in the same fashion that a gentleman of the eighteenth century carried a sword. The poems had become as closely identified with his daily being as his habit of buying canvases in secondhand shops to hang on the walls of his apartment, or to give away to friends. "My pictures blacken in their frames," he wrote:

As night comes on,
And youthful maids and wrinkled dames
Are now all one.

Death of the day! A sterner death
  Did worse before;
The fairest form, the sweetest breath
  Away he bore.

That degree of serenity and of self-knowledge which Landor expresses so well and learned so late, places him in the company of those few poets whose gifts outlast the excitements of their youth and survive the triumphs, the humiliations, the self-deceptions, and the glories of false pride which are, too often, the sum of human experiences during middle age. Landor's wisdom was of a sort that was incommunicable in any of his activities except that of writing verse; certainly it was not related to the continued mismanagement of his large income which spared him only the extremes of poverty, nor to his long-sustained quarrels with a number of his relatives. His unworldliness, his impulsive fits of anger and of generosity possessed the charms of youthful innocence; the poise he achieved was in his poetry: there, the world he saw was neither broken nor misinterpreted. How clearly the misadventures of his life are resolved within it, and how brilliantly in *The Casket* his wisdom illuminates what in less gifted writers is merely the darkness of old age!

Sure, 'tis time to have resign'd
All the dainties of the mind,
And to take a little rest
After Life's too lengthen'd feast.
Why then turn the casket-key?
What is there within to see?
Whose is this dark twisted hair?
Whose this other, crisp and fair?
Whose the slender ring? now broken
Undesignedly, a token,
Love said *mine;* and Friendship said
So I fear; and shook her head.

The ease of statement and its restraint, the finality of accent, the turn of an excellent conceit—all of which distinguish the mark of a true style in poetry are there. It is what we think of when we attempt to describe those qualities of style which are distinctly separate from the more spectacular and less enduring qualities of a highly seasoned personal mannerism in writing verse. We are not concerned with the poem's originality, but with the authenticity of its expression. It is this quality that the greater number of Landor's shorter poems convey, and their abundance indicates a writer of greater stature than can be brought to light within the pages of an anthology.

Someone among Landor's late contemporaries—his name is unimportant and has been forgotten—linked Landor's reputation and his artistry with that of Goethe's, a rash comparison which was smiled upon at the time as a flattering and overly enthusiastic compliment; perhaps it was, for we must accept the presence of Landor without a *Faust*, without a *Werther*, without a *Wilhelm Meister*, and without a Weimar and an Eckermann. Yet both men preserved within their writings the formal graces of the century in which they were born, and both lived through an age that first welcomed and then slowly recovered from its period of Sturm und Drang. Though Landor did not possess the steadiness of mind and of character that we acknowledge in the existence of Goethe's major works, if we remember the particular qualities of Goethe's lyrics, a comparison of them and their felicities to the later poems of Landor is not totally inept nor unconvincing.

In the failure of his dramatic sketches Landor has a position not far removed from the robust company of Byron and Robert Browning; in the successes of his *Imaginary Conversations* he is of that long list of writers who in each age gratify the tastes of a single generation and leave few traces of their remains behind them; it is only in the excellence of the poems which he wrote without ambition, and with little hope of gaining the attention of posterity, that his reputation has earned the respect and the neglect of isolation. To say that he was not unconscious of his position is an understatement, for in his last years, an awareness of its singularity had become the source of the remaining vestige of his pride; and if the world has been slow to recognize the true and enduring merits that were his, surely the voice of his shade in whatever world it may inhabit would be the last voice heard to speak in accents of disappointment or complaint.

1944, 1947, 1971

IMMORTALITY AND THE WHITE KNIGHT OF LEWIS CARROLL'S ALICE

What though the radiance which was once so bright
Be now for ever taken from my sight,
Though nothing can bring back the hour
Of splendour in the grass, of glory in the flower;
We will grieve not, rather find
Strength in what remains behind;
In the primal sympathy
Which having been must ever be . . .

—Wordsworth, *Intimations of Immortality from Recollections of Early Childhood.*

"Then you keep moving round, I suppose?" said Alice.

"Exactly so," said the Hatter: "as the things get used up."

"But what happens when you come to the beginning again?" Alice ventured to ask.

"Suppose we change the subject," the March Hare interrupted, yawning. "I'm getting tired of this. I vote the young lady tells us a story."

"I'm afraid I don't know one," said Alice, rather alarmed at the proposal.

"Then the Dormouse shall!" they both cried. "Wake up, Dormouse!"

—Lewis Carroll, *Alice's Adventures in Wonderland*

It is in like manner and with no intentional disrespect to literature itself, that each generation from Pindar's day to this changes the subject slightly and tells its story. I would like to suggest that even the Dormouse's story as it was told on a fine mid-Victorian afternoon is not entirely irrelevant to the subject of Wordsworth's *Ode* on immortality. We remember that the Dormouse spoke of three sisters who had been living at the bottom of a well (to be exact, it was a treacle well) and that they drew (they had been learning how to draw) all manner of things from it, everything that began with *M*, such as mousetrap, and the moon, memory and muchness: and today, as we reread the *Ode*, memory and muchness disturb us most, and from these we progress toward Wordsworth's moon who with delight looked round her when the heavens were bare.

If one rereads the poem for the sake of recapturing the associations it once held, it is likely to contain memories which its long title half-unconsciously revives; and none of us, I think, can hold Wordsworth or the *Ode* wholly responsible for this phenomenon. For most of us the earliest reading of the poem had its beginning in a school classroom, with Wordsworth read (as Alice's Gryphon might well recall) at odd moments between the study of those superior branches of learning which include Ambition, Distraction, Uglification, and Derision. My own recollection of the *Ode* is surrounded by the images of a boys' preparatory school, where, behind a desk, a young, thin, nervous, red-headed Scotsman sat—and it was he who instructed us in English poetry, basketball, and tennis. I remember him reciting Shakespeare and *The Jabberwocky* with a recklessness that matched his leaps and rushes on the concrete tennis court—and in his reading of Wordsworth's *Ode,* he accented a touch of malice (which all of us shared in reciting the poets of the Lake School) by a slight exaggeration of his Edinburgh burr; one could hear it clearly as he read aloud:

> Our birth is but a sleep and a forgetting:
> The Soul that rises with us, our life's Star,
> Hath had elsewhere its setting
> And cometh from afar . . .

As one heard the *rrs,* the atmosphere increased its tension, for it was part of our unspoken agreement not to laugh aloud at Wordsworth's famous *Ode.* Without knowing why, we felt immensely superior to the image of the lank and grey-haired, long-nosed, elderly poet whose head leaned with a weak, womanish tilt out of the darkness of a photo engraving which faced the title page of Wordsworth's *Poetical Works;* it was an unvoiced pact between us to read him with an air of prep-school skepticism, and to justify our attitude by frequently reciting:

> "O mercy!" to myself I cried,
> "If Lucy should be dead!"

Yet we could not dismiss him utterly; for the *Ode* was almost certain to turn up in awkward places: its title would reappear in questioning footnotes in schoolbook anthologies of English verse and scrawled in chalk upon the classroom blackboard. From a sense of duty to his students (and the power exerted by college entrance boards), our instructor persisted in the revival of the *Ode* on hectographed sheets of paper that were rapidly circulated around the room during the weighted silence of a moment which always precedes a written examination. Who wrote it and what did the poem mean, and what, oh what, was Wordsworth's philosophy? This last we agreed, if not completely understood, was called "Pantheism," and was of heavier substance than anything that went by the name of philosophy in the poetry of Shelley, Keats, or Byron, and one could prove it (if I remember correctly) by contrasting two skylark poems in which it was shown that Shelley lost himself in Nature, while Wordsworth, in a trying hour, was found. It was agreed that Wordsworth somehow achieved salvation and, if less attractive than Byron or Coleridge, was out of danger—was safe and not to be questioned in open controversy; it was as though Wordsworth's recollections of childhood had begun at the very moment when the pleasures of our own had vanished. From a last reading of his *Ode* one went to college, leaving the memories of *The Solitary Reaper, The Reverie of Poor Susan, To a Skylark, I Travelled Among Unknown Men,* and fragmentary stanzas of *Resolution and Independence,* floating and yet heard distinctly within the recesses of the inner ear.

To speak of Wordsworth and his *Ode* again today is like asking oneself the question that Alice ventured: "But what happens when you come to the beginning again?" So much has happened to Wordsworth and ourselves that a true beginning is difficult to find: one road winds backward to the first decade of the nineteenth century in which the *Ode* was written, another to what we mean when we speak of poetry at all, and still another to Alice herself and to her childhood which was overshadowed by the unnamed presence of Wordsworth among the trees of that dark forest where the White Knight recited his ballad of *The Aged, Aged Man.*

Since I confess a predilection for the second and third of three possible beginnings, I shall speak of the first only as it serves to illuminate the darkness surrounding Alice as "she leant against a tree . . . listening in a half-dream to the melancholy music of the song." The first road recalls a number of familiar images, images of Rousseau and of the Fall of the Bastille, the title page of Blake's *Songs of Innocence,* Mr. Thomas Day's adopted daughter, Sabrina, the educated orphan, whose innate goodness was severely tested by her foster father ("It is said that he dropped hot sealing wax on her arms to inure her to pain, and fired blank cartridges at her petticoats to train her in self-control."), images of Mr. Day's Sandford and Merton, Miss Maria Edgeworth's Lazy Lawrence, and among them that dark eyed, semitragic child of genius, Hartley Coleridge, of whom it has been so often said that he was the living prototype of the child within the *Ode:*

> Behold the child among his new-born blisses,
> A six years' Darling of a pigmy size!

These and a hundred other pictures crowd the scene, filling a decade of unresolved Napoleonic Wars: Miss Austen's precocious girls with clear heads and cool fingers trip between them—and everywhere the hope of the world was seen in a child's face, the child no longer stained by sin, the guiltless child, and the innocent, even idiot boy was believed to possess the secret of human happiness. The reflected likeness of that child may be seen in the pallid, soot-streaked features of Smike and Oliver Twist who followed after, and after them, came the pink cheeked, Maypole dancing figurines of Miss Kate Greenaway; and a distinct resemblance to the child's behavior may be found among the heroes of social novels, ranging their separate ways through the fiction of the twentieth century.

Returning to the *Ode* itself and the moment of its birth, we would agree, I think, that its so-called philosophic generalities had been given the particulars of light, shade, depth, color, and motion in a number of Wordsworth's earlier poems: *Her Eyes Are Wild*, *We Are Seven*, *The Sparrow's Nest*, *The Reverie of Poor Susan*, *Michael*, and *I Travelled Among Unknown Men*, were of the same world that was viewed so hopefully in the opening stanzas of the *Ode*. His readers were familiar with its terms; they knew its "Fountains, Meadows, Hills, and Groves," they shared the emotion implied by the use of each abstract noun within the *Ode:* each joy, each grief, each bliss, each soul, each glory; and, I think, we may grant that they were as well prepared to read the poem as he was to write. Even the difficult concept of human immortality was expressed in a language that Wordsworth's early readers (with the aid of his prefatory note) could accept and welcome, and as they rediscovered it within the *Ode*, it seemed to fall into place as effortlessly as sunlight upon the earth. So much then, for our first beginning, which in itself could be expanded into a volume of considerable size and weight. From what we know of the *Ode* and its predecessors, we are reasonably safe in saying that it summed up a number of the beliefs and observations which had been already exposed to light in eloquent passages of *The Prelude* and which had taken form in the first ten stanzas of *Resolution and Independence*.

Our second beginning contains a few remarks on the general nature of what we talk about when we speak of poetry at all; and here, I think, that if Alice's White Knight were brought in to join us, he would insist that such remarks should be called "warnings." That is not their name, of course; nor does the present occasion speak with the urgency of air-raid sirens and threats, yet something very like a "warning" is sounded every time an interpretation of poetry takes place. Unless one is actually reading the poem, hearing it, perceiving it, and is aware (for the time being) of certain hitherto unnamed emotional responses, the warning that one hears is "What does the poem mean?"—then, a moment later—"Is the poem poetry?" From then onward we can tell you what poetry is called or has been called, but not what it is: I am inclined to think that the Wordsworth who wrote the *Ode* called it "natural piety," and that the White Knight called it "my own invention." The Gryphon and the Mock Turtle (since they were obviously concerned with matters of educational importance) undoubtedly called whatever poems they read by the name of "lessons," and most of us, like Alice, tend to respect such formidable creatures who had received the best of educations and who wept, who hid their faces in their paws at the slightest recollection of their past experiences. The pity was that lessons lessened from day to day—and that for them there had passed away a glory from the earth.

I, for one, am willing to believe that whatever the something is that is first thought of as poetry and is then given, like the White Knight's ballad, a number of different names—I believe that the kind of poetry we carry seriously in mind soon acquires a quality that resembles an independent life, a being which springs from and yet finds a place apart from all other things in this imperfect world. As we read it, the poem exists beyond the time and the occasion that prompted its arrival; and there are moments when the poem seems to exist even beyond the gifts, the skills, the ambitions, and intentions of the person who wrote it. There are times when one might almost say that the life of a poem depends upon the varieties of misconception taking place around it; and if we are willing to agree that the play *Hamlet* may be read (quite as one reads the best of Shakespeare's tragedies) as a dramatic poem, surely that example should be a warning to us all. Like Hamlet's father's ghost who walks within it, the play itself still walks the earth to haunt the wariest of its interpreters. Despite the number of footnotes—or is it because of them?—that almost crowd the text of *Hamlet* off the printed page, its central being remains remarkably alive; and while it may be great joy for us to speculate on the names that it may be called, including semantics, psychology, social science, or education, the independent power of life within the play is undiminished.

So it is when we approach any work conceived by human imagination: from the imperfect sources of human life, even from violent action and disorder, a selection of shapes and sounds, color and motion takes place, and we recognize that something has been done which is self-contained and active. These remarks or "warnings" are not, of course, "my own invention"; they have been spoken with far greater accuracy long ago and they may be found by those who have eyes to read them in Homer's story of the creation of Achilles' shield.

The shield was an extremely cunning work of art, and its multitudinous figures resembled life so closely that the shield in its entire being seemed a mirror of the very world Achilles and his enemies had known; and we must remember that Achilles wore it to protect his body from a fatal wound. Was the shield self-knowledge? I suspect that is one of the names that it might be called.

But as I turn from Homer back to Wordsworth, and from Wordsworth to Alice, I cannot prove that Alice herself had read the whole of the famous *Ode* that asserts the promise of immortality. Others have spoken (and among them, William Empson) of Alice's perceptive wit in voicing criticism, yet I can say that her interpreter, who disguised himself as "Lewis Carroll," was not unfamiliar with the world of childhood that the Lake Poets celebrated and held before the eyes of their admirers. We know that his criticism of it was fully conscious (one has but to read the parodies he wrote while an undergraduate at Oxford), but we also know that he accepted the major premise of the *Ode*, even the vision, or rather one of those words which begin with *M*—the memory of the happy moment associated with the past—and if the theme of the *Ode* is closely related to the theme of growing up, certainly the theme of Alice's adventures is of the same character, and is, if anything, illuminated by a greater number of precise steps onward from childhood to maturity.

The first expression of Alice's concern about growing up reached its crisis in her interview with the Caterpillar. She was in deep trouble, and she did not, of course, wish to grow up too fast, yet she wished to be more than her three inches high. It was no wonder that the Caterpillar instructed her to recite Robert Southey's *The Old Man's Comforts*, an eminently respectable poem that had appeared in the *Youth's Magazine* for February 1816, and since that time, it had been memorized by an entire generation of proper children. If her recitation of *Father William* did not recall the image of Wordsworth directly, the memory of Southey recalled him at his weakest, bringing to mind the unhappy *Peter Bell* who, after a wild career, saw goodness in an ass's skin and became an honest man. From him we turn to Wordsworth's *Idiot Boy* and to *Simon Lee* and from *Simon Lee* we return to Robert Southey, the most devoted and least gifted of Wordsworth's three great friends. One remembers Dorothy Wordsworth and Coleridge readily enough, but Southey (not without cause) is as readily forgotten; and if it were not for Alice, who would care to read Southey's unconscious parody of Wordsworth's philosophic attitudes? Who would waste his time reading:

> In the days of my youth, I remember'd my God!
> And He hath not forgotten my age.

To these lines Alice quickly replied:

> Do you think I can listen all day to such stuff?
> Be off, or I'll kick you down stairs!

And then said timidly, "some of the words have got altered": indeed they have, and very lively words they have become. I doubt if any critic of Alice's day would have dared to go half as far as her imperfect memory carried her; and if her words "got altered," they certainly transformed the kindly, senile, sweet old Father William. Was the association also that of another William, a William Wordsworth who succeeded Southey as Poet Laureate, traveling where "other palms are won," beyond the *Ode;* was Father William the elderly poet who made petulant yet shrewd inquiries to an admirer concerning the welfare of his American investments? Perhaps Alice did not intend to go as far as that, yet her remarkably feminine (one almost says "feline") perceptions were aroused, and at the very least, her Father William knew the value of commercial enterprise and the jargon of salesmanship:

> "You are old," said the youth, "as I mentioned before.
> And have grown most uncommonly fat;
> Yet you turned a back-somersault in at the door—
> Pray, what is the reason of that?"
>
> "In my youth," said the sage, as he shook his grey locks,
> "I kept all my limbs very supple
> By the use of this ointment—one shilling the box—
> Allow me to sell you a couple?"

The altered words had done their work; the recitation was not quite right. Was it fair? was it cruel? was it ethical? Alice herself was not troubled by these questions; her subconscious will had voiced its criticism, and to those who had enjoyed her version of *Father William* all questions of justice and morality were made to seem as irrelevant as the memory of conscious right and wrong within the action of a dream. But the authoritative, masculine Caterpillar who had been brought up to respect the philosophy of the Lake Poets was sure that she was wrong from beginning to end, and said so.

I shall not attempt to enlarge upon the intentions which inspired flaws in Alice's memory; we know only that she was neither deaf nor blind and that something had happened to Father William between the date of Wordsworth's *Ode* and Alice's arrival on the scene that was none too lovely to contemplate. We also know that Alice's Father William had been read and still continues to be read by thousands who had never heard of Southey's *The Old Man's Com-*

forts, and what is more important, those very readers grow restless and uncomfortable as they read the following lines from Wordsworth's *Ode.*

> The Youth, who daily farther from the east
> Must travel, still is Nature's Priest,
> And by the vision splendid
> Is on his way attended . . .

Surely, the youth in Sir John Tenniel's drawing of Father William's son (and Sir John's illustrations of Alice's adventures are not to be ignored) was a portrait of a singularly dull young man. Was he the Idiot Boy, was he Michael's son, was he Nature's Priest? Perhaps not, perhaps he was none of these, but his likeness to his brothers is scarcely short of being fatal.

Meanwhile Alice's encounter with the Caterpillar had prepared her for a more important and later crisis in growing up, and here at last, we come upon her in the dark forest attended by the White Knight whose foolish face was lit by a faint smile. The White Knight was about to sing his ballad.

> "It's long," said the Knight, "but it's very, *very* beautiful. Everybody that hears me sing it—either it brings the *tears* into their eyes, or else—"
> "Or else what?" said Alice, for the Knight had made a sudden pause.
> "Or else it doesn't, you know," replied the Knight.

The old Knight was very kindly, very gentle; he had great difficulty in staying on his horse; he was perhaps the meanest flower of knighthood; he was all too human—and there in the dark forest, and with the Knight reminding us of tears, we almost hear the strains of *Resolution and Independence:*

> Thanks to the human heart by which we live,
> Thanks to its tenderness, its joys and fears,
> To me the meanest flower that blows can give
> Thoughts that do often lie too deep for tears.

Resolution and Independence which is a far better poem than the *Ode,* and which was foreshadowed by the *Ode,* closely approached the climax of Wordsworth's poetic life; and if the poem moves in the direction of Wordsworth's maturity, a recollection of it also guides the reader in the direction of Alice with the White Knight at her side at evening in the forest. We are being prepared for the burlesque of *Resolution and Independence* in the White Knight's ballad of an aged, aged man, "the oldest man . . . that ever wore grey hairs."

I'll tell thee everything I can:
  There's little to relate.
I saw an aged, aged man,
  A-sitting on a gate.
"Who are you, aged man?" I said.
  "And how is it you live?"
And his answer trickled through my head,
  Like water through a sieve.

By the time the Knight completes the singing of his ballad, we are well past the *Ode*, stepping through it to the other side, quite as Alice once walked, or half-climbed, through the looking glass. Meanwhile Lewis Carroll's criticism of Wordsworth had shifted its position of attack from indirect reference to explicit parody of a particular poem. Across that merest space from the *Ode* to contemplation of the Leech-gatherer (which is almost impossible to measure because it is so near, so far) the first of our beginnings with its images of Rousseau and the guiltless face of childhood ("A Presence which is not to be put by.") seems to tremble and dissolve as though London Bridge itself were about to fall. But Alice had already heard the crash that followed her conversation with Humpty Dumpty, and the continuous failure of well-intentioned, adult (though sometimes rude) authority no longer troubled her.

If Alice after her visit with the White Knight had begun to grow up, it was in spite of and in a totally different way than Father William and the Aged Man approved. What if she had known something of the same world that Wordsworth's *Ode* had opened to other children (and certainly to their parents and schoolmasters) of her day? The words, somehow, were not the same, and the vision of the Lake Poets had shifted its perspective—and here we must remember that Alice was a heroine and not a hero. From the White Knight she had learned of what poetry might be called, but her perceptions were becoming critical in the sense that she was soon to have other things than poetry to fill her mind. She had to say good-by to the White Knight, leap to the Eighth Square, and after a moment of dismay, be glad at least to wear a crown upon her head. Her reward was that Queen Victoria thoroughly enjoyed her adventures, for the Queen had known and witnessed the failures of masculine authority, and the weaknesses of the speculative, or as Wordsworth would have said, "the philosophic mind." Surely, her advisers and ministers had changed and fallen since she first came as a girl—scarcely a young woman—to wear the crown. There had been Grey and Melbourne, Palmerston and Peel, Derby and Lord Russell—and as for other changes, that troublesome Reform Bill was like the battle between the Lion and the Unicorn—but the Queen had outlived them all. She had outlived her Poet Laureates, Southey and Wordsworth—and the arrival of Tennyson would, no doubt, bring other changes. As for a style, a language, a fashion being laughed at, one had only to remember that in the century before Alice had been born, John Gay's *The Beggar's Opera* laughed Italian opera off the London stage.

But after this much is said of Wordsworth and Alice, why was it, granting the usual changes in poetic taste and fashion, that Wordsworth's *Ode* and its successor, *Resolution and Independence*, became so vulnerable to Alice's remarks? Unlike Achilles' shield, Wordsworth's *Ode* is by no means self-contained; it tends to fall apart, and even the most casual reader of it notices a change of temper, sensibility, and feeling that divide its opening stanzas from its last. Whatever the cause of this defect may be, surely no poet of Wordsworth's stature ever stumbled so blindly into so many traps as he. The most important of these was his undue speculation in prose on the philosophic sources of his poetry. His own definitions of poetry haunted him for fifty years of his long life, and even now, they continue to haunt academic discussions of his remains. Every schoolboy can cheerfully quote and requote his eloquent phrases concerning "the spontaneous overflow of powerful feeling," yet I suspect that Wordsworth's lack of impulsiveness coupled with the mere desire to "overflow," explains many a dull passage in *The Prelude* and *The Excursion.* There can be little doubt that he accepted the role of being a poet with admirable seriousness, and in reading Dorothy Wordsworth's *Grasmere Journal* (1802) one can see that he approached his task with a strenuous immensity of purpose that is unequaled in English literature. In the closing stanzas of the *Ode* and through certain passages of *Resolution and Independence*, he proved his ability to make his observation, his experience, his emotions, his insights, and his thinking flow as though they traveled in a single stream, yet his longer poems contained elements of greatness rather than the completed structure of great poetry. We can sight their far distance from the self-contained design of a true poem by contrasting them with *Lycidas* and *Samson Agonistes*. Did his effort to acquire a "philosophic mind" stand in the way of his development to full maturity? The effort rewarded him with a cloak of authority which became transparent in the merest glance from Alice's candid eye.

In defense of Wordsworth, one can reply that Alice, despite her wit, despite her sharpness, lacked a perception into the tragic aspect of life that Wordsworth saw; she knew terror, but not grief; she had little concern for things outside the ranges of her immediate vision; she was a practical young female, caught, for the moment, in the mortal coils of growing up, and it is doubtful if, in her life beyond her journey through the looking glass, one would find her meditating on the values of poetry.

Admitting that the difficulties of Wordsworth's verse are those of memory and muchness, there are glimpses throughout it of that something, which for me, whatever name it takes, is poetry. For poetry, as I read it, is only incidentally concerned with such abstractions as "the philosophic mind," or history, or science: it need not quarrel with them, it should not quarrel with them—and on occasion, it should be aware of them to its own advantage. It has been said often enough that literary expression (being what it is) is always vitally concerned with what we call our senses—but here we must not forget our sixth sense, intelligence, for poetry must always contain something to delight the mind. Too often we credit the superior critic (and among superior critics Alice should not be forgotten) with an order of intelligence that is not to be found in poetry; this may be an unspoken hint, but it is implied. Although differences of opinion may be expressed between them, no such division exists between them, no such division exists between the gifted poet and his commentators. It is intelligence in its heightened sense, and in, I think, the best meaning of the term, that enters all poetry worthy of our attention; it implies an awareness and a sensibility reflected in the poem itself, and however subconscious or deliberate its offices may be, it imposes those limitations that are sometimes separately regarded as poetic form; it is sensible of ethics and of the devotional spirit, and for the individual poet as well as the reader of his poetry it sometimes illuminates the darkened path toward a true knowledge of mankind.

Since this discussion threatens to expand beyond all thought of Wordsworth's *Ode* and Alice, I fear I shall return to all three of my beginnings; and it is time (if the March Hare still has his watch) for someone else to tell a story.

1941, 1944

ROBERT BROWNING: AN "ESCAPED VICTORIAN"

Aye you're a man that! ye old mesmerizer
Tryin' your meanin' in seventy swadelin's,
One must of needs be a hang'd early riser
To catch you at worm turning. Holy Odd's bodykins!

***

Here's to you, Old Hippety-Hop o' the accents,
True to the Truth's sake and crafty dissector,
You grabbed at the gold sure; had no need to pack cents
Into your versicles.
Clear sight's elector!

—Ezra Pound, *Personae*

In speaking of "frigid fancy" I referred to the particular passage only. But Browning has, I think, many frigidities. Any untruth to nature, to human nature, is frigid. Now he has got a great deal of what came in with Kingsley and the Broad Church school, a way of talking (and making his people talk) with the air and spirit of a man bouncing up from the table with his mouth full of bread and cheese and saying that he meant to stand no blasted nonsense.

—Letter to R. W. Dixon from Gerard Manley Hopkins, 12 October 1881

Hang it all, Robert Browning, there can be
but the one "Sordello."

—Ezra Pound, *Canto II*

The above quotations are enough to open a renewed discussion of Robert Browning. At this moment of writing there is a deep and peculiar silence surrounding the mention of Browning's name: [1] and in that silence, one thinks of the Browning societies, "the Browning clubs," that extended in small groups westward from nightcurtained rooms in London across the American continent seventy years ago. From these one hears the ghostly chatter and earnest "dying fall" of female voices. And in the present darker silence, one also hears prep school and college classes, devoted to Victorian poets, recite the

[1] *Selected Poems of Robert Browning*, with an Introduction by Horace Gregory. New York: Holt, Rinehart & Winston, Rinehart Editions, 1956.

name of Browning, and a voice dictating an assignment of readings from his many poems. There is also floating knowledge of "the Brownings," the romantic legend of his marriage to Elizabeth Barrett, of *Sonnets from the Portuguese* (which is still sold today in various mock vellum and leather gift editions), of Wimpole Street, and of Miss Barrett's thoroughly Bloomsbury cocker spaniel Flush. The rest of the silence is as dense as the Camberwell and Kensington fogs which irritated the membranes of Browning's throat, which choked his speech, which made him fancy, even as far away as Florence or Rome, that he was victim of a persistent asthma from which there was no escape. To renew discussion, one must pry open fog-blanked doors and windows.

At the beginning one should find an answer to Hopkins's charges, for in their direction lies the key to twentieth-century prejudice against Browning, and they are all the more damaging because they contain an important half-truth. Browning, the major Victorian he at last revealed himself to be, had great blemishes. His "frigidities," as Hopkins called them, betrayed themselves by a forced illusion of human heartiness, a blustering air of determined and frightening cheerfulness, the kind of writing that made possible his best-known lines in his song from *Pippa Passes:*

> The hill-side's dew-pearled;
> The lark's on the wing;
> The snail's on the thorn:
> God's in his heaven—
> All's right with the world!

By these means and through the lips of an innocent child, a child not unlike Dickens's Little Nell, Browning's conscious mind righted the world. It would be wrong to say that he did not believe the song he made her sing, and there is a Broad-Church heartiness, an indiscriminate embrace of God and all the conditions of the human lot, that enters the very spirit of the song. It makes us think of the warm American handclasp (and in Italy, Browning was often mistaken for an American) that conceals the cold heart, the inarticulate loneliness—the wish to be Oh, *so* friendly, *so* homespun, *so* eager to call everyone by the first name—and beneath it, a deadly chill. This was one of the ways that Browning in his life as well as in his poetry faced the world; it made a crude balance of how "to get along," to meet "morning at seven," to accept and then shake off the bad dreams of the night before. It was a demonstration of rightness, a will not to give in, and it displayed a thick coating of insensibility—even to some degree an insensibility to poetic art. As for the bread-and-cheese image that Hopkins fired at Browning's head, there are lines to justify it. In *Bells and Pomegranates VII, Dramatic Romances and Lyrics,* among *Garden Fancies* (1845) is the following passage:

> Then I went in-doors, brought out a loaf,
> Half a cheese, and a bottle of Chablis:
> Lay on the grass and forgot the oaf
> Over a jolly chapter of Rabelais.

So far Hopkins's charges against Browning hold their ground, but we should remember that Hopkins, too, was a Victorian, reacting violently, because of his conversion to the Roman Church, to all signs of the Anglican Broad Church, and that he was also fighting a rear-guard action against certain of his major contemporaries. The daytime, bouncing Browning was anathema to him. Browning's show of levity was of a blustering quality that offended Hopkins's standards of seriousness in the writing of poetry, whose strictures were as sharp as Lewis Carroll's parody of Wordsworth's *Resolution and Independence* in the latter pages of *Through the Looking-Glass,* in which the famous "Leech-gatherer" was transformed into an "aged man,/A-sitting on a gate." In their criticism, these two Oxonians, Carroll (otherwise the Reverand Charles Lutwidge Dodgson, Mathematical Lecturer of Christ Church) and Hopkins had certain likenesses: both distrusted a show of bigness and broad reaches of emotion; both were skeptical of inflated literary reputations. Carroll saw in Wordsworth the product of a world as unlike Christ Church as St. John's College, Cambridge; from Hopkins's point of view, Browning, the special student from University College, London, was seen at a distance that was even greater. But Carroll's parody does not destroy the larger, and inner, values of Wordsworth's poem; it is a record of its minor flaws. In the same fashion, Hopkins's charges against Browning do not apply to the deeper, less conscious elements of Browning's poetry. As a contemporary, Browning was a disturbing influence who plunged with the awkwardness of a cheerful whale in and out of the deeper channels of Victorian consciousness. What Hopkins saw was a Browning whose very presence seemed to confuse serious concern in the writing of poetry at all.

Certainly Browning had little of the outward appearance of being a poet. As a man he looked decidedly what he was—an energetic, dark skinned, almost flashily dressed, pushing creation of London's suburban middle class, wearing lemon-colored gloves, not quite a gentleman, who when young and in London frequented the gaudy dinner parties at which the actor, William Macready, Dickens, Forster, and Fox were guests.[2] He had been to neither Cambridge nor Oxford, nor

[2] On one of his early visits to the house of his friendly critic, Fox, Browning, when told by the critic's young daughter that her father was

had he gone to Eton or Harrow. His father, an official in a bank, gave him the resources of a large library he had collected and sent him to a local day school at Camberwell, after which young Browning became a restless special student at University College, London. His actual tutors were his parents, and he treasured his father's library of six thousand volumes to the end of his life.

The examples of Shelley, of Keats, and of Walter Savage Landor loomed large before young Browning. In his teens, as his fragmentary early poem *Pauline* shows, Shelley was the object of his infatuation. His father and mother had become Camberwell Dissenters, and for a brief adolescent period Browning stepped beyond them into Shelley's enthusiastic atheism. But of more lasting heritage were the colonial strain in his father's family and the Wiedemann (German and perhaps Jewish) strain in his mother's ancestry. On his father's side the poet's grandmother was a Creole, and West Indian properties were among the sources of the Browning family fortunes. These streams of memory within the Browning family circle were lasting enough to give the poet a sense of difference from sons of other prosperous Londoners, of which his brisk good looks and dark skin were external evidence. They also pointed the way toward his slightly foreign manner in London company, his lack of deep attachment to island England—and most significantly to his marriage with Elizabeth Barrett, whose family wealth came directly from West Indian holdings.

Literally the complexion of Browning's heritage was of strongly different color from the generally English world before his eyes and through which he had to make his way. It was to place him among those English poets—Byron, Shelley, and Landor—who were also European poets, self-willed exiles from England, and who chose the cities of the south, of Italy, as spiritual homes. "Open my heart and on it see/ Graved inside it, Italy!" had deeper meaning than the majority of Browning's vigorously expressed confessions. The statement showed one of the most enduring of his affinities; and in respect to Camberwell, the southeast London suburb where he was born, it gave him a sense of distance that was almost American.

Among Victorians, Browning is the least English of English poets; he is at a measurable distance from Tennyson as well as from his late contemporary (then unknown as a poet) Thomas Hardy. More than

---

not at home, walked into the music room and played the piano until the critic returned. His aggressive manner may well have offended many, but one can imagine how lively and yet reassuring it must have been to Elizabeth Barrett confined to her rooms in Wimpole Street. His briskness cheered her on, and flared to anger against her only when he fancied she neglected the care of their infant son, "Pen."

that, the occasionally obscure passages in his earlier long poems separated him from the immediate Victorian scene. His *Paracelsus* gained a reading among his early friends and a kindly acceptance of the fact that he was a poet—but who were the friends? They, too, were not precisely of the "right" complexion: W. J. Fox, editor, critic, and journalist, was a member of the Dickens circle; so was Macready, the actor; but, popular as these men were, they were not of a company that established literary reputations. Alfred Domett, the famous "Waring" of Browning's memorable poem, had accepted a political post in New Zealand, and loyal as he was to Browning, had no commanding voice in British criticism.[3] Macready went so far as to produce Browning's play *Strafford*, but he could not extend his good wishes beyond the short run of the play. Dickens's cordiality was that of a busy, much sought-after novelist and platform celebrity; Browning's brisk, middle-class manner and appearance did not offend him in the least, but Dickens was not the man to promote the fortunes of contemporary poets.

The spectacular elopement with Elizabeth Barrett, six years his senior, to Italy (and both poets were well beyond the ages of Romeo and Juliet) gave Browning a singular poetic notoriety; yet the move placed him again out of keeping with conventionally English sights and sounds. For over twenty years his peculiarly un-English elements were reinforced by living in Italy, and with them so was his own way of speaking English, his rhythms and intonations, and these were to affect the accents of his major verse. His innovations of sound and language were to remain unmodified by English spoken on native soil; and in a strange sense, paradoxical as it may seem, he became the greatest of Italy's mid-nineteenth-century poets.

So far as his daily behavior revealed him, he was a rather more than proper middle-class Victorian. As the husband of Elizabeth Barrett, the most popular of England's woman poets, and as the father of their only son, he was a domestic hero. The romantic marriage was not unwise, for he restored an invalid to health and shielded from gossip of the world his wife's habit of taking drugs. She returned his affec-

[3] In the entire range of English poetry, *Waring* is a poem of which there is only one of a kind. In its Victorian setting it is a remarkable portrait of the adventurous man of the world, a figure which brings to mind such men as Sir Richard Burton, as well as the many who represented Her Majesty's Empire around the globe. But the poem is also a celebration of masculine friendships surviving through periods of long separation; in this latter sense it applies to the kind of friendships made in the army during two world wars and chance renewals of them in European and American cities. Through a strange circumstance, perhaps a half-ironic turn of destiny, Alfred Domett, Browning's "Waring," was also the great-uncle of Ernest Dowson, the *Yellow Book* poet, who wrote of Cynara, who died young, and whose temperament was anything but cheerful and robust.

tion; and if the letters they exchanged can no longer be regarded as classic examples of their kind, the feeling that inspired them endured until her death. They shared her income, and later both received a more generous allowance from an income left them by her cousin. Browning accepted whatever embarrassments arose from this situation with exemplary courage. Despite the romantic legend of their elopement, the two poets who received visitors to Italy were commonplace—amazingly so. And on the rarity of a visit from Tennyson, they listened half the night and with wide-eyed patience to *his* reading of *Maud,* which Tennyson so heartily enjoyed. Like many Victorians, Browning had no love of romantic candor, particularly when the subject of sex rose to the surface. After his wife's death he was intrusted with Thomas Lovell Beddoes's manuscripts; when he read them in the company of Edmund Gosse, he was so deeply shocked that he insisted that Edmund Gosse edit them. The box that held the manuscripts was eventually lost; fortunately another friend, Dykes Campbell, had copied the majority of them before they disappeared. The story of the box illustrates the daylight side of Browning's character, of his need as a domestic Victorian to thrust unpleasant revelations into the shadows. Fortunately that need did not extend to the suppression of his own *Porphyria's Lover,* his *Bad Dreams,* his *Childe Roland to the Dark Tower Came.* In the best of his poetry, he did not disclaim the sight of darker truths.

2

With the worst that can be said of Browning safely behind us, an actual rereading of his poems comes into view. At this a contemporary reader might well say, "Like other Victorians, the man wrote too much." The reader would be wrong. Among the peculiarities of Browning's genius was an inability to rewrite successfully a poem or a play; sturdily he wrote his way through dramatic narratives, lyrics, plays in verse. The writing of a play in five days was scarcely a task for him; yet he had no talent for revamping it. He would move on through it, failure or half-success as it might be, to a better piece of writing. Talent, that lesser gift for writing verse, was scarcely his; nor was he, like Tennyson, whose genius was of a very different order, an able craftsman and a professional poet. He was very nearly an example of "the divine amateur," self-taught, doing his own reading, choosing, as he confessed, Landor for his master. He moved toward a distinction of style rather than polish; he needed room and, since for many years his readers were few, he got it. In that sense the silence around him was large; there would be small loss should he try to fill it. He began to fill the silence with his play *Strafford.*

Although Macready, actor-manager-producer, set up the play behind the footlights, where it glimmered and faded for five performances, it was ill-timed. Its year was 1837, the year that William IV died and Victoria became queen. A historical play that displayed a king, Charles I, as possessing all too human frailties in treatment of his loyal servant Strafford, was decidedly uncheerful at a moment when "Silly Billy," William IV, had brought in more than enough lack of respect for the British crown. The times were nervous; and the young queen-to-be was scarcely known. What was overlooked in the play were the strokes of genius in recreating the characters of Charles, his French-born queen, Pym, and Strafford. When the play is reread today the majority of its lines are fresh and clean, and though Browning lacked theatrical skill in presenting his scenes, there is no doubt that he possessed, even at this early date, a historical imagination of the first order. Certainly he had read Clarendon's *History of the Rebellion* with unsurpassed insight. The play was a true tragedy: Strafford's heroism had its mortal flaws; he failed to know himself as well as his loved king, nor could he check himself when he was roused to anger. Nor did the play show taint of mock-Shakespearean melodrama. In these respects Browning as dramatist was superior to the later Tennyson who wrote *Becket;* and if Tennyson was more successful with the public (as he was), it was because he had learned to make everything he wrote seem directly analogous to the feeling of his day. In contrast to Tennyson's *Becket, Strafford* seems to be a half-forgotten forerunner of twentieth-century poetic drama.

But *Strafford* was also a forerunner of Browning's many dramatic lyrics, romances, monologues, represented at length by his novel in verse, *The Ring and the Book.* In the exercise of his historical imagination, Browning had greater scope than Sir Walter Scott. The scope included Biblical as well as Greek antiquity; guided by Vasari's *Lives of the Painters,* it ranged through lesser-known channels of the Italian Renaissance; and, with Vasari left behind, Browning's imagination invaded passages where the Renaissance shaded into the baroque, the baroque into the rococo. Its present tense revealed a Dickensian London in *Christmas Eve,* and in *Waring,* the brilliant portrait of a Victorian friendship. And in this historical connection, Browning was the first Englishman of notable stature to appreciate, to understand, Stendhal's *The Red and the Black.* He was perhaps the only Victorian who was acutely aware of the then obscured genius of the eighteenth-century poet Christopher Smart. In Browning's case, the sum of these temporal ranges was to produce an effect of timelessness. Was this his intention? One finds a convincing, affirmative answer to that question in his "Abt Vogler," the German priest who, having made a musical instrument, the Vogler organ, looks backward at eighteenth-century Rome and sees "rampired walls of gold as transparent as glass" leading to a further image of "a great illumination . . ./Outlining round and round Rome's dome from space to spire." Abt Vogler's image was one of ultimate creation, the moment of revealed religious truth, the epiphany, "the showing forth," and the poem ends with the return to earth again.

In the half century between the writing of *Strafford* and his last poems Browning found room in which to create a large cast of characters, and in doing so he anticipated W. B. Yeats's idea of the poet in 1909. "All my life," Yeats wrote in his *Autobiography*, "I have been haunted with the idea that the poet should know all classes of men as one of themselves. Some day setting out to find knowledge, like some pilgrim to the Holy Land, he will become the most romantic characters. He will play with all masks." [4] Browning in his own day could find kinship with Landor's *Imaginary Conversations*, written in prose, which proved that his long-sustained tributes to Landor, even to the assistance he gave to Landor in that elderly poet's last years, was more than lip service. But Browning's position also provided Ezra Pound with an example—shown in Pound's many adaptations from poets writing in other languages than English and in Pound's conception, illustrated in his *Cantos*—that "All ages are contemporaneous." As Yeats turned to Landor ("And I may dine at Journey's end/ With Landor and with Donne."), in like fashion Pound held to an affinity with Browning. Browning's major productions can now be seen as a bridge between the writings of Shelley and Landor and the major poetry of our own day—and not the least important feature of his example was that his total contribution became a carrier of European culture back to England and westward to the United States. Of all nineteenth-century poets who wrote in English, none equaled the richness and the scope of Browning's cultural references.

With the magnitude of Browning's contribution held in mind, we are not surprised that the broadest, the most enthusiastic acceptance of his poetry first came from readers in the United States. To read through Browning's collected works was very like an extended holi-

[4] Browning's series of poems in *Men and Women*, his *Parleyings with Certain People* illustrate how he anticipated Yeats's remarks and also show his affinity to the kind of writings to be found in Landor's *Imaginary Conversations*. Pound's *Homage to Sextus Propertius* has a debt to Browning insofar as it is a re-creation of Propertius as well as an adaptation of some of Propertius's poems. The Latin poet is one of Pound's "masks" and one of his "characters" in the same sense that Andrea del Sarto and the many characters of *The Ring and the Book* are among Browning's creations. Yeats was affected by Landor's diction as well as by his general choice of Landor as a master; Pound's choice of Browning as a master does not mean that the younger poet was influenced by the elder's language; yet in other respects the fact that Pound followed Browning's example is clear enough.

day in Southern Europe, including weekend tours to Greece and the Holy Land. It is not without significance that his books of poems were eagerly pirated by American publishers. They stimulated American curiosity and had the immediate effect of being cultural *Baedekers.* They were actually reprinted in the Railway Guide of the Chicago & Alton Railroad. The bored (and frequently bewildered) traveler presumably might be inspired to travel farther and farther into cultural space to patronize, after a journey eastward to Boston or New York, the steamship lines. Many of Henry James's traveling Americans, his "passionate pilgrims," were of that temper. And it could be said today as then that Browning himself had many attributes of a "passionate pilgrim." Consistently enough, the Brownings in Rome and Florence had American friends, including the William Wetmore Storys, and Browning's son married a Chicago heiress. The Protestant, unchurched Christianity of Browning also held its appeal to Americans; so far, even his least understanding readers could grasp the spirit of what he had to say.

3

If Browning today has lost some of his prestige as a "psychological poet," he still retains his stature as an innovator in the general field of psychological fiction; without being an influence upon the writings of Henry James, he pointed some few of the directions toward which James moved. Instinctively Browning plotted the extremes of human passions; one says "instinctively," because the darker, more profound aspects of his poetry seem less conscious than his professed optimism, as though in his searchings for truth he could not suppress the darkness, the existence of human failure, the recurrent presence of what he called "bad dreams." Like those of his contemporary, Dickens, his writings were a release of energy; he was not able, and wisely did not care, "to talk about his art." He encouraged Browning societies to arrive at any interpretation of his poetry they chose; since he had had his say, they were free to make what they could of his contradictions. He did go so far as to insist that "*How They Brought the Good News from Ghent to Aix*" had "no sort of historical foundation," that it was written on shipboard without the aid of maps. His comment was a rare exception to his rule.

What business had he then to write, since he professed his optimism, *Childe Roland to the Dark Tower Came?* Of all Victorian poems, it is the deepest step downward to the shores of hell, that area between the feigned madness of Edgar in *King Lear* and the actual madness of Lear himself. At the very least its images are those of Purgatory.[5]

[5] Although some few of the images in *Childe Roland* recall scenes in Dante's *Inferno* and *Purgatorio,* Browning's ventures to the shores of Hell

Porphyria's Lover is of the same company, and so is the stilled, half-gloried-in radiance of *Evelyn Hope*. The shrewdness of the speaker in *My Last Duchess* represents the same extreme away from Browning's daylight world. To be true to the mirror he held up to life and to be true to his own knowledge of the world, he could not, did not, deny an active force of evil. In the writing of these poems, he struck a balance that gave singular force to all else he had to say. From "the great illumination" of Abt Vogler to the Purgatory of Childe Roland, Browning's entire field of vision fell into place. The gradations of his scale were in *The Ring and the Book* and in the many books of poems that began with *Paracelsus* in 1835 and ended with *Asolando* in 1889.

4

In choosing Browning as a Titan among his masters, in electing him the greatest inventor in the writing of Victorian English, Ezra Pound granted him a stature not unlike his estimate of Whitman—with this difference, Pound did not permit Whitman to guide his hand. The likeness between Whitman and Browning is obvious enough: both poets needed room in which to write, large areas of space and time; had they been painters, they would have painted nothing less than murals. Other likeness exist in that both were nineteenth-century Dissenters, vigorously Protestant; both, so far as the very speech of poetry was concerned, were innovators; and both created a style, rather than the finer contours of an art. One thinks of them as moving through and beyond the provinces of art to a style that has all the intention and appearances of being artless. Beyond this point the resemblance fades away.

Pound also found merit in Browning's strenuous levity, the very trait that so profoundly distressed and annoyed Hopkins, which at its worst is a lapse in taste and a sign of false vigor ruthlessly applied. Taken at its best, its infusion of strength, of being devil-may-careless, has rewarding values, and in Browning's verse it carried him beyond all usual treatment of historical décor and saved him from being merely clever. His double and breakneck rhymes, his skipping of accents were and still are a relief to readers of poetry; in their day they were certainly tonic contrasts to the smoother flowing lines of Tennyson; one is artlessly jolted awake. At its best Browning's levity refreshes one as completely as the cantos of *Don Juan*.

Browning's levity has still another aspect; in his minor writings it produced a number of memorable verses and lines, and often those one wishes to forget. The verses fall into the definition George Orwell so brilliantly gave to Kipling's verse, which he called "good-

are distinctly unlike Dante's. They have no relation to Dante's structure of the universe; Browning's scenes are of an individual subconscious.

bad poetry." Some of them were no doubt Browning's substitutes for writing light verse; they are in his *Cavalier Tunes;* and notably they include his *Incident of the French Camp* and "*How They Brought the Good News from Ghent to Aix.*" In refusing to give the "*Good News*" topographical and historical importance, Browning was right: the essential meanings of the poem were in its galloping noises, in the very din it wakened in the reader's ear, and in the relationship between the rider and his horse. His best sustained effort in this medium was his *Pied Piper of Hamelin,* the rhymed narrative that he wrote for the amusement of William Macready's young son.[6] Surely this was a kind of writing that quickly acquired a life of its own and does us small honor to patronize or be, as critics, hypocritical or needlessly snobbish concerning its merits. In the writing of his "good-bad poetry" Browning freed himself from the discretions and mediocrities of his contemporaries; his "good-bad" verses were primarily histrionic, and they released the same kind of energy that Dickens showed in the writing of his novels. In all probability Kipling himself owed a debt to Browning's galloping rhymes and rhythms.

As Swinburne wrote of Ben Jonson, placing him among "the giants of energy and invention," so Browning takes his place among the more immediate ancestors of modern poetry. Like Swinburne's Jonson, it can be said of Browning:

> There is something heroic and magnificent in his lifelong dedication of all his gifts and all his powers to the service of the art he had elected as the business of all his life and the aim of all his aspiration. And the result was also magnificent: the flowers of his growing have every quality but one which belongs to the rarest and finest among flowers: they have colour, form, variety, fertility, vigour: the one thing they want is fragrance.[7]

The incident of Browning's death had an appropriate setting. It came in a brief illness on a visit to his newly married son at Venice. Through his wife's fortune, "Pen" Browning had acquired the great-halled Ca' Rezzonico, now a Venetian public building and museum. The palace on the Grand Canal was as spacious in its grandeur as Browning's lifework, his many books of poems, his hopes, his daylight reveries; it could nearly house the vast number of his characters. His interment in Westminster Abbey, 31 December 1889, nineteen days later, was an anticlimax.

1956

[6] Perhaps the universality of the *Pied Piper's* appeal lies in its power to evoke memories of the Children's Crusade (1212).

[7] *A Study of Ben Jonson*, 1889.

CURATE KILVERT: "DIVINE AMATEUR"

In Britain at the present hour, there is a cult devoted to the writings of the Rev. Francis Kilvert (1840–1879), who kept a diary which now, in its recent discovery and editing by William Plomer, seems fated for an immortality.[1] The regions, Wiltshire and Radnorshire, where he served as curate, are known as "Kilvert Country," for he gave to transient happenings an air of imperishable life and his visits to the cottages of their poor and aged, his picnics with the young seem to acquire a unique importance. Kilvert, as his *Diary* shows, was possessed by a peculiar demon: he had a periscopic eye that revealed with immense clarity and candor (through some "might think me mad") his own emotions as well as things and people around him. In his view the beauty of natural things became slightly more than life-size, its outlines sharper, its colors brighter than in its every day manifestations, whether the periscope turned its head toward a girl's face or a cloud in the sky.

Even the distance of a hundred years has not dimmed the following John Clare-like vision:

> Going down Chain Alley I saw a pair of dark beautiful eyes looking softly and lovingly through the dusk, earnest and eager to be recognized, and the slight delicate girlish figure of the Flower of the Border stood within her grandmother's door, her round olive cheeks shaded by her rich clusters of dark curls. A happy smile broke over her beautiful face, as she looked up shyly and spoke. When I came back a little before midnight the house was dark, but as I passed under the windows I heard the child's voice speaking in the bedroom. Chain Alley is a dangerous terrible neighborhood for a beautiful girl to be reared in.

If this is effective, how much more so is the scene when Kilvert's minute particulars are shown in action:

> He shot a rabbit with his beautiful rook-rifle like a long saloon pistol. The old rooks were all scared away, sailing round at an immense height in the blue sky, and it was pitiable to see the young rooks bewildered wheeling and fluttering helplessly from tree to

[1] *Kilvert's Diary*, edited and introduced by William Plomer. New York: The Macmillan Company, 1947.

tree, and perching, only to be tumbled bleeding with a dull thud into the deep nettle beds below, by the ceaseless and relentless crack, crack of the beautiful cruel little rifles, or to see them stagger after the shot, hold on as long as possible and then, weak from loss of blood, stumble from their perch, and flutter down, catching at every bough, and perhaps run along the ground terrified and bewildered, in the agonies of a broken wing.

This is Kilvertian prose: it is vivid and splendid, the prose of a Victorian "man of feeling"—right for its purpose of showing the horror of "blood-sports" and making further commentary redundant.

2

Though Kilvert had attended Wadham College, Oxford, during the days of the Tractarians, he had no heart for heated religious controversy and theological passions. In temperament, he was Anglican Broad Church: and perhaps he stressed it by adding to his rubicund features the growth of a square-cut beard. The young curate's father, Rector of Lamgley Burrell, was a clergyman of another sort. The elder Kilvert had been an admiring friend of John Henry Newman, lived much at ease, and not unlike the sporting parson in the old song, *Tally-Ho*, would "throw his surplice over his head," to spend most of a country day in trout fishing. Young Kilvert's enjoyments were in vigorous walking, "romps" with young ladies, and robust dancing. He accepted the post of curate in the Vicar Venable's parish in Radnorshire, Wales, and was fascinated by the efforts of a convert to Roman Catholicism, "Father Ignatius," to build a Benedictine monastery in a Welsh wilderness. He was attracted by the man's wild shyness, for in this he found an affinity to his own impulses, his own rambles through the woods, his own desires to hide his face.

At Clyro, Kilvert was the ideal pastoral visitor. His bearded smile was welcome at every cottage. He loved the sick, the poor, the idiotic —and those gone mad: and they loved him. He delighted in looking at children, small girls in particular, and this was a Victorian recreation he shared with his famous contemporary "Lewis Carroll." When among the minor gentry, he liked strolling with young ladies and their mammas, and joined them in their taste for sugar-coated tracts and "Ouida's" romances. He entertained them by giving "Penny Readings" of verse from a lectern.

Yet there were further and deeper turns in the progress of the curate's pleasures. On rounds of pastoral visits, lightly clad cottage matrons exhibited the bare buttocks of their young daughters for his approval, and he noted with vicarious interest how one father, on coming home evenings, would strip his daughter naked for her daily whipping. On a Saturday night visit to one of his cottage children, he wrote:

> Being tub night Polly with great celerity and satisfaction stripped herself naked to her drawers before me and was very anxious to take off her drawers too for my benefit, but her grandmother would not allow her. As it happened the drawers in question were so inadequately constructed that it made uncommonly little difference whether they were off or on, and there was a most interesting view from the rear.

At a bathing beach, the same Victorian pleasures greeted Kilvert. He watched little girls out wading with skirts lifted above their waists, and he "fell in love" with them by the dozens. At the homes of the well-to-do, at parlor tableaux, he saw them, scantily dressed, where they were encouraged to assume voluptuously "sweet" attitudes. As Kilvert describes them these scenes are revealed, since they are enlarged, as being less coy than instinctively sexual, and more girlish than innocent—a part of nature not to be ignored. Today, his joy in watching small girls bathing shows us still another view of Victorian child worship, the mindless delight that Victorians found in weeping over the deaths of Dickens's Little Nell and Tennyson's May Queen. In this he completed a gallery of pictures that at one social extreme, included Sir John Millais's portrait of his grandson blowing bubbles, (which not surprisingly became an advertisement for soap), and at the other, crude engravings of half-naked child-laborers in coal mines and factories. Yet even here his revelations transcend the moment, for in its details his *Diary* has the faithfulness of Dutch flower painting; there is something indelible in the arrangement of the following things: and one notes how an image of drifting naiads seems to float within it:

> And there by the old green road side and on the bank of a little rushing brook the wild snowdrops, the 'Fair Maids of February,' grew in myriads with closed eyes and hanging heads. How white and pure and stainless they looked in the deepening twilight. They grew among the thorns and ragged bushes, peeping through the dead leaves and dry tussocks of bleached and withered grass . . . contrasting their pure white blossoms with the moist black earth.

Here one is also carried back, by subtle associations, to his earlier picture, "The Flower of the Border," where Chain Alley was as fearful a place to be "reared in" as among "thorns and ragged bushes." And by this path, there is an unforced hint of death in "bleached" and "withered" and "black earth," and the suggestion is all the better because it is so lightly stressed, so literally natural.

3

But there were still deeper chambers known to the young curate's psyche. And these stood open at night, waiting in his dreams:

I dreamt that I dreamt that Mr and Mrs Venables tried to murder me. We were all together in a small room and they were both trying to poison me, but I was aware of their intention and baffled them repeatedly. At length, Mr Venables put me off my guard, came round fondling me, and suddenly clapped his hand on my neck behind said, 'It's of no use, Mr Kilvert. You're done for.'

I felt the poison beginning to work and burn in my neck. I knew it was all over and started up in fury and despair. I flew at him savagely. The scene suddenly changed to the organ loft in Hardenhuish Church. Mr Venables, seeing me coming at him, burst out at the door. Close outside the door was standing the Holy Ghost. He knocked him from the top to the bottom of the stairs, rolling head over heels, rushed downstairs himself, mounted his horse and fled away, I after him.

The dream within a dream excited me to such a state of fury, that in the outer dream I determined to murder Mr Venables. Accordingly I lay in wait for him with a pickaxe on the Vicarage lawn at Clyro, hewed an immense and hideous hole through his head, and kicked his face till it was so horribly mutilated, crushed and disfigured as to be past recognition. Then the spirit of the dream changed. Mrs Venables became her old natural self again. 'Wasn't it enough,' she said, looking at me reproachfully, 'that you should have hewed that hole through his head, but you must go and kick his face so that I don't know him again?'

At this moment, Mr Bevan, the Vicar of Hay, came in. 'Well,' he said to me, 'you *have* done it now. You have made a pretty mess of it.'

Today, when waiting rooms entering onto the psychiatrist's office are frequently overcrowded, almost everyone may be allowed to interpret Kilvert's dream within a dream. Much of it is obvious enough. And its violence is in keeping with his account of how young rooks meet their deaths. But I think less spectacular associations released by the dream also have meaning. At the time of the dream, he was about to give up his pastoral duties at Clyro; his kindly Vicar Venables and his wife, with gifts and cheerful sentiments, were speeding his departure. What resentments could the young curate have against his Vicar? They came, I think, from two hidden sources: one was a fear-filled regret at leaving Clyro; the other was a profound gap in temperament between the Venables and Kilvert. Contrasted with their emotionally immature curate, the Venables knew their way about the world; they had the kind of urban connections Kilvert lacked; Venables's brother had been one of Thackeray's friends.

"I do loathe London," Kilvert once wrote; he remained the complete countryman, wary of city evils, represented in his eyes by a Burlington Arcade photograph dealer whose main traffic was in an under-the-counter sale of "French" obscene pictures. The distance between the curate and Vicar was great indeed. One also feels that the urbane manners of the Venables Vicarage hemmed Kilvert in; he needed rapid walking down country roads to let off steam. He had probably reached the bursting point at the time of his nightmare.

Whatever else may be said of Kilvert, he was no hypocrite, and though he hoped posterity would discover his writings, there are no signs, anywhere in his *Diary*, of a compromise with public taste. One is convinced that he transcended all personal vanities by not falsifying whatever his eye directed him to write. In that sense he remains one of a small company, the writer content with a lack of immediate publication, the nearly perfect example of the divine amateur.

1947, 1971

THE ROMANTIC INVENTIONS OF VERNON LEE

I have before me a battered leather-bound Tauchnitz edition of Vernon Lee's *Genius Loci* and *The Enchanted Woods* reprinted in a single volume at Leipzig in 1906. The book had been bought by a friend of mine in a secondhand book shop in New York where the name of Vernon Lee is better known among book dealers on Fourth Avenue than among booksellers on Madison Avenue, or in present day Florence, Rome, Paris, and London. But even among the more learned, the associations of her pen name are those of notes of travel on the European continent, of essays on the subjects of war, psychology and esthetics, all equally outmoded and placed between books on the supernatural and art. In this odd company few know or care that the name Vernon Lee was the *persona* behind which Violet Paget, a woman of French birth and English–Welsh parentage, lived and wrote. I shall say more of her life later; my true concern is with her inventions, her fiction, her short stories and novels; and of her place, though generally unknown today, in imaginative literature.

Pasted on the flyleaf of the book before me is a sheet of note paper and engraved in the upper right-hand corner is: "Il Palmerino San Gervasio Florence" which is obviously the writer's address, and below it in faded black-brownish script the following words: "With Vernon Lee's sincere detestation of the silly and tiresome mania for unmeaning autographs." When the book came into my hands its pages, though bound in leather, were uncut. Evidence is that the unknown and probably deceased American traveler who had been admitted to Miss Paget's apartment was not encouraged (after securing the sheet of note paper) to read the book; Miss Paget had seen through the motives of the request that had come to her: she was not flattered; she was not amused. I mention this incident because it does reveal, if for a glimpse only, of the *persona*, Vernon Lee; it was one not likely to be deceived by the vanities and distractions of literary flattery and fame; it did not smile back at facile admirations and courtesies.

Yet before I speak of her fiction, a few words should be said of her studies in Italian art, of her essays on traveling through Italy and France, Switzerland, and of the Germany that then existed, open to sightseers where troops of adolescents were guided by schoolteachers, the Germany that welcomed the eager as well as the bored traveler from England and the United States, before 1914.

In her travel essays which so readily gave her a Tauchnitz reputation, Vernon Lee spoke to the upper forehead of the middle-brow traveler who was on holiday in Europe. It can be assumed that those who read her travel essays had been to British boarding schools or to American academies. And in thinking of Vernon Lee's readers I also assume that most of them were women who in the rush of boarding a Channel boat or a Cunard Liner had half forgotten everything they knew. To them the main travel routes to and through the Continent were familiar enough; the usual guidebooks had been read, the usual maps had been consulted, and after the flurry of departure, hours of ennui threatened the traveler. But the same traveler was one in whom memories of a nineteenth-century education were reawakened by Tauchnitz editions of Vernon Lee's travel essays; the essays, as they pointed routes to lesser known quarters of traveled places, evoked dimmed yet famous names that had been neglected between leaving school and booking transportation across the water.

During an idle day on shipboard or a rainy day in a hotel, the Tauchnitz Vernon Lee became an English-without-a-foreign-accent counselor who spoke of places within short drives or walks from railway stations and hotels. Guided by Vernon Lee, the traveler gazed upward at the Lion on his tall pillar at St. Mark's in Venice and after that was free to enjoy an hour seated in the shade at Florian's.

Her remarks on Venice, Pisa or Bayeux revived both easy and learned associations with art, music, literature. After reading several of her travel volumes, the charmed (and sometimes charming) traveler was well enough informed to impress less sophisticated friends or relations; a husband or lover could be stirred to admiration; a wealthy aunt could be convinced that the money spent on her niece's education had been a memorable investment. With Vernon Lee's opinions in her head, even the most absent-minded of strolling travelers was permitted to voice a dislike of a tourist-eye view of Venice, to find its shopkeepers too smoothly professional in offering their wares; at Pisa and with an artful mention of Keats's death in Rome, Shelley's odes could be recalled, and at Bayeux the traveler could contrast the art of Degas with that of the famous tapestry. At Wetzlar in Germany the traveler could seek out and afterward recite details of the interior of the house where Werther met his Charlotte and impress her hearers with slightly acid comments on Goethe's genius.

My picture of Vernon Lee's readers is not as fanciful as it may seem. In the autobiographies of Gertrude Atherton and Edith Wharton who moved in circles where Vernon Lee's essays on travel were known and were a topic of discussion, the general atmosphere I have just described prevailed. Mrs. Atherton and Mrs. Wharton took the view that the best writings of Vernon Lee (which included her fiction) had less popular appreciation than they deserved. Edith Wharton was of course the more discriminating judge of her qualities; she had been very nearly snubbed by Miss Paget in her suburban villa outside Florence, but with persistence came to know her and was happy to be among the few Americans—James McNeill Whistler was another—who were admitted to the circle of her acquaintances. Berenson, the watchful critic of Renaissance painting was still another. Both Mrs. Atherton and Mrs. Wharton valued her writings for cherished and knowledgeable reasons; they knew her as an accomplished literary artist, as an intellectual whose erudition equaled her imaginative wit, and one whose prose was worthy of tactful emulation.

But to return for the last time to Vernon Lee's readers who were the restless bright young people of the day when King Edward VII stepped to the throne. This was the day when a few professed and many yearned to understand the poetry of Robert Browning; he was their poet for the same reasons that T. S. Eliot's poems and plays yield so much speculation and commentary in colleges today. To know Browning even at the risk of misinterpretation was the pleasure of the cultured few; to explain and enlarge upon an obscure passage in *Sordello* were proofs of a cultural interest above the ordinary. The traveler who had been to Rome, to Florence and to Venice may have carried her learning lightly, yet listened intently to explicit readings of Browning's verse and then felt that further education was not futile. They knew their Virgil, their Horace, their Petrarch, Dante, Goethe with more firmness and a deeper, if not more scholarly, sense of recognition than their descendants at finishing schools and colleges today. They had their share in the cultural drift of Vernon Lee's essays. Governesses and tutors had prepared them patiently for all that the acceptable young woman of the age should know. In general knowledge they were closer to the high-brow standards of the two World War generations than many of us would care to admit, yet none claimed for her learning more than the casual distinction of chatting brightly at the dinner table; they were no more or less than the cultivated heiresses of British right to rule the world.

In Vernon Lee's *Vanitas*, a volume of short stories, there is a likely description of those who read her travel sketches. If we remove her heroine from the particulars of the story, if we take her not for what she is within it, but rather as the species of young woman who rents a villa for a season and is seen at dinner parties, her presence in that setting is true to type and kind:

She had never learned to talk slang, or to take up vulgar attitudes, or to tell impossible stories; and she had never lost a silly habit of blushing at expressions and anecdotes which she did not reprove other women for using and relating . . . She liked putting on pretty frocks, arranging pretty furniture, driving in well got up carriages, eating good dinners, laughing a great deal, and dancing a great deal, and that was all.[1]

This no more than a glimpse of her, and the lady in the story happens to be un-English; she was one of those Americans who so frequently appear in the novels of Henry James and of Edith Wharton, and who has made an "international" marriage—but as a type she is of the world that Vernon Lee knew so well and for whom she wrote her essays.

2

When I began my reading of Vernon Lee I vaguely felt an affinity, difficult to define, between her writings and those of Virginia Woolf's. Was it possible that the daughter of Leslie Stephen had been impressed by a notable forerunner of the kind of essay she wrote in *The Death of the Moth, The Leaning Tower* and *Street Hauntings?*

We must approach the question of affinity between these two writers by an unfamiliar path, and admit before we start that they had different, and, at times, contrasting minds and sensibilities. Virginia Woolf deliberately employed common sense whenever she spoke of ghosts, and as she did so a matter-of-fact, stiff-backed manner commands her prose as though she had been on the point of saying "nonsense" loudly to her hearers.[2] She had no patience with, no time for wayward flights of superstition. As the reader of her stories will soon discover, ghosts are boldly listed in Vernon Lee's dramatis personae. They are the instruments of fate, of the furies that cross the careers of her characters. They are among the signs of evil—and active evil—that possess the unwary; they haunt the scene; they invade the body and half-innocent imaginations of guilty souls. Here is ground where the two writers seem to part decisively: yet the moment one admits this difference, what of Virginia Woolf's *Orlando*? The line of difference persists but the theme of possession remains; there *is* an affinity in imaginative quality between the two writers as though their agreement not to meet had been one of making a separate invasion of a like territory of fiction.

This invasion of the same terrain by Virginia Woolf and Vernon

[1] From *Legend of Madame Krasinka.*

[2] See Virginia Woolf's essay on Sterne's ghost in *The Moment.*

Lee comes to light in her essay on *Limbo;* a masterly little essay it is, yet it is, like many of her occasional pieces, too short a ledge on which to rest the weight of a posthumous reputation. Her essay reflects among other things her thoughts on the nature of genius which was a subject that often attracted the critical sensibility of Virginia Woolf. In her essay *A Room of One's Own,* that almost forgotten series of lectures on women's rights written when Votes for Women was a gallant Liberal cause, she hovered over and around the subject of poetic genius. She speculated as to how and why it was that she remembered whole stanzas of poems by Tennyson and Christina Rossetti and could not hold in her memory more than a line or two written by poets of her day. She tried to find a reason for the persistent wilfullness of her memory: she said that living poets express a feeling that is actually being made and torn "out of us" at the moment of reading, and then since she felt this reason insufficient, decided to blame the unromantic advent of the First World War for the lack of poetry in the air.

Something like the same problem with its questions entered Vernon Lee's discussion of Limbo, yet she had found by a fresh reading of Dante's lines:

Poerocche gente di molto valore
Conobbi che in quel Limbo eran sospesi

a more forthright answer to it. It would seem that Vernon Lee had an advantage over the earnest lecturer on the genius of her sex; a look down and backward into Limbo is a deeper experience than the Fabian vista of women's rights. She had decided that genius was organic and had nothing to do with machinery, that it was a living organism, that genius itself was immortal but men of genius were mortal—which was a sensible though brilliant middle step in her inquiry. Within her view of genius Vernon Lee placed the element of charm, which is not the whole of genius by any means, but is one of those elements too frequently forgotten by the majority of twentieth-century critics. She had no sentimental regard for the mute inglorious Miltons of Thomas Gray; to her they were mute and inglorious because they lack the charm, the spell-invoking quality that has always been an enduring element of poetic genius, and following her lead through Dante's mention of Unchristianed Babies she found a way of considering the charm of youth. Her recollections of that particular kind of charm had at their center a grass-grown children's garden with a toy house, a "Rabbit's Villa" in it, and for the moment one is almost deceived into thinking one is reading a passage from the first chapter of Virginia Woolf's *The Waves.* Her Limbo includes the world of "might have been" and she illuminates her discovery of it by quoting Christina Rossetti's brother in a dramatic and frightening, penetrating line:

Look in my face: My name is *Might-have-been.*

It was in much the same fashion and with the same sense of loss that Virginia Woolf interwove her images of falling leaves in her novel *The Waves.* The difference is that Vernon Lee never stressed (while Virginia Woolf employed) the techniques and sensibility of symbolism; in this difference the line of distinction between the two writers is clear enough for anyone to read, to understand. In passages of prose where Virginia Woolf has diffused her brilliance and does not arrive at a logical decision, parallel passages in Vernon Lee's prose show the elder woman exerting a conscious will to make up her mind. At worst Vernon Lee's style was florid in the manner of the late Victorians who with less wisdom than intuition followed in the esthetic footsteps of Walter Pater, yet Vernon Lee never lost her way in these dubious pastures for more than the briefest of holiday excursions; the young Van Wyck Brooks was impressed by the sharpness and grace of her learning and wit and the aging Bernard Shaw in a review of her polemics against the First World War sat up and cheered the lucidity of her mind and spirit.[3] It was not without significance that Shaw's praise appeared in the very ancestor of the periodical in which so many of Virginia Woolf's essays came into print, which was an elder weekly called *The Nation,* the combative Liberal parent of *The New Statesman.*

In the years slightly before and during World War I, the years in which Virginia Woolf revealed the gifts of her imagination and her poise among distinguished writers of the day, the fame and gifts of her forerunner, Vernon Lee, were passing into the shadows of a villa in Italy. During the First World War Vernon Lee was bold enough to let it be known that she did not approve of war; this error was political and yet it was consistent with her position of being an observer of the Italian scene. Her polemics against war fell into discredit and neglect, but what is relevant to us is that her unpopular opinions temporarily sentenced her to the Limbo of which she had written so well; at the time of her death, in February 1935, she was as nearly forgotten as any writer of her abilities could be.

3

It was a clever, bookish, studious child who in 1880 had written *Studies of the Eighteenth Century in Italy,* and she was a child born of a mother who outlived, victoriously it seemed, two less spirited, less vigorous husbands; Violet Paget was the daughter of the second

[3] A review of *Satan the Master.*

union and was born in Boulogne, France in 1856. The household soon moved to Italy and a son by the first marriage, Eugene Lee-Hamilton shared it.

Lee-Hamilton was both the light and shadow of the family. Like the sons of some few other old families of England's northern boundaries, he had been trained to enter the diplomatic services. From the time of the ambitiously successful Tudor kings, sons of these families stood at variance from the policies of Court and Parliament; their conservatism held claims to an ancient heritage; it was their privilege, so they felt, to be first critics of whomever became the Prime Minister and to accept lesser posts in the foreign service as a duty to an elder Roman Catholic disestablished order. Wilfrid Blunt was one of these and so was Eugene Lee-Hamilton; like Blunt he was a junior member of the British legation in Paris when the city fell to the Germans in 1870. The generals of the German occupation drove members of the British Embassy out of Paris into refuge and starvation;[4] in this sense the War of 1870 was a preview of what happened during World War II, and Lee-Hamilton, as he escaped to Portugal and later to his mother and half sister in Florence, was among those who were not equal to the occasion. He took to a wheeled bed from which he refused to move for twenty years; he was the invalided Phoenix of the family, its poet, its commentator on world and literary affairs when he chose to speak, and his physicians permitted him to speak only at far-spaced and briefest intervals, his words were of first and of final authority. His half sister was both his guardian and his servant.

Lee-Hamilton was not fated to die in his wheeled bed; when his twenty-year reign over it had been completed, he rose from his rest, visited the United States and married a young English woman; they had one child, a daughter, who died in infancy and shortly after her death, Lee-Hamilton languished into the grave. Edith Wharton, inaccurate as she was in reporting the bald facts and dates concerning her acquaintance with Lee-Hamilton, was correct when she wrote of the extremes of his invalidism and his vigor. When he visited her on his journey to the United States, he talked and rode a bicycle in and around her Long Island estate as though he were possessed by the spirit of an eighteen-year-old boy. The professional psychiatrist may find ready answers to the peculiarities of his behavior.

His half sister was in a position to know the extremes of his temperament well. In his passion for literary distinction he published two books of verse and was among the first of Violet Paget's serious critics,[5] for the invalid had time for careful reading and critical medi-

[4] According to Lee-Hamilton's account, but this is not substantiated by Wilfrid Scawen Blunt's *My Diaries, 1888–1914*.

[5] The very first was her mother.

tation. There can be no doubt that the relationship between half brother and sister was of daily, almost hourly intimacy; there is no need to think that their interviews were always those of painful anxiety or of sickroom boredom; moments of lassitude and speculations on guilt and love were reserved for Lee-Hamilton's pallid sonnets.[6] After reading his literary exercises in verse, done in the approved manner of Walter Pater's young men recently arrived from Oxford, after summing up a few facts of his curious career, Eugene Lee-Hamilton seems to have been a latter-day version of Bramwell Bronte, and as such, demon and all, was an invaluable asset to a gifted younger half sister.

He may or may not have contributed to Violet Paget's odd and sometimes profound storeroom of knowledge which she called a "lumber room filled with cobwebs" that is so evident in her *Studies of the Eighteenth Century in Italy*. But there can be no doubt that he upheld for her, by demanding that she read to him aloud, the standards of Walter Pater's esthetics, an admiration for Pater's essays on the Renaissance, and that he taught her a hatred of war, as well as a distrust of many things which were German and yet reserved for her an appreciation of Winkelmann and Goethe. Did she become possessed by him? Or he by her? Neither can be proved—except that as a writer she was the stronger of the two; she visibly outgrew him and lived to write fiction in which the forces of divine good and satanic evil act out their drama, in which the themes of dual personality and demonic possession are the mainsprings of action.

4

Thus by a roundabout route we come to the shorter fiction of the young woman who adopted in conservative nineteenth-century fashion the semimasculine pen name of Vernon Lee. "Vernon" recalled from a short distance Violet, and the latter part of the pseudonym was a literal transcription of the hyphenated prelude to her elder half brother's surname. One can read into this choice of a pen name some hint of family solidarity and intimacy—how much or how little it is impossible to say. No reviewers of Vernon Lee's early books were deceived into thinking their author was a man; the disguise was transparent and it was probably intended to be so; it was enough, however, to ward off intimate questions that touched upon

[6] Of which a few lines from his *Lethe* are sufficient to show their character:

> I had a dream of Lethe, of the brink
> Of leaden waters, whither many bore
> Dead, pallid loves, while others, old and sore,
> Brought but their tottering selves, in haste to drink.
> And, having drunk, they plunged, and seemed to sink
> Their load of love or guilt for evermore . . .

Violet Paget's private life; that was not the world's business; her books provided all the answers she cared to give.

Within the twenty-five years after 1881, the publication date of her *Studies of the Eighteenth Century in Italy*, a number of short novels and stories appeared under the pen name of Vernon Lee. The first was a by-product of her *Studies, The Prince of a 100 Soups*, a narrative inspired by her readings in Carlo Gozzi, the tales of E. T. A. Hoffmann, and the Italian comedy of masks. She offered the narrative as a tribute to her love of the Italian puppet show and of the commedia dell'arte. Today this little extravaganza reveals no more than a glittering flow of narration and girlish, high-spirited facility; Vernon Lee had no gift for the writing of fantastic comedy; her wit, her gifts were of another kind; nor could she present her modern "problem novel," [7] her *Miss Brown* in enduring prose. These early books were fluttering demonstrations of a talent for writing; they are of interest only to the biographer who may wish to pierce the veil of Vernon Lee's personality by way of reading her early ventures into fiction. Yet among these first attempts in 1883 and in 1884 she did succeed in drawing upon the true sources of her gifts. But if genius can find a definition within writing of less than monumental scope, genius was hers, and something more than the flicker of its

[7] *Miss Brown* (1884) has on its dedication page the following inscription: "To Henry James I dedicate for good-luck my first attempt at a novel." Violet Paget had considered herself a protégé of Henry James, and before he had a chance to read *Miss Brown*, it is highly probable that James thought so too. But the book proved to be something of an embarrassment. Its opening pages showed the influence of a middle period Jamesian style; yet beyond them, the book took on the character of a skittish, wholly girlish satire on the Pre-Raphaelite poets and painters, at home in London's Hammersmith and Kensington, abroad in Tuscan villas in Italy. The story is not unlike that of Shaw's *Pygmalion* (which may have been partially inspired by it): a rich young Englishman of the Pre-Raphaelite Brotherhood took a fancy to a certain Miss Brown, a servant-governess in the household of another Pre-Raphaelite stationed in Italy. The girl—half Italian, half Scots, and an orphan—was then brought to England to be "educated as a lady," with the hope of becoming her protector's wife. Miss Brown, newly educated and introduced to the esthetic, socialistic, and moral vagaries of the Pre-Raphaelite circle, soon became a "problem" to her benevolent yet effeminate lover and his friends. She had grown into a tough-minded pre-Shavian heroine, a "Madonna of the Glaciers," who, not without a chill of distaste and disillusionment, at last consented to marry her wealthy admirer. The book has its highest moments of burlesque in its near portraits of the Ionides family, the Anglo-Greek friends of James McNeil Whistler, the poet Swinburne, and of "Janey," the wife of William Morris. Although *Miss Brown* could be counted as a brilliant *roman à clef* for a writer under thirty, today its distinction is that of "a period piece" to be placed on the shelf alongside *The Green Carnation* and Gilbert and Sullivan's *Patience*.

presence came into being in a short novel *Ottilie*, and a biography *The Countess of Albany.*

Ottilie has for its subtitle "An Eighteenth Century Idyl." There was probably a slight hint of irony in Vernon Lee's choice of "Idyl" to describe the nature of her provincial romance set within an imaginary Franconia a hundred years before *Ottilie* was written. It would be easy to say that its young author was all too obviously an enthusiastic reader of the *Tales of Hoffmann*, the *Sorrows of Werther*, and of *Adolphe* by Benjamin Constant that she was, and her romance does not disguise its literary heritage. But it was also written as though its author had never read an English novel; the romance could have been presented as a rarely felicitous translation from French, Italian, or German and few critics would have suspected a hoax. In her preface of 1883 Vernon Lee laid claim only to being an essayist, not a writer of romantic tales or novels; she confessed to being haunted by the spirits of men and women whose names she had read in historical researches and could not dispel their presence in her imagination; this she insisted was the *raison d'être* of *Ottilie.*

So much for the prudence and candor with which Vernon Lee submitted her romance of *Ottilie* to the public. As to why it can be reread today with pleasure, interest, and a sense of rediscovery is another matter. Up to the moment that she wrote her idyl no writer in English of the nineteenth century with the exceptions of three Americans, Edgar Allan Poe, Fitz-James O'Brien and Herman Melville and one Anglo-Irishman, Sheridan Le Fanu, had entered so deeply into the psychology of incestuous human relationships as Vernon Lee. *Ottilie*, in its external calmness of confessing a brotherly-sisterly relationship of guilt and love is scarcely a Gothic novel; her manner of presenting the theme of possession, of one psyche haunted by another, is too serene to reflect the fires of hell which burn so violently in the pages of Hoffmann and of Poe. Behind the three figures of Ottilie, her lover and her brother, stands the unnamed figure of Johann Joachim Winkelmann whose studies in Greek and Latin and whose journey to Italy inspired Goethe and whose writing brought a belated awareness of the Renaissance and neoclassicism into Germany. The heady results of Renaissance passion in conflict with cool drafts of neoclassic attitudes both imported from Italy worked curious magic in the Sturm und Drang of Germanic literature of which Ottilie's brother was the catalyst and Ottilie the victim. The three figures in the romance are possessed by forces greater than themselves; none escapes the working of destiny. Within its genre we have had few examples in twentieth-century fiction to equal *Ottilie:* to find them we must turn to *The Blood of the Walsungs* of Thomas Mann, to *Les Enfants Terribles* of Jean Cocteau.

No less accomplished in its telling of complex emotions in a steady voice is Vernon Lee's biography of Louise, Princess of Stolberg, who at eighteen had married the middle-aged, dissolute, exiled Bonnie Prince Charlie and became the Countess of Albany residing in Florence. The book appeared in a series, long since forgotten, of "famous women" which contained commissioned biographies of such notables as Margaret Fuller, George Sand and Mary Wollstonecraft; the series was one of those noble ventures, like "men of letters" series, which publishers every quarter century or so are led into sponsoring and which for the most part show how dull gifted writers can be in fulfilling the terms of a contract to write on the subject of their great predecessors. The majority of such brief lives and studies cram the dusty corners of secondhand bookshops mercifully hidden from the opinions of posterity.

Vernon Lee's *Countess of Albany* has none of the atmosphere which usually surrounds a commissioned duty to write a brief study of a heroine in the arts, politics, or letters; in 1885 it puzzled one reviewer who protested that Louise, Princess of Stolberg was not famous enough, that she was no more nor less than an unfortunate princess whom historians of England, as well as of Italy, slighted or ignored. In 1885 Vernon Lee's *Countess* was as unlike books of its kind as it is today; the book was and still is freshly written as though its author had been haunted by a little princess who became (under the alcoholic guardianship of Charles Edward) the platonic mistress of the Italian poet, Alfieri. Alfieri, as Vernon Lee portrayed him, was one who had the passions of another Henri Beyle, who might well have stepped out of an autobiographical passage of *The Charterhouse of Parma*. Famous or not Louise d'Albany, as she was known, was in an utterly fantastic situation between two men, one, her husband, who was an aging heir to a lost throne and the other a poet at war with himself, consumed by the ironic emotions of intellectual and all too fleshly loves. Neither eighteenth-century Rome nor Florence had witnessed a more complex, ghost-ridden, potentially violent love affair. Louise d'Albany was a heroine made for Vernon Lee; she survived both her Prince and her fiery-haired poet, and grew to look at seventy like a squat, fat, unwieldy housekeeper, who waddled through the streets of Florence draped in a red shawl.

Not the least of her stories is *Prince Alberic and the Snake Lady*, a story within a story and which has at its center a legend that echoes the tales brought from the East into southern Europe by the Crusaders to the Holy Land. The snake in the legend is of an origin which is of the East and is not to be confused unwittingly with the serpent of Eden's garden. This snake descends from the benevolent dragons of the East and is the heiress of Good, now transformed in the Christian world to Evil. It is this mutation of the snake lady and her magic qualities, compounded of both Good and Evil which endows Vernon Lee's version of the legend with its undercurrents of inherited fears and ecstasies. Beneath the charms of what seem to be no more than a Gothic fairy tale, deeper realities exist, and behind their psychological revelations, lies the conflict of Western taboos against the religions of the East. No one has told the story of the snake-dragon with more persuasion than Vernon Lee.

A foil to the legend of Prince Alberic is a fifteenth-century story, *A Wedding Chest* which tells of the romance behind the painted panel of the chest, described in the Catalogue of the Smith Museum, Leeds, England, as "The Triumph of Love." This sanguinary little romance is filled with the bloodstained shadows of fifteenth-century Italian courtship and revenge; and lively ghosts they are, breathing the passions of holy and profane love with the violence of John Webster's tragedies. Scarcely less memorable is Vernon Lee's version of a legend concerning Domenico Neroni, a painter whose name is scarcely mentioned by Vasari, and who was, as she described him in her *Renaissance Fancies and Studies*, a fifteenth-century seeker of pagan perfection. His journey into the ancient world is one that invokes pagan spirits and rituals. As in the story of Prince Alberic, the soul of its protagonist is possessed by forces of a world that exist behind the world of every day reality.

Amour Dure, *Dionea*, and *A Wicked Voice* are all within the charmed circle of Vernon Lee's Italy; each has the singular marks of her authority. The particular spell cast by Dionea the Genoese, the spell of the Uranian Venus, is of Mediterranean probability and not of the Irish Sea nor the English Channel; the province in Vernon Lee's "world Atlas" is of Southern Europe; and the haunting echoes of the voice heard in *A Wicked Voice* are of a kind that are appropriate only to Venetian gardens, the canals and night-shadowed, narrowly turning streets of Venice. In Vernon Lee's *Hauntings* the spirit of place haunts the reader, and in reading her stories I am at times reminded of a little English woman I once knew, who after securing a hard-won master's degree at Oxford was for many years a governess–tutor of well-to-do-American girls in Germany. She guided her charges up and down the Rhine, an eager, round-eyed Lorelei who spoke Oxford German. Of people she could remember almost nothing; names and faces quickly vanished beyond the reaches of her memory. "I am haunted by places," she would say half wistfully, "Stuttgart and Ulm, Nurmberg and Frankfort, the stones of their streets, the roofs of their houses are in my dreams; I am possessed by them, they own me." In the same fashion Vernon Lee's tales and romances are possessed by genii of time and place as well as the personality of their author. It is through her eyes that a present generation of readers at home or abroad may set their blue guidebooks aside to rediscover Europe. And if the Italy they find is unlike any other Italy in English fiction, it is because no English writer since Vernon Lee (and I am aware of the Italys of Henry James, E. M. Forster, Norman Douglas, and D. H. Lawrence, all excellent of their various kinds) has peopled Italy with such enduring ghosts and shades. One sees them glimmering in Rome's fountains, one sees them pace the waters of the Arno, and hears echoes of their voices across the Grand Canal; they are moonlit visitors.

Perhaps no Mediterranean cycle of romances and legends is complete without an image, however ironic and fantastic, of Don Juan. In her *Virgin of Seven Daggers* both Don Juan and Spain arrive and with them a brimming lake of Hell's fires. Her Don Juan is not perhaps the greatest of the heroes who have answered to his name, but he is vivid enough, and his presence is enriched by the grace of the *Virgin of the Seven Daggers.* And with Don Juan the reader has a last and memorable look into the resources of Vernon Lee's baroque imagination.

1954, 1971

WILLIAM ERNEST HENLEY'S CAREER

Where is William Ernest Henley and where are the Henley evenings at the house on the road to Richmond in suburban London, a quarter-hour's walk for young men who strolled through spring twilight out from Bedford Park? *Invictus* is, of course, still remembered by those who are given to reciting verse in a loud voice, but many of the young men are gone, and if many of their names are to be recalled, they are to be found only in the files of their chief's magazines, the once famous *Observer* and the *New Review;* and today even Henley's luminaries whose fame outdistanced his, Wells of *The Time Machine*, young Kipling of the *Barrack-Room Ballads* and *Captains Courageous,* the J. M. Barrie who wrote *Sentimental Tommy*, and Bernard Shaw who once held promise of becoming a music critic, are scarcely known for what they looked like then. As for Henley himself, it is quite as though posterity had committed a special act of forgetting him and his once highly burnished reputation, his skill in marshaling the forces of literary warfare, his influence upon young men who saw him as master, chief, idol or demigod of their generation.

It would be well, if only for a moment, to look at Henley as though he were actually restored in flesh—not the poet who wrote unrhymed verse (which seemed so "realistic" in its day) as well as ballades, triolets, and rondeaus—but as quite another kind of literary being, the careerist, the Tory critic, the hero and instructor, if you will, of young men who practiced the art of writing virulent prose. The stage directions for the scene are any afternoon or evening between 1889 and 1898; it is a room in Henley's fine house on the road to Richmond, and he is there for everyone to see. His great physique, the golden, wiry beard and hair, shoulders and upper torso thrust across a desk, or resting its full weight upon the low back of a chair, would never fail to impress his visitors with the momentousness, the urgency of all he had to say. To those who saw him in this proximity, the very atmosphere seemed charged with light, and for them it was no effort to remember the complaint of Robert Louis Stevenson's wife who had said that Henley's energy endangered Robert's health and that his friendship drove her husband to the verge of physical exhaustion.

Behind the physical presence and the impression that it left upon the imagination of Henley's young admirers, there are a few biographical facts that increased the growth of a heroic legend. Henley was born in 1849 and was the son of an unprosperous Gloucester printer and secondhand bookseller, and in addition to the fears of poverty, he suffered the privations of an incurable disease. In early adolescence, tuberculosis of the bone had maimed one foot and subsequently destroyed it. As he neared maturity, the other foot was threatened and to stave off the immediate danger of its amputation, Henley, penniless, friendless, and yet without despair made a pilgrimage from Gloucester to Edinburgh, there to make a direct appeal to the great surgeon, Joseph Lister, who became interested in his case and promptly installed him for treatment in a hospital. It was from Lister's hospital that Henley wrote to London editors, and Sir Leslie Stephen, in particular, was stirred by the forthright character of a personality which appeared between the lines of a short letter. In February 1875, when Sir Leslie had found occasion to visit Edinburgh, he did not forget Henley, and bringing Robert Louis Stevenson with him, called at Lister's hospital in search of the young man whose letters had awakened such lively interest. The interview was an extraordinary success. Within an hour Henley gratified the promise that Sir Leslie had discerned in the brief letters, and at the same time, Stevenson's curiosity was transfigured into admiration for a man who so cheerfully and vigorously surmounted physical pain and economic hardship. Stevenson entered the friendship with unusual sensibility and understanding for, he too, continued to survive the threat of long illnesses. In discovering Henley he had found someone whose laughter was contagious and whose masculinity was the very complement of his own fragile graces, of his velvet-coated ease and slippered ardors.

When at last, and this was two years later, Henley arrived in London, he came as the true heir of a Danish Anglo-Saxon family of Henleys and was, for those who saw him, the reincarnation of a Norse hero, whose ready, short-clipped phrases struck the ground as though they were as many thunderbolts. His first venture, *London*, a satirical weekly, chose the aging Gladstone as its foil, Gladstone who was then a huge white whale swimming to its rest in warm and comfortably expanding Liberal waters. *London*'s harpoons effected little damage to the whale, but drew attention to the forceful stance and skill of a new personality in British journalism, and from an editorial office Henley emerged to receive the rewards of public recognition.

It was during the following ten years that Henley developed a remarkable aptitude for endowing the work of his contemporaries with the brilliance of his own vitality; Austin Dobson and Alice Meynell profited greatly by his advice and championship, and with the assistance of Charles Whibley, one of his young disciples, Henley became Stevenson's literary agent, lending his energy to the support of Stevenson's early ventures in romantic fiction. When *London* perished under him (an untimely death) he sought out commissions for free-lance criticism and in a series of reviews reignited the smoldering reputation of George Meredith; he converted the *Magazine of Art* into a testing field for his esthetic convictions and in its pages he introduced the art of Rodin to the intelligence of the British public. By the time he accepted his position as editor of the *Scots Observer*, his policies for assuming a virtual dictatorship of British letters had attained full growth; and the paper was founded for the express purpose of becoming his personal vehicle.

Surely, no editor had ever received his commission on better terms than Henley's when he stepped into the office of the *Scots Observer*. Its owner was Fitz-Roy Bell, a well-to-do Scots lawyer who felt it his duty to restore Edinburgh's intellectual glory which had notably diminished since the days when Wilson and Lockhart commanded the fortunes of *Blackwood's Magazine*. Bell had read Henley's reviews and in them saw those qualities of leadership that might well equal or extend beyond the critical successes of a *Christopher North;* Bell was prepared to be generous with a man who showed every promise of filling the place that had been long left vacant by Wilson's death; the weekly journal was handsomely subsidized, and soon the wide pages of beautifully balanced type, which distinguished the *Scots Observer* from all other periodicals of its day appeared on the library tables of the British intellectuals, of the Oxford don or undergraduate, of young men in the consular service, or the librarian—all who professed to have an interest in the latest turn of critical opinion in literature.

Self-educated and endowed with the strong will of those who climb out of poverty into the professional classes, Henley's articles of faith were those of trenchant individualism. It was characteristic of him to choose Disraeli as his political model, and in this choice lay the sources of his early strength and weakness. Through this association he earned the dislike and open distrust of the thoughtful Wilfrid Scawen Blunt, and secured the protection of the nimble-witted politician, young George Wyndham. To Henley, Disraeli's drive toward the expansion of British Imperial power in the Near East had all the fascination of a search for hidden treasure. Yet Henley's defense of Disraeli shows clearly enough his uneasy relationship to the object of his admiration, for the means that the statesman used ran counter to Henley's forthright disposition; and the young editor was caught in the net of semidisillusionment which traps so many men of literary talent who follow too closely the sinuous path of political conversion.

It is, therefore, scarcely surprising to learn that a number of his contemporaries, while accepting his aid and friendship, soon adopted the habit of describing him as a literary pirate, and that Stevenson half-affectionately modeled "Long John Silver" in Henley's image. Even the least discerning of his acquaintances saw in his worship of physical strength a compensatory impulse toward balancing his own physical disabilities—and that impulse soon showed its nakedness as it translated itself into editorial tyranny. From the very start of Henley's career on the *Observer*, he had used the periodical as a training school for his young men, young men who displayed either personal loyalty to himself or unusual promise of pursuing a literary apprenticeship as stern as his own had been and as prolific. Once they had proved their usefulness, the young men were then trained to submit to Henley's explicit orders: "Never again use that detestable word, 'stylist,' if you would be an officer of mine" he wrote to Vernon Blackburn, and the instruction was like an order of the day.

Henley's successful leadership, however, built castles of sand against an eventual and seemingly inevitable storm. As Blunt observed, he was "a bitter talker, but a sayer of good things," and as he grew older, the bitterness increased; his quarrels became more frequent, and were, at times, patently unnecessary. He had been among the first to champion and to publish the poetry of W. B. Yeats, and he could not refrain from the urge of rewriting the poems that had been submitted to him. I doubt if the exercise of this prerogative deeply stirred the currents of Yeats's enmity, but in after years, when Yeats wrote of the time that he also frequented the Henley evenings, one finds his enthusiasm for Henley's gifts considerably cooled. He remarked that he had been comforted by the knowledge that Henley also rewrote Kipling's verse, but it is significant that Yeats recalls on the very same page of his *Autobiography* an encounter with a former member of Henley's once formidable reviewing staff:

> I met him in Paris, very sad and, I think, very poor. "Nobody will employ me now," he said. "Your master is gone," I answered, "and you are like the spear in an old Irish story that had to be kept dipped in poppy-juice that it might not go about killing people on its own account."

Henley's falling out with Bernard Shaw was a matter of far more serious concern; Henley was among the first to recognize the potential qualities of Shaw's work; and with a commanding, impatient, enthusiastic gesture of approval, Henley insisted that Shaw write his essays in musical criticism for the *Observer.* Shaw immediately agreed to contribute a series of commentaries on current events in music and all went well until the question of Richard Wagner's latest work arose. In London, appreciation of Wagner's symphonic operas had been nursed to shrill and feverish heights by members of the Pre-Raphaelite Brotherhood, all of whom were marked targets for Henley's bitterest scorn. In a weekly article commissioned by the *Observer* Shaw spoke well of Wagner and Henley accepted it; but when the piece appeared in print Shaw found that his praise of Wagner had been changed to censure by Henley's unmistakable turn of phrasing. Shaw cut short his friendship with the *Observer*'s editor, and the break was final. From that time onward he chose to overlook Henley's merits and to dismiss him (not without kindly patronage) as unimportant, as a minor poet to whom matter meant little and manner everything.

Throughout Henley's long-extended quarrel with the Pre-Raphaelite Brotherhood, he held the position of a man whose tastes were austere and positive, but whose judgment in phrasing them reduced a sound and intelligent thesis to the levels of petty controversy. One can understand and readily underscore his dislike of the rhetoric which so lavishly embellished Rossetti's sonnets in *The House of Life:* and there can be small doubt that Henley would have welcomed Gerard Manley Hopkins's remarks upon the infirmities of Swinburne's diction, particularly in the observation that had been made to Canon Dixon as early as the winter of 1881:

> Swinburne is a strange phenomenon: His poetry seems a powerful effort at establishing a new standard of poetical diction, of the rhetoric of poetry; but to waive every other objection it is essentially archaic, biblical a good deal, and so on: now that is a thing that can never last. . . .

In turn one can approve of Henley's stricture as he wrote: "An artist is he who knows how to select and to inspire the results of his selection," a remark which anticipates by a quarter century Ezra Pound's advice to his followers in *A Retrospect* republished in 1918:

> We shall have fewer painted adjectives impending the shock . . . As for myself, I want it so, austere, direct, free from emotional slither . . . In the art of Daniel and Cavalcanti, I have seen that precision which I miss in the Victorians—that explicit rendering, be it of external nature, or of emotion.

But it must be admitted that Henley seemed to be a shade too openly preoccupied with the popular successes through which the Pre-Raphaelite Brotherhood exerted its influence. An occasion presented itself for him to attack Rossetti's privately printed magazine, the *Germ*, and with a recklessness that brought him little honor, he remarked:

> Dante Rossetti imagined the *Germ*, made the *Germ* possible, floated the *Germ*, and in the long run died of the *Germ*. The engineer "hoist with his own petard" was never better exampled than in Dante Rossetti and the magazine which excused his lapses and made him an amateur for the term of his natural life.

To this day one is tempted to believe that the humorless invectives Henley employed to crush his adversaries restored them to admiration among sensitive and uncritical readers, and it is not at all improbable that the violence of his abuse momentarily elevated the Rossettis, Dante Gabriel and his industrious brother, William, to the eminence of literary martyrdom. Like the unfortunate Robert Buchanan, whose essay, *The Fleshly School of Poetry*, had achieved sufficient notoriety to condemn the critical reputation of its author, Henley seemed to have "fought because he could not think."

Meanwhile many doubts concerning the seriousness of Pre-Raphaelite scholarship had been set in motion by John Churton Collins, one of Henley's friends, whose long report on the state of learning at Oxford and Cambridge universities contained a withering list of errors that had caught his eye in Sir Edmund Gosse's studies in English literature which had been published under the imposing title, *From Shakespeare to Pope*. In speaking of John Churton Collins in this particular place I hope I may be pardoned for seeming to digress from the downward stream of Henley's career in journalism. The two men had like temperamental affinities, and if Henley's tyrannies had made it far too easy for a succeeding generation to forget his energy and courage, the memory of Collins's name and reputation have been lost in an obscurity so deep that they awaken greater curiosity than a sober interest in the values he represented. In memoirs written by minor figures of late Victorian celebrity Collins is remembered chiefly as the man who once insulted "poor Gosse" by listing the many errors he had made—and the single appreciation of Collins's weight in modern criticism finds its voice in T. S. Eliot's essay on Cyril Tourneur.

Collins entered the field of critical scholarship by a road no less difficult than Henley's journey from Lister's hospital to London. As an undergraduate at Balliol, Collins had shown extraordinary promise, but he left Oxford without taking his degree and came down to London to face poverty and the dreary routine of teaching classical literature at Scoone's Training School for Indian and Civil Service. An appointment to lecture in the University Extension system came to him as an act of deliverance from Scoones, yet nine-tenths of his waking hours were spent on lecture platforms, for he had joined a small army of bright young men who were sent with lecture notes in one hand and a watch in the other to distribute the mysteries of learning, classical or otherwise, to large middle-class audiences throughout London and its neighboring boroughs. The position, if it could be called such, was scarcely one that enhanced his authority in the writing of critical articles; anything he wrote was likely to be viewed (which it was) as taking root from an extramural source, and when his critical report on the universities appeared in the pages of the *Quarterly Review* for December 1886, Collins was a man of thirty-eight, and the many years of talk in lecture halls, of hasty note-taking, of being hard-pressed for time had left their ugly scars upon his prose.

It was all too easy to dismiss Collins's passion for reform in the universities as seeming heretical in the sense Gosse wished his strictures to be read, for Collins vehemently distrusted the value of teaching literature in the manner of the German philologists, a method which then dominated professional scholarship at Oxford and Cambridge; and at the other extreme, Collins with equal vehemence also distrusted the loose, drawling, drawing-room manner of Gosse's entry into literary criticism. In the light of Collins's excellent studies in the literature of the sixteenth and seventeenth centuries, including his revaluation of John Dryden which was the first and is still the most impressive study of its kind in modern criticism, there is little doubt that the best of his work has improved with the passage of time. One finds it salutary to quote or underline a passage from his essay on the study of classical literature in the universities:

> Classical literature can never become extinct, but it can lose its vogue, it can become the almost exclusive possession of mere scholars, it can cease to be influential . . . Philology cannot save it. It must be linked with life to live, with the incarnation of that of which it too is the incarnation, to prevail. Associate it as poetry with poetry, as oratory with oratory, as criticism with criticism and it will be vital and mighty.

Collins's early friendship with Swinburne which had been broken by the intervention of Sir Edmund Gosse, bore the fruits of his studies in dramatic poetry, and his was perhaps the first of many rediscoveries of John Donne which continued from his day into the first quarter of the twentieth century.

Among the many reasons why Collins's ventures into criticism failed to attract the readers of its day and is left for us to rediscover in its oblivion, is that Collins, in his position as a radical Conservative, stood aside from the larger currents of popular feeling which warmed and nourished Gladstone's retreat in Liberal waters; to attack Gosse's scholarship was to attack by implication the rise of liberal opinion in Great Britain, and Collins's brusque dismissal of William Rossetti's scholarship also implied to the casual reader a counterthrust at the entire Pre-Raphaelite Brotherhood, including the robust and vigorously combative William Morris who had served so notoriously as a figurehead in the ranks of Socialism.

Another important cause of Collins's failure to move easily among his contemporaries, and here his fate with Henley's carried its burden to posterity, was his unguarded and probably unconscious love of controversy for its own sake, an emotion which in its awkward sincerity, quite as William Hazlitt's urgency to confess his domestic misfortunes, still embarrasses the reader. The lack of an early success in his career clouded the last few years of Collins's life, for even his appointment to a chair at the University of Birmingham had come too late, and he had felt, not without reason, that his literary remains would be forgotten.

Nor were the closing years of Henley's life less unfortunate in their Cassandra-like decline into disfavor; as his sense of personal loss increased with the death of a young daughter, his quarrels became even more frequent and ill-advised, yet however cynical he may have become, he was not as Stevenson implied (a hint that touched off a series of erratic estrangements between the two men) a man bent upon filling his purse at the cost of literature. Even the later *Observer*, which had changed its prefix from *Scots* to *National* and the more impressive *New Review* which followed it, refused to compromise its values by publishing work that could be described as merely cheap or popular. Whatever excesses in tactlessness or anger he may have indulged in at the expense of critical sanity and justice, Henley, the editor, remained the watchful, energetic guardian of what was then a new and unknown generation in English letters—and in that office he was incorruptible, if not serene.

Perhaps it was a self-destructive impulse, and surely it was one nurtured in bitterness, that led Henley to write his essay on Robert Louis Stevenson for the pages of the *Pall Mall Magazine*. After a moment of hesitation, Henley agreed to review Graham Balfour's official biography, *The Life of Robert Louis Stevenson*, for *Pall Mall*'s book section, but as he began to write he soon discovered that Stevenson's death had not resolved the emotional difficulties which had unsettled the latter years of their relationship; his patience broke, and his essay rambled into an unsavory reminiscence of old quarrels. In reply to Henley's ill-timed recklessness and critical irrelevancies, the British public was willing to accept Oscar Wilde's remark that so nearly touched the source of Henley's weakness: "He has always thought too much about himself which is wise; and written too much about others that is foolish."

Henley's essay on Stevenson was the last of his controversial appearances, and in the year of his death, two years later, in 1903, he felt that he had survived all his disciples, and certainly, he had lived beyond his short span of great literary fame. One rereads his famous *Invictus* as one might read an ironic epitaph on a hard-won and ill-poised integrity—and last of all, one hears the failing echo of a spent career. He was not the master of his fate, for the ambitions of the world had been too much with him, its glories were of the transitory powers emanating from an editor's desk and chair; they were of the visions that floated across proof sheets waiting correction under the lamp, and their illusion of an enduring life had vanished almost as soon as Henley's body had found its rest within the grave.

1933, 1944

W. B. YEATS AND THE MASK OF JONATHAN SWIFT

All my life I have been haunted with the idea that the poet should know all classes of men as one of themselves. Some day setting out to find knowledge, like some pilgrim to The Holy Land he will become the most romantic characters. He will play with all masks.

—Yeats, *The Autobiography*

Put off that mask of burning gold
With emerald eyes
O no my dear, you make so bold
To find if hearts be wild and wise
And yet not cold.

—Yeats, *The Mask*

I declare this tower is my symbol: I declare
This winding, gyring, spiring treadmill of a stair is my ancestral stair:
That Goldsmith and the Dean, Berkeley and Burke have travelled there:
Swift beating on his breast in sibylline frenzy blind
Because the heart in his blood-sodden breast has dragged him down into mankind.

—Yeats, *The Winding Stair*

In rereading the poetry of William Butler Yeats's last decade, one need not and, indeed, one should not believe everything one sees and hears. The last and fourth period of Yeats's creative life was in some respects his most fruitful period; surely it brought to him his years of widest fame and seemed to uncover new sources of his matured imagination—and yet, even as we recognize and pay tribute to his gifts as a lyric poet, we should not overlook his talent as an actor, an actor who richly cultivated his poetic attitudes, who wore many masks and spoke in many voices, and whose work at proper intervals contained, as he himself would have been pleased to say, "the fascination of the difficult."

Remembering his autobiographies, from the earliest *Reveries over Childhood and Youth* to the last of his published reminiscences, *Dramatis Personae*, and not forgetting George Moore's *Hail and*

Farewell, no actor of Yeats's long day (not even Sir Henry Irving) ever played a role with a more luxurious show of temperament and delight than the Yeatsian performance behind a mask. And here, as always, when we are surprised by some fresh turn of true ingeniousness, we cannot help but admire the brilliant display of energy and art by which he evaded the pitfalls of his fondest imitators. One enjoys the skill with which he acquired even the latest devices of his youngest contemporaries, including W. H. Auden and Stephen Spender, and yet retained authority, choosing for himself the center of the stage.

It is with these reservations that one attempts to discriminate between the dramatic gesture and the poetic realities of Yeats's last appearances, between Yeats's love of the histrionic manner for its own sake and the genuine choice of a mask his daemon sought to wear. In the years between 1928 and 1939, it was all too plain that Yeats's earlier identities with William Blake and with Mallarmé had become shopworn and that the mask of Shelley had long been tossed aside; and here it should be confessed that these impersonations were far less successful than the young Irishman's ability to assume the personae of the Gaelic myth; and though Yeats never relinquished the touchstones of what he conceived to be Blake's mysteries, extending their power in his latter years to adaptations of the *Upanishads*, he abandoned the gaudy trappings of a Blake revived and costumed by the Pre-Raphaelites for those of that "dirty old man," "that horrible spirit" who had been St. Patrick's most notorious Dean.

Even to the casual eye, the elder Yeats's identity with Swift is not without its own contrasts and denials. In rereading Yeats's prose, one soon learns to distrust the flourish with which he introduced evocative, and sometimes semiesoteric names, each name accompanied by that touch of rhetoric (borrowed from Walter Pater who had been his godfather in prose) which is at once the mark of a true style as well as the mannerism which always threatens to destroy it. He seemed always to have loved great names for their own sake, but his particular fondness was reserved for those that carried weight within a world of Anglo-Irish culture; he spoke of Helen and Pythagoras, Oisin and Leda, Christ and Cuchulain, Plotinus and Solomon, and against these he balanced another set of names and associations: Ibsen and G. B. Shaw, Madame Blavatsky and J. M. Synge, Fabian socialism and French symbolism, Lionel Johnson and Ezra Pound—with this list of names in mind one becomes aware that no modern poet has inhabited or walked through so many schools and movements to his own advantage. In recognizing Yeats's intention to wear the mask of Swift, one must not look for signs of an absolute consistency; nor should one expect to find a literal analogy that would yield a comparison of *Gulliver's Travels* with the major poems of Yeats's last decade. The true identity is at once more subtle and more obvious, and the first (perhaps unconscious) step in that direction came as early as 1926 with the writing of the third section of *The Tower:*

It is time that I wrote my will;
I choose upstanding men
That climb the streams until
The fountain leap, and at dawn
Drop their cast at the side
Of dripping stone; I declare
They shall inherit my pride,
The pride of a people that were
Bound neither to Cause nor to State,
Neither to slaves that were spat on,
Nor to the tyrants that spat,
The people of Burke and Grattan
That gave, though free to refuse—
Pride, like that of the morn,
When the headlong light is loose,
Or that of the fabulous horn,
Or that of the sudden shower
When all streams are dry,
Or that of the hour
When the swan must fix his eye
Upon a fading gleam,
Float out upon a long
Last reach of glittering stream
And there sing his last song.[1]

The presence, the heritage that Yeats recalled to mind was of Protestant, Anglo-Irish, eighteenth-century Dublin, and in terms of that heritage he was about to write his will; and, as we shall soon discover, the line included the names of Swift and Goldsmith as well as those of Burke and Grattan, running forward in time to welcome and embrace the memories of Charles Stewart Parnell and Roger Casement. This line, however inclusive it may seem, is a road that does not permit excursions into the far sea lanes of *Gulliver's Travels*, nor into the writing cabinets and dossiers of Queen Anne's court, nor does it reveal the secret of India's forest philosophers so artfully hidden between the leaves of the *Upanishads*, but down that very road one readily unearths the long neglected verses of Dean Swift. It has been frequently observed that distances in time have little meaning in the streets of Dublin or on narrow highways in provincial Ireland; Dublin's eighteenth-century speech and architecture, and in

[1] *The Collected Poems of W. B. Yeats*. London: Macmillan and Co., Limited, 1933. (Subsequent quotations are also from this edition.)

the provinces beyond the English pale, the shades of Druid seers and heroes share an equal martyrdom with Christian saints and victims of political misfortune. Even the merest glance at James Joyce's *Finnegans Wake* uncovers the rich and closely woven texture of an Irish past and present; heroes of lost centuries have a persistent, continuous, contemporaneous life within the fabric, so in the elder Yeats's discovery of Swift, the fruitful years of Swift's deanship at St. Patrick's seem at a mere arm's length from twentieth-century O'Connell Street in Dublin.

Another indication of how variously alive that fabric was in Yeats's memory is generously stated in J. A. Symons's article *Wilde at Oxford.* In speaking of John Pentland Mahaffy, called "The Admirable Crichton" of Trinity College (and who was one of Wilde's lecturers at Trinity), Symons wrote:

> Above all his hobbies he prized what he called the art of the conversation. It was an "art" for which Dublin in the seventies provided an ample field of exercise, for the eighteenth century still survived in the Irish capital, and not only because the noble houses of Merrion Square and its neighborhood were occupied by men who could afford an eighteenth century lavishness of hospitality. Socially Dublin was more compact, and yet more inclusive than London then; it was dominated, not by an aristocracy rich enough to hold itself out of contact with the middle class, nor an aloof legendary Queen, but by the Vice Regal Court and its garrison of younger sons, who fraternized more or less on terms of equality with the Protestant ascendancy of law, medicine, church and university. Large dinner parties were a daily occurrence; they formed a stage on which any man of character might make his mark.[2]

Among other things, one realizes here why Yeats's admiration for the mercurial Oscar Wilde was never broken—and why, though ruins and shades of the eighteenth century were still to be found in Dublin's streets sixty years later, the scene had grown comparatively dull and dirty. Although much remained of Yeats's youth, the glittering days of the Viceregal court were gone, and following them, the excitements and the diversions of the Gaelic Renaissance had also paled; the First World War (to say the least) had left its mark on Dublin and all Ireland: The Abbey Theatre was not what it had been; the semicommunist Irish Republicans were among the newest heroes, and there was reason enough for elder men of Anglo-Irish derivation, particularly those who had long memories, to identify themselves with images of bitterness and of loss.

Granting all this, one might still ask the question: Where does Swift come in? Why among the many masks through which Yeats

[2] *Horizon,* April 1941.

spoke does the mask of Swift assume particular importance? From another source than those that I have mentioned we begin to arrive at an answer through J. M. Hone's witty and intelligent appraisal of Yeats's politics; speaking of the time when Yeats served his term as a senator in Cosgrave's government, following the Irish "Troubles" of 1916–1921, Hone recalls a story of how Yeats replied to those who asked him the name of his political party. Was he an old Parnellite? Was he a Republican? Was it up Cosgrave and down De Valera? Yeats said calmly: "I am a Whig"—and laughter, derision, and confusion followed his remark. But the value of the joke which associated Senator William Butler Yeats with the Protestant land-owning aristocracy in Ireland had more than a touch of Yeats's customary shrewdness in it; it brought back to mind memories of Dean Swift's political ironies, and with it the same quality of fear and distrust that unseated Swift at the court of Queen Anne when the Duchess of Somerset had but to whisper the word "atheist" and the would-be councilor of the Queen's ministers was exiled to the Deanery of St. Patrick's. Again Yeats had prepared himself (and perhaps the end in view was still unconscious) for the role of Swift in twentieth-century Dublin; and, so far as Yeats was concerned, the part carried with it no direct or immediate political responsibilities; he was left free to modify the role, however, whenever he chose, for the lines to be spoken were too difficult, too harsh, too abstract for Yeats's Dublin contemporaries—it required a true act of poetic imagination to revive the bold, coarse-fibered image of Swift's personality on the Abbey stage in November 1930.

In the introduction to his play, *The Words upon the Window-Pane,* Yeats wrote:

> What shall occupy our imagination? We must, I think, decide among . . . three ideas of national life: that of Swift; that of a great Italian of his day; that of modern England. If the Garrets and the Cellars listen I may throw light upon the matter, and I hope if all the time I seem to be thinking of something else I shall be forgiven. I must speak of things that come out of the common consciousness, where every thought is like a bell with many echoes. . . . Now I read Swift for months together, Burke and Berkeley less often but always with excitement, and Goldsmith lures and waits. I collect materials for my thought and work, for some of my identification of my beliefs with the nation itself, of its own permanent form, in that one Irish century that escaped from darkness and confusion, I seek an image of the modern mind's discovery of itself. I would that our fifteenth, sixteenth, or even our seventeenth century had been the clear mirror, but fate decided against us. . . . Swift haunts me; he is always just around the corner.[3]

[3] *Wheels and Butterflies,* by William Butler Yeats. New York: The Macmillan Company, 1935.

"Swift haunts me"—the phrase reminds one of the way Swift haunts the first page of *Finnegans Wake*, for Swift is a demimyth of Irish consciousness, a name, a legend in itself as well as the author of the *Drapier Letters*. One may well wonder how Yeats spent "months together" reading Swift; we know from the introduction to *The Words upon the Window-Pane* that he read the Fourth Drapier Letter and the *Discourse of the Contest and Dissensions Between the Nobles and the Commons in Athens and Rome*, a Whig document that contained a definition of three tyrannies, the One, the Few and the Many—and what is even more important, we know that he had also reread Swift's poetry. We can well understand how the unsolved mysteries of Swift's relationships to Vanessa and Stella stimulated the love of mystery for its own sake in Yeats's imagination—mysteries, by the way, that are as intractable as the problem of Hamlet's melancholy, and which offer an excuse for reinterpretation every time Shakespeare's play makes its reappearance on the stage. Yeats's particular interest in the question: Was Swift mad? is of the same quality that marked his pursuit of Swedenborg which he followed with delight for so many years; the importance here was that he rediscovered a mystery in eighteenth-century Dublin, and that in his effort to reinterpret it, he was led to a reading of Swift's *Verses to Vanessa* and *Stella's Birthday Poems*. Even in Dublin, where the memories of Swift have greater vitality than in any other place on earth, a rereading of his poetry carries with it the charm of verse that has been neglected; one had to seek out the poems in eighteenth-century editions, and that semiesoteric search alone would insure Yeats's interest for many "months together."

Thanks to Harold Williams's definitive edition of *The Poems of Jonathan Swift* we need not speculate too darkly upon the nature of Yeats's reading which prepared him for the performance of his last impressive role. The poems themselves bring to light the complexities of Swift's relationship to Queen Anne's court, to his friends in London, to Sir William Temple's excellent library (where the young Swift completed his literary education), to the Irish people, to politics in general, to Stella and Vanessa—and (which is perhaps the most important relationship of all) the relationship of Swift to his own verse.

Here one remembers Dr. Johnson's telling of the story how Dryden remarked: "Cousin Swift, you will never be a poet"; and in rereading the strained and lifeless *Pindaric Odes* inscribed to Sir William Temple, to King William and to the Athenian Society which young Swift wrote and Dryden read, we tend to believe that the elder poet's harsh sounding judgment seems singularly mild. Until Swift grew to active manhood, the writing of verse remained one of the larger elements in his complex of frustrations; in the presence of metrical numbers his imagination, his wit, his intelligence turned to stone, the lines of verse falling heavily across the page, spent and inert. The frequently quoted lines:

> My hate, whose lash just heaven has long decreed
> Shall on a day make sin and folly bleed;

were written at the age of twenty-six and lie hidden in an incredibly dull and abstracted series of couplets addressed *To Mr. Congreve.* It was not until Swift reached the age of forty-one that he wrote his first true poem, his second version of *Baucis and Philemon, Imitated, From the Eighth Book of Ovid.* Even the first version of the poem, written two years earlier, seems to have broken the spell of dullness which hung over him as he wrote verse, and it is significant that he broke the spell by discarding his attempts to write heroic verse. Swift adapted the story of a peasant's hut transformed into a shrine to a lively scene in Kent, the peasant's cottage changed into a village church, but this was no mere imitation of Ovid's *Baucis;* the fire, the inspiration that Swift had caught and adapted to his own use was the coarse, homely vein in Ovid which gave certain passages in his *Metamorphoses* an air of mock innocence and mock heroic charm, and it was at this point that Ovid closely resembled Plautus, which sharply differentiated his work from the larger and more richly elaborated structures of Virgil's *Aeneid* as well as the urban and polished brilliance of Horace's *Augustan Odes.* (And here, in a parenthesis, we need not forget the elder Yeats's desire to identify his work with the coarser fibers of Irish life, of which the rewriting of his poem *The Dedication to a Book of Stories Selected from the Irish Novelists* in the 1933 edition of his *Collected Poems* is a noteworthy example:

> I also bear a bell-branch full of ease.
>
> I tore it from green boughs winds tore and tossed
> Until the sap of summer had grown weary!
> I tore it from the barren boughs of Eire,
> That country where a man can be so crossed;
> Can be so battered, badgered and destroyed
> That he's a loveless man. . . .

In these lines the image of Swift's hand guiding Yeats's is all too clear.) The next twenty years of Swift's activity in writing verse, roughly the years 1719 to 1739, relieved the burden of his own inadequacy in the composition of poetry. He had found a poetic style in which he could be master; it was a style in which the lively, almost antipoetic wealth of realistic detail anticipated the narrative poetry of George Crabbe. Although the brief *A Description of the Morning* and *A Description of a City Shower* were exceptions to the rule, his characteristic verse form followed the metrics of Butler's *Hudibras;* it was a form peculiarly suited to his temperament, and as he adapted it to his own needs, he could resume it or shake it off with all the ease of wearing an old, comfortable, and somewhat dirty dressing gown. Rather than seeming to be an overly strict or inhibiting discipline, the rhyming couplets gave him freedom to exercise his wit on a dull morning, to vent his anger, or to pay tribute to a friend.

Perhaps it is not too much to say that Yeats sought for a like freedom in his latter years, a freedom to use a vigorous masculine speech in verse with the same air that the aristocrat always meets the peasant on common ground—for both have always been outside the circle embracing middle-class society, since one is as much above the law as the other is below it. Here one remembers the miserable, dull-witted, brutish Irish peasants that enter Swift's mock pastorals, and with it one recalls a story told by Swift's publisher, George Faulkner, who described his author's method of correcting proofs for the Dublin edition of Swift's works in 1744. The proofs were read to two menservants, "Which if they did not comprehend, he would alter and amend, until they understood it perfectly well, and then would say, 'This will do; for I write to the Vulgar, more than to the learned.'" There is a clear connection between the ironic wit of this story and another that Yeats wrote in a letter to Dorothy Wellesley, 23 December, 1936:

> Hate is a kind of "passive suffering" but indignation is a kind of joy. "When I am told that somebody is my brother protestant," said Swift, "I remember that the rat is a fellow creature"; that seems to me a joyous saying.

From this we move to other analogies between Swift's position in Dublin as Dean of St. Patrick's and Yeats's reputation in Ireland during the 1930s. Yeats's later poems, *The Tower, The Winding Stair, Words for Music Perhaps,* were better known in London and in New York than in the place where they were written and first saw light. He could almost say as Swift wrote to Charles Ford: ". . . it is an infamous Case indeed to be neglected in Dublin when a man may converse with the best Company in London." In the broadest sense, he was again like Swift in that he seemed an apparition walking up and down familiar Dublin streets, exiled at home, a "Whig," slightly out of time and place, and like Swift he was both a Protestant interpreter of Ireland to a literate public in London, and the spokesman of an Anglo-Irish world to a nation of diffident, poverty-stricken, predominantly Roman Catholic people on his own soil.

If the mask of Swift was becoming to the years in which Yeats resumed his identity with the national life of the Irish people, one need not interpret all that both men had to say in terms of sexual impotence and personal, ungoverned loss of temper. Certain recent critics of both Yeats and Swift have found much to admire in rage and passion for their own sake; and they have frequently quoted Yeats's desire to be a "foolish, passionate old man" with the hope, perhaps, of emulating him when they themselves are "old and grey and full of sleep." But Swift, even at an early age, had learned to sublimate personal frustration in moral passion as he wrote "the evil to be avoided is tyranny, that is to say, the summa imperii, or unlimited power solely in the hands of the one, the few, or the many . . ." and in his middle years, the defeat of his ambitions at Queen Anne's court found its cure in his identity with the unhappy Irish as he composed the *Drapier Letters*. While it would be absurd to assume that Yeats's "lust and rage" in his last years contained a proof of moral passion comparable to Swift's, or to claim that the sources of his rage were identical with those of the mask he wore, his *Saeva Indignatio* has a justification in his great gifts as a poet. Neither Yeats's *Blood and the Moon* nor Swift's masterpiece in verse, *On the Death of Dr. Swift,* is remembered solely because of the bitterness or rage some few of their lines imply: the latter survives because of Swift's observant, realistic eye and wit; and in Yeats's poem one realizes more than all else the power of his imaginative insight, as well as the appropriate uses of an imagery that lent distinction to his poetic style since the writing of *The Tower* in 1926. In the guise of Swift, Yeats well understood the role of seeming on occasion foolish, blasphemous, tortured, half mad, holding in his heart, as a lighted candle, the frenzy of Dionysus. It is in this atmosphere and setting that one discovers the Crazy Jane songs, partly stimulated, of course, by Yeats's devotion to Spiritualism, that furthest, that last extreme of the Protestant attitude which develops from each man being his own priest and confessor to the logical conclusion (if logic can be applied to any aspect of religious faith) of being his own medium, echoing the voices of spirits from the dead.

In this connection, one might well ask the question: Who is Crazy Jane? And is she Ireland? Perhaps not, that would make too great a claim upon her identity. She is more accurately "of Ireland," quoting in her twentieth song a fragment of an old catch sung for at least six centuries on Irish soil:

> "*I am of Ireland,*
> *And the Holy Land of Ireland,*
> *And time runs on,*" *cried she.*
> "*Come out of charity,*
> *Come dance with me in Ireland.*"

One man, one man alone
In that outlandish gear,
One solitary man
Of all that rambled there
Had turned his stately head.

In *The Words upon the Window-Pane,* Swift's presence on the stage is through the lips of Mrs. Henderson, a spiritualist medium, and Mrs. Henderson's control, Lulu, speaks of "that bad old man in the corner," who is Swift, and of the young lady who through Lulu's eyes is in fancy dress, "hair all in curls—all bent down on the floor near that old man with glasses." There is a strong resemblance between the "solitary man" in outlandish gear and Lulu's Swift—he may not be the same man, but the resemblance is strong enough to establish a family relationship, and though Crazy Jane is not Vanessa, her solitary man will not dance with her no more than Swift yields to the demands of Vanessa's love. The dramatic action of both scenes is the same. The solitary man replies to Crazy Jane:

"The fiddlers are all thumbs,
Or the fiddle-string accursed,
The drums and the kettledrums
And the trumpets all are burst,
And the trombone," cried he,
"The trumpet and the trombone,"
"And cocked a malicious eye,
"But time runs on, runs on."

As we keep in mind the solitary man's refrain "But time runs on, runs on," his family resemblance to Swift does not diminish in the rereading of *Stella's Birthday* written in 1724—that admirable poem compounded of masculine malice, wit, grace, tenderness, and love:

Beauty and Wit, too sad a truth,
Have always been confin'd to Youth:
The God of Wit, and Beauty's Queen,
He Twenty-one and She Fifteen:
No Poet ever sweetly sung,
Unless he were like *Phoebus,* young;
Nor ever Nymph inspir'd to Rhyme,
Unless, like *Venus,* in her Prime.
At Fifty-six, if this be true,
Am I a Poet fit for you?
Or at the Age of Forty-three,
Are you a Subject fit for me?
Adieu bright Wit, and radiant Eyes;
You must be grave, and I be wise.
Our Fate in vain we would oppose,

But I'll be still your Friend in Prose:
Esteem and Friendship to express,
Will not require Poetic Dress;
And if the Muse deny her Aid
To have them *sung* they may be *said*.

But, *Stella*, say, what evil Tongue
Reports you are no longer young?
That *Time* sits with his Scythe to mow
Where erst sate *Cupid* with his Bow;
That half your Locks are turn'd to Grey;
I'll ne'er believe a Word they say.
'Tis true, but let it not be known,
My Eyes are somewhat dimmish grown;
For Nature, always in the Right,
To your Decays adapts my sight,
And Wrinkles undistinguish'd pass,
For I'm asham'd to use a Glass;
And till I see them with these Eyes
Whoever says you have them, lyes.

No Length of Time can make you quit
Honour and Virtue, Sense and Wit,
Thus you may still be young to me,
While I can better *hear* than *see;*
Oh, ne'er may Fortune shew her Spight,
To make me *deaf*, and mend my *Sight*.[4]

To change the metaphor back from sight to hearing, surely "The fiddlers are all thumbs, / Or the fiddle-string accursed"—but who, again, is Crazy Jane? While her relationships to the men of whom she speaks place her by broad analogy within the same world that witnessed the Irish "Troubles" of 1916–21 and the years of De Valera's rise to power, she is clearly not Stella, nor of the line to which Burke and Grattan belonged. She is of that underworld that Burns saw when he wrote *The Jolly Beggars,* and her language has a half romantic, half neoclassic turn of eloquence. Since Yeats's reading, like all of Anglo-Irish Dublin's, always returned with a fixed, yet casual, eye upon the literature of the eighteenth century, we need not be surprised to find another Crazy Jane in Tomkin's obscure anthology of *Poems on Various Subjects*, London, 1804. Her author was M. G. Lewis, Esq. M. P.[5] and under her name we find these lines:

Why, fair maid, in ev'ry feature,
Are such signs of fear express'd?

[4] *The Poems of Jonathan Swift*, edited by Harold Williams. Oxford: The Clarendon Press, 1937.

[5] Lewis later became famous as the author of *The Monk* (1796).

Can a wand'ring wretched creature
  With such terrors fill thy breast?
Do my frenzied looks alarm thee?
  Trust me, sweet—thy fears are vain
Not for Kingdoms would I harm thee,
  Shun not then poor Crazy Jane.

Dost thou weep to see my anguish?
  Mark me! and avoid my woe;
When men flatter, sigh and languish,
  Think them false—I found them so:
For I lov'd—Oh! so sincerely.
  None could ever love again:
But the youth I lov'd so dearly,
  Stole the wits of Crazy Jane.

. . . .

Now forlorn and broken-hearted,
  And with frenzied thoughts beset;
On that spot where last we parted,
  On that spot where first we met.
Still I sing my love-lorn ditty,
  Still I slowly pace the plain;
While each passerby in pity
  Cries—God help thee, Crazy Jane!

Following poor Jane's "frenzied looks" what an excellent companion she makes for "Swift beating on his breast in sybylline frenzy blind / Because the heart in his blood-sodden breast had dragged him down into mankind"!—and with her cry through Yeats's lips, "All things remain in God," the scene rounds to completion upon a darkening stage.

In re-creating the figure of Crazy Jane, Yeats also displayed his greatest contradiction in assuming the role of Swift in twentieth-century Ireland. If Jane's unhappy plight recalls Ireland's past and present—and even now, perhaps a large part of Ireland's future—it also recalls the familiar burdens of Thomas Moore's *Irish Melodies.* Readers of Yeats's early poems, particularly those who remember *The Lake Isle of Innisfree,* can recognize at once the impure, almost maudlin strain that Yeats had inherited from "The harp that once through Tara's halls / The soul of music shed." That Yeats in his latter years was able to go behind the *Irish Melodies,* tracing their music to a relatively pure, less tarnished source, is, of course, among the signs of his true genius. But if one reads those poems of the Crazy Jane cycle that are less successful than the best, a note of pathos and ill-timed heroics sounds all too clearly on the ear. The obvious flaw in Yeats's performance of a great role was his inability to see the mock-heroic aspects of Swift's life and work, the mock hero whose shade overhears the gossip of Queen Anne's court in his verses *On the Death of Dr. Swift.* No one in his right senses would lay great claims for Swift's ability as a lyric poet, so here in Yeats's disability to realize fully the mock-heroic character of Swift's verse as well as the moral passion which ran beneath its lines, we find Yeats at his weakest, attempting to transform an essentially ironic role into terms of tragedy.

If Yeats's identity with Swift cannot be held responsible for the best of all his work (a list which should include *In Memory of Major Robert Gregory*, *An Irish Airman Foresees His Death*, *Sailing to Byzantium*, and *The Tower* itself, as well as a half-dozen poems selected from *The Winding Stair*) the mask helped to sustain his energy as he approached death through the distractions of old age. Swift's late maturity was in itself a heartening example, and the vigor of Swift's intellect was in truth "the strength that gives our blood and state magnanimity of its own desire," an abstract, moral passion that Yeats did not possess, but could, on occasion, simulate with the superior graces of an accomplished actor. In *The Words upon the Window-Pane* one hears Yeats's Swift echoing the words of Job and Sophocles' chorus from *Oedipus at Colonus:*

> Never to have lived is best, ancient writers say;
> Never to have drawn the breath of life, never to have
> looked into the light of day,

as his will overpowers Mrs. Henderson, shouting, "Perish the day on which I was born!"—which remains, even at its best, an uncontrolled mixture of tragi-comic associations. The play is not a tragedy, yet it points the direction, if one remembers Yeats's translation of *Oedipus at Colonus*, of his furthest reach toward an understanding of a tragic situation in human life, and for Yeats it seemed to be (or rather, this is the impression his play leaves upon the reader) a statement of the purge that relieves the terrors of old age. For the rest, we hear the remote, perhaps the very last, intonations of Yeats's voice through the mask of Swift in *Under Ben Bulben*, which Dorothy Wellesley tells us was first given the uninspired title *His Convictions:*

> Irish poets, learn your trade,
> Sing whatever is well made,
> Scorn the sort now growing up
> All out of shape from toe to top,
> Their unremembering hearts and heads
> Base-born products of base beds.
> Sing the peasantry, and then
> Hard-riding country gentlemen,

The holiness of monks, and after
Porter-drinkers' randy laughter;
Sing the lords and ladies gay
That were beaten into clay
Through seven heroic centuries;
Cast your mind on other days . . .

The verse is not Yeats at his best; the metrics rattle onward with few pauses to their stop until they arrive at the truly excellent:

Cast a cold eye
On life, on death.
Horseman, pass by!

Yeats had outworn the mask with his death; the play was over and the curtains drawn.

1942, 1944

YEATS REVISITED: "THE CHAMBERED NAUTILUS"

W. B. Yeats's *Autobiography* belongs on the same shelf with Ruskin's haunting and rare *Praeterita*.[1] If to the hasty reader Yeats's book seems to contain an unwarranted number of mystifications and ambiguities, he should remember that if Yeats had not been a very great poet, he would have been known in Ireland as one of the greatest charlatans of his day. The ignorant and bigoted in Dublin streets half believed he had "an evil eye." They had heard he dabbled in magic spells and if they chanced to see him down the street, they crossed themselves. A careful rereading of his *Autobiography* shows that he regarded his life as fiction in symbolist prose, his poems as ultimate truths.

The association of Yeats's name with symbolism began as early as 1900, and in London that relationship was strengthened by the writings of Arthur Symons, who had praised him as an heir of the French Symbolists. During those early days of his career, Symons was his necessary friend and critic. Between that time and 1914, Yeats's fame as a poet of "The Celtic Twilight" had worn somewhat thin; it had attracted the appetite of moths and was motheaten. For the moment he seemed better known as the director of the successful Abbey Theatre, and as such he had become vulnerable to George Moore's caricature of him in the first volume of *Hail and Farewell.* Moore took pride in being known as a follower of Zola, a stance directly opposed to that of poetry and symbolism. Yeats was in danger and he probably knew it. Any direct reply to Moore's *Hail and Farewell* would place him on Moore's level and make him seem ridiculous. He took the wiser course of ignoring Moore's distorted picture of his activities in the Irish Movement and of his friendship with Lady Gregory. Instead of a public quarrel with Moore he chose to write and publish the first section of his autobiography, *Reveries over Childhood and Youth*, a document that recreated the legend of himself as an Anglo-Irish poet, rather than that of the Abbey Theatre's alert and able chief director. He chose to remember that he came of a seafaring, military, landowning family; that though his father

1 *The Autobiography of William Butler Yeats*, Consisting of *Reveries over Childhood and Youth*, *The Trembling of the Veil*, and *Dramatis Personae.* New York: The Macmillan Company, 1938.

was a painter and an artist, he was also an intellectual and a Puritan. The *Reveries* were to be read by "Those Few People Mainly Personal Friends Who Have Read All That I Have Written." The slender book was an early step toward Yeats's later practice of remaking himself, and was behind his impulse when he wrote in his 1914 volume of verse, *Responsibilities,* "There's more enterprise in walking naked."

Later he was to say:

> The friends that have it I do wrong
> Whenever I remake a song,
> Should know what issue is at stake:
> It is myself that I remake.

His action was like that of the chambered nautilus, and to return to his prose, it had the intonations of Dublin table talk, with commas, semicolons and periods floating in air, and added to it, a flourish borrowed from Walter Pater. Not unlike Suetonius's *Lives of the Twelve Caesars,* his *Reveries* are a mixture of legend, fact, and fable; and in their re-creations of a poetic temperament and destiny, they anticipated the confessions of James Joyce's *Portrait of the Artist as a Young Man.* Consciously or not the first two sections of Yeats's *Autobiography,* the *Reveries* and *The Trembling of the Veil,* reflect his mastery, in prose, of the symbolist technique: the arts of suggestion and of association, the art of sustaining beyond and behind all material things, the authority of a vision are there. Pater's two laws also prevailed: the necessity "to burn with a hard, gemlike flame," and (which was an echo from Gautier) the fact that "all art aspires to a condition of music." (These were to become laws in the Yeatsian esthetic. Later he added a few others: "Spring vegetables may be over, they have not been refuted. I am Blake's disciple, not Hegel's: 'contraries are positive. A negation is not a contrary.' ") And without loss of personality and a personally speaking voice, he had learned the art of remaking himself.

The Trembling of the Veil, its title taken from a phrase of Mallarmé's, came eight years after Yeats's *Responsibilities.* He had improved upon his learning of symbolist doctrines from Arthur Symons. Both the book of poems and the latest section of his autobiography were proof of his quoted epitaph: "In dreams begin responsibilities." From the wells of his sublunar memory, he revived the members of a "Tragic Generation": Lionel Johnson, John Synge, Oscar Wilde, Henley. Yeats had become the nearly perfect (one can almost say "Proustian") writer of anecdotes. He retold and improved upon one of Wilde's set pieces in conversation, saying at the same time that the memory of what he heard was better than his written story. Like Bernard Shaw, Yeats kept open a place in his heart for Oscar Wilde, for to the Anglo-Irish when "No Oscar ruled the table," conversation grew dull and spiritless. And truly enough the conversational wit of Wilde's plays was a bridge, spanning the gap of nearly a hundred years, between the wit of Sheridan and Shaw. Wilde had relit the footlights of a tradition that dated back to Congreve and Oliver Goldsmith. To writers of Yeats's generation the debt to Wilde's theatrical presence was enormous.

In his autobiography as in his verse (note *The Circus Animals' Desertion*) he had perfected the craft of building ivory towers from heaps of rubbish, of making bricks out of broken glass and mud-stained fragments of old rags. From Madame Blavatsky's dubiously engineered séances, as well as her *Isis Unveiled*, he was to write his play, *The Words upon the Window-Pane;* and from the oracular nonsense of Alastair Crowley (who was called "The Great Beast" by an angry magistrate who had failed to secure a conviction of fraud against him) Yeats drew imagery for the writing of *The Second Coming*. In his *Trembling of the Veil* was proof enough of Yeats's flirtations with theosophy, but more than that the book was proof of his sustained poetic stature, its mark of greatness. He had transformed his experience with charlatans into a larger vision of the world. In 1923, the year after it appeared, he received "the bounty of Sweden," the Nobel Prize. George Moore's attempts to ridicule him were well forgotten. In Dublin, Yeats—Senator William Butler Yeats of the new Irish Free State—had become a public figure. The need of creating a further legend of his life had vanished. And that is why the last third of his collected *Autobiography* lacks energy and flavor; he reserved his strength for his last poems, for the remaking of some of his early verse, for collections of his essays, and writing of such lectures as *On the Boiler*.

1954

"THE NOCTURNAL TRAVELLER": WALTER DE LA MARE

The poetry and prose of Walter de la Mare lean over a bridge of years from the last century into our own. Among some of the things of which his writings tell us are the peculiar haunting memories that the environment of the nineteenth century still holds. Twenty years ago, it was easy to insist that we had thoroughly outgrown, or had outrun, even the memory of late nineteenth-century décor; of course we had not; we were still possessed, half-sleeping in our dreams, by mechanical Speed and Progress.

As for De la Mare, he continued to write, in the same fashion he had made his own, stories and rhymes for children, two novels, *The Memoirs of a Midget* and *The Return*, books of short stories, poems —and he appeared to devote his leisure moments to the making of anthologies, collections of verse and prose which did not in the least resemble the usual piecing together of other men's wits and genius, but were books of imaginative insight and discovery. It had become De la Mare's way to approach his readers by an entrance through the nursery (a popular path, if one is at all successful—and a very dangerous one) in his anthologies. The path is clear in his *Come Hither*, a collection of rhymes, poems, and verses, so arranged as to introduce children to the reading of poetry. That was its thoroughly innocent disguise; it did not pretend to teach children how to read poetry, nor to find a moral hidden within a poem, nor how to find a meaning that a poem might contain. The concealed plot of the book was to awaken whatever is meant by the word "imagination." I don't know how many people have given the book to children, or read it aloud to them; I suspect that many have intended to make a gift of it to a child and then kept it themselves, or presented it to older children than the child they originally had in mind; it is a book in which imagination remains unglossed—for to people who have no poetic imagination, "imagination" keeps children awake at night and guides them in the telling of frightfully neurotic lies.

I have spoken of the dangers De la Mare has run in approaching his readers through the doors of the nursery, and his writings are distinctly affected by that approach. Others have entered through the same door: Edward Lear, Lewis Carroll, and, with measurable damage, so have Robert Louis Stevenson and J. M. Barrie. In the cases of Lear and Lewis Carroll the mask of childhood offered an appropriate release for the genius of the writers behind the mask, yet neither men, in spite of the popular success of their books for children, were professional writers. They were not afflicted by the professional need to write for children, which can become a great and crippling affliction. The convention of writing of and for children did not injure Stevenson's *A Child's Garden of Verses*, nor did it mar the adventurous wanderings toward *Treasure Island;* even Dr. Jekyll and Mr. Hyde, the downward look into the mystery of dual personality and the play of forces of good and evil within it, remained unharmed by the convention of childhood memories, insights, desires. *Dr. Jekyll and Mr. Hyde*, founded on the famous case of Deacon Brodie of Edinburgh,[1] kept Stevenson within the charmed circle of his childhood memories—but when his perception revealed an identity other than that which childhood memory permitted, the convention of writing stories for Victorian boys and girls crippled his hand—and the result was an abortive masterpiece, *The Master of Ballantrae*. Stevenson feared to give his readers an adult answer to his final variation of the good vs. evil theme. The same fears, the same curse afflicted J. M. Barrie's *Peter Pan.* The truth that Barrie so valiantly discovered, the desire for eternal sexless youth, failed of its translation into other than sentimental terms; a frightening charm still permeates the movement of the play, a charm that remains unpurged of its essential fears and premonitions of disaster.

These are the dangers that De la Mare chose to run, and at his second best he is not quite free of them. One convention of the nursery is charm; and the second best invades the verses of *Nod.* Charm is there:

> His drowsy flock streams on before him,
> Their fleece charged with gold,
> To where the sun's last beam leans low
> On Nod the shepherd's fold.
>
> . . . .
>
> His lambs outnumber a noon's roses,
> Yet, when night's shadows fall,
> His blind old sheep-dog, Slumber-soon,
> Misses not one of all.

[1] I was told of Stevenson's debt to the case of Deacon Brodie by William Roughead—that classic authority on Edinburgh crime. Both Charles Whibley and Roughead have written brilliantly on the subject of Brodie—and indeed, he was one of the most attractive of what Henry James calls "Roughead's nefarious characters." The right side of Brodie was firmly attached to his duties to the Presbyterian Church and to his craftsmanship in the making of furniture—his left (after nine o'clock at night) was devoted to Edinburgh's underworld. At the gallows, his last words were: "Ladies and gentlemen, what is death but a leap in the dark!"

The musical art that went into the making of these two stanzas is nearly flawless; there is a rocking movement in the lines, and the line falls to rest, yet the result is oversweet and coy, and the sign of danger is in the name of the shepherd's dog, "Slumber-soon." All usual expectations are gratified; everything is safely, noiselessly at rest—but everything is a shade too artfully, too safely said. One does not quite believe it; it is too professional, too pat. It is when De la Mare's charm has more than itself to recommend it that its internal strength endures beyond its artfulness. Within the blue and white China walls of the nursery, a good Dr. Jekyll is in need of the evil and crooked shadow of a Mr. Hyde behind him. In that shadow the secret of De la Mare's magic lies. The shadow is behind all things within the nursery, behind all green and grey stone garden walls, and in that shadow is concealed much of what De la Mare has to say. He has written somewhere that it is the meaning that exists, not in words, but *between* them which is so important, so difficult to make clear. And for the lyric poet, more than half the meaning of a poem is in its music:

> And when I crumble who will remember
> That lady of the West country?

Disassociated from the rest of the line, the word "crumble" is almost ridiculous, but to hear its association with "remember" and to associate it with the wearing away of a headstone in a churchyard, is to understand that an act of magic has been performed, and it is the kind of felicity of which De la Mare is a master. I doubt whether these two lines would make sense in any other language than that of English.

2

And what of the stories that De la Mare has written? His excellence is to be found in four of them: *Seaton's Aunt*, *Miss Duveen*, *The Three Friends*, *The Green Room*. In three of them, the spell exerted by another century than ours casts its shadow across the page; it haunts each story. That spell is what Max Beerbohm has caught in his cheerfully wry caricature of him sitting in a Victorian parlor at the footstool of a formidable maiden lady, but it is also the same aspect of De la Mare's prose writings that places them in the genre of the short stories of Joseph Sheridan Le Fanu, whose *In a Glass Darkly* has been revived and reprinted, whose *Uncle Silas* has received the respect and admiration of Elizabeth Bowen. It is the genre of which James's *The Turn of the Screw* is a famous illustration; the best of De la Mare's stories depend upon the intense, and subtle perceptions of concealed guilt, ambitions, desires; they are revelations of the hidden will to power that so often corrodes the mind, and love is transformed into the desire to possess wholly the psyche of the loved one. It has been De la Mare's achievement in this genre to arrive upon the scene with a deceptively innocent eye: in telling the story of poor Seaton devoured by an implacable Aunt, he has the air of calmly reciting a fragment of schoolboy memoirs, and in *Miss Duveen* there is the figure of a lonely child, housed with an unsympathetic grandmother, who finds an affinity with the unloved old maid, a neighbor, Miss Duveen. Miss Duveen has lost her wits and knows she has, but she has retained her moments of intuitive knowledge which are shared by the lonely boy. Miss Duveen's ancient sins are sins of family pride and vanity—and the sin of maidenly diffidence, the most delicate and insidious sin of all, which is so often called "modesty" and which grew like a weed in many green and rainswept Victorian gardens. As the boy grows older he sees Miss Duveen drifting toward madness;

I began to see we were ridiculous friends, especially as she came now in ever dingier and absurder in clothes. She even looked hungry, and not quite clean, as well as ill; and she talked more to her phantoms than to me when once we met.

When the boy learns that Miss Duveen's friends have been compelled to put her away, there were no tears:

But I know now that the news, in spite of a vague sorrow, greatly relieved me. I should be at ease in the garden again, came the thought—no longer fear to look ridiculous, and grow hot when our neighbour was mentioned, or be saddled with her company beside the stream.

This is the end of an early friendship and the end of the story, and I quote directly from it to show how simply, firmly, precisely De la Mare purges *Miss Duveen* of all false sentiment and how securely he steps out of the trap where lesser writers however honestly inspired, have lost their poise.

Of all three stories in which the shadow of *time past* falls across the page, *The Green Room* is an obvious tour de force, yet it is of a kind that could be practiced only by a poet of De la Mare's extraordinary skill in making verse that serves his purpose in defining the characters of an inept, self-centered poetess and her posthumous, well intentioned, naive editor. A less perceptive, less artful writer than De la Mare would have been content to make his ghostly, romantic heroine no more than an outrageously bad poet, for in the writing of this story the temptation is to make her the objective of satire, which would have destroyed the power she held over her editor and completely alienated the best of his good intentions. For De la Mare's purpose her verse must be good enough to deceive the young, the enthusiastic reader who thinks he is reading poetry when he is reading the effusions of a strong-willed, self-possessed young woman—her verses have the attractions of a lady in love and in distress and of lyric facility, if not art, that so often pass for poetry among those who do not read verse too often or too well. This was the kind of mock-poetic presence which in every age makes its appearance somewhere either in verse or fiction on a respectable publisher's list and which ten years later fills the darker shelves of the secondhand bookseller. In this case the ghost happens to be of early nineteenth-century origins, one who is very nearly another Emily Brontë, but is not, yet is powerful enough to haunt the imagination of the editor who discovers her manuscript in the library of a rare book shop; his encounter with it has all the force and, of course, all the illusion of an actual love affair.

One can read into this story several ethical conclusions: one can say that good intentions are of little value to an editor or critic, that vague young men are too easily possessed by strong-willed young women, that one should distinguish between the ghost of reality and reality itself, that the projection of a self-centered personality must not be mistaken for literary art—but it is among the rules of De la Mare's art to stress none of these; these conclusions are left to the will and temperament of the reader; it is enough for De la Mare to evoke the dual presence of unearthly and worldly reality, and despite the charms of his external gifts in telling a story, to reveal the flaws, not without a suggestion of evil, which are concealed within human action and emotion.

The best key to the central meaning, so artfully hidden in a number of De la Mare's stories, is found in one of the shortest of them all, *The Three Friends,* in which two elderly men discuss the problem of "afterlife" and personal immortality. The comic scene includes a friendly barmaid. Of worldly being Mr. Eaves remarks:

> I might change in a score of ways . . . I might fall ill . . . I might come into some money; marry again. God bless me, I might *die!* But there, that is in the "after-life"; that's all over; no escape; nothing. I can't even die. I'm just meself, Miss Lacey; Sully, old friend. Just meself for ever and ever . . . it's just what Mr. Sully says . . . it's my sentence. Eh, Sully? wasn't that it? My sentence?
>
> Sentence! Oh, no! You! cried Miss Lacey . . . You've never done no harm, Mr. Eaves!

It is not my intention to transform De la Mare into an existentialist philosopher, yet it is of some moment that this Mr. Eaves conceives of an immortality as "no escape" from what he is; "it isn't what you do . . . It's what you are"; which observation was arrived at long before Jean-Paul Sartre wrote *No Exit.* There is no comfort in the best writings of De la Mare for softhearted children and their parents; if and when he is whimsical, whatever exists between his lines, or on the other side of a green tinted mirror of the world, it has in it somewhere the chill of ice, or the rational touch of snow.

3

As one returns from De la Mare's stories to his poems, it is no more than the necessary step from one form of writing to another; the qualities of both fancy and imagination remain the same, and no writer of his day, with the possible exception of W. B. Yeats, has relied so completely upon the resources of imaginative power. In this sense, as well as in other affinities, De la Mare is a Romantic poet in the best European tradition. It is an association that permits him to measure his standards for lyric verse by the writings of Poe, Beddoes, and Darley as well as those of Robert Herrick, Thomas Campion, and Thomas Hardy; his coolness, his "reason," has less affinity with the strictly neoclassic poets than with the "sons of Ben Jonson," who had little in common with the sterner virtues of either Milton or Dryden, and whose conception of classical form was not restricted by varieties of blank verse and the heroic couplet.

All this is another way of saying that De la Mare is a traditional lyric poet "with a difference"; that in England today and with Edith Sitwell and Dylan Thomas he fills the vacuum created by the failure of younger poets to grow beyond the promises of talent and the writing of further essays on Ezra Pound and T. S. Eliot; this is not to belittle Eliot's stature as a poet nor to forget his tribute written in verse to De la Mare,[2] but to define, as best I can, the peculiar

[2] From *Tribute to Walter de la Mare: on His Seventy-fifth Birthday*. London: Faber and Faber, 1948. Part of which is:

When the familiar scene is suddenly strange
Or the well known is what we have yet to learn
And two worlds meet, and interest, and change;

When the nocturnal traveller can arouse
Dogs cower, flitter bats, and owls range
At the witches' sabbath of the maiden aunts;

When the noc[t]urnal traveller can arouse
No sleeper by his call; or when by chance
An empty face peers from an empty house;

By whom, and by what means, was this designed?
The whispered incantation which allows
Free passage to the phantoms of the mind?

By you; by those deceptive cadences
Wherewith the common measure is refined,
By conscious art practised with natural ease;

eminence which De la Mare's poetry holds in England, and the sense of relief and of assurance that the public feels in reading it. Those who read De la Mare's poems are confident that they are reading poetry: verse and rhyme are there; read aloud, the poems sound like poems; they look like poems; they seem familiar to the ear and eye. This particular kind of public confidence has given De la Mare's poetry the outward semblance of being a safe choice for reading aloud to children, to one's near relatives, or to one's self.

It is on a second or third reading of the poems that a sense of difference arrives; the poems seem so effortless, so "right," so rhymed with ease that what De la Mare is actually saying has a way of sliding beneath the surface of his lines; one almost expects a platitude, or at best a well-worn sentiment, but what one finds is decidedly something else, of which the poem called *Away* is a memorable choice and from which after a second reading, it is difficult to dislodge its meaning and music from one's ear and mind:

There is no sorrow
Time heals never;
No loss, betrayal,
Beyond repair.
Balm for the soul, then,
Though grave shall sever
Lover from loved
And all they share;
See, the sweet sun shines,
The shower is over,
Flowers preen their beauty,
The day how fair!

Brood not too closely
On love, or duty;
Friends long forgotten
May wait you where
Life with death
Brings all to an issue;
None will long mourn for you,
Pray for you, miss you,
Your place left vacant,
You not there.[3]

The sentiment of the second stanza is not the usual conclusion to the lines which precede it; on first reading, one is caught up, shielded

By the delicate, invisible web you wove—
The inexplicable mystery of sound.

[3] *Collected Poems* by Walter de la Mare. New York: Henry Holt and Company, 1941.

and reassured by the general tone of optimism which gilds the surface of the opening stanza; it contains but a single warning of what is to follow: "Though grave shall sever/Lover from loved/And all they share"; one is also caught up in the delights of hearing De la Mare's play of inner rhymes, so that the reversal of sentiment from easy consolation and daylit brightness to a dark speculation falls as a surprise; the poem is no longer easy and familiar.

More delicate, yet more adventurous in form, and more precise in the placing of separate word and phrase is *Autumn* (in *Collected Poems*):

There is a wind where the rose was;
Cold rain where swept grass was;
  And clouds like sheep
  Stream o'er the steep
Grey skies where the lark was.

Nought gold where your hair was;
Nought where your hand was;
  But phantom, forlorn,
  Beneath the thorn,
Your ghost where your face was.

Sad winds where your voice was;
Tears, tears where my heart was;
  And ever with me,
  Child, ever with me,
Silence where hope was.

The progress from the usual observation to the particulars of deeper feeling and sentiment carries the meaning of both poems; both poems show, honorably enough, a philosophic debt to Hardy; one recalls Hardy's *The Garden Seat*, and *Transformations*. The debt is strictly philosophic and not a literal exchange of "influences" at work between two poets. Hardy's view of nature held for its precedent Wordsworth's pantheism, yet it was a face of nature transformed by what Hardy called a "plethoric growth of knowledge simultaneously with the stunting of wisdom." To Hardy the turn of the nineteenth century into the twentieth and the events of World War I brought the threat of a "new Dark Age," which, as he phrased it, showed in "The barbarization of taste" and "the unabashed cultivation of selfishness in all classes." The phrasing of Hardy's criticism carries the accents of an elderly Victorian, but the sense of what he said is not without a note of prophecy; his view of nature in *The Last Chrysanthemum* "is but one mask of many worn / By the Great Face Behind," and the transformation of human energy—a more particular, yet darker view than Wordsworth's—entered Hardy's trees and grasses.

Hardy's rule for the recapturing of wisdom included a recognition of a psychic relationship of men and women to other forms of life, even to inanimate things and places, and from this philosophic root De la Mare has made his own field, "pasture" one almost says, his world of psychological and metaphysical reality.

In the creation of his field of vision, his view is singular and minute in detail, an independent view that remains unconcerned with fashions in writing verse and one that has been sustained since the publication of his first book of poems, his *Songs of Childhood.* As in his prose, so in his poems, he does not speak to teach, but to reveal: and this distinction is, I believe, an important one. It is true that some of his stories are as delicately poised, as penetrating, as *revealing* as some of the shorter writings of Henry James; their psychological subtlety is no less effective, their art no less in evidence; they lack only the strong fibers of an ethical, a moral fabric that sustain the inner meanings as well as the larger aspects of James's novels. De la Mare's relationship to James and Hardy may be compared to Robert Herrick's relationships to Donne and Ben Jonson; one cannot claim for Herrick the metaphysical powers of Donne, nor the large worldliness of Jonson's wit, yet Herrick, on his occasions, wrote with great excellence *Rex Tragicus, or Christ Going to His Cross* and the complex *Corinna's Going a Maying,* one of the masterpieces of English verse.

In De la Mare's poetry wit is allied to revelation; it appears in the lines of one of his childhood rhymes, his "Poor Jim Jay / [Who] Got stuck fast / In Yesterday," which resolves itself into a metaphysic of time and space. And why does De la Mare place his childhood rhymes so prominently within his field of vision? The first answer should be that he enjoys the wit of doing so, the wit of revealing a metaphysic where it is least expected, but the second answer, which lies behind it, is of profound relevance to the central meaning of more than half his poems. In giving a lecture at the Rugby School in 1919, De la Mare said, "A child, a visionary, lives in eternity; a man in time, a boy—sheer youthfulness—in the moment." Among his later poems, under the title of *The Chart,* are these four lines:

> That grave small face, but twelve hours here,
> Maps secrets larger than the seas',
> In hieroglyphics more austere,
> And older far than Rameses'.[4]

[4] *Winged Chariot and Other Poems* by Walter de la Mare. London: Faber and Faber, 1951.

To be childish in the sense that De la Mare presents childhood vision is to exist before temporal consciousness distorts the knowledgeable world; his is a clarity of vision that Lewis Carroll shared in his adventures with Alice, of things seen at the level of a grass blade. It is De la Mare's poetic conceit that the antiquities, Egyptian or Druid, including Stonehenge and the recent ruins of World War II, which brood over England today, contribute to a sense of the past. This is not easy to define, nor is a literal interpretation of the landscape within his poems desirable; yet no recent poem of English countryside is more appropriate than the lines to *The Ruinous Abbey* (in *Winged Chariot and Other Poems*):

> Stilled the meek glory of thy music
> Now only the wild linnets sing
> Along the confusion of thy ruins
> And to cold echo sing.
>
> Quenched the wan purple of thy windows,
> The light-thinned saffron and the red;
> Now only on the sword of thy dominion
> Eve's glittering gold is shed.
>
> Oh, all the fair rites of thy religion!—
> Gone now the pomp, the ashen grief;
> Lily of Easter and wax of Christmas;
> Grey water, chrism, and sheaf!
>
> Lift up thy relics to Orion;
> Display thy green attire to the sun;
> Forgot thy tombs, forgot thy names and places;
> Thy peace forever won!

The undertone of De la Mare's irony in the peace that is found beyond names and places and the rites of religion is faint but clear; the very organlike tones of the poem cover it, yet it is there, quite as, in an early poem, "Your ghost [is] where your face was." And, of course, the same watchful art pervades the poem, guides its music and selects the phrase.

No poet in elder age since Yeats has kept his art more watchful and alive than De la Mare has; and like Yeats, he has mastered his privilege to write in the full richness of the lyrical tradition of English verse, a privilege which leaves him free with that freedom which comes only through the mastery of form, to draw upon the resources of memory, and with these resources, to speak in accents of authority, and that few poets of the past or of our own century possess. It is improbable that a young poet, however gifted, could have written the following lines of *She Said* (in *Winged Chariot and Other Poems*):

She said, "I will come back again
  As soon as breaks the morn."
But the lark was wearying of the blue,
  The dew dry on the thorn,
  And all was still forlorn.

She said, "I will come back again,
  At the first quick stroke of noon."
But the birds were hid in the shade from the heat
  When the clock tolled, No: *but soon!*
  And then beat slowly on.

She said, "Yes, I'll be back again
  Before the sun has set."
But the sweetest promises often made
  Are the easiest to forget,
  No matter grief and fret . . .

That moon, now silvering in the east,
  One shadow casts—my own.
Thought I, my friend, how often we
Have shared this solitude. And see,
  Midnight will soon draw on,
When the last leaf of hope is fallen,
And silence haunts heart's vacancy,
And even pining's done.

The observation in this poem is drawn from memory and the experience of time, and the metaphysics of time and space have been among the recurrent themes of De la Mare's poetry. It is consistent with the character of De la Mare's wit that it should recall in the title of his long poem *Winged Chariot* Andrew Marvell's lines *To His Coy Mistress,* and without effort, a familiar association of time is presented to the reader. Once that association with Marvell's lines is struck, it is De la Mare's wit that guides the poem. It is easy enough to say that the poem is neither narrative nor dramatic in design: it is rather, a meditative poem, a monologue on time, which implies, through the most artful of disguises, the progress of a spiritual autobiography behind it. No one but De la Mare could or would make a poem of this kind; and few poets of this century would trust their technical skill to the writing of a long poem in the rhymed *terza rima,* and this with all possible variations upon that form. One can be safe in saying that there is not a dull line in it, that the technical brilliance of the poem often threatens to outshine its metaphysics and that it has the dangerous air of being a tour de force. Like all of De la Mare's writing at its best it demands more than a single reading; yet even in quotation some measure of its depth may be glimpsed in the following passage:

> The very soul's at gaze, as if in trance:
> Poised like a condor in the Andean night,
> When scarp and snowdrift, height of pinnacled height,
> Transmute with wonder the first morning light.
>
> So, in its innocence, love breaks upon sight.
>
> Hatred, dread, horror, too. As books relate:—
> Thyestes when his own son's flesh he ate;
> First stare at his iron cage of Bajazet;
> And Oedipus—when parricide's his fate.

These lines have a variety and crispness that have been achieved by few poets since Pope wrote his *Moral Essays* in heroic couplets; and De la Mare's technical achievement is of like quality:

> So, out of morning mist earth's flowers arise,
> Reflecting tintless daybreak in the skies;
> And, soon, the whole calm orient with its dyes.
>
> And even in bleak Winter one may go
> Out of night's waking dreams and see the snow
> In solemn glory on the fields below.
> How happy he whose 'numbers' well as sweet,
> Their rhythms in tacit concert with their feet,
> And measure 'time,' with no less hushed a beat . . .
>
> And clepsydra—the clock that Plato knew,
> Tolling the varying hours each season through;
> Oozing on, drop by drop, in liquid flow,
> Its voice scarce audible, bell-like and low
> As Juliet's communings with her Romeo.
>
> More silent yet; pure solace to the sight—
> The dwindling candle with her pensive light
> Metes out the leaden watches of the night,
> And, in that service, from herself takes flight.

I shall leave to other readers and critics the pleasure of finding the uses and ambiguities which De la Mare plays upon a favorite word like "sweet"; I shall leave to others the rediscovery of his felicity in choosing adjectives that seem as innocent at "tintless" and "pensive," and are so indisputably right in the way he places them. I am more concerned with the quality of wit which is revealed and is central to the character of his imagination in his last remark upon the candle: "And in that service, from herself takes flight." It is such lines as these that the particular, the peculiar quality of De la Mare's genius finds its expression; the same presence is felt in his *Memoirs of a Midget,* which has become a classic of its kind, and in the short story *Miss Duveen;* it is an act of revelation, with the least possible commentary, ethical or otherwise, which concerns the nature of the world that he has seen as if in a vision, for more than three quarters of a century. Undoubtedly, *Winged Chariot* is the best of De la Mare's longer poems, but it is also among the very few excellent long poems written in the twentieth century. Since, in a poem of this kind the full life of a poet's imaginative being is implied in the making of it, it has an authority that is not to be measured by its external brilliance nor the actual time spent in writing it. To other poets—and De la Mare is a poet's poet as well as one whose lyrics and narratives have caught and held the attention of the popular ear —his example reasserts the presence of magic in poetry which is commonly sought for and rarely found.

1951, 1961

THE DYING GLADIATORS

THE ISOLATION OF ISAAC ROSENBERG

> We begin with high culture at the Egyptians. A land of high, profound, austere philosophy—their art expressed their priestly natures. Art went hand in hand with their religion, grave and austere. With a profound knowledge of form and perfect craftsmanship, all their energies were directed to express deity, an abstraction of simple, solemn profundity, the omnipresent spirit. Their art was angular and severe.
>
> —Isaac Rosenberg, from *Art*, a lecture delivered in 1914

The young man who wrote these lines was a poet; he had been attending classes in drawing and painting at the Slade School in London, and he was now beginning to discover that the seriousness of his intentions and the practice of them had turned from the visual arts to those of writing poetry. In fragmentary essays,[1] in letters to friends and patrons he had begun to think for himself, to observe the peculiar nature of his place in the world, for his position was peculiar: his home was in the East End of London; he was a Jew, and his education at the Art School of Birkbeck College and at the Slade had been far removed from the usual British preparation at Oxford and Cambridge for the study and writing of poetry. In his letters and papers there is no evidence that he had known either D. H. Lawrence or Gaudier-Brzeska, yet among his immediate contemporaries the miner's son and the young French sculptor who moved so restlessly in "artistic circles" of London's Chelsea held positions that were analogous to his. Both Gaudier-Brzeska and Lawrence would have accepted Rosenberg's remarks upon nature: "Whatever the subject, nature is always our resort, a basis for creation. To feel and interpret nature, to project ourself beyond nature through nature, and yet convince of our faithfulness to the sensation, is imagination." But there should be no mystery as to why the three young men, so nearly of an age (Lawrence born in 1885 was Rosenberg's senior by a mere five years) did not meet. Of the three Rosenberg was the least known figure; his promise was known to Edward Marsh, to Gordon Bot-

[1] One of the best of the essays under the title of "Emerson" appeared seventeen years after Rosenberg's death in *Scrutiny: A Quarterly Review*, March 1935. The essay is a brief but incisive commentary on Walt Whitman's debt to the poetry and idealism of Emerson.

tomley, and to Henry Tonks, the painter, who was George Moore's old friend, and these men represented a world that stood at considerable distance from the friendship of Gaudier-Brzeska with Ezra Pound. In the *Georgian Poetry* anthologies which were modestly edited by Edward Marsh, signifying his presence only by the initials "E. M.," neither Lawrence nor Rosenberg was consistently published; Lawrence had attacked the "Georgian" standards of poetry in letters to Edward Marsh as early as 1913, and Rosenberg, who was almost as critical a contributor to the anthologies as Lawrence in his discriminations concerning the poetry of Rupert Brooke, grew friendly with Marsh after Marsh's relationship with Lawrence had turned distinctly cool. But perhaps distance between Rosenberg and his two contemporaries was that invisible distance (which cannot be measured in geographical terms) between Stepney in London's East End and the West End's semi-Bohemian Chelsea as they existed before the First World War. That distance, which was neither purely racial nor of poverty alone, but combined the qualities and unhappy relationships of both, was enough to isolate and to obscure the early development of Rosenberg's talent.[2]

The isolation in which Rosenberg wrote was not entirely to his disadvantage. Compensations are to be found in the seriousness and independence with which he regarded the important decisions he made in respect to the art he practiced, often in ill-health, until death in action while serving as a private in the British army cut short his career on 1 April 1918. A happier situation would have modified and perhaps charmed away his conviction that "art . . . intensifies life," his conviction that "you can only talk round literature"; it was his temperament to approach questions of painting and of writing at the level of deeply rooted or radical values, and to show discontent at anything less than the standard of poems he hoped to write. In *The Collected Works of Isaac Rosenberg*, edited by Gordon Bottomley and Denys Harding, a single volume, published in London by Chatto & Windus in 1937, the illustrations are half-tone reproductions of Rosenberg's paintings and drawings. Given another temperament than Rosenberg revealed in his poetry and prose, his gifts in the graphic and plastic arts would have assured him an "easy living" among those who earned a livelihood in the almost commercial art of portrait painting. At twenty-one he had mastered what now appears to have been the Slade School manner, the style of Sir William Rothenstein's popular drawings which served as illustrations to Sir William's *Men and Memories*. A chalk drawing of a blonde girl's head, the

[2] How keenly Rosenberg felt his isolation is shown in one of his poems, *Spiritual Isolation*, a poem of Job-like character, which transcended the emotions of self-pity in its religious theme.

detail of a reclining figure with its eyelids closed and three self-portraits seem to have been done with happily accomplished facility. But when we turn to the *Portrait of the Artist's Father* something more than the Slade School manner shows its hand. The figure is a conventionally placed head and shoulders in full front view against a dark background; the head is bald, the right eyebrow slightly raised over heavily lidded eyes, the pale light of the forehead and high cheekbones contrasted by the darker tones of a neatly trimmed mustache and beard, and around the throat a coarsely woven cloth held in place by the top button of a well-worn jacket. It is not a facile portrait, but one that obviously selects elements of dignity and plastic strength rather than qualities of charm and of ease in presenting its subject. It has something of the "priestly nature," "grave and austere" that Rosenberg sought for in his definition of Egyptian art; the painting was far better than others that his editors saw fit to reproduce, yet one understands why, even at their best, Rosenberg's gifts in painting could not satisfy the demands he made upon them. They fell short of being first-rate, and the fact that they did left him depressed and restless, and he would break appointments with friends and patrons rather than show them his latest paintings.

His painting was, of course, suffering from the same complaint that had afflicted the entire field of British art, a complaint which betrayed the uneasy marriage of the literary imagination with graphic forms. Exceptions to this particular disease were and still are rare and only the art of Constable and Turner, and an occasional portrait by a master of the eighteenth-century school are among them. Rosenberg struggled against what he called the "contemporary influence"; he distrusted English "charm," and he preferred "the romantic way" of Rossetti back to Pre-Raphaelite beginnings to the contemporary influence at work in British schools which so quickly reduced all adaptations of postimpressionism to illustration, to poster, and, at last, commercial art. He became all too well aware that the artist who depends on his art for his living must be an advertiser. And advertising was not what he proposed to do.

2

With these thoughts in mind Rosenberg returned to the writing of poetry. His very early poems—and some written as early as 1905—bear the marks of having been written easily and were on the level of readily acceptable magazine verse, the kind of verse which in 1905 and today, forty years later, is often published in literary magazines, and which, not unlike his drawings and sketches, could have earned him popular praise. Outwardly "formal" verse was of easy accomplishment for him, but he had been reading Keats and he had been reading Donne, and from his interests in Rossetti he turned for a short time to the poetry of Francis Thompson, a natural choice of "art . . . hand in hand with religion," since the discovery of Gerard Manley Hopkins was yet to come, Thompson best represented a late Victorian synthesis of religion and poetry in English verse. Thompson, however, was too soft, too yielding for any permanent hold upon Rosenberg's admiration, and Rosenberg had spoken with contempt of an age that regarded Keats as being "simply sensuous." Rosenberg was beginning to distinguish in his brilliant essay *On a Door Knocker* the difference between a superficial, popular romanticism and poetic reality:

> This is essentially an age of romance. . . . The philistine has become the romanticist, and the poet the philistine . . . incongruity that might be a Japanese fantasy. The ragged newsboy bartering news and information to the gentleman in the high hat. The gentleman in the high hat benevolently making a picture of himself for us to enjoy the spectacle and see, this charming young lady decked out as a draper's front window as if this were some merry carnival.

This paradox serves as an introduction to the ambiguous uses and qualities of a familiar object, the door knocker; the door knocker then:

> . . . is a type of prostitution, for it is sold to all men; of helplessness, for it lies where all can wreak their will on it; of power, for it sets great forces in motion; of aristocracy, for it is lordly and imperious; of democracy, for it makes no distinction between low and high; of wealth, for, like gold, it is the means of opening doors. . . .

And Rosenberg, as he sat down to write new poems that he sent in letters to friends or printed privately in three little pamphlets, made a further observation: "Very few people say what they mean, though they may say what they think."

3

At the time of this resolution to write new poems came the war and his enlistment in the British army. Among his ambitions was to write a play in verse, an ambition common to many "modern" poets in England, Ireland, and the United States since 1893 when Ellen Terry met with such success in a production of Tennyson's *Becket.* But whatever gifts Rosenberg possessed, they were not of the theater, nor could he relate his themes of Hebraic origin to the disciplines of writing dramatic verse. Figures of Moses, of Saul, of Lilith, and at last, a vaguely conceived and heretical Unicorn in scenes with Nubians and Amazons crowded the pages he sent to Gordon Bottomley to read. What he accomplished here was not the first draft toward writing a play, but flexibility and a fresh approach to the writing of blank verse. He had rejected smoothness in writing verse; "Regular rhythms I do not like much," he wrote to Edward Marsh, and he made the choice of seeming obscure and being "experimental." It was his purpose to write out of and within the Jewish tradition, which in itself, aside from Milton's contribution to an almost Hebraic literature in *Paradise Lost*, was an "experimental" task in English verse; the nature of Rosenberg's intention is shown in:

Through these pale cold days
What dark faces burn
Out of three thousand years,
And their wild eyes yearn,

While underneath their brows
Like waifs their spirits grope
For the pools of Hebron again—
For Lebanon's summer slope.

They leave these blond still days
In dust behind their tread
They see with living eyes
How long they have been dead.

His intentions were further realized in *Chagrin* with its first lines:

Caught still as Absalom,
Surely the air hangs
From swayless cloud-boughs,
Like hair of Absalom
Caught and hanging still.

The imagery has the same formation and is of the same world that had been seen in glimpses in an earlier and far less successful poem *Night and Day:*

Though the sun's face be on high,
Yet his fiery feet do lie
Fixed on earth . . .

The kind of promise that Rosenberg holds for those who read him is of knowing that a consistent order of poetic reality existed behind his superficial obscurities. Among its elements was his way of looking at the physical world, another was the traditional aspects of his race and its religion:

They who bowed to the Bull god
Whose wings roofed Babylon,
In endless hosts darkened
The bright-heavened Lebanon.

The following lines from another poem are of the same origin:

No blossom burst before its time,
No angel passes by the door,
But from old Chaos shoots the bough
While we grow ripe for heaven.

4

Since his death a few of Rosenberg's shorter poems have been reprinted in various anthologies which bring him back to mind as a "war poet," a survivor of the same moment and of like associations that surround the memory of Wilfred Owen; and of the two poets, Owen has remained in the more fortunate position. In latter-day revivals of Owen's name, the author of "I, too, saw God through mud—" has perhaps suffered the curse of being overrated, for like Rosenberg, his writings were cut short by death in military action in 1918. Owen was less radical, but also less fragmentary in his accomplishment than Rosenberg; in reading Owen, the reward is one of finding four or five completed poems that seem to exist for themselves alone; in reading Rosenberg, one finds the occasional line or the intractable phrase, or the presence of an isolated imagination that has evidence of life beyond the accomplishments of art. One has confidence that the coarser fibers of Rosenberg's poems were the necessary complements of what he had to say in poems that showed his hatred of war as well as the religious center of his being. His *August, 1914* is characteristic of the "war poems" that he had begun to write:

What in our lives is burnt
In the fire of this?
The heart's dear granary?
The much we shall miss?

Three lives hath one life—
Iron, honey, gold.

The gold, the honey gone—
Left is the hard and cold.

Iron are our lives
Molten right through our youth,
A burnt space through ripe fields
A fair mouth's broken tooth.

There is little self-pity in these lines, and unlike Owen, Rosenberg with his hopes of accomplishment fixed upon the "grave" and "austere" had no concern for

the pity of war.
The Poetry is in the pity.

Rosenberg held to a darker faith:

Moses, from whose loins I sprung,
Lit by a lamp in his blood
Ten immutable rules, a moon
For mutable lampless men.

His darkness, whether in sight of trench warfare or in London's streets, was lighted only by such fragmentary lines as these:

Our eyes no longer sail the tidal streets,
Nor harbor where the hours like petals float
By sensual treasures glittering through thin walls
Of women's eyes and colour's mystery.
. . . .
God gives to glisten in an angel's hair
These he has gardened, for they please his eyes.

The imperfections in these lines are obvious enough; the repetitions of "eyes" within them are not placed with the necessary skill to build the lines into a finished poem. The merits are in the phrases, "tidal streets," the "thin walls of women's eyes," and the simple use of "gardened."

If Rosenberg did not accomplish all that his poetry and prose implied, he leaves behind him a high standard of poetic responsibility. It is clear that like Owen he had broken with the popular criteria that had been accepted for poetry written before 1914. His example to younger poets of more than a generation later lies in his concern for values in poetry that dismissed immediate influences, and sought out with appropriate seriousness the central forces, which in his life were religious, of poetic imagination, and character.

1937, 1961

RUPERT BROOKE AT GRANTCHESTER

Fifty years ago, the best known poet to contribute to the celebrated series of anthologies, *Georgian Poetry*, was Rupert Brooke. The series, which ran to five volumes published between 1912 and 1922, was edited by Edward Marsh, Winston Churchill's secretary, a glittering young-man-about-London who knew everyone, from Lady Diana Manners to D. H. Lawrence. Marsh was also the enthusiastic patron of promising English painters and young poets known as "Georgian", and among this set (which included Lawrence, John Drinkwater, Harold Munro, John Masefield, Walter de la Mare and Robert Graves), Rupert Brooke not only shone, but dazzled.

More, perhaps, than anyone else in England, Brooke seemed to represent all that was new and heroic in the rising generation. All too soon his heroism was put to the test of World War I. In April 1915, his name appeared on the casualty list, and the gilded legends of his beauty and talent spread wherever English poetry was admired.

It is perhaps surprising that his biography (completed shortly before Christopher Hassall's death in 1966) is the first full-length portrait of Rupert Brooke that we have.[1] Yet the book seems to have enduring literary interest. Georgian poetry, which fell out of fashion in the 1930s, is now undergoing not only a critical reassessment—partly because of the recent reascendency of Robert Graves—but also something of a revival.

The Georgians wrote verse out of a distinctly English countryside tradition, which was consciously more English than the associations of a word like "British." In England there is a renewed effort to write something easily recognized as island English verse. In that island there is also a revival of highly conventional verse forms, of which today the light verse of John Betjeman is a conspicuous example. The aftereffects of reading Betjeman's verse is like the aftermath of looking at genre painting. Sentimental and pictorial as they may be, certain poems by both Brooke and Betjeman are as popular and as neatly rooted in an English tradition as the "English unofficial rose" that Brooke remembered in his garden at Grantchester.

Because of its bulk and weight, Hassall's *Rupert Brooke* has the

[1] *Rupert Brooke: A Biography*, by Christopher Vernon Hassall. London: Faber and Faber, 1964.

appearance of an old-fashioned "official" biography. Because of the poet's family connections, the worlds of William Morris's Socialism and of Rugby and Cambridge move into view. The famous Stracheys and the Keyneses are there; so is Sir Leslie Stephen and his daughter, Virginia (afterwards Virginia Woolf), who is witnessed as a child playing with little Rupert Brooke at the seashore. These scenes restore the day when Cambridge Liberalism, with its elder Whig tradition dating back to Horace Walpole, was semifashionable—it was as though a Phrygian cap were only half-concealed beneath a mortarboard or a tall silk hat.

It is little wonder that Rupert Brooke, schooled at Rugby, where his father was a housemaster, found himself at King's College, Cambridge, and was predisposed toward Fabianism. Nor is it surprising that he won competition prizes for writing verse in a Liberal paper, *The Westminster Gazette,* edited by J. A. Spender, Stephen Spender's uncle.

At King's College, Brooke's amazing good looks— "His skin was like a girl's," people said; "he was beautiful rather than handsome"—coupled with a lighthearted, easy talent for writing verse—gained instant recognition. He was in heady revolt against Victorian dogmas, and particularly against his mother's domineering, shrill and coldly-voiced homilies. And his quarrels with his mother retarded his emotional maturity. ("Why are you so unsatisfactory?" she wrote in February 1913, when told of his planned tour of America. "Is it my fault?") With girls he betrayed his likeness to the Greek boy, Narcissus. During these early years his clinging, alternately warm and cold, attachments to two young women were unhappy—especially the long, painful affair with Kathleen ("Ka") Cox, whom he called "the best thing I found in life," but who was not unlike himself in her incapacity for mature relationships with men. He failed to charm some women—notably that famous Fabian, Beatrice Webb, who wrongly and solemnly distrusted the sincerity of his Fabianism.

Since Brooke moved swiftly within the *Zeitgeist* of the few short years he lived, of at least as great an interest as his love affairs is the influence of the Cambridge philosopher, G. E. Moore, upon his behavior and his poetry. Moore believed that religious dogma was not only untrue but unnecessary, that a good state of mind was to know exactly what one feels at a given split second of time—a celebration of an eternal moment. Brooke accepted these ideas and embodied them in two popular poems, *The Great Lover* and *Dining-Room Tea.* Brooke was also quick to reject the "art-for-art's sake" platitudes of the 1890s. "Art," he wrote, "isn't the thing that makes one happy or miserable: it's Life. Art is only a shadow, a second-rate Substitute . . . and the best of all is to live poetry. It "even keeps one young."

To remain forever young was his desire, a wish that was ironically granted by his death at 27. He died of blood poisoning aboard ship while on duty in the Aegean as a sublieutenant in the Royal Navy, and was buried the same day—23 April 1915—on the island of Skyros.

Meanwhile, his writings contributed generously to the glory of youth and physical beauty. At a moment when German expressionism had its earliest and scarcely articulate beginnings, Brooke, though uninfluenced by German fashions, was a buoyant, out-of-doors expressionist strolling barefooted, not too far from Cambridge, at Grantchester, the place that became the title of his "masterpiece," as he called it, a memorable, sentimental venture into light verse.[2]

During the war years, and for a short time after, his voice was the voice of youth. His Cambridge-bred primitivism, his delight in walking barefoot or shedding all his clothes were taken as signs of revolt against middle-class Victorian ethos. Young people were thrilled at being shocked by him. It was appropriate that the title, *This Side of Paradise*, of F. Scott Fitzgerald's first novel was a quotation from one of the most engaging of Brooke's South Sea poems.

Brooke made a cult of friendships, and he conducted its rituals in the manner of a glorified Boy Scout. Self-invited, and with a friend or two, he would invade London to "camp out" overnight, or for a weekend, on the floors and furniture of Edward Marsh's flat.

Beneath the conventional surfaces of his good looks and his popularity at King's College, Cambridge, there were signs of an approaching "crack-up." His early attachments to painfully plain featured young women were fearfully inept, and yet he seemed to demand from them the intimacies of maternal affection and forgiveness. "The Great Lover" he hoped to be in verse was in pathetic contrast to reality. He wavered in his decisions of what to make of himself; was

[2] I believe Brooke's *Grantchester* can be called "confessional." During the late 1960s certain critics of poetry began to speak of "confessional verse" as though it were a special form invented during the mid-twentieth century. Actually the genre began a long time ago, and a classic masterpiece is Pope's *Epistle to Dr. Arbuthnot*. In this tradition there is Wordsworth's *Prelude* as well as a large number of Yeats's poems. It certainly includes Byron's *Childe Harold* and *Don Juan*, and at more recent date, Auden's Don Juanish autobiography in his *Letters from Iceland*. And here it is appropriate to include John Betjeman's candid, disarmingly sincere *Summoned by Bells*—an autobiography in verse. Betjeman's art of understatement is in full evidence; the rather longish poem is likely to haunt the reader's memory—and who knows?—*Summoned by Bells* may be one of the few poems by which the present age of English verse will be remembered. From an American point of view, in 1971, it seems unfortunate that Betjeman is not England's Poet Laureate; one feels that he would have filled that particular office with great ease and melancholy wit.

he to be a talking, active Fabian, a Cambridge don, or, as he remarked half-bitterly, "a minor poet"?

The tradition of English verse in which Brooke was most at home was broadly Byronic. In this he anticipated the early Auden. But in the line of tradition before and after Byron, Brooke's chosen affinities were Marlowe and Webster, Donne, Milton, Andrew Marvell, Praed and A. E. Housman. These were his consciously acquired masters.

He had already plunged deep into readings of poetry. At the very least, he had become a learned postadolescent. (After his death, Virginia Woolf, who was not one of his ardent admirers, commented on his extraordinary learning.) He was, however, fast slipping away from Fabianism and with a sense of the ridiculous he drew a sketch of one of his Fabian colleagues:

> I lent him Mr. Arthur Symons on the French Symbolists & Decadents. He read it, very earnestly. "Do you know," he confided to me as we sat reading in the garden, "I can't help thinking these fellows are rather dangerous. You know when a man begins seeing things that aren't *there* . . . well, I mean, he may see *anything*, one feels!" He beamed at me patiently through his spectacles. I did not know what to say; so turned the conversation onto fluctuations in unemployment.

Perhaps unconsciously he knew he was fated to go on reading and writing poetry. His awareness of excellent writing began to mature, and he was one of the few young men of his generation to appreciate the poetry of Arthur Symons's friend W. B. Yeats.

The reciting of poetry, the writing of his own occasional verse, and a meeting with one of the prettiest girls in London, a young actress, Cathleen Nesbitt, who was most unlike other women he had met, were tonic to his troubled psyche. Under her spell he began to emerge from his earlier trials with women, the living nightmare of his restless narcissism which he had called his "foodless and sleepless hell." He was in need of holiday from himself, from Europe—even from England. His friendship with Miss Nesbitt soon became the prelude to his light affairs with native girls of the South Seas, which as some of us are likely to remember, were the occasions and pastel tinted backdrops of his tripping and gaily metered metaphysics. Rereading him today, it is easy to see that his peculiar genius had its best expression in the writing of verse that celebrated, with an evanescent sheen, an eternal passing moment:

> Hasten, hand in human hand,
> Down the dark, the flowered way,
> Along the whiteness of the sand,

And in the water's soft caress
Wash the mind of foolishness,
Mamua, until the day.
Spend the glittering moonlight there
Pursuing down the soundless deep
Limbs that gleam and shadowy hair,
Or floating lazy, half-asleep.
Dive and double and follow after,
Snare in flowers, and kiss, and call,
With lips that fade, and human laughter
And faces individual,
Well this side of Paradise! [3]

More of the same authority and spirit are to be found in this passage from *Retrospect:*

Love, in you, went passing by,
Penetrative, remote, and rare,
Like a bird in the wide air,
And, as the bird, it left no trace
In the heaven of your face. . . .
All about you was the light
That dims the greying end of night;
Desire was the unrisen sun,
Joy the day not yet begun,
With tree whispering to tree,
Without wind, quietly.
Wisdom slept within your hair,
And Long-Suffering was there,
And, in the flowing of your dress,
Undiscerning Tenderness.

This was verse of a kind and temper no other Georgian writer could hope to master. Soft and amorphous as Brooke's diction and imagery too often were (a fault he shared with other Georgians), the quality of his verse, its surface brilliance, was closer to Marvell's and Lovelace's writings than to the verse of his contemporaries. Surely no one can deny his skill. An example of his very nearly matchless verve and wit may be shown in the following lines from *The Old Vicarage, Grantchester,* calling up the spirit of Lord Byron in the foreground:

Still in the dawnlit waters cool
His ghostly Lordship swims his pool,
And tries the strokes, essays the tricks,
Long learnt on Hellespont, or Styx.

[3] *The Collected Poems of Rupert Brooke,* with an introduction by George Edward Woodberry. New York: John Lane Company, 1915. (Subsequent quotations are also from this edition.)

Dan Chaucer hears his river still
Chatter beneath a phantom mill.
Tennyson notes, with studious eye,
How Cambridge waters hurry by . . .
And in that garden, black and white,
Creep whispers through the grass all night;
And spectral dance, before the dawn,
A hundred Vicars down the lawn;
Curates, long dust, will come and go
On lissom, clerical, printless toe;
And oft between the boughs is seen
The sly shade of a Rural Dean. . . .

Perhaps it is well to note that *Grantchester* had an earlier title, *The Sentimental Exile*, and that throughout its length, teetered on the verge of shameless bathos. Yet Brooke's art rescued the poem from its fall; his genius always arrived just in time to make *Grantchester* the remarkable thing it was and is, a unique and perennially youthful apparition, in any well-made anthology of light verse.

Careful readers of his letters are almost certain to discover that *Grantchester* was essential Brooke: parochial, intensely personal and boyishly appealing. Written at a café table in Berlin on a sweltering summer day in 1912 the poem was one of the first of his great successes in guiding the flow and turn of the octosyllabic couplet. The inspiration came at a moment when he was nearing an emotional crisis. His affair with Katherine Cox had been going badly; he had recently failed at gaining a fellowship at King's College. The day was out of joint. "Conversational German" frayed his nerves.

Then, as though he were in a trance, and like a waterfall, came the final version of the poem. Within that hour he was the poet of "Little England," who, with a half ironic, seraphic smile, distrusted everything not wholly Grantchester, the place he had chosen as his retreat from Cambridge social life as well as from his mother's house at Rugby.

Two years later, when he came to write his famous *The Soldier* sonnet—"body of England, breathing English air"—his straight-eyed patriotism, even his chauvinism were well-known aspects of his character. The best years of his writing, like "trailing clouds of glory," seemed far behind him. Yet, as poet, he had won fame enough. Even Ezra Pound, who had slight regard for Georgian poets, had a good word for him.

In Virginia Woolf's view he was "somehow a mixture of scholar and man of action, and . . . his poetry was the brilliant by-product of energies not yet turned upon their object." She then went on to wonder "and to question still: what would he have been, what would he have done?" Today, a half-century later, her speculative questions, apt as they then seemed to be, are less pertinent, almost irrelevant.

Scarcely more than a week before Brooke's death in the Aegean, Dean Inge from his pulpit in St. Paul's read aloud his sonnet, *The Soldier*. The reading touched off the sensational blaze of Brooke's popularity in England. That fire was to be sustained for many years.

Before his enlistment in the navy he had written his will. In event of his death, the royalties earned from his poems were to be equally shared by three poets, Lascelles Abercrombie, Wilfrid Wilson Gibson, and Walter de la Mare. This provision was characteristic of Brooke's generosity, and since the three poets needed money more urgently than he, it was also a clear indication that his early devotion to Fabianism was not mere lip service. Even here, his gesture turned out to be one of heroic proportions. Beyond all expectations, the small volume of his collected poems was launched on its own phenomenal career of popularity. The total income from its sales mounted to a fortune. Seldom have the good intentions of a giver been more completely and ideally realized.

1964, 1971

LONDON'S NATIONAL PORTRAIT GALLERY: 1934

The National Portrait Gallery looks like a bank, a square, gray-stone, sturdy annex to the more imposing façade of the National Gallery. Its foundations seem rooted in rock and iron under Trafalgar Square; it is permanent and safe, a good place to lock up valuables, standing withdrawn, yet in full sight of Nelson's monument and it is just around the corner from the quick tide of traffic that circles Piccadilly. Perhaps it is actually a bank, and its tall chambers are safety vaults to house the dead, the famous dead in their familiar attitudes of life. The Gallery, then, is rather less a gallery than a compromise between a public library and a national churchyard where one may trace the origin of the million faces seen on the streets of London, faces at noon at Waterloo Station, in Soho, the Thames Embankment, or down the Strand.

One looks for history here and not for art; and the atmosphere, like so much (too much) of English painting, is literary. Pay your sixpence, walk up the stairs; the way is broad and the halls are empty. As one enters a wide reception hall, members of the present royal family and a wide semicircle of diplomats in World War treaty conferences are quickly passed by. These figures, spread on canvas and framed in heavy gilt, are wooden creatures, and are far less lively than our memory of them in the feature sections of illustrated newspapers. Strangely enough, history begins with an American by an American—the Sargent portrait of Henry James.

Somehow the reproductions of this familiar head, shoulders, and upper torso have never done the original canvas justice. Seeing him here, quite as Sargent left him, James seems to dominate the room, and, for a moment, seems more English than his peers. His head is John Bull's head—round and full-blooded, bald—and was this why the Suffragists slashed at the canvas? They were in a hurry to get things done and slashed in fury, but, had they looked longer, they would have discerned a gaze of defiance, most un-English, in the candid eyes that met their own. They would have seen that the left thumb, hooked into the armhole of the vest, showed an aggressiveness beyond mere male complacency after a Sunday dinner. In this gesture he betrays that moment of boldness which comes to every timid man and he seems determined, despite long sentences and longer fits of shyness, to be heard at last and honored in a foreign land. One almost hears the hesitant, persistently low voice echoing across drawing rooms where James imagined himself unwanted, and in spite of silences which cleared his way, ignored. Pale Sir Edmund Gosse, beside him on the wall, is infinitely more assured than he, for Sir Edmund could well afford a show of modesty, and could peer nearsightedly into the faces of many friends at tea, friends who brought him praise and fame and offered him posts of authority on lecture platforms and in literary weeklies.

Across the room from Gosse and James is a young woman who would remain unrecognized were it not that her name appears in brass below the portrait. She is Marian Evans and this likeness of her was painted, I would say, before "George Eliot" gave her a weighty reputation. Here she has sunlit yellow hair and a red rose and white complexion. The heavy features that we know so well, the half-closed eyes and heavy lips, the face that seems to be the proper image of her who wrote in semiclassic beef-and-pudding prose, are of a later sitting. Perhaps the signs of heaviness are here, but they can be mistaken for robust health and prematernal animal calmness, as yet untouched by years of hard-won dignity and the lack of a fixed social position in society. The face that smiles down at us seems now reflected in the faces of the lower middle classes. These very features, sharpened slightly and less smiling, are to be found in the faces of barmaids and ribbon clerks, and those women who are stationed behind glass cages in restaurants and hotels. These, like the face above us seem preternaturally calm, yet they retain their calmness with a grim edge of resistance to the memory of Victorian womanhood. They tower over the little men surrounding them and stand guard over fleets of deferential bellboys and suave waiters. Efficient management is in the air, and through each swift action British serenity (so it seems) must be maintained.

George Eliot, however, is not the only woman in the room. Here are the Brontë sisters, and, among others, a certain mother and daughter who effect a singular contrast in personality. Of course, the two are Mary Wollstonecraft and Mary Shelley, and, if the mother has an obvious advantage, some credit must be given to John Opie, her portrait painter. Human warmth entered each canvas as he touched it with his brush, and the woman before him was a nearly perfect model for his talent. He did not, however, invent the rich lips and generous mouth, nor the warm light that radiated from her body. It was she who transmuted something of her own warmth to the chilly blood of William Godwin; and it was she who changed him, as though by some chemic miracle, into a lover. His humanitarianism was of the kind that fed itself upon abstractions; whatever emotions he possessed were quick to die and found their substitute in silent anger and martyred pride. Her death gave him the solace of human grief, yet after it, there was nothing left but the spiritless desire to gain an income from the inheritance of his wealthy son-in-law.

It would be easy to dismiss the pretentious portrait of Mary Shelley as so much vanity and outmoded affectation. The thin lips are curved into a simper that is the worst of all possible substitutes for a smile. It is obvious that Mary Shelley was acting the part of a grand lady seated at a writing table: the red curtain behind her, the fashionable black dress, the writing implements in ordered disarray about her, were details chosen for posterity to admire. The table reminds us that she was a novelist in her own right as well as the widow of a famous poet, but the rich, heavy furniture and the smart dress also remind us that she was the mother of a son who was to inherit a baronet's title and a respectable fortune.

The grand lady was not too vain, nor was she affected without good reason. In the past she had learned to fear gossip and ill fame, and she knew well, I think, that outward appearances too often fix the world's opinion of a woman. Perhaps she had premonition that the pose struck by the grand lady in the portrait would gain respect in the Victorian age that was to follow hers. She had, moreover, the task of making her dead husband's poetry seem more suitable to the title that her son would bear, and perhaps, if such were possible, less obscure. She used what means she could to build a posthumous reputation for the poetry that had not yet found its widest audience, and, I think, it is not too much to say that the portrait is among the unconscious contributions to that end. At last she had won security and now would not relinquish it; something of that deliberate coolness that guided her father's elaborate but unsuccessful plans toward making a livelihood ran in her blood and she was not to fail.

Now that a hundred years have left Haydon's tragedy behind us, it is no longer necessary to apologize for the fantastic discrepancy between his finished work and its price for being what Haydon was —a painter with a "literary" imagination; yet his portrait of Wordsworth is more convincing than all other attempts to paint the poet, and the original canvas is far more effective than any of its reproductions. The experience of seeing it on a wall is not unlike that of meeting Sargent's Henry James. Haydon, I think, loved Wordsworth with a pure heart; and by that I mean that both men met for a brief moment on common ground. Both shared a sense of awe concerning the importance of their work, their duty to themselves, their art, their nation, and the world.

Haydon's Wordsworth stands with dark mountain clouds behind

him. The head and shoulders of the gaunt figure are bent forward in heavy reverie. The eyes gaze downward on a distant earth below, and under the hawklike nose the left side of a distorted lip is suddenly revealed. This revelation of the twisted lip is a surprise, for here one sees, or rather feels, an element of deep self-pity that was to counterbalance its discontent by the sonorous music of—shall we call it—"epic pantheism"? Even the sonnets of the later Wordsworth contain an "epic" quality; the simple world of mountains, hills, and trees grown very large; and it is still the largest world that England ever knew.

This vision of a large world, so a friend has told me, is a rare experience in English art. Milton shared it and Byron embellished his possession of it in the ironic cantos of *Don Juan*. Both Blake and Shelley held outlines of this vision in the mind's eye, yet neither lived to see the edifice completed. And Hardy in his great Victorian ruin, *The Dynasts*, again looked upward and saw its rounded hemispheres. And it is not too much to say that the same vision haunted D. H. Lawrence, and in his painting the grand manner revealed itself once more. Perhaps the sight of a like vision led to Haydon's suicide. He could not guide his hand to encompass that thing he valued most, but as he saw its semblance rise in Wordsworth he sketched a detail and preserved it for posterity.

Here, in this room, set in glass cases on a center table, rest the life masks of Keats and Blake. Keats is the prototype of the "little" Londoner one sees on the less crowded thoroughfares; the sensitive lips, the delicately veined eyelids, are of the type. But these whom we meet now have no release in words for the sensibilities that are revealed in a graceful inflection of the voice or in a final gesture of the hand. They stand at bookstalls in Bloomsbury or wander, black-hatted, through Soho Square. They are to be found under the shelter of a German bookshop near Charing Cross and some admit a recent conversion to Communism. But it is the type that we rediscover, and not the poet, for the poets of England's twentieth century wear other masks with which to face the world.

Contrast to Keats lies in the head of Blake; here is the compact jaw, and the full lips set in a straight line, as though the muscles of the face were controlled by some centrifugal force. Here one may well imagine a tenacity of purpose seldom discovered in those erratic flashes of genius which illuminate his poetry. The face is a self-righteous face which is the moral aspect of true heresy; by gazing inward he saw that godlike image of his own strength, but the effort demanded more than human effort could sustain, and his prophetic books, if one regards them as works of art, remain stillborn.

After a circuit of the many faces in this room, a circuit extending backward from the end of the nineteenth century to its beginning, one says good-bye by stopping for a moment at the large, dark portrait of Leigh Hunt. There is no denying the man's charm, nor the attraction of the intelligent brown eyes with their quick appeal to human sympathy. It would be difficult to refuse him anything, or to remember that he had once borrowed money from you. Many of his friends could testify to his liberal service in their cause. His praise of their poetry came from his lips as easily as most men breathed the fragrance of spring air. The benevolent quickness in his eyes made praise such as his a special gift, a gift to be offered and accepted without embarrassment. In return he asked the right to live, to smile as he smiles here, dependent on your good humor, your purse, your willingness to respond with human tolerance to human weakness.

Upstairs, the eighteenth century revives itself again. The more or less predictable knowledge of the world's affairs is written large in the faces that Sir Joshua Reynolds knew so well, and in them we see again those signs of maturity that the nineteenth century discloses in the features of its scientists alone: Faraday, Owen, Huxley, Darwin. We have learned rather too well the eighteenth-century attitude of elegance, its love of fine linen and brocaded velvets. And because of this we are not prepared to see the restlessness that animates the room: Matt Prior looking up from his busy writing table as though about to speak; Bonnie Prince Charlie, as a boy, breathless, as though he had run into the room and were about to leave again at once; Laurence Sterne sitting on the edge of a chair, forcing a heavy white-lipped smile in a brief interview. Despite their courtesy, despite a background which reveals a succession of calm Georgian interiors, there is something almost American in their demand for movement. Tobias Smollett, with his red nose and shrewd blue eyes, seems about to ask a question and turn away, and there, of course, is a theatrical portrait of David Garrick, trying his best to represent tragedy, melodrama, comedy, and farce with both eyes wide and staring into nowhere. This is not (as one might suppose, seeing each reproduction of a canvas separately) a quiet room, for the entire company seems to move in a dozen swirls and eddies. We are mistaken, I think, if we consider the prose of the *Spectator* or the verse of Pope's *Epistles* as living apart from the conversation that was overheard at coffeehouses and at card tables.

Speaking of conversation and its entry into literature, one thinks of Boswell's famous *Life*, and from this memory of it we turn to Reynold's excellent portrait of the early Johnson.

The early Johnson is by no means a young man; he is on the nether side of middle age, retaining, with characteristic tenacity, the vigor of forty-five. The coarse-grained skin is pale and its pallor is accentuated by the dark background that Reynolds chose for this three-quarter profile of his friend. Again one does not ask too much of "art" in the National Portrait Gallery, but I suspect that the portrait is among the best of Reynolds's work. The profile is very like a cameo or medallion, and certainly in its clear outline of forehead, nose, lips, chin, and naked throat it resembles the classic head on a Roman coin. And to this outline Reynolds had added his peculiar gift of scientific observation; with admirable candor he has painted in the nearsighted eye narrowing to a painful squint—the face is almost blind. The physical handicap is balanced against the strength of the broad neck, which is reinforced by the dignity of the strong curving line extending down from upper forehead to the open shirt front below the throat.

As we walked upward, leaving the eighteenth century behind us in a lower gallery, the circle of English life grows smaller, and we are facing, more often than not, effigies of men and women whose activity, hopes, ambitions, began and ended in a life at court. Here is the court life of the Stuarts, and beyond them are found glimpses of the Tudors. History and legend have done well by them and they belong at this distant date to the mythology of a deeply nourished tradition. It is well to note the mixture of strength and kindliness in Cromwell's features, and amusing to recognize family resemblance to Charles the Second in the faces of the children embraced by his court ladies. But as we leave the room, we are reminded that the London street below us has little kinship to the intimacies of a life long vanished from the chambers of Old Whitehall. Nor does the skill of a Van Dyck revive those passions for which men died in a lost cause.

As we descend the stairs, the halls of the square building seem more deserted than before. The portraits seem to lock themselves within their separate chambers, and again, as one steps out to sunshine and Piccadilly, the impression of leaving a huge safety vault returns. The faces in the street, however, seem less strange, and, if your road homeward is lost, someone with Dr. Johnson's courteous compassion in his voice will point the way.

1934, 1944

VIRGINIA WOOLF: THE SPIRIT OF TIME AND PLACE

In reading Virginia Woolf at her very best—which includes *Mrs. Dalloway, To the Lighthouse, The Waves* and certain of her essays in her two *Common Readers* as well as in the present volume [1]—it is necessary to dust off and repolish that tarnished, dented, much abused word that has become an article of kitchenware in criticism. The word is "genius." [2] It is necessary, I believe, to say that genius,

[1] *The Death of the Moth*, by Virginia Woolf. New York: Harcourt, Brace & Co., 1942.

[2] Today Virginia Woolf's writings seem less brilliant than they did during the 1930s and 1940s. And time has also dimmed the glitter of Lytton Strachey's eccentricities and mannerisms (and he was one of her dearest friends). Yet it is she who remains "the genius" of the Cambridge-Bloomsbury group, with G. E. Moore and E. M. Forster as its godfathers. So far, *The Waves* (1931)—proclaimed her best novel by her husband and publisher, Leonard Woolf—seems to have weathered changes in literary taste. Surely it is a far better book than its predecessor *Orlando*, which today resembles a historical charade in fancy dress with V. Sackville-West photographed as its hero-heroine. Its prose is dubious—not witty enough to please the sophisticated reader, nor deft enough to please the reader of light verse: ". . . we glance at Orlando standing by the window, we must admit that he had eyes like drenched violets, so large that the water seemed to have brimmed in them and widened them; and a brow like the swelling of a marble dome pressed between the two blank medallions which were his temples. . . ." One is never sure whether this is parody or not; is it false poetics, or is the prose merely arch and coy? Yet it is the style of *Orlando*.

In *The Waves*, in what she called her "unintelligible book," Virginia Woolf's experiments were of a more serious nature—so was her theme, that of people being haunted by childhood memories, and so was its inner purpose—to write a book in memory of her brother, Julian Thoby Stephen who died in 1906, and whom, according to Michael Holroyd (Strachey's biographer), "Lytton venerated and idealized." In her *A Writer's Diary* she went on to explain how she worked on *The Waves*, gathering together fragmentary "images" that "only suggest." "Thus I hope to have kept the sound of the sea and the birds, dawn and garden subconsciously present, doing their work underground." With these biographical hints drawn from Michael Holroyd (Holroyd pointing out that Lytton was the model for Neville in *The Waves* and Thoby Stephen the model for Percival) and those hints (not noted by Holroyd) also explain the mention of Catullus in the book—which hitherto seemed inappropriate; for it now looks as though Mrs. Woolf wanted to suggest that Lytton's "deification" of Thoby as well as her own grief for his early death recalled Catullus's famous lines for better or worse, means that the writer whose gifts have earned the once-coveted and shining title is the spirit of a particular time and place, a tutelar deity whose radiance sheds an unflickering, beneficent light within temple walls. Mrs. Woolf's gifts, however else we may define them, were of that quality; their residence was Bloomsbury in London and not too far from the dark and yet Alexandrian outlines of the British Museum; the moment which they suffused with pallid and clear illumination on library walls or in guest bedrooms of a country house on holidays or at eight o'clock dinner parties in the city was of the period that we now recall as existing precariously between two major wars. It was that time and place through which Mrs. Woolf's spirit moved and to which the spirit brought its endowments of sensibility and grace.

Virginia Woolf's American publishers have thoughtfully issued E. M. Forster's tributary lecture on Virginia Woolf to accompany the posthumous collection of her essays, *The Death of the Moth,* a volume, by the way, which might well have been published as a third series of confidences to her *Common Reader.* E. M. Forster's tribute, delivered in the Senate House at Cambridge on 28 May 1941, is of a sort that only he could have spoken, for the author of *Abinger Harvest* and *A Passage to India* is another branch of the same tree which Henry James had planted in London soil and whose roots were the source of nourishment for the gifts of Dorothy Richardson as well as his own and those of Virginia Woolf.[3] His remarks are of more penetrating eloquence than her notations on his novels in the present collection of her essays, but he has, we reflect, the advantage of the last word. As she inquires, somewhat impatiently, of Mr. Forster's work, "What next?" he proceeds calmly to celebrate the pervading charms of her personality, its freedom within the limitations she imposed, its unexpected turns of laughter, its sudden responsiveness—and despite its air of seeming guardedly aloof—before an audience of women, its virtues as a "lady" who lived upon her income of five hundred pounds a year, for she could not pretend that her mother turned a mangle, and she herself, unlike Mrs. Giles of Durham, "had never stood at the washtub." Those of us who have read *A Room of One's Own* would find it difficult, I think, not to recognize the personality that Mr. Forster breathes to life in an hour's lecture, and that same personality resumes its character in an essay on *Middlebrow* which Virginia Woolf's husband saw fit

---

at his brother's grave. Memory of Catullus's poem strengthens the fine last four pages of *The Waves.* And the concluding passages of the book certainly justify placing it above Virginia Woolf's other novels.

[3] *Virginia Woolf,* by E. M. Forster. New York: Harcourt, Brace & Co., 1942.

to include in *The Death of the Moth;* nor does one quarrel with Forster's carefully, adroitly balanced peroration in which he says "she gave acute pleasure in new ways, she pushed the light of the English language a little farther against darkness."

Whatever Forster says in his brief talk reflects the sensibility of an elder inhabitant of Virginia Woolf's world as well as one who traveled beyond its sphere; so far we may be assured of his wisdom and his poise, and he has said more within the hour and some thirty-seven small, wide-margined pages than many another solemn eyed essayist could say in a hundred large sheets of fine, closely printed type. But for my part, I find myself thinking less of Virginia Woolf as a "lady" and as a "woman," than as a daughter of Sir Leslie Stephen, the slightly ink-stained figure who in her youth was surrounded by gentlemen of late-Victorian celebrity; one thinks of Meredith, of Ruskin, of the American Ambassador, James Russell Lowell, of Robert Louis Stevenson, and, of course, Sir Edmund Gosse; one thinks of books lining the walls of a capacious library, and with them the names of writers who reappear in the pages of Virginia Woolf's novels and essays: Sir Walter Scott, Keats, Shelley, Coleridge, Shakespeare, Horace Walpole, Edward Gibbon—but the list would grow tedious and seem inexhaustible. One begins to wonder if, after all, after writing *A Room of One's Own* and *To the Lighthouse,* she had made an escape from Sir Leslie's house and the gentlemen who came for tea? She believed she did, and there is written evidence of an exit left behind her, but a door remains open, and still one wonders, if she did escape, how far?

Far enough, one says at first, to discover a singular melody for her own prose, and Leonard Woolf, in editing this latest of her posthumous volumes, remarks upon her care in rewriting and revising the merest reviews sent off to the London *Times* Literary Supplement and the *New Statesman.* That melody, one may trust, was her great concern, and it sounded as she rehearsed and played it with the noise and chiming of many little bells.

Sometimes the bells rang sharply and clearly, striking their notes of nearly absolute finality in the newly published pieces on Horace Walpole, Sara Coleridge, and *Street Haunting,* but on occasion—and it is usually an occasion when the subject of the piece happens to be a romantic poet, Coleridge, or Shelley, or a Shakespearean play—the little bells ring so persistently that they seem to cover something left unsaid. Are these the moments when the escape from Sir Leslie's threshold was incomplete? When the open door behind her made it imperative that she remember Coleridge and Shelley? And because she must remember, therefore the bells chimed insistently, over and over with not too much to say?

Whether or not these questions can be answered with the directness that one might desire, it is plain enough that with few exceptions Virginia Woolf is at her happiest as she recaptures a moment of the eighteenth century viewed always in the light of her own day. As one reads her interpretations of Walpole and Cole, of *The Historian and "The Gibbon,"* her escape seems certain; and in *Street Haunting: A London Adventure* her spirit resumes its character of genius. We are certain also that in the generation between two wars it was she who revived the so-called "familiar essay" which began its life in the formal prose of Addison, which reappeared, or rather culminated one period of its existence, in Charles Lamb's *Elia,* and then breathed fitfully until Max Beerbohm arrived in London. It is that heritage which one rediscovers in *The Death of the Moth,* and it seems natural, even in a literary sense, for her to have selected the eighteenth century as one point of its origin, a birthplace, perhaps, of her identity. The sensibility which she expressed to the admiration of her contemporaries had its likeness in the Age of Sensibility itself.

In her essays she was a mistress of what often has been called an "outmoded" form, and if one admits that the familiar essay was among the vehicles of her genius, one need not concern one's self too deeply over the question of her ability in literary criticism. She was not, I believe, vastly disturbed by problems of the intellect, and because she was not, one may find one of several reasons for her lack of ease in the presence of Coleridge. She exerted an influence in literary matters because of her gifts and her intelligence, and because her artistry embraced the arts of persuasion and of charm. It is only when her criticism appears to be incidental to the portrait of a literary figure that it becomes convincing to the eye, and when the portrait is lacking, and when the criticism takes the form of a set argument, the illumination fades, and we hear only the ringing of her small bells.

It may seem strange that her essays on Henry James, George Moore, and E. M. Forster are less good than the others, and that her *Letter to a Young Poet* offers no more than what Polonius would say. The question of her escape from what was once Sir Leslie Stephen's threshold and the distance between it and her room in Bloomsbury returns in a slightly different guise. She seems to be reminded, half unwillingly, of her duties to the many books piled high against the wall, of her obligation to the names of Chaucer, Shakespeare, Tennyson, Keats, Byron, of upholding among her contemporaries, both young and old, a judgment that weights the page with its list of names. The names, as we know, perhaps too well, are familiars of discourse on literary subjects, but as she used them to stress the failures of contemporary literature, they remain mere counters of discussion. In these papers one feels that she is not the fortunate genius who writes with such brilliancy of Coleridge's daughter, Sara—and the question is: Has her genius found itself again because it was spoken in the voices of two daughters of famous men, one the daughter of a poet and philosopher, the other the daughter of a knighted literary critic?

In closing this third volume of Virginia Woolf's addresses to her *Common Reader* one is impelled to say that no reading of her best work can be called complete without a knowledge of it, without the delight of hearing her genius speak again. And in her essay that re-creates the magic of walking city streets at evening, "streets haunting" as she called it, written in 1930, one finds a premonition of her own death, and her true epitaph:

> The sights we see and the sounds we hear now have none of the quality of the past, nor have we any share in the serenity of the person who, six months ago, stood precisely where we stand now. His is the happiness of death; ours the insecurity of life. He has no future; the future is even now invading our peace. It is only when we look at the past and take from it the element of uncertainty that we can enjoy perfect peace.

1942, 1971

THE SPEAKING VOICE OF D. H. LAWRENCE

"I shall live just as blithely, unbought and unsold," wrote D. H. Lawrence in 1925. And in this remark there is a note of prophecy that describes the curious nature of his survival during the half dozen years following his death. Perhaps none of the earlier objections to his work has been removed since 1930, yet his influence has endured in the kind of fame that Matthew Arnold perceived in Shelley's reputation which was both legend and literature and both "ideal" and "ridiculous." Much of Lawrence's ardent pamphleteering is now outmoded. And nothing seems to have grown so clearly out of fashion in a few short years than Lawrence's specific lectures on sex and obscenity. Today they seem to have gone to the same place reserved in memory for the events of early postwar Europe and America. Yet even in his most perishable writing the character of his influence remains.

However and wherever Lawrence is reread, whether in scattered posthumous papers,[1] or in the poems, short stories, or in the novels, it is the speaking voice that is heard clearest and remembered. We then recall Lawrence's letters, which seem always to renew at each date line a briefly interrupted conversation, and with them we remember David Garnett's little sketches of how he worked: writing as he cooked his meals or sat in one corner of a room while others talked, writing as he unpacked boxes and suitcases, writing almost as he moved and breathed, as though the traveling of his hand across paper were the very reflex of his being. Surely, this prodigality was "art for my sake" and was the visible power of the thing he called his "demon" which is to say that much of it was scarcely art at all. Artfulness was sometimes deftly concealed within the larger rhythm of conversation; and sometimes his "demon" was called upon to gratify an urgently explicit demand of form: These moments are identified with the writing of *Sons and Lovers* as well as the writing of a half dozen poems and three or four short stories, but in the rest of everything he wrote the more flexible rule of "art for my sake" was applied and satisfied.

[1] *Phoenix, The Posthumous Papers of D. H. Lawrence.* New York: The Viking Press, 1936.

Lawrence, of course, was by no means unaware of what was happening; he had read his critics and matched his wit with theirs:

> For me, give me a little splendour, and I'll leave perfection to the small fry. . . . Ugh, Mr. Muir, think how horrible for us all, if I were perfect! or even if I had "perfect" gifts! Isn't splendour enough for you, Mr. Muir? Or do you find the peacock more "perfect" when he is moulting and has lost his tail, and therefore isn't so exaggerated, but is more "down to normal"?—For "perfection" is only one of "the normal" and the "average" in modern thought.[2]

How well he knew that the image of the peacock's tail would fill the reader's eye; and there in the image itself, he had uncovered a fragment of the "splendor" he had sought, and with an eloquent gesture, passed it over to the reader. It was as though he had been saying: Mr. Muir has given me bread and I give you cake. My transformation of Mr. Muir's gift, dear reader, is your reward for reading me. This answer was always Lawrence's reply to authority, whether the authority was the Evangelist, preaching from a Nottinghamshire pulpit, or Roman law concealed within the new laws of the Fascisti, whether it was the British censor or Mr. Muir. But he was always least fortunate whenever he attempted to answer that authority directly: his ingenuity lay in the art of improvised distraction. And in distracted argument he was never more successful than in his reply to Mr. Muir.

With Lawrence's rejection of the average man came his distrust of the society around him: "Only the people we don't meet are the 'real' people," he wrote in *Jimmy and the Desperate Woman*—and his "real" people were "the simple, genuine, direct, spontaneous, unspoilt souls," which, of course, were not to be found among the people Lawrence saw on city streets, not in "London, New York, Paris," for "in the bursten cities, the dead tread heavily through the muddy air," and in each face he saw the same stigmata Blake had witnessed, "marks of weakness, marks of woe." These were his average, "normal" people, branded by service in the World War like Captain Herbertson in *Aaron's Rod*, mutilated by war and sanctified by bourgeois wealth like Chatterley, malformed by ignorance and poverty like the Nottinghamshire miner, or tricked and defeated like the American Indian, "Born with a caul, a black membrane over the

[2] This quotation is from some notes called "Accumulated Mail" published in *The Borzoi, 1925* (New York: Alfred A. Knopf). Lawrence's remarks on "Mr. Muir" refer to a review that Muir had written of *The Rainbow* in the *Nation* (London). "Mr. Muir" was, of course, Edwin Muir, long before he was known as a poet. See essay in this collection, "The Timeless Moment in Modern Verse: Edwin Muir."

face." And as Lawrence traveled, he saw the same disease spread over half the earth—and he was not to be identified with any of that kind, the meek, the humble, or the dead. Though the physical resemblance to Lawrence's speaking voice may be traced throughout his novels, through Paul Morel, Lilly of *Aaron's Rod* or Mellors of *Lady Chatterley's Lover*, he was happiest in another kind of personality; and the image of the bird was best: the mythical phoenix, the peacock, or the Tuscan nightingale. To defend the nightingale (as well as himself) against the "plaintive anthem" of John Keats's *Ode*, he wrote:

> How astonished the nightingale would be if he could be made to realize what sort of answer the poet was answering his song. He would fall off the bough with amazement.
>
> Because a nightingale, when you answer him back, only shouts and sings louder. Suppose a few other nightingales pipe up in the neighboring bushes—as they always do. Then the blue-white sparks of sound go dazzling up to heaven. And suppose you, mere mortal, happen to be sitting on the shady bank having an altercation with the mistress of your heart, hammer and tongs, then the chief nightingale swells and goes at it like Caruso in the Third Act—simply a brilliant, bursting frenzy of music, singing you down, till you simply can't hear yourself speak to quarrel.[3]

Of course, the nightingale was the very thing Lawrence wished himself to be, the thing apart from the quarreling couple on the shady bank and his "art for my sake" had for its model the work of a creature who:

> . . . sings with a ringing, pinching vividness and a pristine assertiveness that makes a mere man stand still. A kind of brilliant calling and interweaving of glittering exclamation such as must have been heard on the first day of creation.

This was the splendor that was Lawrence's great concern, the "bursting frenzy of music" that emanated from a source within the body, and was itself the body, the physical being of a living creature. The lack of that physical force was his definition of modern tragedy, and it was the same emptiness he had witnessed in the lives of the civilized people who surrounded him. In that self-pitying, sad, silent company he had seen the image of Paul Morel, his early self of *Sons and Lovers:*

> . . . left in the end naked of everything, with the drift toward death . . . It's the tragedy of thousands of young men in England.

But Lawrence's instructions to live the splendid life always had the tendency to oversimplify the cure for complex (and human) silences and fears. They were all too much like telling friends and

[3] In "The Nightingale" from *Phoenix.*

neighbors to be natural, to "go be a man." His work had all the skill and all the confident lack of knowledge of one who had carefully trained himself to conduct an orchestra by ear. Throughout Lawrence's verse and prose a dominant rhythm persists above loose phrasing and verbal monotony; his ear had been trained to catch the idiomatic inflection of English speech, avoiding always the outmoded rhythms of literary usage. In this respect his work shares the vitality of Whitman's verse and Melville's prose, and like theirs it contains the same self-taught art that controlled its imagery.

Even the most casual reader of Lawrence will soon become aware of how deliberately he avoided the urban image and how through prose and verse there is a literal predominance of "birds, beast, and flowers." And as their number increases, how tropical they seem, and we remember that his need for physical well-being followed the hot course of the sun. But it is characteristic of Lawrence's imagery that its action remains suspended in utter darkness or in the full floodlight of noon; and though it is frequently breathing and alive, it seldom extends its force to an actual climax. How many of his images start bravely and end in helplessness, as though they could not carry the burden of their swelling heat and color to move elsewhere! And this same helplessness enters the majority of his many poems, all incomplete, all lacking in the distinction of verbal action to give them motion and finality. How many of his novels end with the promise of a life beyond them yet to be fulfilled in the next novel, perhaps, but for the moment still unwritten! Only in *Sons and Lovers*, and in a few of the short stories do we find a definite space of time and action brought to an ultimate conclusion—only in these and in three or four of the *Last Poems*. The rest of his work leans heavily into the future, as though the next page to be written would complete the large design of which his fragments were pencil sketches from the living model.

I suspect that this very characteristic of incompleted action is responsible for the air of expectancy which welcomed the publication of each posthumous volume of letters, stories, poems, essays, or incidental papers. Lawrence in death seemed still in flight around the globe and it has been difficult to think of him as a middle-aged writer dying nerveless and exhausted in a sunlit room in Southern France. The biographies of Lawrence, his self-imposed exile from England, the disorder among camp followers of the Lawrence household may be used as sources for a facile parallel to Shelley's death and the legends which grew out of it. But how eagerly Lawrence would have hated Shelley and would have cheerfully denied all he had written, and did in fact answer his *To a Skylark* in the same language in which he replied to Keats's nightingale:

"Hail to thee, blithe Spirit!—bird thou never wert." Why should he insist on the bodilessness of beauty when we cannot know of any save embodied beauty? Who would wish that the skylark were not a bird, but a spirit? If the whistling skylark were a spirit, then we should all wish to be spirits. Which were impious and flippant.

We need not stop to consider the flaws in Lawrence's heavy-footed questioning, for in this reply there is implied an entire century's increased distrust of Platonic reasoning. Between Shelley and Lawrence arose the shadow of Nietzsche's Zarathustra, who said as he descended from the mountain:

> To blaspheme the earth is now the dreadfulest sin. . . . Man is a rope stretched between the animal and the Superman. . . . Aye, for the game of creating, my brethren, there is needed a holy Yea unto Life. . . .

Lawrence's great error, of course, was to echo the sound of Zarathustra's warning without clear knowledge of the myth from which Nietzsche's hero had sprung, and lacking this knowledge he could not stride into another world that lay beyond good and evil. The literary heritage of the early nineteenth century had come down to him by way of Herman Melville and Walt Whitman. As he entered the latter phases of his career, traces of Whitman's eloquence spread throughout his writing, yet he was always to reject Whitman's democracy with uneasy violence. Whatever was to remain revolutionary in Lawrence's thinking was something that resembled philosophic anarchy. In a recently discovered paper, *Democracy*, written in 1923, he used Whitman as his text, in both praise and blame, to reiterate his distrust of a bourgeois democracy and its possession of property. His rejection of authority included a consistent denial of Marx as well as Plato, of Aquinas as well as Judaism and all law of church and state.

Yet in this wide negation of authority lies one secret of his influence with a younger generation of postwar writers. To deny bourgeois authority and to leave England was to break down the barriers of class and national prejudice that had seemed impassable before 1918, or rather, had remained unbroken for nearly a hundred years. He had survived many forms of British bourgeois hostility which brought with them the lack of a large reading public, persecution from the War Office, and the action of the British censor as well as charges of religious heresy. And there was ample evidence to convict him on any or all of these charges of public disfavor. His reply was that he alone remained alive in a dead world, a world in which the memory of its millions killed in a World War had spread the shadow of mass murder as well as lonely suicide over the furthest reaches of Anglo-Saxon civilization. And when his own death came, he made his own choices in preparation for it, convincing himself and those who read him that he had chosen the path of stilled and dark waters into oblivion.

Almost with his last breath he was to say, "For man the vast marvel is to be alive. For man, as for flower, and beast and bird . . ." and this reassurance in the goodness of physical being from someone whose self-taught and imperfect gifts alone sustained his eloquence, created a hero for a generation that feared the stillness of its own despair. It is not without perception that T. S. Eliot as well as others have read the warning of disease in Lawrence's heresies of behavior and craftsmanship. We know only too well his many failures, and among them we learn his refusal to abide by the truth of his observation in writing a brilliant analysis of Baron Corvo's *Hadrian the Seventh:* "A man must keep his earnestness nimble to escape ridicule." Yet his insight was never more profound nor more direct than when he associated Whitman with his own name, for it is through the work of Lawrence that the younger men in his generation of British writers have learned the actual significance of Whitman's enduring reputation. Like Whitman, Lawrence left behind him no model of technique that would serve to crystallize the style of prose or poetry in those who followed him. Lawrence's influence as a teacher was irrevocably bad; surely his literal imitators, like Horace Traubel's discipleship of Whitman, illustrate the master's flaws until their burlesque becomes so clear that pity or contempt deflects all criticism. Such imitation is the pathetic attempt to reproduce the absence of form, as though the devoted student had amputated his arm to simulate the sensation of his master's missing hand. Lawrence's real strength, like his invisible presence living "blithely, unbought and unsold," is explicit only in the combined force of his legend with a small selection from his prolific work of less than twenty years, and from these fragments we learn again how vividly he revived the memory of the maker in English literature, restoring the moment of vision and insight as a mark of genius in English prose and poetry.

1942, 1971

WYNDHAM LEWIS: "THE ARTIST AT WAR WITH HIMSELF"

Of a company which includes the names of Joyce and Pound, T. E. Hulme and T. S. Eliot, Wyndham Lewis was the most trenchant *avant-gardist* of them all. Now that his merits have been summed up with appropriate brightness by Hugh Kenner, *Wyndham Lewis* (1954), and with more painstaking seriousness by Geoffrey Wagner, *Wyndham Lewis* (1957), one sees him as unique as ever: prophetic, yet often wrong in his opinions, learned, yet almost righteously "self-made," hardheaded, yet unshrewd. In the arts he practiced fiction, painting, philosophy, criticism, journalism; he came at everything the hard way and with distinction.

He went to Rugby and London's Slade School of art; Paris, where he heard Bergson lecture at the Sorbonne, was his university; [1] his

[1] Is it both irreverent and irrelevant to remember that Lewis was born on board a British ship of which his father was captain in the Bay of Fundy? I think not. Sometimes the accident of place of birth or the legend of it, takes on curious meaning to what follows after in a man's career. As artist, critic, satirist, novelist, journalist, Lewis was a "displaced" figure in British art. After one year at Rugby (according to Geoffrey Wagner) and a year at the Slade School, he spent the next six years studying painting in Munich and in Paris; he saw something of the Netherlands and Spain—and in 1909 came back to England. Mr. Wagner is very right indeed as he observes how deeply Munich's Witzblatter affected Lewis's graphic art, and as deeply as Paris, became his university. Lewis, so it then seemed, had broken through and with the tradition of British art.

The legend of his being born at sea, his self-made Continental education and his belief in both is enough to account for Lewis's sense of other-worldliness from the London world he saw, that sense which drew him toward the orbit in which T. E. Hulme, Ezra Pound, Gaudier-Brzeska, and later T. S. Eliot moved. In spite of Lewis's intellectual conversion to abstractions and cubism in the graphic arts, his painting, like so much of British paintings, held to "ideas" of painting rather than to the resources of paint and line within themselves. Anyone who looks at Lewis's self-portraits, at his portraits of his friends, Pound and Eliot, will find a center of interest in the subject, rather than in the esthetic quality of the painting itself. However deeply Lewis was affected by European schools that came after postimpressionism, at last he remained within the tradition of British "literary" art. He, of course, never yielded to the "sweetness" of commercial art; his "ideas" rejected the "smooth," the facile, the false compromises to meet popular appeal. His failure was a failure of talent, not of critical years from 1909 to 1928 in London can be called by those who care for art "the Wyndham Lewis era" in Britain's capital. Like a last, phenomenally alive recruit in Cromwell's army, he conducted guerrilla warfare against British concepts of time and art, against popular brands of socialism, against ill-defined emotions and loose thinking. His assaults were carried on from the invisible ramparts he erected in Soho restaurants or behind the gates of the British Muesum; he invaded whole squares of Bloomsbury, and skirted the Thames Embankment down into Chelsea, and on the edges of Kensington at Notting Hill took Ford Madox Ford's house by storm. Mr. Kenner describes it:

> Mr. Ford Madox Ford—then Hueffer—was at the top of the stairs, pink, and aghast that his privacy and his luncheon with the original of Christopher Tietjens should be invaded by a silent steeple-headed figure wearing a huge black cape. The figure mounted the stairs, saying nothing. From beneath the cape it produced and flourished crumpled rolls of manuscript, which it pressed into Ford's unnerved hands. More wads of paper appeared from beneath the hat, from inside the waistcoat, from the pockets of the long-tailed coat. Ford numbly accepted them. All the time the figure said nothing. At last it went slowly down the stairs, without a word, and vanished.

In these singular engagements, at times accompanied by Ezra Pound, his strategy dismissed the arts of tact, and presented itself in the little magazines he edited: *Blast*, *Tyro* and *The Enemy;* the portraits that he painted were, more often than not, received as insults by their sitters rather than compliments; under strain of sitting for Lewis, Ronald Firbank tripped and hovered behind Lewis's shoulder to direct hopelessly, unsuccessfully, the drawing of his features upon paper. Lewis, as always, was genial enough, but decidedly intractable; he was a man of genius who possessed no talents.

In his own painting and in his criticism of modern art Lewis was a lion in wolf's clothing, his fangs bared in harsh, dark lines. From Whistler's example he evolved an ungentle art of making enemies; the last of his little magazines, *The Enemy*, revealed that debt, yet Lewis, unlike the famous American painter, was not a man of high-pitched sensibility. With matchless energy he entered and rode the violent "Machine Age" *Zeitgeist* of the early twentieth century and called it Vorticism, an explosive compound of ideas derived from Sorel, Nietzsche, and Bergson, capped with the dogmatic brilliance of Ezra Pound's young friend, T. E. Hulme. The shock was

---

perception of what his painting might have been—but at this point, the antiartist in Lewis comes forward in his painting, and as a scientist might solve a problem, so Lewis's forms take on geometric contours.

that when Lewis descended from his Vorticist chariot he showed the archetypical face of a twentieth-century Dr. Johnson, one who distrusted humanitarian ideals, yet stood for all the moral values of truculent individualism.

His first novel, *Tarr*, the writing of which was interrupted by World War I, has been imitated by younger novelists from 1918 to the present day; superficially it was another version of Bernard Shaw's early play, *The Philanderer*, in actuality, it was a nearly superhuman effort to introduce "the novel of ideas" to English readers; it proved to anyone who could think at all that the arch-Bohemian concealed a bourgeois heart and soul and that witless violence lurks in the shadows of romantic ardors. To reread it is to find it a book of more endurance than those which have attempted to improve upon it; it is among the half-dozen English novels of the present century written entirely without clichés.

But the apotheosis of the prose that Lewis so strenuously carved out as his own in *Tarr*, is in his volume of short stories, *The Wild Body;* his stern, serio-comic wit has never shown to better advantage than in his telling of the adventures of an Englishmen in Brittany; the book is not merely Lewis at his best, but at least four of the stories, including *The Death of the Ankou*, are among the classics of twentieth-century fiction.

Unfortunately, after writing at his best, Lewis with vigorous candor, proceeded to explain them out of existence; one does not care to deny Lewis's purpose to make his stories illustrate "the root of the comic" as he does in an essay on *The Meaning of the Wild Body*, but one comes away with the conviction that Lewis, prior to 1928, wrote unevenly but far better than he knew.

The phenomenon of Wyndham Lewis involves, as Kenner suggests, an Olympian quarrel with itself; a turn of ego, untouched by vanity, which prompted him to the extremes of self-criticism, and to attempt verbal acts of satire, like *The Apes of God* and *The Childermass*, which were far beyond the resources of his prose. To be successful, Lewis's weighty fantasies in satire would have had to equal in prose Pope's *Dunciad*. Failing of that high reach, Lewis's Apes were considerably less agile than Swift's Yahoos.

From these Lewis turned to overt polemics, to unpopular political opinions, steering close to pro-Hitler sentiments and allowing the public to take his measure as a dangerous crank; the fact that he rejected socialism in all its forms was underrated and ignored, and in 1939 he was forced to write *The Hitler Cult* to correct the impression that he favored the Nazi state. Like many Europeans who had seen the horrors of World War I he became an unwary, unguarded partisan of peace; his wars were of a moral and esthetic order; they concerned the artist, the metaphysics of time, Western culture, and the ancient failings of human intellect. Under the stresses of public disfavor, many of his writings became powerfully dull.

In 1937 the first signs of Lewis's recovery began with his autobiography, *Blasting and Bombardiering*, a book shot through with excellent brief portraits of Joyce and Eliot and Pound—but Lewis himself is nearly made invisible as he presumed to wear the cloak of belligerent opinions. Mr. Kenner has much to say in favor of his novel *The Revenge for Love*, published in 1954, yet the book, formed with greater skill than *Tarr*, has less concentrated force than *The Wild Body*. Lewis at his best requires a small canvas in which each detail of the piece stands in relief and that is why some of the stories in *Rotting Hill*, satires of recent Britain in the toils of socialism, have more effective brilliance than his longer essays in the novel.

In 1951 word had been sent out that Wyndham Lewis had gone blind: "Milton," he said, "had his daughters; I have my dictaphone." In his manly fashion he proceeded to make the best possible use of his misfortune, to live internally, to say more to his dictaphone than he wrote in the past, and not to part with the self-lashing demon who at times all but destroyed him, yet kept him in his latter years alive. The internal war in Lewis was between the artist who made his work possible at all and the moral critic who held all works of imagination in high doubt.

In his last years, Lewis's dictaphone brought him memorable rewards. In those years came the most prophetic of his books of essays, *The Writer and The Absolute* (1952). "It is dangerous to live," he wrote, "but to write is much more so—" and with this statement he faced the situation of the serious artist. As for the writer of the twentieth century, he stated that position with equal clarity:

> The writer can never hope to go of a morning into his working room with the same carefree detachment with which the man of science enters his—free to investigate our most moronic peculiarities without protest, or to devise how best to wipe us out in bulk by means of radiation or atomic fission. A relative freedom can be attained by the writer if he comes in a fairly mild period. He has in many periods enjoyed it.

He glanced toward the United States and New York:

> Contemporary New York might almost be regarded as a madly materialist maritime republic—Carthaginian in its contempt for the writer.

There is more truth than bitterness in that remark—and an American paradox exists within it. So long as he is ignored, the American writer is "free." The present American habit of ignoring or merely patronizing poets as though they were neurotic children has given them a "freedom" far greater than poets enjoy in various capitals of Europe, including always, the Soviet Union. If in the United States, the poet compromises his gifts by yielding to the demands of "publicity," public favor, fashionable groups, he has only himself to blame.

In *The Writer and The Absolute*, Lewis clearly defined the various positions held by André Malraux, Sartre, and George Orwell. He saw Malraux, the writer, vanishing into direct political action—"escape through action," so Lewis wrote. He saw Sartre's existentialism as twentieth-century nihilism, driving Sartre to feverish efforts to find a wide public among the bewildered, ignorant young who throng cafés, and are detached for the moment only from society—he saw Sartre drifting into a flirtatious union with Communism. From Lewis's thoroughly accurate observation of Sartre's position, further observations may be drawn. The twentieth-century nihilist with his heritage of Hegel, Marx, and Freud finds it difficult to attract sustained attention from younger readers. Younger readers, however ignorant, grow up—and the greater majority grow up and away from attitudes of adolescent disillusionment and nihilism. Abandoned elder nihilists then find themselves drawn closer and closer to the orbit of Communism. To the writer the Soviet Union has always offered the illusion of notoriety among millions of readers as a substitute for individual excellence and fame. Journalists like Sartre find this illusion irresistible—they yield to it, and are exploited by the Super State. How pitifully wrong they are is shown by the courage of Pasternak, who though living within the Soviet Union, gained his freedom as a writer in the world outside it. What Sartre lacks is courage.

Lewis's own courage and clarity of vision led him to a mature and I believe enduring estimate of Orwell's writings, and how Orwell's socialism and hasty conversion to Communism came from the springs of inverted snobbery. Lewis is right in concluding that Orwell's conversion to and later rejection of Communism (shown in his autobiographies and novels) are marred by "timely" thinking and writing, and art now outmoded. As Lewis remarks, the single proof of Orwell's integrity as artist is in his fable *Animal Farm*, which is likely to remain as an undying reminder—a warning—of totalitarian horror.

It is appropriate that the last image of Lewis should resemble that of Tiresias—his isolation in blindness shedding light in a world with which he had never found the terms of peace. In the *avant-garde* of one age he became the seer of the next, and like Tiresias achieved a semi-Olympian authority.

1957, 1961

THE BLACK-STOCKINGED BAIT AND DYLAN THOMAS

Though the mere occasion may seem irrelevant, I shall never forget the hour I first read a book of Dylan Thomas's verse and prose. The book was Thomas's third book, *The Map of Love*, and the scene was a little bookshop in sight of the British Museum in London; the time was August of 1939. I had just come from meeting a fellow American in that very street, a little woman with rosy cheeks, tightly curled black hair beneath a hat of artificial primroses and violets; her innocent and yet birdlike eyes were wide with excitement. Without stopping for breath she told me of the Moscow-Berlin pact: "It may mean peace," she said, "and it may mean war, and of course the Russians are always strong for peace." Back at home the little woman's vocation was teaching the social sciences in a girls' college, and her war-threatened holiday in London had given her new notes on "world affairs" to carry back with her to the United States. The British Museum was already locked to visitors as though Bloomsbury gloom (with the aid of His Majesty's armed guards) had sealed its doors forever. My American lady's plump and gloved hands—the gloves were dove grey and beautifully tailored—fluttered in half suppressed delight as though they had accidentally touched the "pulse of the world," and she, the lady, were another Pandora who at the moment had opened the fatal box. Since I had an uncheerful view of the times which to me seem to have begun their wars in 1914 (the date by the way of Dylan Thomas's birth) I was in no mood to share the lady's elation at the very latest "news"; such turns of history had been in "progress" for a long while, and I needed elation of another sort. I abruptly turned away from her, entered a glass-fronted shop and started to read *The Map of Love* displayed on the counter. Obviously the book could not be read at a glance, it would deserve more than several readings, and with this thought in mind, I bought it.

2

Since that afternoon in 1939 which now seems so long ago and labeled with "events" and premonitions, the Anglo-Welsh poet, Dylan Thomas, has become—and not without justice and discrimination—the most thoroughly, if not most widely, read poet of his generation in England.[1] Perhaps he is a "war poet," but I seriously doubt that kind of relevance attached to his poems and to his name—or rather it is of the same kind of relevance which attended my meeting with a teacher of social sciences in London and the purchase of *The Map of Love*. The scene out of which Dylan Thomas emerges as the central figure may be given the general title of "neoromanticism," a scene in which the later poems of W. B. Yeats and of Edith Sitwell (and it is not without grace of temperamental affinity that Miss Sitwell praised Thomas's early *25 Poems*) provided a precedent for the arrival of Dylan Thomas. Other precedents exist in the richness of Welsh poetry itself, and in the annual festivals in Wales of poetry read aloud. Still other sources are to be found (particularly in Thomas's devotional poems, the *Vision and Prayer* cycle in *Deaths and Entrances*) in *The Temple* of George Herbert, for *The Temple* is not unknown to Welsh readers of English devotional poetry. Nor should a true "ancestor" of younger Welsh writers in England be forgotten—Arthur Machen, whose imaginative writings have gone through at least four cycles of neglect and appreciation, and are as cheerfully alive today as ever. But the "neoromantic" scene has still other figures, in which Walter de la Mare extends a heritage from Beddoes, John Clare, Poe, and Darley; and as one turns from the elder poets, the American Hart Crane and the Anglo-Irish George Barker seem to be immediate "forerunners" of the kind of lyricism that Dylan Thomas found congenial to his gifts. One should also include Henry Treece and Vernon Watkins among Thomas's immediate contemporaries, who, like Barker, reach toward a richness of expression that had been denied such poets as MacNeice and C. Day Lewis, who are often betrayed by their facility into the charms of writing "magazine verse," or colorful epithets, which may amuse or shock the eye, but fail to attach their brilliance to profound centers of human emotion or intellectual meaning. The overtly journalistic and admittedly "neoclassic" school which discovered *A Hope for Poetry* before 1939 has suffered reverses. Of that "elder" generation, W. H. Auden, by virtue of his wit and his professional skill, seems to be the sole survivor of what was "fashionable" not so many years ago.

[1] In 1946 New Directions (New York) published *The Selected Writings of Dylan Thomas*, edited and with an introduction by John L. Sweeney. The book contains forty-seven of Thomas's poems, four short stories, and the first and last chapters of *Portrait of the Artist as a Young Dog*. It is an excellently proportioned and well-modulated selection of Thomas's writings. Sweeney, in his introduction, emerges as one of the most discerning critics of contemporary verse. His prose is distinguished by wit and clarity, and no one who reads criticism for enjoyment as well as information can afford to ignore his commentary on Dylan Thomas.

3

The term neoromanticism does not, of course, define the specific nature of Dylan Thomas's or any other poet's poems, but it does indicate the more general atmosphere and heritage to which a poet's writings may belong; such terms as classical and romantic are always in danger of being used as weapons of abuse or as tarnished laurels, and as we come close to an actual reading of Thomas's poems, another term, symbolism, rises into view. This is all very well, but since Arthur Symons published *The Symbolic Movement in Literature* in 1899, conscious elements of symbolism and the techniques employed by the symbolists have entered the main streams of poetry in English on both sides of the Atlantic. In respect to Thomas's poems one can say this: that which so closely resembles the technique of symbolic poetry in his poems is of the same nature that guided W. B. Yeats in his re-creations of the Celtic myth that he drew from the lives of those around him and himself, and drew also from the writings of Dr. Douglas Hyde and Standish O'Grady. In Yeats's poems the French symbolists served as examples, as "guides," rather than "masters"—and it is safer to conclude that he did not follow them literally, but in a more active sense, attracted some features of their technique to the centers of his imaginative being. Anyone who has read the sources of a literature sprung from "the myth," and particularly the North Druid myth, soon becomes aware of their likeness to some features of so-called "modern" symbolist poetry in English. Thomas's poems, including *The Hunchback in the Park* and *Among those Killed in the Dawn Raid was a Man Aged a Hundred,* show something of the same method that Yeats employed, a "drawing power," a fusion of "mythological" reality with individual perception. And it is to be noted that Thomas's word order often carries within it characteristically Welsh phrasing.

One index to Thomas is found in his book of autobiographical short stories, *Portrait of the Artist as a Young Dog,* and its first story, *The Peaches,* is a view of things seen and heard in many of Thomas's poems. The "place" of the story is a countryside in Wales, and the "time" is childhood, literally the "time" when things are seen for the first time and at first hand. The description of "the best room" in a farmhouse has the very elements, the "keepings," and one almost says the "furnishings" of a number of Thomas's poems; they are the centers out of which Thomas's characteristic imagery springs and to which it returns:

The best room smelt of moth-balls and fur and damp and dead plants and stale, sour air. Two glass cases on wooden coffin-boxes lined the window wall. You looked at the weed-grown vegetable garden through a stuffed fox's legs, over a partridge's head, along the red-paint-stained breast of a stiff wild duck. A case of china and pewter, trinkets, teeth, family brooches, stood beyond the bandy table; there was a large oil lamp on the patchwork tablecloth, a Bible with a clasp, a tall vase with a draped woman about to bathe on it, and a framed photograph of Annie, Uncle Jim, and Gwilyn smiling in front of a fern-pot. On the mantelpiece were two clocks, some dogs, brass candlesticks, a shepherdess, a man in a kilt, and a tinted photograph of Annie, with high hair and her breasts coming out . . .[1]

Another paragraph from the same story has other characteristic "keepings" which are brought to light again in Thomas's poems:

I remembered the demon in the story, with his wings and hooks, who clung like a bat to my hair as I battled up and down Wales after a tall, wise, golden, royal girl from Swansea Convent. I tried to remember her true name, her proper, long, black-stockinged legs, her giggle and paper curls . . .

And still another scene from the story has a farm boy preaching a sermon from a wagon used as a pulpit. It is perhaps gratuitous to remark the well sustained prose rhythm, the shrewd yet innocent blasphemy, and the wit that is contained in the following passage:

I sat on the hay and stared at Gwilym preaching, and heard his voice rise and crack and sink to a whisper and break into singing and Welch and ring triumphantly and be wild and meek. The sun through a hole, shone on his praying shoulders, and he said: "O God, Thou art everywhere all a time, in the dew of the morning, in the frost of the evening, in the field and the town, in the preacher and the sinner, in the sparrow and the big buzzard. Thou canst see everything, right down deep in our hearts; Thou canst see us when the sun is gone; Thou canst see us when there aren't any stars, in the gravy blackness, in the deep, deep, deep, deep pit; Thou canst see and spy and watch us all the time, in the little black corners, in the big cowboys' prairies, under the blankets when we're snoring fast, in the terrible shadows, pitch black, pitch black; Thou canst see everything we do, in the night and the day, in the day and the night, everything, everything; Thou canst see all the time. O God mun, you're like a bloody cat."

In the above quotations one also begins to see the limitations and ranges of Thomas's vocabulary: "black" is among Thomas's favored adjectives, and the subjective associations of the *Ballad of the Long-legged Bait* (which is included in *Deaths and Entrances*) are clearly shown in the phrase, "proper, long, black-stockinged legs." The

[1] *Portrait of the Artist as a Young Dog*, by Dylan Thomas. New York: New Directions, 1940. (Subsequent quotations are also from this edition.)

"myth" of the *Ballad* is taken from a familiar group of North Druid myths, and "myth" or story is also implied in one of Walter de la Mare's poems. Thomas, by drawing it to the center of his own imagination—an example offered by the poems of De la Mare as well as Yeats—has made the "myth" his own. The mock sermon provides a precedent for the *Vision and Prayer* cycle in *Deaths and Entrances*, for blasphemy, whether in the best or worst sense, always admits the consciousness and the reality of religious being—and therefore, T. S. Eliot's *The Hippopotamus* has its place in forecasting the arrival of *Ash-Wednesday*. The relationship between Thomas's prose and poetry may be shown by comparing the first passage I have quoted with a few lines from his early poem, *In Memory of Ann Jones*, which was not retained in his *Collected Poems:*

> Morning smack of the spade that wakes up sleep,
> Shakes a desolate boy who slits his throat
> In the dark of the coffin and shed dry leaves
> That breaks one bone to light with a judgement clout,
> After a feast of rear-stuffed time and thistles
> In a room with a stuffed fox and a stale fern.

There has been some talk of "Freudian imagery" in more than a few of Thomas's poems, and certainly Thomas has shown no fear in employing sexual imagery of which the elegy, *The Tombstone Told When She Died* is a magnificent illustration:

> The tombstone told when she died
> Her two surnames stopped me still.
> A virgin married at rest.
> She married in this pouring place,
> That I struck one day by luck,
> Before I heard in my mother's side
> Or saw in the looking-glass shell
> The rain through her cold heart speak
> And the sun killed in her face.
> More the thick stone cannot tell.
>
> Before she lay on a stranger's bed
> With a hand plunged through her hair,
> Or that rainy tongue beat back
> Though the devilish years and innocent deaths
> To the room of a secret child
> Among men later I heard it said
> She cried her white-dressed limbs were bare
> And her red lips were kissed black,
> She wept in her pain and made mouths,
> Talked and tore though her eyes smiled.

I who saw in a hurried film
Death and this mad heroine
Meet once on a mortal wall
Heard her speak through the chipped beak
Of the stone bird guarding her:
I died before bedtime came
But my womb was bellowing
And I felt with my bare fall
A blazing red harsh head tear up
And the dear floods of his hair.[2]

Is this poem more Freudian than a poem by Blake or D. H. Lawrence or some passages that may be found in the poetry of Coleridge? I would say no more and no less. This is not to underestimate the general influence of Freud upon the poetic imagery of twentieth-century writings in both prose and verse; and I may as well add, as a matter of opinion, that twentieth-century claims for the "modernity" of sex have been greatly exaggerated.

4

In the foregoing paragraphs I have attempted to show something of Dylan Thomas's regional identities, the charm of his highly individual imagination as well as his affinity to a larger, unevenly gifted body of neoromantic literature. Among his elders only Yeats, Edith Sitwell and Walter de la Mare are poets of greater and more mature accomplishments than he; the others, including George Barker and Henry Treece, who seem to have responded to the same impulses that have moved Thomas (and Barker's early poems preceded Thomas's and were in print before Thomas's style had taken form), have fallen prey to the forces of "easy writing" and a tendency toward disintegration. *Death and Entrances,* was, I think, Thomas's best single book of poems published before his *Collected Poems* in 1953.

In *Death and Entrances* (1946) came the unmistakable signs of Thomas's poetic genius, his poems under the title of *Vision and Prayer* and his *Fern Hill.* In the tradition of English Romantic poetry, *Fern Hill* takes its place beside Wordsworth's *Tintern Abbey.* Both poems are rare in their power to re-create the spell of memory and the world of nature seen through the eyes of childhood. In this respect both convey similar emotions to the reader. The publication of Thomas's *Collected Poems* later reinforces this conclusion. In the year of his death, 1953, and in a prefatory note to his *Collected Poems,* Thomas wrote: "These poems, with all their crudities, doubts, and confusions, are written for the love of Man and in praise of

[2] *The Collected Poems of Dylan Thomas.* New York: A New Directions Book, 1953. (Subsequent quotations are also from this edition.)

God, and I'd be a damn' fool if they weren't." The statement showed his advancing maturity, his critical wit. Better than his critics he knew his flaws, but he also knew his great promise of an immortality.

There was no faked piety in Thomas's prefatory note. In his *Collected Poems,* the poems of *Vision and Prayer* with their George Herbert-like verse forms, reached their conclusion in the magnificent lyric written in memory of the death of his father, *Do Not Go Gentle Into That Good Night,* which, by the way, is an example of the French villanelle in English verse. The themes of purification by fire and rebirth are implicit in *Vision and Prayer* and beyond them came the denial of spiritual death in *Do Not Go Gentle.* In one sense the poem stands as Thomas's own epitaph.

During the last year of his life in the romantic confusions of his lecture tours, his violent readings of his poetry, his ill-health, his Welsh humors, he was very like an actor playing against the backdrop of a stormy night. He had succeeded in completing his role of lyric poet in a storm-ridden age of wars and threats of wars—one who was disguised one moment as an eternally boyish Welsh bard, and in the next, as Lear's prolix and witty Fool who saw and knew "the dying of the light."

5

Any revaluation of Dylan Thomas's writings should be prefaced by the remark that he was "a child of genius" in the double sense of this ambiguous phrase. His father, a Welsh schoolmaster, who drank his life away at bars in public houses, had a spark of the same genius running through his veins—and he gave his young son a love of poetry to which he added the ambition to write it supremely well.

The elder Thomas was erudite in his devotions and poor in cash; his wife came from a Welsh farming family, and it was she who provided in what might have been a pedantic literary heritage a touch of earth and outdoor nature. She was also a chapel-goer. And in the chapel there was always the invisible flutter of angels' wings and the smell of brimstone emanating from the Devil. All these, and the tinsel of provincial showmanship, made up the elements, the very dynamics, the heady dialectics of good and evil in Dylan Thomas's life and poetry.

Many of us in New York can still remember Dylan Thomas, the showman, the stout, perky little Welshman, in clothes that could never quite fit him, strutting the lecture platform, reading poems in a high-pitched voice. He called himself "a second-rate Charles Laughton," but the showman was also a second-rate Dylan Thomas, who loved to play comic bits in amateur theatricals back home in Wales, who loved to play the dog, the pig, or King Lear's Fool before his inferiors in places like the White Horse Tavern downtown on Hudson Street.

In these performances he was the roaring boy, "the ringtailed roarer," whose style of acting was to influence the platform manners of Theodore Roethke, and afterward, those of the "Beatnik" poets. In his public role (so FitzGibbon informs us in his biography of Dylan Thomas) Thomas frequently repeated his youthful attempts to be like his father, a cigarette hanging from his lips dribbling ashes to the floor, and a pint mug of beer held in the grip of his right hand. Since much of his public life had been spent in pub-crawling, whether in London or New York, it was the second-rate Dylan Thomas—and tenth-rate alcoholic clown—that urban entertainment-seekers saw. Yet even in the extremes of childish play-acting, there was rather more than a hint of tragic loss, that off-stage, in the wings, there was something fine being destroyed.

In *Selected Letters of Dylan Thomas*, edited by his biographer, Constantine FitzGibbon, the tensions and dynamics of Thomas's life off-stage as against the image of his public life are made clear. Though the roaring boy does not wholly vanish, in the *Letters*, when asking for favors, he is sometimes painfully coy, striking tail-between-the-legs attitudes, and fervent in his apologies for wrong doings. Yet even here we are closer to the essential Thomas than the sight of him lurching through the streets or at the bar. And we are drawn—through his wit—very much closer to the poet who wrote miraculous, and, at times, hilarious short stories and was the maker of some of the best poems written in our century.

FitzGibbon's great find is in the letters written to Pamela Hansford Johnson when Thomas was under twenty-one, she a year or two older, and they thought themselves in love with one another. He criticized her verse and wrote about his own; he advanced his literary likes and dislikes, and of his ambitions to grow out and away from provincial Wales: "It's impossible for me to tell you how much I want to get out of it, out of narrowness and dirtiness, out of the eternal ugliness of the Welsh people . . . And I will get out."

To those critics who have overstressed Freudian influences on Thomas's writings, here is his serious and convincing answer: "I am in the path of Blake . . . The greatest description I know of our own 'earthiness' is to be found in John Donne's 'Devotions,' where he describes man as earth of the earth, his body earth, his hair a wild shrub growing out of the land . . . Every idea, intuitive or intellectual, can be imaged or translated in terms of the body, its flesh, skin, blood, sinews, veins, glands, organs, cells, or senses."

Like many other youthful poets, Thomas underrated Wordsworth: "But Wordsworth was a tea-time bore, the verbose, the humourless, the platitudinary reporter of Nature in her dullest moods." Yet if one thinks of Thomas's *Poem in October* and his *Fern Hill* there is evidence that he read two of Wordsworth's poems with strict attention, and honestly enough, he confesses: "I admit the Immortality Ode is better than anything he ever did (with the exception of the pantheistic creed expressed in Tintern Abbey)."

Thomas held to a complex, visceral inward-looking pantheism of his own making: "I believe in the writing of poetry from the flesh, and, generally, from the dead flesh. So many modern poets take the living flesh as their object, and by dissecting, turn it into a carcass. I prefer to take the dead flesh, and, by any positivity of faith and belief that is in me, build up a living flesh from it." This was the play, one against the other, of death and life, Thomas's opposites; a dialectic that he probably learned from William Blake. This was again illustrated when he chose John Donne's phrase, "Death and Entrances" as the title for the best of his single books of poems. "Entrances" in this sense carries the associations of rebirth.

Thomas rejected the tenets of surrealism: "Automatic writing is worthless as literature," he wrote, "however interesting it may be to the psychologist & pathologist." Thomas then went on: "My facility . . . is . . . in reality, tremendously hard work. I write at the speed of two lines an hour. I have written hundreds of poems, & each one has taken me a great many painful, brain-racking and sweaty hours."

Thomas was a poet of minute particulars. "Beauty," he said, "is the sense of unity in diversity . . . One should take first an empty brain and a full heart to every poem one reads." Then he sensibly adds, "an impossible task. The only possible way lies in the reading & re-reading, preferably aloud, of any new poem that strikes one as holding some or however little value . . . Each genuine poet has his own standards, his own codes of appreciation, his own aura," a truism he revealed in his appreciation of George Herbert and Christina Rossetti. "Everything is wrong," he added, "that forbids the freedom of the individual," and in this statement, he sounded his own strength, his independence, his freedom from all literary groups and movements.

In his writings he was never to relinquish that source of strength which is one of the primary reasons why certain of his poems are likely to be read "as long as forever is." It was in the practice of his independence that he created his singular relationships to nature as well as to the universe: "It is my aim as an artist . . . to prove beyond doubt to myself that the flesh that covers me is the flesh that covers the sun, that the blood in my lungs is the blood that goes up and down in a tree."

And without the self-pitying whines of how one can be "alienated" from society, he continued: "Artists, as far as I can gather, have set out, however unconsciously, to prove one of two things; either that they are mad in a sane world, or that they are sane in a mad world. It has been given to the few"—Thomas obviously counted himself among them—"to make a perfect fusion of madness and sanity, and all is sane except what we make mad, and all is mad except what we make sane." What is important here is the stress that, by placing it last, Thomas gives to the word "sane." So far as his poetry was concerned, and this included his vision of the universe, he refused to find a haven in madness.

In his poetry at its best there is "a perfect fusion" of the opposites, a precarious welding together of the two extremes—a "dead body" and "the soul": "Looking on one dead, we should say, there lies beauty, for it has housed beauty, the soul being beautiful . . . if only I could say with Blake, Death to me is no more than going into another room. How easy, too, it is to say that; there is as much charlatanism in a poet as there is in an astrologer, and it may be that the genuineness and the value of the one is the genuineness and value of the other; both have a love and awe of the miraculous world."

The precocious boy who wrote with prophetic knowledge of the poetry he had promised himself to write, spoke of death with such familiarity, it was as if he knew his time for the making of poetry was very short. There were moments when he felt himself to be a Welsh Rimbaud. With his father beside him dying of cancer, he had a strong pre-knowledge of death's presence on earth. He met this presence with the Romantic violence of his villanelle *Do Not Go Gentle Into That Good Night.*

But what of all his poems? Do they place him, as some of his admirers once thought, with John Keats, with Donne? Of course not. Despite their power, despite their findings in a world of marvels, Thomas's particulars, his womblike imagery, his overripe phrasing close in upon one, they create the feelings of claustrophobia, whereas the particulars of Keats and Donne open outward into a greater universe. It was the concentric character of Thomas's intensely personal language that caused his poems to move inward from the world of nature out of which they drew their imagery. Yet Thomas's accomplishment was a marvel in itself; and that was why a tragic sense of loss attended the news of his early death. And a likely immortality may be found in his re-creations of a pastoral childhood at Fern Hill, a childhood to be rediscovered by young readers of poetry in many future generations.

1947, 1961, 1971

THE TIMELESS MOMENT IN MODERN VERSE: EDWIN MUIR

In anthologies and studies of contemporary poetry it is the unexpected poems and poets who are increasingly evoked. Of these the least heralded, yet most rewarding, is Edwin Muir (1887–1959): his best poems are short, and in contemporary company, resemble no one else's. The poems stand quite alone, and in their outward dress, innocent of fashionable twentieth-century devices. Read carefully, their character is both traditional and unique.

And who was Edwin Muir? In answering that question one begins to describe the unusual nature and source of the poems he wrote. He and his wife, Willa, were generally known as the translators of the tales and parables of Franz Kafka into English; it is not much to say it was they who made Kafka famous. Muir's limited celebrity from his own writing came very late, and at no time in his brief career of fame was he other than a soft-spoken, slender, shy, self-effacing man. The extraordinary thing about him was the youthful, almost saintly brilliance of his gaze glancing through the surrounding veil of his modesty. In the early 1950s, on his short visit to the United States, it was as though the external Muir, a man of letters and mild-voiced lecturer, shielded and half-concealed an internal presence, one of the best of twentieth-century Scottish poets.

The internal Muir, the poet, whom his wife was fond of calling "an extremely early Christian," was born on a farm in the Orkneys, that low-hilled chain of islands, off Scotland, not far from Norway, where the provinces of the Scandinavians and the Scots-Irish almost touch each other. Rich as these unfamiliar farmlands were in spoken myths and legends, the Orkneys were not known for raising poets. Muir was a child of that environment, and from it springs his *An Autobiography* published in 1955, as well as the revised edition of his poems.[1] The autobiography provides a valuable backdrop to the poems, a far better exegesis of their visionary content than a conventional critical analysis would yield. If the best of the poems are not as well known as they should be, the self-told story of his life gives us a few of the causes why.

[1] *Collected Poems* by Edwin Muir, with a preface by T. S. Eliot. New York: Oxford University Press, 1965.

The writing and publication of Muir's poems is of recent date in his career. During his adolescence the migration of his family south to Glasgow was a journey into brutish slums, ill-health and death. The elder members of the family were wiped out and beyond his rural schooling, Muir's education was of his own finding, his native taste, and his austere, though imaginative, discernment. He earned his keep by holding precarious clerkships in beer-bottling and bone factories and last in a shipbuilder's office—all this an unlikely apprentice service for a future poet and literary essayist.

In these surroundings, it was not extraordinary that he became converted to socialism; what was unusual was his quick discovery that Marxism was not for him, and with this conviction, he turned to A. R. Orage's startling periodical, *The New Age,* which advocated Maj. C. H. Douglas's Social Credit. This choice was significant, for Orage was an editor of vivid perceptions and fine intuitions: with the same insight with which he guided Muir, he encouraged the early work of T. S. Eliot, Ezra Pound, Dylan Thomas, and Katherine Mansfield. When young Muir wrote him, asking for advice, he freely gave it, and accepted a weekly column of Muir's prose for *The New Age.*

Meanwhile, the poet in Muir had made independent soundings and discoveries in Scottish and English poetry, and among English poets, Wordsworth's example of plain speech that articulated feeling "too deep for tears" left its mark. Wordsworth as model was a warning against the use of emotional trivialities and Scottish provincialisms in verse. Such teaching was excellent for Muir, and so was the discipline of verbal simplicity. The only harm that came from Wordsworth's influence (and this is a reason why some readers have underestimated Muir) is the colorless, atonal utterance that damps his poetry whenever it falls short of its best.

Muir had begun by writing prose. As he wrote later:

I produced . . . a sort of pinchbeck Nietzschean prose peppered with exclamation marks. I should be astonished at the perversity with which, against my natural inclinations, my judgment . . . I clung to a philosophy so little suited to a clerk in a beer-bottling factory, if I did not realize that it was a "compensation" without which I should have found it hard to face life at all.

In 1920 H. L. Mencken reprinted Muir's "Nietzschean prose" from the columns of *The New Age* under the ironical title *We Moderns* in a little green book. As Muir in 1954 was glad to confess, his *We Moderns* had long fallen out of print, yet between the lines of its affected style and wit, there was an intelligence that never confused the humane values of poetry and art with those of power politics. His brief Nietzschean fever thoroughly inoculated him against all future contamination, either from the Fascist right or the Communist left.

Encouraged by Orage, the Muirs, husband and wife, ventured to London, and then into Europe, on a career of translations from the German and of literary journalism. Unlike most such writings, Muir's reviews and critical pieces had a particularly serious and inquiring air; he was well prepared to make his discovery of Kafka. In this country, his prose caught the attention of Van Wyck Brooks, literary editor of *The Freeman*, who persuaded him to contribute his middle-European travelogues to that journal, including his sketches of Prague. It was through their experiences in Europe that Muir was able to shake off the last vestiges of Scottish provincialism and to find his place as a citizen of the world, unique of his kind, with the visionary eye of a poet.

At an age when most poets had lost their first flush of inspiration, Muir had just begun. His published verse is without juvenilia; no youthful or experimental imperfections mar its lines; to the present reader, its only flaws are shadows cast by Wordsworthian matter-of-factness and lack of color, but when the shadows vanish his poems have an air of eternal freshness, an "early-Christian" touch and truthfulness that Giotto's frescos have, as in the following lines from his *The Annunciation:*

> The angel and the girl are met.
> Earth was the only meeting place.
> For the embodied never yet
> Traveled beyond the shore of space.
> The eternal spirits in freedom go.
>
> See, they have come together, see
> While the destroying minutes flow,
> Each reflects the other's face
> Till heaven in hers and earth in his
> Shine steady there. He's come to her
> From far beyond the farthest star. . . .

No poet of our day has been able to emulate the primitive character of the Scottish Border ballads wtih the quiet authority and distinction mastered by Edwin Muir. At their best his lines have the concentrated action and clarity of *Sir Patrick Spens*, as well as Robert Burns's "The trumpets sound, the banners fly,/The glittering spears are ranked ready . . ." and Sir Walter Scott's "Proud Maisie is in the wood,/Walking so early;/Sweet Robin sits on the bush,/Singing so rarely." This is of the same power of vision and art that began to enter Muir's poetry in 1934. Note these lines on heraldic beasts:

> Who curbed the lion long ago
> And penned him in this towering field
> And reared him wingless in the sky?

And quenched the dragon's burning eye,
Chaining him here to make a show,
The faithful guardian of the shield?

A fabulous wave far back in Time
Flung these calm trophies to this shore
That looks out on a different sea.
These relics of a buried war,
Empty as shape and cold as rhyme,
Gaze now on fabulous wars to be.

Something very like a hint foretelling World War II may be found within these lines, but quite as important as the warning is the transcendental quality of Muir's imagination. There is metaphysical tension and strength in *The Animals*, a vision that probably had its source in a memory of childhood on the farm:

They do not live in the world,
Are not in time and space.
From birth to death hurled
No word do they have, not one
To plant a foot upon,
Were never in any place.
For with names the world was called
Out of the empty air,
With names was built and walled,
Line and circle and square,
Dust and emerald;
Snatched from deceiving death
By the articulate breath.
But these have never trod
Twice the familiar track,
Never never turned back
Into the memoried day.
All is new and near
In the unchanging Here
Of the fifth great day of God.
That shall remain the same,
Never shall pass away.

On the sixth day we came.

Nor as he changes the setting to a Greek environment is his vision less penetrating. Here is the deep vista of *Orpheus' Dream:*

At last to turn our heads and see
The poor ghost of Eurydice
Still sitting in her silver chair,
Alone in Hades' empty hall.

The same depths are reached in *The Horses*, one of the poems T. S. Eliot greatly admired, where there is a sight of our world returned to "long-lost archaic companionship" after the devastations of the next great war, a look forward into a future that closely resembles mankind's beginnings.

Among Muir's very last poems, there is the strange and magical fable, *The Two Sisters*, which re-creates in modern poetry the sense of destiny so often felt in rereading older Scottish songs and ballads:

> Her beauty was so rare,
> It wore her body down
> With leading through the air
> That marvel not her own.
> At last to set it free
> From enmity of change
> And time's incontinence
> To drink from beauty's bone,
> Snatching her last defence,
> She locked it in the sea.
>
> The other, not content
> That fault of hers should bring
> Grief and mismanagement
> To make an end of grace
> And snap the slender ring,
> Pulled death down on her head,
> Completed destiny.
> So each from her own place,
> These ladies put to sea
> To join the intrepid dead.

Surely here is proof enough that Muir in casting off mere provincial mannerisms and dialects has made his own language that restores the strength of a Scottish tradition (which for centuries has held its own in metaphysics) and given it universal character and meaning.

1965

ON GEORGE MOORE AND REGIONALISM IN FICTION

In America, the literary fashions of the 1880s and the 1890s which had been imported from continental Europe and its islands, enjoyed an irresponsible and certainly indecorous old age until the years immediately following the First World War. This has been particularly true of our relations to British literature of *Yellow Book* origins and to the tradition of Flaubert, and in this respect we have been slower than the Germans. Someone—I believe it was D. H. Lawrence—said that Thomas Mann was "the last sick sufferer from the complaint of Flaubert," but Flaubert was not generally appreciated as a serious novelist in the United States until 1919! By that time, we had belatedly discovered George Moore—and not the George Moore who has always and still deserves a measure of our attention, but he who had written *Confessions of a Young Man*, the George Moore who had so flagrantly enjoyed the liberties he had taken in writing and re-editing his dead life. We embraced his foolishness, his indiscretions; and we shared, vicariously, of course, his love of shocking those who were supposedly a shade more innocent than he. We enjoyed half-seriously his belated impersonations of Huysmans, Pater, Wilde, and Gautier—but admiration of this kind grew chilly beyond the third decade of the present century, and at the moment of his death in 1933, his literary remains had begun to fall, soundlessly and with scant honors, into the semiobscurity in which they rest today.

If one makes allowances for the slight embarrassments which attend a revival of recently outmoded literary figures, a rereading of George Moore's early novels is by no means difficult. The only difficulty that arises is the possible mistake of taking their author too seriously, but one does not stop reading; something is there that outlives the moment of its creation. One decides to follow the heroine of *A Mummer's Wife* to her last fifth of gin in a London slum, one pauses to take another look (and not without amusement) at Lewis Seymour in *A Modern Lover* boldly posed naked (he was to represent a dancing faun) in Mrs. Bentham's drawing room. One then recalls how swiftly and how skillfully Moore introduced the latest fashions in French naturalism to the subscribers of London's circulating libraries. This was in the early 1880s and at a moment when the very thought of translating Zola into English for the enlightenment of the British public seemed both highly experimental and morally dangerous. Perhaps a reason why the libraries (after a brief dispute) decided to accept Moore was that it must have been as difficult to take Moore seriously then as it is today. Moore earnestly defended his lack of humor, but the spirit which his early books convey has the charm, the occasional turn of brilliant observation, the eagerness, the sensitivity of the obviously immature, yet gifted writer.

One agrees that the circulating libraries took small risk in allowing *A Modern Lover* and *A Mummer's Wife* to pass from hand to hand among young British matrons or their housemaids. The books may well have been shocking, but the incidents that were artfully contrived to shock us are so innocently, so boyishly confided and so lightly placed and stressed; they had the air of being "entertainments," rather than the weighted arguments that would blast the family hearth or endanger the Stock Exchange. Despite the skill with which Moore handled the formulas of naturalism, despite his exact descriptions of airless and shabby rooms or fog darkened streets, his scenes of Paris and of London lack emotional reality, quite as they lack the realities of verbal warmth and density and color. It was not until his third novel was written, *A Drama in Muslin,* in 1886, that one could possibly discern a third-dimensional quality at work; there, the scene is well within the English pale of Ireland, and is circumscribed by journeys to and from Dublin's viceregal court, the parlors of the Shelbourne Hotel, and Anglo-Irish estates and country houses.

Since I believe that George Moore was indisputably an Irish writer rather than an Irishman who had acquired British poise, the occasion arises for a brief commentary on the regional aspects of naturalism in fiction. One should not be surprised to find Moore at his best on Irish soil, for the premise of his consciously acquired art (the realistic novel in its latest form) almost demanded that he should have been; but before I enlarge upon the Anglo-Irish character of Moore's work, what seems both a truism and a paradox in the esthetics of realism should be given a hearing.

The realistic novel, as we have known it, is of protean shapes; it is of many tongues and of many varieties, depths, and colors. It is easy to agree that Fielding, Gogol, Tolstoy, Balzac, Flaubert, Dickens, Nexö, Dreiser, and the Thomas Mann who wrote his *Buddenbrooks* were realistic novelists. The mask that realism wears is international and yet the hidden limitations of the realistic novel are regional. The best and most far-reaching examples of its art depends upon an intimate awareness to a particular environment; the particulars of human behavior present their immediate problems to the author and reader alike, for both must feel the external truth of what is being said and done. It has taken a Second World War with its news of a north-eastern front extending into the far reaches of the Russian plains to endow Tolstoy's *War and Peace* with a renewed vitality for the American reader. And those readers who cannot carry in the mind's eye the omnipresent, yellow-grey density of fog in nineteenth-century London would also fail to grasp the full meaning of the theme and its variations in Dickens's masterpiece, *Bleak House.* As one follows the mutations of realism and its heirs in the novels of Zola in France, of George Moore in Ireland, of Dreiser, Sherwood Anderson, and James T. Farrell in the American Middle West, the writer's awareness of a particular time and place seems to increase; he tends to grow more and more dependent upon the realities of an environment and a region that he knows well, and with this knowledge, he conveys the strength of his convictions to his reader. To the foreign reader he demands an effort in the direction of an accurate translation—and lacking that effort, the best of his serious writing is likely to become transformed into a novel of exotic charm, as though it were a trip to a strange place, in which the wilds of urban Chicago, New York, or Paris, may assume (to the reader's eye) the same attraction that is felt in reading an account of a journey to the source of an unknown river in Brazil. In this sense, many a realistic novel offers the blandishments of an "escape" for the bored or harried reader; and, often enough, the very rich have enjoyed the exotic charms of a novel relating the misfortunes of the very poor.

George Moore's eager and enthusiastic practice of the arts of realism, even today, has an air of seeming fresh and adventurous. He did not seem to move at a measured pace, but to leap and to dive, swimming through gaps in his own intentions by hasty adaptations of scenes and episodes from the novels by Flaubert and Zola; the water was cold, but he churned its surface until it sparkled. If the successes of *A Modern Lover* and *A Mummer's Wife* did not bring him fame, they suddenly illuminated the curious aura of notoriety that was always to be associated with the mention of his name; and the phenomenon deceived a number of his critics, Virginia Woolf among them, into thinking that his gifts were exclusively those which enabled him to write his fictional autobiographies; and there is little to show that he himself was not equally deceived, for George Moore, as his *Confessions* and his *Memoirs of My Dead Life* so plainly testify, was unable to make a clear distinction between notoriety and fame. A transitory burst of candor meant as much to him as an arduous search for truth, and he mistook the surprise he caused by the first for the most difficult achievements of the latter. It was candor that betrayed Moore's lack of true worldliness; and his confidences, whispered aloud for all the world to hear ("Moore never kissed but told"), left him naked to the rebukes of his more seriously minded contemporaries. Bernard Shaw's stage directions and prefaces to his plays, even when they had the air of taking the reader or spectator into personal confidence, never failed of their objective in social criticism; in Moore's voice, the personal aside was less clearly directed and controlled, and however often it ridiculed the canons of Victorian respectability, it frequently lapsed into what seemed to be the utterance of a deliberately phrased faux pas.

But between the writing of his first two novels and his *Confessions of a Young Man,* Moore wrote the earliest of three books that merit our attention, *A Drama in Muslin,* and, as if to strengthen and support my argument that Moore's work was at its happiest at home, the book was actually written in Ireland. The training he had received in Paris (for the city of Paris had been his university and Manet, Turgenev, and Zola may be regarded as his instructors) began to bear the fruits of his industry. Within ten years he had been transformed from an Anglo-Irish dilettante, born to an estate that yielded several hundreds of pounds per annum, into an industrious novelist and man of letters—and in Dublin he possessed the advantage gained by a lack of celebrity at home. If in a later generation, Joyce saw the Dublin of his *Ulysses* with a steadier and more deeply penetrating eye than Moore, we should remember that Moore was there before him, viewing the city with a gaze of youthful detachment and a true concern for the arts of prose. In *A Drama in Muslin,* Moore's acknowledged spokesman is a Mr. John Harding, a novelist, who drifts, almost unseen, through Dublin streets and through the reception rooms of the Shelbourne Hotel; he is an object of admiration for Moore's plain featured, shy, and humorless little heroine, Alice Barton, but the admiration does not grow into love, for Mr. Harding remains her self-appointed guardian and educator.

In rereading *A Drama in Muslin* one half envies those who discovered Moore as a promising young novelist in the 1880s; as in *A Modern Lover* and *A Mummer's Wife* his lack of maturity was again turned to his advantage; and even today, one feels that his sensibilities heralded the awakening of a new spirit in modern fiction. The marriage market of an Anglo-Irish gentry at Dublin's viceregal court was the object of Moore's concern and ironic observation; the court is gone, and the immediate occasion for Moore's protest against the fate of innocent and badly educated young men and women, paired off and sold at the marriage market by ambitious mothers and bankrupt fathers has long since passed. But to view sex clearly as a marketable social commodity was a position taken up by Bernard Shaw a few years later in *Mrs. Warren's Profession,* and close juxtapositions of extreme wealth and extreme poverty which created so much dramatic and intellectual excitemant in Shaw's early plays have their première in *A Drama in Muslin*. If Turgenev had read and admired Maria Edgeworth and learned from her a measure of the skill required in writing a realistic novel of social irony, Moore had been no less assiduous in taking hints from Turgenev's discoveries in reading *Castle Rackrent* and *The Absentee*. An inspired cycle of literary apprenticeships had come to a full round and returned to its source within the English pale in Ireland. But Moore's sensibilities were also tuned to receive all the protests of a youthful generation that had been caught in the net of elderly ambitions, mistakes, and Victorian hypocrisies.

It is not just to say that Moore lacked art in the writing of *A Drama in Muslin;* yet its atmosphere of something we call an artless charm pervades throughout the narrative; we enjoy it in much the same spirit that we find pleasure in witnessing an earnest and enthusiastic rehearsal of a play in a small town six weeks before its arrival ten doors west of Broadway; the director is inspired and is willing to risk a few experiments in technique that an older and perhaps wiser man would consciously avoid and the actors are doing better (if one makes allowances for awkward pauses and incomplete gestures) than they know. The episodic and simultaneous shift of scene between a landowner bargaining with rebellious tenants, and his wife bargaining for the sale of his pretty daughter is a venture into the experimental techniques of realistic fiction that has been continued from the day *A Drama in Muslin* first appeared to the writing of John Dos Passos's *42nd Parallel*. The characters of Mrs. Barton, the scheming mother, who learns too late the feminine unwisdom of turning each rival mother with a girl for sale into an enemy, the stupid beauty, her daughter Olive, her husband, the landlord who fancies himself a painter of unrecognized talents, the young Lord Kilcarney, the "catch" of the Dublin season, who is besieged alike by rapacious mothers and starving tenants, are memorably and sensitively drawn. Moore's improvisions were those of an exceptionally bright student of realistic fiction who had suddenly usurped the master's place and had become for one brief hour the teacher, and if not the philosopher, the guide. In sensibility he had advanced beyond all other younger novelists of his day; only the mature Henry James with his virtually unread and certainly unappreciated *Princess Casamassima* overshadowed him, and in the position he had won, he attained a freedom of eloquence and a quickness of perception which in many of his later novels and in their numerous revisions were either stilled or blotted from the page.

In *A Drama in Muslin* he had found almost too much to say on too many varied subjects, but all were related to his discontent of living in Ireland:

The Dublin streets [he wrote] stare the vacant and helpless stare of a beggar selling matches on a doorstep. . . . On either side of you, there is bawling ignorance or plaintive decay. . . . We are in a land of echoes and shadows. . . . Is there a girl or young man in Dublin who has read a play of Shakespeare, a novel of Balzac, a poem of Shelly? Is there one who could say for certain that Leonardo da Vinci was neither a comic-singer nor patriot?—No. Like children, the young and old, run hither and thither, seeking in Liddell oblivion of the Land League. Catholic in name, they curse the Pope for not helping them in their affliction; moralists by tradition, they accept at their parties women who parade their lovers to the town from the top of a tramcar. In Dublin there is baptism in tea and communion in a cutlet.

The discontent that Moore displayed was salutary and one feels that he expressed it with deeper penetration into the lives of a people than the kind of social criticism he had to offer later in the pages of *Esther Waters* and *Evelyn Innes.* One does not easily forget the scene in which the weak and bewildered young Lord Kilcarney wanders alone on the stone embankments of the Liffey in the small, dark hours of the morning, pursued by promises of ambitious mothers with marriageable daughters and harried by threats of economic ruin promised with equal vehemence by Parnell and the Land League.

Looking backward and in that glance reviewing the social dramas of Bernard Shaw, the pamphlets and speeches of the Fabian Society, the domestic novels of Arnold Bennett, and the H. G. Wells of *Mr. Polly* and *Tono-Bungay,* the flashes of youthful insight which illuminate the narrative of *A Drama in Muslin* seem at this distance to have acquired the prophetic intonations of a Delphic oracle. As the novel closes, one reads the following description of Ashbourne Crescent in London:

To some this air of dull well-to-do-ness may seem as intolerable, as obscene in its way as the look of melancholy silliness which the Dubliners and their dirty city wear so unintermittently. One is the inevitable decay which must precede an outburst of national energy; the other is the smug optimism, that fund of materialism, on which a nation lives, and which in truth represents the bulwarks wherewith civilisation defends itself against those sempiternal storms which, like atmospheric convulsions, by destroying, renew the tired life of man. And the Ashbourne Crescent, with its bright brass knockers, its white-capped maidservant, and spotless oilcloths, will in the dim future pass away before some great tide of revolution that is now gathering strength far away, deep down and out of sight in the heart of the nation, is probable enough; but it is certainly now, in all its cheapness and vulgarity, more than anything else representative, though the length and breadth of the land be searched, of the genius of Empire that has been glorious through the long tale that nine hundred years have to tell. . . .

It is in Ashbourne Crescent that Moore's solemn and candid heroine became a successful lady novelist and it was there, happily wedded to a physican, that she came to rest; the comedy was over, and Moore's little study in social irony had a satisfactory and plausible conclusion.

Moore's return to Ireland at the end of the century (as everyone who has read his *Hail and Farewell* remembers) had been inspired by W. B. Yeats's enthusiasm and his urgent propaganda for a Celtic Renaissance in literature. By this time Moore's celebrity in London was well established, and the temperamental differences which always existed and were never resolved between the two men, had been shrewdly put aside by Yeats with the purpose of using Moore's gifts and notoriety to support a worthy cause. I happen to believe that Yeats's invitation came to Moore at a critical moment in his career, that it prolonged his creative life by another decade, and we, as readers of Moore's half-forgotten novels, are enriched by a rediscovery of *The Lake* and *The Untilled Field*. Among Moore's weaknesses as a mature writer (and despite his industry) was his infinite capacity for being bored; the boredom was all the more insidious because Moore lacked sufficient self-knowledge to realize its effect upon his work. The curse of dullness which is so brilliantly absent from his early novels and his scenes of life in Ireland, begins its round in the pages of *Esther Waters* and is resumed after the completion of *Hail and Farewell* to continue till the end of his life which closed so inauspiciously with *Aphrodite in Aulis* and *The Pastoral Loves of Daphnis and Chloe* and *Peronnik the Fool*. When Yeats's invitation came, Moore had the need to be prodded back to the centers of his discontent, to be made aware of them in such fashion that his active sensibilities could be reawakened. I am not prepared to say that Yeats fully perceived the importance of his urgent invitation to George Moore; I suspect not, I suspect that he was too deeply concerned with his own relationship to the Celtic Renaissance to realize that he had granted Moore more than a passing favor. I am inclined to believe that their subsequent quarrels had at their source an esthetic (and therefore far less flagrantly personal) cause of disagreement than certain passages in *Hail and Farewell* and Yeats's *Dramatis Personae* would seem to indicate. Moore was an excellently well-trained and sensitive critic of modern painting while Yeats was a notably inept one; Moore was a naïvely schooled and indifferent critic of verse which his *Anthology of Pure Poetry* proved to all the world, while Yeats in his own voice as a poet commanded an authority that was and still remains superior to almost everything that Moore might have to say concerning poetry. It is impossible to speak of Yeats's work without acknowledging the far reach inward to the realities of subjective being while the delights of reading Moore's prose are those which are gained by reading the observations of a man who has been inspired by the presence of an active world around him.

But whatever the causes of Moore's reawakening of energy may have been, the stories which Moore included in *The Untilled Field* remain as fresh today as in the hour that he wrote them to be translated into Irish in 1900. The spirit in which he composed them was cheerfully stressed in his preface to the Carra Edition of *The Untilled Field* in 1923:

> . . . I wrote "The Wedding Gown," "Alms-Giving," "The Clerk's Quest," and "So On He Fares," in English rather than in Anglo-Irish, for of what help would that pretty idiom, in which we catch the last accents of the original language, be to Tiagh Donoghue, my translator? . . . but these first stories begot a desire to paint the portrait of my country, and this could only be done in a Catholic atmosphere. . . . "The Exile" rose up in my mind quickly, and before putting the finishing hand to it I began "Home Sickness." The village of Duncannon in the story set me thinking of the villages around Dublin, and I wrote "Some Parishioners," "Patchwork," "The Wedding Feast," and "The Window." The somewhat harsh rule of Father Maguire set me thinking of a gentler type of priest, and the pathetic figure of Father MacTurnan tempted me. I wrote "A Letter to Rome" and "A Play-House in the Waste"; and as fast as these stories were written they were translated into Irish. . . .

With the aid of a literal translation (done by T. W. Rolleston) of a few of the stories back into their original English, Moore edited *The Untilled Field* for British and American publication; Gaelic imagery had strengthened the original text, and the stories were, as he wrote, "much improved by their bath in Irish. 'She had a face such as one sees in a fox' . . . how much better than 'She had a fox-like face.' "

The little stories, sketches, and a novelette, *The Wild Goose* which are listed in the contents of *The Untilled Field* were never widely read, and Moore himself confessed that he had half-forgotten their existence because he was so soon engaged in writing a sequel to them in *The Lake*. Perhaps the lack of appreciation they received injured Moore's vanity, but it is more likely, that coming as they did from a semiconscious source of inspiration, Moore underrated their importance, and presented them with a display of too much modesty. Something of their true quality is suggested in the speech of the anonymous spectator who tells the story of the blind man in *Alms-Giving:*

> The new leaves were beginning in the high branches. I was sitting where sparrows were building their nests, and very soon I seemed to see further into life than I had ever seen before. "We're here," I said, "for the purpose of learning what life is, and the blind beggar has taught me a great deal, something that I could not have learnt out of a book, a deeper truth than any book contains. . . ."

In this spirit Moore created his Father Maguire, the stupidly domineering priest, Father MacTurnan, the innocent and heroically humane Father of his parish and with them there is the remarkable Biddy M'Hale who caused Father Maguire so much trouble by donating the money for a window in his new church and following him, there is the story of *The Wild Goose,* the repatriated Anglo-Irish newspaperman, whose career as a politician in Ireland has its broad analogy to the career of Parnell, and among the best of the shorter pieces is *The Wedding Gown* in which Moore's sensibility reminds one of the qualities that are discovered in rereading the tales of Hans Christian Andersen. In his introduction to the Carra Edition of *The Untilled Field,* it was characteristic of the later Moore to claim that his Irish stories served as a precedent for John Synge's *The Playboy of the Western World,* but whether they did or not (and I suspect that they did not) the quality of their prose and the sensitivity of their observations foreshadowed the writing of Joyce's *Dubliners. The Untilled Field* contains no story as well controlled or as delicately contrived as Joyce's little masterpiece *The Dead,* but the reaches of *The Untilled Field* closely approximate the intentions and accomplishments of Joyce's stories, and with the exception of Joyce's *The Dead* and *A Little Cloud,* Moore's stories are markedly superior.

To us who read Moore at a trans-Atlantic distance and at a time when his once spectacular introduction of literary modes and attitudes seem outworn, an interesting and seemingly farfetched analogy—a parallel, if you will—between George Moore and Sherwood Anderson comes to mind. For a moment, the parallel seems curious rather than exact, but the more I think of it, the closer the work of the two writers falls together, and the analogy which seemed to span too great a distance between them reveals something that results in a just understanding and estimate of their contributions, each separately, to a national literature.

Like Moore, Anderson indulged himself in a wealth of semi-autobiographical reminiscence and extolled the merits of candor above those of truth, and like Moore's autobiographies, Anderson's memoirs and storyteller's stories seem less like actual confessions than works of fiction that had been released from the disciplines employed by writing a short story or a novel. To a notable degree both men as writers lost themselves among the high arches and corridors of the palace of art. In later life, Moore returned to his early and ill-advised worship of Walter Pater, and his habits of industry kept him chained to the task of writing the books which now seemed fated for oblivion. With equal misfortune, Anderson's love of the perfect phrase, the prose sentence, and paragraph that remain an eternal delight to the eye and ear seems to have sterilized the gifts that promised so brilliant a future in the two volumes of his short stories, *Winesburg, Ohio* and *The Triumph of the Egg*. If Moore's source of inspiration lay within the English pale surrounding Dublin, certainly the sources of the sensibilities that Anderson so memorably expressed may be found within an equally small circumference of Midwestern small towns, railway junctions, and farm lands; and the resemblance between the work of the two men increases as one remembers the debt that a younger generation of writers owed to them. To the same degree that *A Drama in Muslin, The Untilled Field,* and *The Lake* anticipated the discernments of a new literary generation in Anglo-Irish—and indeed, British—literature, Anderson's early short stories preceded the now familiar complex of youthful sensibility and a concern for artful presentation, of naturalism and of individual candor that is so strongly marked in the early writings of Hemingway, Faulkner, and Dos Passos. Both elder writers possessed the impulse "to see further into life," something that could not be learned out of a book and was "a deeper truth than any book contains." This impulse is, of course, by no means an uncommon impulse in any generation, but Moore's and Anderson's discovery and expression of it, set an example for the young writers who came after them.

It would be easy to regard Moore's long career in writing prose a failure, and it is certainly easy for me to repeat that the expectations he awakened were never quite fulfilled, that the very terms of his art (those of the naturalistic novel) left him discontented, that he never perceived fully the richness and value of his Irish origins even as they were displayed in his own writing. The almost fatal lack of knowing fully his true identity with Ireland cut him off from those sources of feeling which might have resulted in work of lesser scope than he enjoyed, and would have been of more mature and lasting satisfaction. Easy as it may be to enlarge his failures and dimmed as Moore's reputation seems today, the scales of a final judgment still tip in his favor. I have repeatedly spoken of his sensibility, and I have done so because everything he wrote reflects the writer whose art is guided by feeling rather than the deeper inward reaches of emotion.

Few writers survive the trials of writing their autobiographies—a last farewell that should be taken late in life—and Moore, after his confessions and memoirs of a dead life, retained enough energy to write his third and best, *Hail and Farewell,* which overshadowed the merits of his more pretentious novels. The sensibility of which I speak had its moments of a significant hold on the imagination and its presence distinguishes Moore from all other writers of prose in English who suffered the transition which carried them from the nineteenth century into the twentieth. One thinks of Moore's survival in much the same terms as Father Oliver's swim to safety in the closing pages of *The Lake:*

A long mile of water lay between him and Joycetown, but there was a courage he had never felt before in his heart, and a strength he had never felt before in his limbs. Once he stood up in the water, sorry that the crossing was not longer. "Perhaps I shall have had enough of it before I get there"; and he turned on his side and swam half a mile before changing his stroke. He changed it and got on his back because he was beginning to feel cold and tired, and soon after he began to think that it would be about as much as he could do to reach the shore. A little later he was swimming frog-fashion, but the change did not seem to rest him, and seeing the shore still a long way off he began to think that perhaps after all he would find his end in the lake. His mind set on it, however, that the lake should be foiled, he struggled on, and when the water shallowed he felt he had come to the end of his strength.

"Another hundred yards would have done for me," he said, and he was so cold that he could not think, and sought his clothes vaguely, sitting down to rest from time to time among the rocks.

"How cold are thy baths, Apollo" is the phrase that returns to mind whenever one thinks of Moore; and in a literature of Anglo-Irish origins, we think of him as one who shook himself free, if only for a brief hour, of the chilling waters of Apollo, and who is now on the fortunate shores of an immortality.

1944

H. G. WELLS: A WREATH FOR THE LIBERAL TRADITION

Several years ago I invited a British poet out to lunch. I chose an Armenian restaurant in the upper twenties on Lexington Avenue, that section of New York where behind half-curtained windows one can almost fancy a return to the Soho in London of twenty-five years ago. Certainly the atmosphere was of other times, other places than the moment and place where we found our seats, and of a slightly foreign air. The setting was contagious; we were in a stage set of somewhere else. The poet's Bloomsbury accent—and he was among the best talkers in London—became more pronounced as the conversation lost its bearings; he was always more persuasive than ultimately convincing, and with a half-glitter from his fine blue eyes—the conversation must be saved—he broke out suddenly with: "Why doesn't someone write something about H. G. Wells?" The question came out of the air and was unanswered by either of us.

I might have said, but didn't, that it is difficult to place Wells anywhere; he can't be put in a corner; he doesn't stay in the nineteenth century where he belongs; he was never a poet or an artist, yet he haunts our feelings and certain sections of our minds. If today he happens to be a ghost in London, he is strangely more alive than the papers where so much of his journalism appeared. Though in his last years his journalism wore his mind thin, he had dearly loved it; after writing "outlines" of history, he continued to write from week to week, "outlines" of world affairs, "outlines" of the universe, and his conclusions, even in the thinnest of his prose, were always more often right than wrong. His friends reported that shortly before his death during the midsummer of 1946 he had grown weary, but he had spoken of fatigue twelve years earlier, and wrote his *Experiment in Autobiography* in anticipation of death; the book gave him as he wrote it, "freedom of mind"; that was what he wanted before death, and he could afford to take it, in a house whose windows looked out over Regent's Park.

Wells was born in 1866. The time and place was Dickens's England and Wells was born into the same social strata where Dickens, fifty-four years earlier, first saw wind-swept or fog-clouded skies above his head. But the particular Wells who haunts us today was born a generation later than his birthdate. It is the idealistic young tutor of biology who "collapsed into literary journalism," who wrote *The Time Machine* and *The First Men on the Moon,* whose step is light and brisk. The ghost had earned godfatherly privileges at one of the rebirths of "science fiction." Imaginary voyages into space, aided by enthusiastic use of the telescope, were notorious and fashionable adventures as early as the seventeenth century. The eighteenth century was not unaware of them; yet the more famous journeys, Defoe's *A New Voyage round the World,* and *Robinson Crusoe* and notably Swift's *Travels by Lemuel Gulliver* chose water as their element. The romances of Jules Verne came earlier than Wells's ventures, but Wells, more brilliantly versed in latter-day popular science than Verne, returned to models provided by Swift and Defoe. Wells's romances, like Defoe's, had the air of being documentary reports, and like Swift's they were parables of life on earth, or rather of life, as far as Wells could discern it, within the complicated, minutely class divided structure of English society. Wells's inspiration for *The Time Machine* began with a paper he wrote to demonstrate the existence of the fourth dimension, the *Universe Rigid,* a stiff, self-conscious essay in popular science which was rejected by Frank Harris, the deep voiced, black haired editor of the *Fortnightly Review.* The fourth dimension was "news" in the 1890s; any mention of it awakened the same curiosity that talk about "relativity" had thirty years ago. It was necessary for Wells to give that topic "life," to give it human relevance, to make his theory felt as well as understood. He solved his problem by converting it into a parable of what might happen if British society were divided into two races: those who ran machines, lived underground, and were scarcely human; and those who lived on the surface of the earth, beautiful, indulged, nearly witless creatures whose voices slurred into musical phrases, all dependent on the labors of their underground slaves, helpless in the presence of machines, and all living, not without fear, in a sunset glow of civilization.

The actual force of Wells's parable developed in terms of social meaning rather than of scientific revelation. Was this social satire? Perhaps; one could read it that way. Was it Swiftian in speculation of human destiny? No; it lacked Swift's nearly tragic vision of human savagery—and lacked Swift's whiplash, his passionate hatred of human folly. Wells's vision was one of warning, because Wells believed that human beings would listen to warnings—if their minds were freed. This belief is at the center of Wells's famous liberalism; it also defines the character of his no less famous optimism. "Freedom of mind" with the security of peace around it, the peace of Plato's idealism, the middle world of ideas in which mankind realized concepts of divine origin defined the utopia Wells held in view. The parable of *The First Men on the Moon* contains the same hope. At the end of the book, Cavor—the scientist from earth held captive by the creatures of the moon—who established communication with the earth from his prison on the moon, is killed by his captors. Unwisely he allowed moon's creatures to learn earth's ambitions toward empire building, to conquer the universe by force, by war. Moon's creatures then found no other alternative but to destroy him, to cut themselves off from barbarous earth. Wells's effort was to warn his readers that wars were held in disrepute by all possible forms of living intelligence except mankind's. *The First Men on the Moon* was published in 1901, the moment when the people of Western civilization held greatest hope for the promises of a new world opening up to them in the progress of a "scientific" twentieth century.

Readers of science fiction today may find *The Time Machine* and Wells's voyage to the moon tame, less highly seasoned than recent romances of the same genre. Science fiction, as we know it now, is the popular, dubiously legitimate, subconscious offspring of violence in current fiction. Its greatest revival came during and after World War II. Its narrative patterns followed earlier designs of the gangster and western romance—its hidden forces, its dehumanized human elements are those of sadistic encounters and destruction. Readers who might be ashamed of (or afraid of) being too strongly attracted by scenes of violence in other forms of litreature could accept science fiction as instructive of future life on the far shores of an "expanding universe." How deliberately the writers of science fiction follow wild west-gangster formulas I do not know; the greatest possibility is that the science fiction writer is not the cynical monster he so often appears to be, but that he has the same hidden enjoyment of thrills and terror which delights the science fiction reader. This is the secret which is shared between them. Beneath the surfaces of recent science fiction, totalitarianian and atomic warfare mount the skies in technicolor profusion; fear of the future is among the dominant emotions awakened by nuclear fission—and if one looks for parables within science fiction, one finds that they point toward victories of a "one world," totalitarian drive to power.

The distance between Wellsian science fiction and its present revivals can be measured by recognizing two extremes of fear: in Wells's books the fear is that mankind will carry into the future its past mistakes, and Wells's warning implies a rejection of the past. The more thoughtful science fiction writers of the 1950s face a more explosive, more lethal, darker future than Wells had in mind, nor do they seem as confident as he did that their warnings can clear, if not purify, the air. This distinction is, I think, important. A dark aura encircles the fantasies of Arthur C. Clarke who is certainly the best of writers in a genre that even today has renewed inspiration from *The Time Machine.* Like the writings of the early Wells, Clarke's short stories and romances are less easy to dismiss as merely science fiction than the work of his fellow craftsmen. Like Wells of *The First Men on the Moon,* the weight of his prose is light, the structure of his stories neat and polished; he is obviously the latest "master" in his chosen genre. His book of stories, *Reach for Tomorrow,* has a variety which extends from the psychological sharpness of *The Parasite* to the topical wit of *Jupiter Five;* it is the first time in many years that John Collier of *Fancies and Goodnights* has had a rival. Under whatever title Clarke's fiction is a delight to read. But the paradox produced by reading too many of Clarke's interstellar space romances is intellectual claustrophobia. One's mind is locked in a future of totalitarian doom. Human loyalties to place and to other human creatures vanish—these are the dark auras of Clarke's wit and inventiveness. Clarke's mad, power-driven scientists are successful; while Wells's devotees of science, equally mad, pay the price for their logical deductions with their lives.

The distinction that Wells's science fiction has, and why *The Time Machine* is still unique with a timelessness of its own, is that Wells held at the center of his writings a protest against darkness—intellectual darkness—and in his science fiction, however out of fashion it may fall, the protest has a resounding note. To clear away the darkness of the past was Wells's effort; to the young H. G. Wells scientific knowledge and inventiveness were the means of leaving Victorian darkness—or any other darkness—in the shadows behind him. If his best writings have an air of "cleanliness" it is because his mind fought the claustrophobia of Victorian lower (very low) middle-class poverty, of group thinking (within a short time he found himself at odds with the Fabians), and, when he had become famous enough to be invited out to dinner, of London literary circles.

2

His *Experiment in Autobiography* (1934) is not the book that it might have been—the fully annotated document of a Victorian-Edwardian literary career, a "success story" of one of the highest paid literary journalists in England, the man who came from nowhere and who for thirty years influenced, and often guided, the liberal thinking of the twentieth century. The first two hundred pages of Wells's *Experiment* are as remarkable as the author himself; yet a warning of the thinness, like that of skimmed-milk prose, which diluted the latter four hundred-odd pages to round-table discussions wearily circulating at two in the morning, is in the book's subtitle, "Discoveries and Conclusions of a Very Ordinary Brain." This was not modesty, nor irony; it was part of Wells's liberal belief that a "very ordinary brain" was one to be valued and respected; yet the phrase has a deeper meaning. Wells grew easily bored at writing about himself, or rather that side of himself which did not preside at a public meeting. And the truth was that the memorable scenes of the first two hundred pages, which included portraits of his mother and father—his mother, educated as a Victorian lady's maid, his father as a country gentleman's gardener—had been written before, but disguised as fiction, in his novel *Tono-Bungay*. The best of the autobiographical Wells is in that novel, his masterpiece of social comedy. If one may speak of "light prose" with something of the same meaning that we speak of "light verse," *Tono-Bungay* has a place of its own in British fiction. But one must distinguish it from the comedy of Dickens's half-Gothic, poetic prose, the hilarity of cosmic scenes in his major novels. One must also remove it from the vicinity of Evelyn Waugh's wit—that is of another vintage. Thackeray's *Vanity Fair* is of no nearer kinship; it has taken nearly fifty years to recognize *Tono-Bungay*'s Edwardian-Wellsian high spirits as another approach to the vanities of Western civilization, nor has the advertising genius of Ponderevo, Wells's chemist who invented "Tono-Bungay," declined; it has grown to much larger proportions in the United States. It is the genius that makes presidential campaigns "the greatest shows on earth" flickering and roaring from TV screens. The new word for it is "publicity."

None of Wells's fiction withstands the test of rereading as admirably as *Tono-Bungay;* it is not merely Wells's best book, it is an Edwardian masterpiece; it has the abundance of the Victorian "three-decker" and yet it is "streamlined" within scarcely four hundred pages. In its own day (1909) it bridged the distance between "the problem novel" and the novel of ideas. Like the novels of E. M. Forster, its argumentative brilliance prepared the way for the intellectual content of D. H. Lawrence's *Women in Love* and the early novels of Aldous Huxley. Beyond its own *Zeitgeist, Tono-Bungay* still opens the door to the largest booth of the twentieth-century's "Vanity Fair" where advertising—the faked poetry of successful careers, industry, and politics ("the poetry of commerce" Wells called it)—is bought and sold. It is significant that Ponderevo, the mock hero-villain of the book, rises from the lower middle classes only to burst in mid-air; he does not escape his doom. The civilization that made his rise possible also had the power to destroy him, to leave him on his deathbed, the victim of an ability to make "quick money." The point is that Ponderevo is trapped by the values he tried to manipulate; he is the inflated "little man," who a generation later was to become Germany's Hitler and France's Laval. Was Wells too mild in making him a comic figure? I think not. He is a figure of Anglo-American derivation; it is better to keep him true to his origins, and to remember that though an analogy to his failure can be drawn from his European heirs, he is seen in the perspective of his own environment. The distinctive features of democracy, with its heritage of parliamentary government, keep our Ponderevos, no matter how large they grow, within range of comic reference.

Ponderevo's nephew and biographer is the thinly disguised, autobiographical Wells, the Wells who sought for "freedom and trackless ways," who very nearly, but not quite, confused definitions of "truth" with those of "science," and felt that beyond art or literature, his duty was to reach toward truth into "the heart of life," to "disentangle" it and to make it "clear."

But as Wells reached toward his "reality," the search was beyond himself, and with loyalty to his Platonic liberalism (though his relationships with women were more ardent, irritable, and paradoxically lonely than Platonic) the view was often beyond visible horizons. During his boyhood his claustrophobia had a hint of agoraphobia in it. Like Trollope's at Harrow, Wells's boyhood humiliations, his poverty, were strongly associated with a world of country houses where he had small rights, if any, to exist. That world was governed (through the grace of his mother) by a Low Church Victorian God. Though the prospect was as delightful as landscapes that Jane Austen knew, Wells was consciously blind to it—and for good reasons. His place was so "low" that the loveliest, broadest landscape turned to desert; yet it would be wrong to say that Wells forgot it; it returns in a vision of the future in *The Time Machine;* it is a "condemned playground" of flowers, grasses, the Liberal gentry, country houses fallen into charming ruins, peopled by creatures "on the intellectual level of . . . five-year-old children" and condemned because of outmoded childish fancies and fears. Was Wells deliberate in his reconstruction—in ruins—of Kentish Up Park where his mother served as housekeeper? He may have been; but it would have been unlike him to turn that deliberation inward to brood upon it; meanwhile the boy, and later the "bright young man," spent his waking hours looking for an escape from a world he knew too well.

Whatever may be said about the culture of late Victorian England it opened several doors at the top of the stairway to an H. G. Wells. The largest was labeled "trade"; the others were "Politics," "Tutoring," "Popular Science," and "Journalism." Art, literature, law, and higher branches of the teaching as well as scientific professions and the Church were jealously reserved (as everyone knew) for those who had attended Public School and the two universities, Oxford and Cambridge. And British culture with its romantic acceptance of world empire as well as a popular notion of evolution, was decidedly eclectic. The failure of his father's shopkeeping closed the door of trade to Wells; for this "bright young man" business was a trap, or rather, the risk of failure in it was too obvious, too clear. The other four doors were less hazardous, more attractive; he retained his interest in politics, and combined the usefulness of the latter three: first as apprentice in a chemist's shop, then as a teaching-scholarship boy, then as tutoring student at the Imperial College of Science and Technology at the University of London, and last as journalist for scientific publications. Wells had no illusions concerning the merits of any class or the need of class distinctions. In England he knew that class hierarchies of the Victorian-Edwardian order were rapidly slipping into the past and he noted that decline in his many novels. Unlike George Orwell of a later generation, his liberalism contained no illusions guided by the promises of Marx; therefore he did not share the disillusionment of the latter-day liberal journalist who had followed him.

Wells's independence was that of the aboriginal British islander, overlaid with the hatred of the Anglo-Saxon for Norman rule. He was a rare British republican with no respect for the Crown. This kind of independence made Wells distrust the promises made by the elite, whether they came from the lips of Fabians, Beatrice and Sidney Webb (he saw Sidney Webb as a good civil servant, but no more), or the lips of Lenin. In spite of his vision of a world state, his spirit was the same as the island English who manned boats and ships at the evacuation of Dunkirk and Dieppe in World War II. The evacuation of British troops across the Channel was the work of thousands who had "ordinary" brains, and their accomplishment converted a military disaster into a civilian and island victory.

And last, what of Wells's literary position? Journalism engulfed it and that he knew as well as any of his critics. In his famous quarrel with Henry James (since he could not eat his cake and reserve the crumbs for art) he took the side of journalism versus art, a position held by his predecessor, the arch-Conservative Kipling as well as his contemporary, the pro-Roman-Church journalist, G. K. Chesterton. The position had no taint of compromise as far as art was mentioned. If James was a snob, Wells stood committed as a Philistine: that was the score. Yet his position had more candor, more sturdiness, and was of tougher moral fiber than those held by Hugh Walpole and Arnold Bennett, the two writers of popular fiction who in their day seemed to rival Wells. Both flirted with art. Both had the journalist's ear and eye for what the public of Edwardian taste would care to read; they were happy victims of a *Zeitgeist* that gave them immediate rewards. Their flirtations with art could not extend their fame, nor could the skills of craftsmanship endure beyond the moment of their deaths. Bennett's *The Old Wives' Tale* remains a somber trophy of "what a writer he might have been!" And Henry James's favored novelist in a large group of younger writers was Hugh Walpole, who is remembered best in a biography that deserves to be cherished by more readers than have discovered it: *Hugh Walpole* by Rupert Hart-Davies. Of Wells's contemporaries among the Fabians, only Bernard Shaw ("a raw, aggressive Dubliner" Wells called him) survives the wreckage of an era—but then Shaw had too much wit to flirt with art. When the necessity came for him to use art, he embraced it as though he held a willing actress in his arms in the glare of footlights on the stage. Shaw being Anglo-Irish, and of no place at all either high or low in the British hierarchy of classes, could afford, though poor enough at the beginning of his career in London, a recklessly shabby, genteel, artistocratic air, the prerogative of a foreigner who wrote with a purity of diction that few of his London or Oxford contemporaries could command.

As far as his writing can carry us, the living Wells is preserved for us in three books, the first published in 1895, the last in 1909, *The Time Machine, The First Men on the Moon* and *Tono-Bungay*. The voluminous other writings are likely to collect dust rather than cause a resurrection of the spirit. His Platonic idea that men could be better than they were still haunts the middle streams of British culture, where, incidentally, the sharp distinctions of Britain's upper middle class have been swept away. Since World War II Britain's internal social revolutions have followed a Wellsian model rather than the Marxian pattern of open class warfare, and the household servant class which his mother represented has disappeared. In America, the spread of Wellsian liberal idealism has taken a less political, but no less characteristic, form. It hangs like a rosy mist whenever and wherever heads of large corporations meet to create new foundations for the giving of grants "for culture." On its material side it retains Ponderevo's faith in the "poetry of commerce"—publicity—and relief from income taxes; in the United States the representatives of Wellsian liberalism are often millionaires. But Wells's restless campaign for enlightenment could never be represented by a firebrand held high against the night. Wells's torch is a rod of neon light, unesthetic as you please, a common fixture, diffusing rays upward against passing clouds in a hopeful sky.

1957, 1961

A FOOTNOTE ON THE HISTORICAL NOVEL

> To deal with history means to abandon oneself to chaos and yet to retain a belief in the ordination and the meaning. It is a very serious talk . . . and perhaps also a tragic one.
>
> —Hermann Hesse, *Magister Ludi*

In English the historical novel has a fascinating heritage. Its godfather, if not its actual progenitor, was Sir Walter Scott; and it is an accepted fact that the *Waverly Novels* rapidly furthered the spread of the romantic movement. If Sir Walter lived today, what a marvelous figure he would make in Hollywood! He would still be living beyond his means and twice as far in debt, being paid in the publicity-ridden, faked gold dollars that Hollywood generates in millions. His unfinished estate at Abbotsford—that living dream of anachronic splendor, even in his day—would be twice as large. A brilliant Scots historian, Donald Carswell, remarked that Sir Walter knew everything about history—except its meaning. And so he did; at his worst, he was the literal begetter of the "costume novel"—which from Sir Walter's day to our own always rises to the top rungs of the "best-seller" lists.

At his own best Sir Walter was scarcely a historical novelist at all. His great novels, *The Heart of Midlothian, Guy Mannering, Rob Roy, Redgauntlet,* the spectacular "morbid" romance, *The Bride of Lammermoor,* very nearly existed in *his* present tense. They were of an immediate, Scottish, eighteenth-century past, alive in the memories of Sir Walter's elder contemporaries. It was in the word of mouth, legendary aspects of Scottish scenes and incidents that Sir Walter's imagination gained authority. Except for his facile skill in story-telling, his famous *Ivanhoe* is bookish claptrap, and the same may be said for many of his other ventures into historical romance, all of which are easily convertible into "costume" narratives. Sir Walter was an avid reader of works in his own genre; nor was he as unsophisticated in his knowledge of human behavior and motives as careless readers of his "costume" narratives may suppose. Proof of his critical insights may be shown in his *Lives of the Novelists* and in his appreciation of M. G. Lewis's *The Monk*—which despite its Spanish setting, is the unique example, and supremely so, of an intensely erotic Gothic novel written on Dutch soil and published in

London in 1796. Sir Walter did not fail to read it in its suppressed first edition. Yet it is also clear that Sir Walter's "costume" novels were written for the family circle—which *The Monk* was not—and he reserved his more deeply felt revelations of life for scenes that he knew well, the country north of Edinburgh and in the city itself.

With the exceptions of Dickens and Thackeray, the popular historical novelists of the Victorian age followed the models created by Sir Walter's costume novels—that line remained unbroken, steering its way under titles that are now forgotten. Only the exceptions—Dickens's *Barnaby Rudge* and *A Tale of Two Cities*, as well as Thackeray's *Henry Esmond*—can be said to contain lives of their own. As historians, both Dickens and Thackeray (and in Dickens's case, half unwillingly) accepted *meanings* of history inspired by Macaulay and Carlyle.[1] These twin distorters of history should not be underestimated in the strength of their influence on the Victorian age; it would have been remarkable (since neither Dickens nor Thackeray were professionals in historical research) if they had completely escaped the dominant, and domineering influences gendered by the two historians. Today, Dickens's *Barnaby Rudge* with its Lord George Gordon riots of 1780 is reread, as it should be, in terms of the Chartists agitations which aroused Dickens's sympathies, yet warned him and his readers against the violence of mob rule; *A Tale of Two Cities* is also reread in the light of social maladjustments in mid-nineteenth-century England—yet its interpretation of the French Revolution stems directly from the teachings of Carlyle. Today Thackeray's *Henry Esmond* is less "historical" in import than psychological, and because it is the most tightly, neatly woven of Thackeray's novels, it holds its place on library shelves. Another exception to the costume novel in British historical romances arrived in 1881 in the publication of J. Henry Shorthouse's *John Inglesant.* This romance whose action extends through the years of the English civil war is a "sport" in British fiction, remarkable for its scenes in Italy as well as in England, a theological novel of the first order, disguised as a romance. In fiction, the Anglican Church has no better brief for its position than *John Inglesant.* If not a major novel, it has the distinction of standing alone among nineteenth-century romances.

In the twentieth century the heirs and heiresses of Sir Walter Scott's romances include many costume novels of the American Civil War—whether from the North or South, they breed by hundreds. In this genre innovations are few, and whatever period in history they choose to represent, incidents, costumes, legends, myths are overblown, enlarged, so it seems for Hollywood production. It is better to speak of them as "entertainments," panoramas of battles, ad-

[1] See Macaulay's *History of England* and Carlyle's *French Revolution.*

venturous love affairs, heroics and histrionics tossed against a huge backdrop called the "past." The most high spirited of these, certainly the most hardy, tough, and yet engaging, is Robert Graves's *I, Claudius*. It has already survived more than a quarter century test of time. But what of more recent contributions to historical fiction that are innovations and not purely "entertainments"?

The best, the most vital of recent innovations in the historical novel are written by Winifred Bryher,[2] one of the few novelists of the present generation who has given pertinent, historical meaning to scenes and incidents of the past. Her four novels, *The Fourteenth of October*, *The Player's Boy*, *Roman Wall*, and *Gate to the Sea*, are short, highly charged analogies to situations and problems of loyalty that bedevil our days and nights. She has the insights of a poet, an extraordinary poet, who with fine discrimination selects an illuminating moment of action, and re-creates it in a metaphor that may be applied to twentieth-century dilemmas and choices. In her novel *The Player's Boy* her story of a changing age may be likened to a change of spirit which fell in darkness over Europe immediately following World War II. For her historical analogy to this mutation she chose the reign of James I in England.

The metamorphosis of James VI of Scotland into James I of England, lord of all Britain and its islands, was the sign of a new age falling, not without disaster, from the old. The histrionic abilities of James outmatched the sunsetting glories of the post-Shakespearean stage; he relished treason plots, and probably inspired several of them. He combined metaphysical wit with courtly love of the young Scots gallants he brought down with him from the north, and if he was, like Nero, an indifferent poet, no one could deny his brilliance on the public stage.

The age was also that of Beaumont and Fletcher, of the years that Sir Walter Raleigh, imprisoned by James, wasted in the Tower, and of the coming of the Puritans, who in a later decade were to close the theaters. It is in this dramatic setting that the action of Bryher's novel spins is plot.

The story is told in the person of James Sands, a player's boy, apprentice to an actor of the old school and who, for an all too brief spring holiday, is under the protection of the poet, Francis Beaumont. The story is Sands's story. Beaumont's story—and as Bryher writes it, it is the story of every highly sensitized, gifted poet who is the heir of one age and moves into the violence and destructive passions of the age that follows it.

[2] Born Winifred Ellerman at Margate, Kent, in 1894. The name Bryher, taken from one of the Scilly Isles, was first assumed as a pen name, later adopted legally.

It is impossible to convey the compact artistry of Bryher's prose without quotation:

> The buildings in Cripplegate were unaltered, but otherwise it was a different street. The bright, clear colors of Elizabeth's day were gone with their wearers. Everything was dark and soft, the hated Spanish influence was as apparent here as at Court. These fine, discreet velvets suggested candlelight and conference, the open air of bowling greens would ruin them, these silver laces would tarnish in the rain. . . . Time tangled; it never ran in a straight scythe cut, as they pretended in the moralities, but lay in loops, like the grass at haying time when the conies scampered for safety, and stem and flower were upside down together.

This passage, beautifully tuned to the imagination of James Sands also shows the metaphysical temper of the book as well as its play, one against the other, of pastoral and urban images. No living writer of historical romances can lay claim to the quality of prose that makes *The Player's Boy* a memorable book.

So far I have deliberately withheld a retelling of the book's idyllic love scenes and the tragic implications of its plot—these are for the fortunate reader of the book to rediscover with the assurance that no page lacks dramatic action.

One of the finest scenes in the book is of the crowds that gather to witness Sir Raleigh's execution and, incidentally, few historical novels I have read have re-created moments of the past with greater accuracy of events and of the men affected by them. The portrait of Francis Beaumont is unmistakably true to the man who joined with Fletcher in writing *The Knight of the Burning Pestle.* The violent ending of the book is appropriate to an age in which James I was the royal actor. James might have had Shakespeare as his court poet, John Donne his chaplain, Lancelot Andrews his intimate advisor in theology, and Bacon his lawyer; his ego dimmed his concern with any of these men. He ignored many of the best writers of his day, and the age fell into violence and darkness.

The violent note on which the novel closes has metaphorical reference to the dark scenes in World War II, scenes of treason and treason trials, and in Europe the aftermath of the German occupation of France. The materialistic Puritans in *The Player's Boy* may be likened to Communists, and the cynical manipulations of James I to insure state rule have their likenesses to bureaucratic state power which threatens the artist in any monolithic state.

Her novel *Gate to the Sea* revives an incident of the fourth century B.C. The scene is the port of Paestum, a town known for the beauty of its rose gardens, a Greek colony on the west shores of the boot of Italy, then recently subjected to the tyranny of new and barbarous invaders, the Lucanians. The central figure of the story is Harmonia, priestess of Hera, goddess of religious song, who has chosen to stay in the conquered city so as to preserve Poseidonian relics and to uphold the elder Greek tradition against ignorance and savagery. The greater majority of her friends had become exiles of Paestum, and Greeks had become slaves of invaders, forbidden to speak their own language, forbidden even to remember their old ways of living, their rites, their customs.

The world of the fourth century B.C. at Paestum was not unlike invaded worlds today: a change had come—not for a promised better world but for a spiritually dead, starving, and bitter one in which loyalties vanished, friends betrayed friends; all feared to speak their minds.

Bryher's art in the telling of Harmonia's story is one of understatement; no incident of her trials and disillusionments seems theatrical or contrived, yet each has the strength of quietly exerted power, and that power is related to the quality of Bryher's prose: it is clear, taut, free of rhetorical gestures; it is poetic, yet austere—and many miles away from the pitfalls of the "mandarin style." No one living today writes prose with more quiet, unstressed authority than Bryher's. In telling the story of her heroine's decision to change her mind, to escape from Paestum, to carry the Poseidonian relics to a shrine beyond the reaches of barbarian conquerers, Bryher unfolds a dramatic narrative with high moments of action without losing poise or clarity.

Harmonia's resolution at the close of Bryher's story is an example of what her prose accomplishes. Rescued by loyal sailors, and thinking of her escape from Paestum, Harmonia reflects:

> Someday she might understand the purpose of their suffering, sitting perhaps in a garden at Salente with—and how strange it would be—nothing to fear. . . . The past was over; some intuition told her that a recognition of this fact was the purpose of her liberation; she had to persuade the exiles that it was false to dream of a return and that they must root themselves in the new region that had offered them shelter with such willingness. She stared across the bay: there was their beach outlined by a rim of foam. . . . Then as a welcome darkness blotted out the city, she saw in the last flash of light the towers and the white gateway through which they had passed to freedom, old, indestructible, facing the masterless sea.

This is a passage that every twentieth-century exile should learn to understand. No living novelist has expressed their situation better.

In Bryher's work one sees in progress a fresh approach in the creation of historical fiction; fiction that implies the use of a historical imagination as well as the art to give it meaning.

1961

PAUL ELMER MORE: THE *SHELBURNE ESSAYS*

> The adventurous soul who today against reigning scientific and pragmatic dogma would maintain no vague and equally one-sided idealism, but the true duality of the one and the many, the absolute and the relative, the permanent and the mutable, will find himself subjected to an intellectual isolation and contempt almost as terrible as the penalties of the inquisition, and quite as effective in producing a silent conformity.
>
> —More, *Shelburne Essays, Seventh Series*

Reading these lines some thirty years later since their writing in 1910, and almost a decade after his death in 1937, and despite his own doubts in the merits of prophecy, it would seem that Paul Elmer More had foretold the fate of his posthumous reputation. His *Shelburne Essays* have dropped out of print, and while the mention of his name reawakens echoes of respect, it recalls, not without embarrassment, the more persistent echoes of a literary quarrel which created unhappy diversions in academic circles a quarter of a century ago. In speaking of Paul Elmer More and his *Shelburne Essays*, it is not my intention to revive the heat of a neohumanist controversy which flourished with such a violent show of ill-feeling that its moral issues were lost in the general confusion surrounding them. It was then agreed that Irving Babbitt, who was More's associate and friend, was the better controversialist, and that his personality with its abrasive force struck fire at more frequent intervals. It was true enough that Babbitt secured the greater number of converts to the neohumanist cause; his zeal was no less than the zeal of an evangelist, and though its sincerity and high seriousness remain unquestioned, the evangelical temper which inspired the pages of his *Rousseau and Romanticism* was too obviously ill-suited to the doctrines of restraint and sanity that he essayed to preach. The decorous lamb of neohumanism appeared upon the scene clothed as a lion, but its disguise which had been so artlessly assumed failed to deceive its ingenious and infinitely more worldly enemies; it was quickly stripped of the garments it had worn with such innocent and unlamblike pride, and was subsequently sacrificed on the altars of literary journalism.

Irving Babbitt's best writings are, of course, noncontroversial—and it would seem an impertinence to defend his essays on the masters of French criticism or his introduction to an English version of *The Dhammapada*. The same may be said of More's *Shelburne Essays*, and it is not my purpose to defend them against an unseen attack, and at a distance of nearly forty years. They have weathered well, if somewhat obscurely, on library shelves, and a renewed acquaintance with then readily dispels the darker clouds of a half-forgotten neo-humanist controversy.

2

It can never be said that More underestimated the powers that he felt were ranged against his point of view, but he saw the prospect of "intellectual isolation and contempt" in almost the same spirit as one who secretly enjoys the prospect of an early martyrdom. We may admire the courage of his stand, but I cannot help but think that his invitation to an "adventurous soul" enjoined his readers to share in the disfavors of defeat, and, if so, he opened an unhappy prospect for the general furtherance of his views. Even with the rewards of an inner serenity in sight, the probability of failure was far too great—and in the very decade in which the *Shelburne Essays* were written, the hopeful first decade of the twentieth century, American life was almost totally preoccupied with the visionary as well as material aspects of success: success in extending the ranges of popular education, success in achieving the practical results of Thomas Alva Edison's researches in his laboratory, success in being admitted to New York's 400, success in being presented at the Court of St. James, success in the distribution of novels until they became best-sellers, success in business, success in building the Panama Canal, and success in American affairs abroad—the success of John Hay's "Open Door" policy in China and President Theodore Roosevelt's successful mediation of the Russo-Japanese War. Against all this, More's invitation seemed more austere than it does today; and it seemed more bleak and less certain of achieving a distant victory than a contemplation of the darkest of Thorstein Veblen's gloomy prophecies. It was not that More's views of the future were too black, but that they held the colorless vistas of white and grey. I may be speaking here of a superficial aspect of More's work, but it is one that is almost certain to catch the eye of an impressionable reader:

I cannot doubt [he wrote in the third series of his *Shelburne Essays*] that there are some in the world today who look back over the long past and watch the toiling of the human race toward peace as a traveller in the Alps may with a telescope follow the mountain-climbers in their slow ascent through the snows of Mont Blanc; or again they watch our labours and painstaking in the valley of the senses and wonder at our grotesque industry; or look upon the striving of men to build a city for the soul amid the uncertainties of this life, as men look at the play of children who build castles and domes in the sands of the seashore and cry out when the advancing waves wash all their hopes away.

If one accepts this as a perspective through which More saw the world, the image of Mont Blanc rises to command a view below it, and at that distance, beyond the intimate noises of beach and shore, and where the cry of a human voice, if heard at all, sounds thin and shrill, one sees a wave advance—is it white or grey?—to wash away the castles in the sand.

It is at this distance, and when he is not at his best, that More sometimes fails to meet the moral issues he discerns; they seem remote, or hypothetical, or merely "literary" in the bad sense of the term, and it is as though More had seen them from the steps of the Widener Library at Harvard or from the windows at Bryn Mawr. Throughout his essays one traces the marks of European travel, yet the paths skirt the great cities of London, Paris, and Berlin in favor of the tourist routes of Switzerland and Italy. The paths were those of an academician's holiday from which he viewed "the unshadowed splendour of Mont Blanc" in a little room with a Tauchnitz Edition of Byron's *Don Juan* in his hand. At these moments the setting always seems as though it were a shade too pleasantly suburban; even in his retreat to Shelburne's rural beauties, there to enjoy a rediscovery of Thoreau's *Walden* in the congenial surroundings of brooks and birds and forest greenery, the atmosphere was very nearly as suburban as many sections of New England are today. For since the turn of the old century into the present, New Hampshire has been the summer residence of the well-to-do from Cambridge and from Boston.

In a sense (and by this I do not mean that life in an American university or college is an "escape from life") academic surroundings seem to promote a slightly suburban air. In America the physical aspects of our centers of learning tend to resemble the country club, and, truly enough, many of its vital social activities are concentrated in undergraduate supper clubs and fraternities that however discouraged reemerge under new names on the campus. By the very nature of the task that it performs, an educational institution does not present the hardiest alternatives for a moral critic of American life; its realities are such that they seem unworldly to the man of affairs. Its true limitations have been seriously discussed by Henry Adams, who did not go so far as to say with John Jay Chapman "that teaching dethrones the intellect," but wrote his *Education* for everyone to read; and the limitations are sufficient to explain why no great novel, no first-rate play, nor even a document comparable to Saint-

Simon's memoirs of the court of Louis XIV can come to life within them.

We may be grateful, I think, that another moral critic of literature, Samuel Johnson, so dismally failed in his teaching a boys' grammar school at Litchfield that he took the road with David Garrick, his ex-pupil, to seek his fortune at his nation's capital. How deeply Johnson loved his London is well known, but his love was not inspired nor enhanced by the fact that London was an easy place for him in which to live. We know that it was not; and by the time that Boswell met him, the poise that he had achieved was at the cost of knowing profoundly the wells of human suffering around him and of tasting their depths reflected in his own soul. At each turn of his career his gifts were tested by conflict or agreement with the best minds of his age. In this respect few moral critics (and More was not among them) have suffered or enjoyed Johnson's particular advantages—and what we value most in Johnson's writings, even in his notes on Shakespeare, is the distinctly unliterary character of his observations. In his notes on Falstaff we find the following comment and we delight in the sharpness and depth of his psychological insight:

> Every man who feels in himself the pain of deformity, however, like this merry knight he may affect to make sport with it among those whom it is his interest to please, is ready to revenge any hint of contempt upon one whom he can use with freedom.

We may feel that in some few of his literary judgments Johnson is steadfastly, and at times, cheerfully wrong. We know the limitations that were imposed by the formidable army of his prejudices, which included a dislike of Fielding and a distrust of Scotsmen and Americans, yet within the world he knew so well (and that world was at his nation's heart and was circumscribed by one of the great cities of modern civilization) the rightness of judgment remains as sound as on the day he wrote his note on one of King Henry's speeches:

> Shakespeare urges this aggravation of the guilt of treachery with great judgment. One of the worst consequences of breach of trust is the diminution of that confidence which makes the happiness of life, and the dissemination of suspicion, which is the poison of society.

We cannot expect to find anything of like derivation in Paul Elmer More's *Shelburne Essays*, and turning westward from Johnson's London, we enter a more rarefied, brighter, harsher, and (if I may say so, even in praise of America's most distinguished humanist) a less distinctly humanized atmosphere.

3

Someone has spoken—it does not matter who, for no doubt many others have made the same observation—of the delightful urbanity of the prose which graces the early *Shelburne Essays*. Urbanity in prose was one of the standards by which the nineteenth century measured its approval of an essay in literary criticism, and an early twentieth-century reaction against the arts of being urbane was natural; urbanity seemed to cover a lack of seriousness, to remind one, if ever so slightly, of the hypocritical heart that knew of neither Freud nor Jung, and yet was satisfied to beat its tattoo securely beneath a tightly buttoned-up frock coat. In reading the *Shelburne Essays* we are aware of their proximity to the Victorian scene in literature, and More could not deny his affection for its lesser figures, its Lionel Johnson, its George Gissing, or a forgotten poetess, Louisa Shore, but however urbane he may have seemed, there is no lack of seriousness in what he had to say. And today, now that the nineteenth century is at a proper distance behind us, we are less frightened by the presence of its urbanity than we were, let us say, twenty-five years ago. To speak of Tennyson or of Longfellow no longer awakens the discomfort that was once felt. We are in a position to see how steadily More viewed the merits and flaws of Longfellow's poetry, how careful he was not to patronize it, or to dismiss its hold upon popular imagination. In reading his essay on Longfellow, one discerns More's mingled debt to an Emersonian habit of speech and his affection for that most urbane of nineteenth-century essayists, Charles Lamb. One sees and hears that heritage throughout the essay, and its eloquence is clearly overheard in the concluding paragraph in which More speaks of Longfellow's adaptations from Dante:

> We need have no fear of paying homage to a poet who wrote such lines as these. And he himself, if he did not, like Dante and his peers build at the great cathedral of song, did at least add to it a fair and homely chapel, where also, to one who comes humbly and reverently, the eternal ages watch and wait.

Perhaps the flourish at the end of his last sentence is still a shade too rhetorical for our taste, but it was said gracefully, and after More had stated plainly that Longfellow's great weakness was in mistaking the offices of fancy for those of imagination. No critic in America has written of Longfellow so searchingly and well, and it is to More's enduring credit that he performed a skillful operation without maiming or disfiguring his patient—and the result (which is something extremely rare in criticism) is that after More has weighed the balance of Longfellow's tarnish and brass against his merits, one returns to a reading of his poetry with a keener, if more strictly limited, appreciation than before.

In his *Shelburne Essays,* More practiced the art of suspending his esthetic and moral judgments, and one awaits, quite as one waits for the fall of an ax, for the place and the moment at which the sharpened edges of his discrimination are going to fall. More's temperament was far too seriously inclined to allow for a play of wit, and on the rare occasions when he did employ it, it arrives with the sensation of an overweighted shock upon the sensibilities of the reader. Something of that shock is felt as one reads his comment on Arthur Symons's verse:

> There are things it were good for a man, even for a decadent poet, not to have written, and these poems to Bianca, with their tortuous effort to find the soul in the ambiguities and unclean curiosities of a swaying will are of them. They are a waste of shame.

Since we are on the subject of More's remarks concerning the "decadence" or symbolism of Symons's poetry I think a word should be said of More's general attitude toward symbolism. As he wrote of Symons's "unclean curiosities," which does seem strong language to apply as one rereads a stanza or two of flaccid and derivative verse, More's position was by no means untenable. The verse is weak and one is not disposed to defend it, but when one comes across More's remark that Baudelaire's poetry is equally "unclean," a warning is sounded that we should not ignore. The same warning is heard as we reread More's attempts to elevate the talents of Lionel Johnson and Lady Augusta Gregory above the poetic gifts of W. B. Yeats. It is not enough to say that More's moral philosophy demanded a consistency that would automatically reject Yeats's poetry and the presence of Baudelaire; that consistency had already suffered a compromise in More's acceptance of Dante Gabriel Rossetti's poetry and James Thomson's poem, *The City of Dreadful Night.* In respect to Baudelaire and Yeats, More's rejection of their poetry has two slightly different faces than the one he presents to Romantic "decadence" in British verse. His language is that of nineteenth-century criticism, and nineteenth-century criticism was not equipped to recognize the techniques in poetry that the early symbolists employed and passed on to their heirs. Another aspect of More's rejection of Yeats and Beaudelaire is more closely related to the thoroughly Protestant character of his morality, and he was always likely to seem capricious or uncertain whenever he spoke of an Irish literature or entered the presence of what Henry Adams discerned at Mont St. Michel and Chartres.

In both word and spirit, More had seen "decadence" at work in a literature that started bravely enough with the Lake Poets, and declined through the course of a century to the less happy moments of Elizabeth Barrett Browning, Swinburne, and William Morris, and there is no need for me to reenlarge upon that kind of "decadence" here. Yet what of the symbolists and their heritage which has affected every major poet who came early or late to his maturity between 1900 and the beginning of the Second World War? We should admit that where More saw merely a continuation of the "decadence" that he perceived so clearly in the doctrines, the verse, and the prose of Oscar Wilde, E. A. Robinson, More's contemporary, had been refreshed by a discovery of Verlaine, and W. B. Yeats had found a touchstone for lyrical impressionism in Mallarmé. Yet the very poets who received the greatest benefit from a youthful enthusiasm in practicing the techniques and attitudes of symbolism, also outgrew them, or so modified the original poetry as stemming solely and directly from its influence. What More underestimated was the hardiness (with all its seeming fraility and lassitude) of the poetic imagination possessed by Yeats. In general, all literary movements, no matter what their names may be, fail to circumscribe the gifts of a writer who is fortunate enough to arrive at his maturity; but the less gifted are always left behind, suffering the limitations of a particular school, or the instructions of an early master.

If More saw little of the strength that was implicit in Yeats's slowly maturing genius, he was by no means uncertain of the values that Hawthorne's imagination brought to light, or the salutary results of reappraising the poetry of George Crabbe. More may have been aware (but this one cannot prove) that his perception of Crabbe's merit had been shared by E. A. Robinson; if it was not, there is still room for speculation as to whether Robinson had read his essay, either as it appeared in a periodical, or after it was gathered into a selection of a *Second Series of Shelburne Essays* in 1905. However that may be, there is a passage in More's essay on Crabbe that parallels and reilluminates one of the major themes of Robinson's poetry. More wrote of Crabbe:

His own early life in a miserable fishing hamlet on the Suffolk coast, under a hard father, his starving years of literary apprenticeship in London, and then for a time the salt bread of a dependency as private chaplain to the Duke of Rutland, acquainted him with many sorrows which years of comparative prosperity could not entirely obliterate. He is at bottom a true Calvinist, showing that peculiar form of fatalism which still finds it possible to magnify free will, and to avoid the limp surrender of determinism. Mankind as a body lies under a fatal burden of suffering and toil, because as a body men are depraved and turn from righteousness; but to the individual man there always remains open a path up from darkness into light, a way out of condemnation into serene peace. And it is with this mixture of judicial aloofness and hungering sympathy that Crabbe dwells on the sadness of long and hopeless waiting, the grief of broken love, the remorse of wasted opportunities, the burden of poverty, the solitude of failure, which run like dark threads through most of his *Tales.*

The setting of Crabbe's verse as More interpreted it recalls the atmosphere of Robinson's poem, *The Man Who Died Twice,* but more important than a general resemblance of human sympathy and insight is More's specific observation that "to the individual man there always remains open a path up from darkness into light, a way out of condemnation into serene peace." This is what the man who died twice has to say even with his last breath:

"Why pity me?"
He asked strangely, "You see that I'm content.
I shall not have to be here very long,
And there's not much that I may do for God
Except to praise him. I shall not annoy you,
Or your misguided pity, with my evangel,
For you must have yours in another dress."

And with a lighter measure of poetic tact and grace, Robinson reiterated the theme in *Archibald's Example:*

"My green hill yonder, where the sun goes down
Without a scratch, was once inhabited
By trees that injured him—an evil trash
That made a cage, and held him while he bled.

"Gone fifty years, I see them as they were
Before they fell. They were a crooked lot
To spoil my sunset, and I saw no time
In fifty years for crooked things to rot.

"Trees, yes; but not a service or a joy
To God or man, for they were thieves of light.
So down they came. Nature and I looked on,
And we were glad when they were out of sight.

"Trees are like men, sometimes; and that being so,
So much for that." He twinkled in his chair,
And looked across the clover to the place
That he remembered when the trees were there.

In his temperamental responsiveness to Crabbe's verse, More is far more persuasive than in his attack on Arthur Symons or in his praise of Elizabeth Gaskell's novels; his moral earnestness which in certain of his essays seems so shrill and out of key resumes its poise as one reads what he had to say on the subject of solitude and Nathaniel Hawthorne. In this essay, and through the twentieth-century's respect for Henry James (whose monograph on Nathaniel Hawthorne in the English Men of Letters series is one of the finest critical biographies in modern literature) and by a path that More felt was the "teaching . . . of the universal protest of the human heart," those limitations, which so frequently had placed him behind the invisible line marked by the first hour struck in the year of 1900, begin to drop away. Speaking as I am from the mid-years of the century that More so heartily mistrusted, and indeed, a measure of his distrust is justified by our experiences in the presence of two World Wars, his illumination of Hawthorne's "philosophic symbolism" (the phrase is his) may seem more fashionable than More himself would have desired. To *The Solitude of Nathaniel Hawthorne* More brought those resources that he had gained in his studies of India's forest philosophers and from his well-considered knowledge of the Orestean cycle in Greek tragedy. How pertinently he wrote of Hawthorne when he said:

> But if Aeschylus and Hawthorne are alike poets of Destiny and of the fateful inheritance of woe, their methods of portraying the power and handiwork of Ate are perfectly distinct. The Athenian too represents Orestes, the last inheritor of the curse, as cut off from the fellowship of mankind; but to recall the Orestean tale, with all its tragic action of murder and matricide and frenzy, is to see in a clearer light the originality of Hawthorne's conception of moral retribution in the disease of inner solitude. There is in difference something, of course, of the constant distinction between classic and modern art; but added to this is the creative idealism of Hawthorne's rare and elusive genius.

This, I believe, is one of the happiest of More's analogies, and as he speaks of Hawthorne's "rare and elusive genius," I doubt if there are many better examples, such as More has given us, of an artist's dual responsibility to life and art. The very theme of his essay seems to have touched a hidden spring in More's imaginative life, and the images that rise from it are those that show the subtle likenesses and contrasts between the peace of solitude and the terrors of human isolation.

It is this vein that More wrote his essay on *Nemesis, or the Divine Envy*, in which the instruction, "Think as a mortal," runs as an obbligato through its theme. The instruction itself is a familiar law of ethical discourse, and if restated baldly it has little meaning to the modern ear, but it was More's intention to renew its life, and as in his essay on Hawthorne's solitude, he calls on the spirit of Aeschylus to illustrate his text:

With implacable zeal the Erinyes hunt down earthly glory that vaunts itself unduly. So in the play of Aeschylus they exclaim: "The vanity of men and their pride that toucheth the sky,—all this melteth at our dark-stoled approach, it wasteth away unhonoured under earth." In these fearful daughters of Night the Greek beheld the penalty that overtakes those who forget in pride or madness to think as mortals: and woe to the man whom some higher law impels to disdain these avenging deities, whether it be a Hamlet of the modern world driven on by conscience and ghostly apparitions, or an Orestes summoned by oracular voices to confront their wrath in pursuance of a sterner duty. And woe to the man whom the gods have endowed with superhuman wisdom, for to him also the grace of heaven is not without peril.

I think I am not far wrong if I assume that the tone of these remarks is scarcely that of one who is merely an accomplished reader in comparative literatures—something else is there, and I believe it to be the voice of a man who had come to speak a sermon. The voice was heard when Samuel Johnson wrote his *Life of Richard Savage*, and it was decidedly less agreeable to the ear of the reader twenty-five years ago than it is today. I think I am not wrong when I say that we are less frightened by More's approach to his subject than in the days of revolt against the Puritan tradition in American literature; to admit that men are less than gods does not infringe, I hope, upon those liberties which have survived the events and the emergencies of the past thirty years.

The preaching of a lay sermon is, of course, a dangerous practice for any modern writer, and his greatest danger (which may arrive as tribute to his gifts) is to become the leader of a literary cult; it was that misfortune which attended the latter years of D. H. Lawrence's life, and within it there are many open trap doors through which the unwary writer falls. To find and perhaps to preach sermons in stones may have done very well for the companions of the melancholy Jaques in Arden's forest, but we remember those sermons best when they were recited as conscious parodies of their devotions, and in that old play it is the clown who rules the scene.

In rereading More it is not difficult to recall that the best of Emerson's prose writings were those that could be read as though they were delivered from a pulpit, and I think there can be little doubt that it was More's intention to strengthen, even though it seemed to narrow, the vein of humanism which runs its course throughout the somewhat amorphous, and certainly all-embracing teachings of Emerson. The failure of Emerson's idealism was one of the contributing causes of the tragic failure of Woodrow Wilson's position at the close of the First World War: could we say that in his moment of pride that Woodrow Wilson failed to think as a mortal?

There is much that might be written of More's quarrel with science in his *Shelburne Essays;* it was not a happy quarrel, and as I have said before, More was not a fortunate controversialist. His concern was that of a moral philosopher whose sensibilities responded to the "truths" that had been revealed to him through literature, and in particular, through the poetic literature of an Anglo-American tradition. Poetic "truth," of course, is of a different order than scientific "truth," and the difference between them has been best said in Basil Willey's study of *The Seventeenth Century Background*:

> For in poetry thought is not pure, it is working in alliance with the feelings and the will. In Bacon's phrase, it "subjects the show of things to the desires of the mind"—which is the exact reverse of the process called science.

It is better to recognize the moral "truths" of literature as a process in reverse of a nonmoral aspect of scientific thinking than to insist, as More did, than an irreconcilable quarrel existed between them. The actual "truth" that More conveys to us (and that reality is implicit in his essays on Nemesis and Hawthorne) needs no apology—but here the question is not an academic one, and is, as it should be, closely related to those ancient "truths" which are constantly refreshed and given an enduring life in poetic literature. Here, the proper relationships between man and man and gods and men are not to be denied: and is it a paradox to say that More realized the fulfillment of his moral "truths" only when he restored the practices of moral criticism to the dignity and seriousness of a fine art?

Someone has said, and with a lightness of inflection that made the statement seem disarming, that poetry itself is a moral art. And so it seems to be in the Protestant tradition of an Anglo-American literature. The statement explains to some degree the depths of More's perception as he regarded the values of Hawthorne's "rare and elusive genius," for Hawthorne, like Henry James, is among those writers of prose whose art existed within a world of poetic realities. In his interpretations of Aeschylus and of India's forest philosophers, Paul Elmer More shared an insight of that world, and in his application of the precepts from ancient sources, one rediscovers their reality in American literature.

One word more. As the present century reaches its meridian, to be humane, and to be aware that the wrath of Nemesis pursues the would-be conquerors of our world are merits that had been forgotten before the arrival of two World Wars. And to be humanitarian in one's desires is associated with too many of the mistakes that we have made. The broad wave of humanitarianism has spread too thinly, for the trials of the present century are not washed away by it, and there is too much evidence of wreckage on its shores. If I may be permitted to dismiss my metaphor and to speak plainly of a conflict between two words that has gone on longer than anyone cares to remember, let us say that the virtues of being humane have more inherent strength and a deeper penetration into a true knowledge of the human spirit than the transient rewards of the humanitarian impulse and its facile disillusionments. But as More once wrote, "these questions that touch man's deepest moral experience are not capable of logical solution; indeed, they lose all reality as soon as they are subjected to dogmatic definition." The knowledge that we truly seek is how to live, and to do so we turn with More to those realities that the Greeks perceived in the presence of Divine Envy and that Hawthorne saw when he wrote his fable of *The Minister's Black Veil.* It is in these terms that the answer must be read, in the very image of Nemesis, in the tragedy of Orestes, in the story of Job's trial, and in the maturity of Adam's knowledge as he left the garden of Eden.

1944

MUTATIONS OF RELIGIOUS FAITH IN MODERN FICTION

Whenever we are about to enter a new decade of our extremely self-conscious twentieth century, a renewed effort is made to sum up the mutations of spiritual faith as they have been expressed in contemporary literature.[1] For the present we seem to be passing through long stretches of unfaith, and the churches have become self-critical, or rather, self-conscious to a high degree. This habit of self-examination had its beginnings, I think, in the nineteenth century, which during its middle years, took an optimistic view: and in the popular mind Darwinian Evolution was proof of Progress as though it were a continuous advancement of enlightened apes and men slowly walking upward on an inclined plane. And parallel to this, Progress was also read into the increase of material wealth and advances in technological development.

In saying this I am, of course, unjust to enlightened intellectuals of the Victorian era, for so far as I know, few of them conceived of Darwinism in such naive terms, but for the moment, I am concerned with a general concept that spread its branches into the popular arts, sciences, and philosophies: and in this area, metaphysics as well as religious faiths were swept into a far corner and almost hidden from view. Promises of change into a better material world filled the air: something very like an earthly, if mechanical, Paradise seemed just about to arrive around the corner. London's Crystal Palace was regarded as a preview of marvels. Even worthy poets were entranced by the hope of continual change. With his accustomed brilliance and skill, Tennyson inverted the popular notion of the upward tilting plane into:

> Not in vain the distance beacons. Forward, forward
>   let us range.
> Let the great world spin forever down the ringing
>   grooves of change.

So much then for the ideas of straight line, continuous change. Let me modify them by saying they more properly describe changes in

[1] If the tone of this piece seems to differ from that of other essays in this book it is well to remember that its source is from an informal discussion of a general group of ideas in a symposium on spiritual problems in today's literature.

fashion rather than changes in art, and they can be applied with more accuracy to strictly mechanical inventions—such as the development of the first gasoline engine to the design of the first motored airplane. Human beings, in the growth and decline of their civilizations, do not move in straight lines backward or forward, or up and down; their movements are not as neatly mechanical as that. "The ringing grooves of change" which Tennyson all too cleverly conceived as an eternal railroad track are irrelevant to the circular, often spiral movements of human imagination and beliefs.

I

I am not, of course, the only one to speak of discontinuous change in cultural developments. W. B. Yeats held to the notion of spiral changes in civilizations, and Paul Valéry remarked many years ago, that literature, as he saw it, was always discontinuous—that what he discerned as new movements in literature did not proceed directly from one another in temporal sequence. One may find an example of Valéry's observation in the sequences of Poe to Whitman, from Whitman to Edwin Arlington Robinson in American poetry. Certainly the contrasting changes in poetry here, which took place between 1840 and 1900 are discontinuous. The mutation did not "progress" in a straight line.

I happen to think that mutations of belief, as they transform the arts are, in reality, a series of intersecting spirals in our culture, and at the point where one intersects the other, we call that transformation in appearance, "change." In this sense, no purely scientific, religious, moral, or even esthetic, work of art exists. This also implies that works of art carry the impress of all-too-human lack of perfection; they are a fusion of impure elements reflecting the character of the civilization that gave them birth.

In my time, perhaps the most influential of writers effecting a change in attitudes toward literature was James Joyce. It is of some importance to remember that he regarded himself as living within a Christian world, and that however violent a critic he became of Irish Catholic bigotries, he remained within the orbit of Roman Catholic associations and references: his blasphemies were actual blasphemies, and the cast of his thinking was theological. The speaker in his *Stephen Hero* was, of course, the early Joyce, whose "Esthetic was in the main 'applied Aquinas.' " From there onward he ruminated over redefinitions of critical terms:

The artist, he imagined, standing in the position of mediator between the world of his experience and the world of his dreams—'a mediator, consequently gifted with two faculties, a selective faculty and a reproductive faculty.' To equate these faculties was the secret of artistic success: the artist who could disentangle the subtle soul of the image from its mesh of defining circumstances most exactly and 're-embody' in artistic circumstances chosen as the most exact for its new office, he was the supreme artist. This perfect coincidence of the two artistic faculties Stephen called poetry and he imagined the domain of an art to be cone-shaped. Again he used it to designate the vast middle region which lies between apex and base, between poetry and the chaos of unremembered writing. Its merit lay in its portrayal of externals: the realm of its princes was the realm of the manners and customs of societies—a spacious realm. But society is itself, he conceived, the complex body in which certain laws are involved and overwrapped and he therefore proclaimed as the realm of the poet the realm of these unalterable laws. Such a theory might easily have led its devisor to the acceptance of spiritual anarchy in literature had he not at the same time insisted on the classical style. A classical style, he said, is the syllogism of art, the only legitimate process from one world to another. Classicism is not the manner of any fixed age or any fixed country: it is a constant state of the artistic mind. It is a temper of security and satisfaction and patience. The romantic temper, so often and so grievously misinterpreted and not more by others than its own, is an insecure, unsatisfied, impatient temper which sees no fit abode here for its ideas and chooses therefore to behold them under insensible figures. As a result of this choice it comes to disregard certain limitations. Its figures are blown to wild adventures, lacking the gravity of solid body, and the mind that has conceived them ends by disowning them. The classical temper on the other hand, ever mindful of limitation, chooses rather to bend upon these present things and so work upon then and fashion them that the quick intelligence may go beyond them to their meaning which is still unuttered.[2]

As everyone knows today, *Ulysses* was the result of Joyce's long thoughts throughout the writing of *Stephen Hero* and *The Portrait of the Artist as a Young Man*—his need for change and a redefinition of terms regarding the novel was proved by his re-creation of the Ulysses myth in Dublin. Clearly enough the spiral intersections of Hebraic, Christian and Greco-Roman cultures may be discerned within the stresses of Stephen's consciousness; and Hebraic-Christian moralities in flux are reevoked during the famous drunken dream scene of the book. It is important, I think, that they serve so prominently here, that in an age of growing unfaith (which describes Joyce's decades as well as ours) rather special stress is placed upon

[2] *Stephen Hero,* by James Joyce. Edited from the manuscript in the Harvard College Library by Theodore Spencer. A new edition incorporating the additional manuscript pages in the Yale University Library, edited by John J. Slocum and Herbert Calhoun. New York: A New Directions Book, 1955.

"the showing-forth" and rituals of spiritual rebirth. In these mutations of religious faith sanctimonious church-going tends to drop out of favor and a more critical, more discriminating spirit enters devotional exercises.

2

It has also been no secret that we are living through seventy years of a "scientific age"—and it was not until recently that a few intellectuals in the United States and England rediscovered that they were still alive in a world where religion and ethics were not totally abandoned. At the very least, a religious cultural heritage still held some meaning. During the past seventy years the emergence of the totalitarian state in Italy, in Germany, in Russia have offered examples of how a political machine—and I use the word "machine" advisedly—assumes absolute power.

The sight of a blacked-out Europe, rained upon by bombs and rockets, was not a reassuring spectacle, particularly, if one had viewed science as among the wonders that had been evolved by man for the betterment of mankind. A hundred years ago, young men and women, faced by the promises that an advancing technology had brought before them, grew doubtful of the kind of security on earth offered them by religion. Today the same measure of doubt enters the thinking of those who believed too blindly in the security attendant upon scientific progress. Doubt has begun to undermine the cheerful tenets of absolute state power, of utilitarianism, and of pragmatism. A popular expression of this reversal of belief is voiced by Malcolm Muggeridge (who once thought of himself as a Marxist):

> I believe that without a God, and the humility that goes therewith, man is in the process of destroying himself, and perhaps his world as well, that having no sense of moral order, he will increasingly find it impossible to create any order whatsoever; that, separated from God, he must either fall into the sin of pride, imagining himself to be God-like, and like Icarus flying disastrously into the Sun, or relapse into animality . . .[3]

If there is any change in the temper of imaginative writing between the dates of 1900–1970, the loss of faith in material and scientific progress is among the elements of that change; it colors our thoughts, hopes, and fears. And in saying this I become aware that in using the phrase "imaginative writing"—which is very broad indeed—I had better begin to limit my discussion to the area of modern fiction; for the poets of Western civilization have for the greater part—and with remarkable consistency—regarded science through the lenses, "opera

[3] *The Listener*, 1 October 1970.

glasses," if you will, of irony and skepticism. Among poets, belief in material philosophies has been extremely rare, and in their writings—whenever attempted—the effort to infuse their language with the shoptalk of science, including that of social science and psychology, has often resulted in strange absurdities. As bizarre—or even more so—as Tennyson's "ringing grooves of change."

But writers of fiction have been less fortunate than the poets. In the majority of cases, their standards of success have been modified by commercial values. However strongly a novelist believes what he writes, his survival often depends upon his ability to cope with the fashions of his day—or with whatever his publisher thinks pleases the public. In both England and the United States the publisher tends to regard a work of fiction in the same light as that of any other piece of perishable merchandise placed on the market. This general rule, to which there are notable exceptions, applies to thousands of volumes published every year.

My concern is not with these great tons and masses of fiction that are offered for sale as though they were products on display in a supermarket. Changes in belief cannot be charted by attempts to make our way through floods of superficial undistinguished commercial writings. On deeper levels than these a few observations can be made. Between 1918 and 1970 the fiction once defined by Zola's "naturalism" died a natural death. Even those who had emulated Zola—the most noteworthy of these being Theodore Dreiser—began to feel that the so-called "natural" laws of biology and environment could not explain all the springs and motives of human action, will, and desire. It is of some interest to observe that in his old age Dreiser created a hero whose virtues were derived from a Quaker heritage in which the American model of conduct was the saintly figure of John Woolman.

3

At the turn of the century, when his novels began to appear, Joseph Conrad, like so many others, was accepted as a realist. Even then, he was regarded as a realist who held to many points of difference from the attitudes of his fellow writers. The almost rugged strictness of his prose was consistent with the unblinking austerities of his moral convictions. Behind him loomed the stern beliefs of the Polish Roman Catholic Church: and he had retained the tensions of its moralities in his writings. The following quotations from his *Lord Jim* will illustrate this point—and these, like my quotation from *Stephen Hero*, are pertinent to the writer's attitude toward life and art:

"He lifted up a long forefinger.

" 'There is only one remedy! One thing alone can us from being ourselves cure!' The finger came down on the desk with a smart rap.

The case which he had made to look so simple before became if possible still simpler—and altogether hopeless. There was a pause. 'Yes,' said I, 'strictly speaking, the question is not how to get cured, but how to live.'

"He approved with his head, a little sadly as it seemed. 'Ja! Ja! In general, adapting the words of your great poet: That is the question . . .' He went on nodding sympathetically. 'How to be! Ach! How to be!'

"He stood up with the tips of his fingers resting on the desk.

" 'We want in so many different ways to be,' he began again. 'This magnificent butterfly finds a little heap of dirt and sits still on it; but man he will never on his heap of mud keep still. He want to be so, and again he want to be so . . .' He moved his hand up, then down. 'He wants to be a saint, and he wants to be a devil—and every time he shuts his eyes he sees himself as a very fine fellow so fine as can never be . . . I a dream . . .'

. . . .

" 'And because you not always can keep your eyes shut there comes the real trouble—the heart-pain—the world-pain. I tell you, my friend, it is not good for you to find you cannot make your dream come true, for the reason that you not strong enough are, or not clever enough. Ja!. . . And all the time you are such a fine fellow, too! . . . How can that be? . . .

. . . .

" 'Yes! Very funny this terrible thing is. A man that is born falls into a dream like a man who falls into the sea. If he tries to climb out into the air as inexperienced people endeavor to do, he drowns—nicht wahr? . . . No! I tell you! The way is to the destructive element submit yourself, and with the exertions of your hands and feet in the water make the deep, deep sea keep you up. So if you ask me—how to be?' "[4]

Conrad's phrase, "the destructive element," caught the attention of his seriously minded contemporaries. It haunted the consciousness of Henry James, who was later to write: "In the destructive immerse. That is the way." It was certainly a way toward making a drastic confrontation with a spiritual problem—or advancing further the difficult "showing-forth" of moral conflicts. On James's part it took decisions of this kind to prepare him for the writing of one of his masterpieces—*The Altar of the Dead*. I should also say that the candle lights and visions in James's famous story were what reflects Swedenborgian imagery that deeply influenced the spiritual life and writings of the three Jameses: Henry, Sr., William, and Henry, Jr. And it is possible that the "fields of light" referred to in *The Altar of the Dead* was an echo of Henry Vaughan's "they are all gone into the

[4] *Lord Jim, A Tale*, by Joseph Conrad. Garden City, New York: Doubleday, Page & Co., 1927.

world of light," for the long Vaughan poem was well known to readers who had been attracted to mysticism, spiritualism, and the findings of the Society of Psychical Research.

In Europe and immediately after its World War I, the apotheosis of naturalism, stripped of its hopes, was reached in Celine's *Journey to the End of Night.* Celine's protagonist was an absolute nihilist, a physician, an unsuccessful practitioner in the slums of Paris, the touch of whose hand upon a patient was the touch of death. In itself the book was a complete negation of the humane spirit—a naturalist document that took a last step downward in a long line of realistic writings that had begun with the *Confessions of Rousseau.* During the 1920s, the forces of naturalism were further dispersed by the arrival of François Mauriac, a theological novelist of the first order, whose *Woman of the Pharisees* came as contra-action to the tenets of realism that preceded it, and is another illustration of changes in the artist's perception as well as of discontinuity in the evolution of literature. And as far as more popular, as well as more superficial movements in French literature were concerned, surrealism had taken the place of naturalistic formulas. Newer formulas created in the name of psychoanalytic analysis were substituted for the earlier, less imaginative, camera lens, day-by-day recording of human behavior, which had been put into practice by Zola and Dreiser.

In America during the late 1930s, it had become evident that naturalism in fiction had literally traveled to the end of night, and that Marxist materialism had revealed itself as antagonistic to imaginative fiction of the twentieth century—unless the meaning of a book could be twisted to serve Marxian ends. Critics of fiction then turned to three sources of newly awakened inspiration: the novels of Henry James, of Herman Melville, and of Franz Kafka. Of these it is of some interest to note that James had gone through three separate stages of interpretation: first, as a psychological novelist, then, as a critic of society, and, third, as a moralist, scrupulous in his attention to Christian ethics. This last stage has had its weight upon younger writers of the 1940s. The latter two writers of fiction were rediscovered as carriers of a biblical and Hebraic heritage and what was first admired in Kafka as realism—and the same interpretation attended early readings of James Joyce's *Ulysses*—became transformed into a glimmering vision of Kafka's religious purpose, with its relationships between man and man and the inaccessibility of God. It was then rediscovered that Melville's contribution to our literature was transcendental in its import. These rediscoveries began to fill the vacuum that had been created through the general collapse of realism.

In Britain, changing attitudes toward religion were heralded by the neo-Catholic satires of Evelyn Waugh—and readers were entertained and refreshed by the startling arrival of his *Vile Bodies*—a revelation of what "Bright Young People" in the set surrounding Lady Diana Manners thought and did during the small hours of the morning. Not since the publication of Thackeray's *Vanity Fair* had the English novel served the purposes of satire so brilliantly and well. Parallel to Waugh's series of novels, came Graham Greene's "entertainments," the best of which was *Brighton Rock,* a neo-Catholic parable in the form of a psychological crime story. But *Sword of Honour,* Waugh's last recording of a changing world through the disasters of World War II, will probably remain the most enduring example of religious fiction written in England during the present century. Among writers in Britain, after the disasters of two world wars, the revivals of faith in Roman Catholicism brought with them two notable reassertions of faith in The Established Church: Charles Williams's essay *The Descent of the Dove,* and in fiction, Anthony Powell's *The Valley of Bones,* an important segmant of his major work, *A Dance to the Music of Time.*

In American writing since 1918 intimations of change in religious attitudes have been less obvious than in Europe—yet even here, signs of a shifting away from nineteenth-century agnosticism are to be found among our more significant novelists. The Roman Catholic boyhood of F. Scott Fitzgerald contributes meaning to the tragic sense of loss, "the Fall," in *The Great Gatsby,* and in William Faulkner's *Light in August* the ineffectuality of the defrocked minister has a powerful undercurrent of inevitable loss with the abandonment of religious authority. Willa Cather's writings also contributed to a reassertation of Christian ethics in American fiction—and the early short stories of J. F. Powers, particularly in his *Prince of Darkness,* have something of the same sensitivity to Roman Catholic moralities.

In showing the existence of a survival of religious feeling within the areas of modern fiction, one should be careful not to overstate the case. The age through which we are living is still one of unfaith, perhaps as dark and as far out of the sight of God as in St. Augustine's century. Through the mutations in cultural climate and the very nature of discontinuity in art, the darkness of an era may still admit small shafts of light. Joyce's *Stephen Hero,* even with his doubts of orthodox faith, saw his way clear toward a preservation of the human spirit:

> The imagination has contemplated intently the truth of the being, of the visible world, and the beauties and splendor of truth has been born. The imagination, though it bury itself fathoms deep in formulas and machinery, has need of these realities which alone give and sustain life and it must await from those chosen centers of civilization the force to live, the security for life, which can come to it only from them. Thus the spirit of man makes a continual affirmation.

1957, 1970

A PORTRAIT OF THE IRISH AS JAMES JOYCE

What of the Irish? The first association is that of sentimental rubbish: pigs and poverty, green harps, broken clay pipes, priests, bogs, pale-colored whiskey, sorrowing mothers, white-skinned half-naked girls, dirt, tears, murder, and maudlin songs. After that, a pious, betraying, shrewd, Godhaunted, Devil-possessed, God-cursed, embittered, timid, brave, lecherous, prudish, naive, innocent, guilt-ridden, proud people—which is a fraction nearer a romantic truth. And added to this was an old idea: "Every Irishman is a King; every Irishman is a poet"—particularly the latter. Evidence of Kingship vanished centuries ago, but the halo of Kingship remained. Scarcely more tangible was the conviction, "Every Irishman, a poet":

Ich am of Irlonde
Ant of the holy londe
   Of Irlonde.
Gode sire, pray ich the,
For of saynte charite,
Come ant dance wyth me
In Irlonde.

This was a fragment of a beggar girl's song—set down by God knows whom. It whined a bit, yet it was poetry and held real music in it. How does it stand with the claim that every Irishman is a poet? Not very strongly. Behind it however was a fanatical belief: poetry and Ireland were one. Past the middle of the seventeenth century, a great half-poet, Jonathan Swift was born in Dublin. Near the middle of the eighteenth century Oliver Goldsmith, outwardly a brave-timid, naive-witty Irishman who talked foolishly, and whenever he had money, tossed it away, wrote *The Deserted Village*, a poem that steadily improves with time. It looked as though the Irish claim were lost. One poet only was the score: and one supremely modest poem. Of course there were poems in Gaelic—but could these make a literature? They were too fragmentary. The fanatical belief persisted, a belief that was the triumph of wild imagination over possibilities: then came Yeats, the excitement of the Celtic Renaissance, and a crowd of minor writers (seemingly descended from Tom Moore), then Bernard Shaw and George Moore (who today is rated lower than he should be) and James Joyce. To the bewilderment of the Irish themselves, the Irish claims came true, and a truth that is extended in the writings of Samuel Beckett. A tradition of belief suddenly paid off: it was like watching a river of quarters and half dollars pour from the opened doors of a two cent slot machine.

The score may now be counted: five writers of the first order: Yeats, Shaw, Joyce, O'Faolain (the short story), Beckett.[1] And these claims are not in terms of money made or of "the Bitch-Goddess Success." They are to be measured in terms of vision, humane compassion (no matter how "coldly Irish" they seem), and strength of character—and ultimately, beyond the provinces of art. Both Yeats and Joyce rested their early claims for superiority not on the skills of their art, but on having mastered them, stressed their claims upon a "showing-forth" of life itself, that is why a study of their lives has its importance toward an understanding of what they wrote.

Although Richard Ellmann's *James Joyce* is probably not the last book he will write, it has the air of being "a masterpiece." In the best sense of the word it is an "official" biography, a large book that reconstructs, year by year, Joyce's life from his birth in Rathmines, near Dublin, 2 February 1882 to his death in the Schwesterhaus, Zurich, 12 January 1941. The book is a tribute to Joyce's memory, and one of the few of its kind in literary history.

Whether Ellmann intended to make James Joyce an archetypical Irishman or not, his book succeeds in making Joyce combine within himself all the contradictory elements in Irish character: his pride playing against his guilt-ridden soul; his blasphemy against Thomism and Jesuit-trained piety; his almost boundless courage against fear of thunderstorms and dogs; his arrogance in the face of good fortune and bad against timidity and shyness with women; his heavy drinking against an ascetic passion for the "hard way" and hard work; his brutality (for his treatment of his brother Stanislaus was no less than brutal) against the extremes of tenderness for other members of his family; his intellectual integrity against a naive clinging to superstitions; his ease in weeping against the power to evoke a comic genius greater than the wits of Sheridan, Goldsmith, Wilde, and Shaw; his poverty against an aristocratic flinging away of money; a love of maudlin Irish songs against a brilliant critical taste in the writing of parodies; his dandyism (for the male Irish even in rags always look "smart") against the wearing of white, easily soiled tennis shoes; his love of perfection and neoclassic pedantry against the wildest flights of imagination in romantic literature. Joyce, as Richard Ellmann so convincingly presents him is the Irish hero—*gloria in excelsis!*

To say that Joyce was a complex human being is an understate-

[1] And now in 1971, to this list I would add a sixth—John Synge, who on rereading shines with more radiance than ever.

ment, and it was a sign of his genius and strength of character that he kept his complexities intact. When Joyce in desperation over the incurable madness of his daughter Lucia forced himself to consult Dr. C. G. Jung, he succeeded in confusing that eminent psychiatrist—but of course, few Irish heroes have spent an afternoon reclining on a psychiatrist's couch. They match their wits, their sins, their guilt against the mouth of a confession box with an Irish priest on the other side of it. It is unlikely that any psychiatrist, however famous, will ever come to know a Joycean Irish hero: the moment he *thinks* he does so, he slips into a trap that even the most ignorant, simple-minded Irish priest would cheerfully avoid. Though the mature Joyce kept away from the confession box himself, and properly called himself a Jesuit, not a Catholic, he advised troubled friends to confess to priests—and not to waste their time and money in psychiatrists' offices.

Joyce matched strength against two talented members of his own family—his prodigal drunken father who reduced his family to living in a Dublin slum, and Stanislaus Joyce, his younger brother, who became a violently bigoted atheist, and the very soul of human virtues. Joyce outcharmed both. Outwardly, Stanislaus was the "strong man," regular in habits, just and coolheaded, kind and loyal; and as his own book, *My Brother's Keeper*, proves, very nearly a writer of the first order. Actually he was the weaker of his father's sons, giving his earnings away to support his sisters, James and James's family; it is significant that his book, his single gift to posterity, even at his death in 1955, remained an unfinished manuscript. James's strength of character from childhood through middle age was masked by youthful arrogance and the charm of one who laughed away the fears of those around him. His own fears (at their darkest) were purged by occasional bouts of heavy drinking. Since he possessed, like his father, a fine voice and a early flawless "ear," a few hours of drinking were topped by a round of songs. Spurred by his father, and trained in Jesuit schools where his father's eloquence secured scholarships for him, Joyce's intellectual disciplines were furthered. Deeply inspired family pride played its part here, as well as intellectual boldness and arrogance. Joyce could not, did not fail the father who wrote an indignant letter to the Pope, protesting against the desertion of Roman Catholic Ireland from Parnell's cause. To logical, sane, uninspired eyes, old John Joyce's railings at the Pope seems willful comic madness, but with full knowledge of Ireland's distress, the sacred person of an Italian Pope meant nothing to an Irish Joyce. James Joyce inherited the strength of his father's wit and arrogance—in the same breath he was "in" the Irish Catholic Church and "out" of it, as individual as Adam, the first created man, and intellectually a Thomist, a follower of Dante and Giambattista Vico and a Jesuit. Joyce was a whole-souled blasphemer (as the Irish so often are), and *not* unlike his younger brother, an earnest, honest, atheist heretic.

While still an undergraduate at University College, Dublin, Joyce wrote an appreciation of Ibsen which had the good fortune to find publication in *The Fortnightly Review* of London—a true accomplishment for a boy of eighteen. In Dublin the essay established him as a genius. More remarkable than the essay itself were the inspiration and the will that arose from it, Joyce's learning of Dano-Norwegian so he could read Ibsen in the original, and then write a letter to Ibsen.

This last action showed that his reputation of being a "genius" in Dublin did not deceive him, that his intentions had seriousness behind them, that he was not to spare himself the rigors of the "hard way," that he would force himself to "make good" the claims of his pride and egotism. His patronizing friend, Oliver Gogarty, was no fool. He felt, rather than perceived, Joyce's hidden strength; he soon learned that he had blundered in offending Joyce's sensibilities, and for that reason feared him. In his insensitive clumsy way, he became obsequious to Joyce. Did he know he would go down to posterity as "stately, plump Buck Mulligan"—the anti-Joyce, the eternal Judas? Of course not. But he felt that something terrible might happen.

W. B. Yeats's handling of Joyce's arrogance showed far deeper insight than Gogarty's. The inner Yeats was as tough as the inner Joyce; Yeats knew the ways of Irish charm and what they concealed, and it is not surprising that the elder poet was the sharpest critic of Joyce's early poems; he did not underrate their sensitivity, their subtle musical innovations, their distinction—his only complaint was that they did not *say* enough. Patiently, and in the face of Joyce's impertinence, he became Joyce's most steadfast champion, passing his writings on to be praised by a young American of his generation, Ezra Pound.

Joyce's various places of exile away from Dublin—Paris, Trieste, Rome, periodic brief stays in London, Zurich—never left Ireland behind, but rather intensified the *presence* of Dublin wherever Joyce lived in wildly extravagant Irish poverty. This was a kind of poverty that always went in debt five pounds after the last penny was spent. The presence was heightened by his heroic "common-law" wife, Nora Barnacle, who was as archetypically Irish as he—his Eve, his mistress-wife-mother, his Molly Bloom, and essentially his Anna Livia Plurabelle, mother of his son Giorgio and his Cassandra-fated daughter, Lucia. These, with Stanislaus (who followed them and so often supported them out of his poor earnings from the language teaching, piece-work factory of the Berlitz School where both brothers were employed) were his true intimates. He could not exist without them, nor they without him. He was their prodigal patriarch. After Joyce's death, Nora found the routine of living full; she had not read his books, but shared the excitement of a precarious "good life," with self-sacrificing patronesses such as Harriet Weaver and Sylvia Beach, the publisher of *Ulysses,* rescuing her "Jim" from ruin. When asked if she remembered visits from André Gide, she looked blank, and then replied, "Sure, if you've been married to the greatest writer in the world you don't remember all the little fellows."

Rather too much than too little has been written of Joyce as the supreme artist of his day.[2] After his death, "the Revolution of the Word" collapsed in fragments of some of the worst writing the world has ever read. The only writer to "come out" of Joyce, and to go his own way, the "hard way," is Samuel Beckett. Joyce left no heirs. His two masterpieces, *Ulysses* and *Finnegans Wake*, are resurrections of the comic spirit of which we have such rare examples as the writings of Rabelais, *Don Quixote, Tristram Shandy,* and *Gulliver's Travels.* That compassionate spirit is humane, not humanitarian. As Joseph Campbell suggests *Finnegans Wake* achieves its universality by being the misadventures of the soul in Purgatory. Yet *Finnegans Wake*'s achievement is precarious. The accent of the book is parochial, and its primary demand upon the reader is to hear it read aloud; its very accent is "of Ireland." If one cares nothing for the Irish and its "monster"-composite-hero, Finnegan-HCE, and is slow to recognize the dazzling beauty of Anna Livia Plurabelle, the true measure of its great achievement is half lost. Even today its danger lies in becoming the unread classic of the twentieth century; it needs an exposition as brilliant as the outline found in the Campbell-Robinson *A Skeleton Key to Finnegans Wake.*

Ellmann's contribution to Joyceana is one that shows the distinctly personal sources of Joyce's writings—a revelation that makes Joyce as "personal" a writer as W. B. Yeats. His missteps are few, and these are related to his tone-deaf readings of Joyce's lyricism. In this respect, Ellmann belongs to the tone-deaf generation of critics who came forward in the 1940s, who accepted the flaws of Pound, Eliot, and Auden as standards of excellence in writing verse and grew to admire flat lines and tone-deaf phrasing. Joyce's gift was nine-tenths auditory—so was his wit. His slight lyrics, underrated by Ellmann, have greater distinction than the best of A. E. Housman.

Since the arrivals of *Ulysses* and *Finnegans Wake* much has happened that has dimmed the shock of the first impact of Joyce's genius. Members of the Joyce Cult are growing old. Today Joyce's

[2] I suspect that the best short essay on *Ulysses* is Joseph Campbell's study, "Contransmagnificandjewbantantiality" in *Studies in the Literary Imagination,* vol. 3, no. 2, October 1970. (Atlanta, Georgia; Georgia State University.)

prestige is academic. What remains? Experiment for art's sake is dead. One must look further. Joyce as the great forerunner in twentieth-century literature reveals another aspect. His writings are still God-haunted; he is the forerunner of a renewed theological approach to life. In this lies the secret of his endurance. His art was the means, the embodiment of his secret, the heart of his example in reading Dante's *Divine Comedy*. *Ulysses* and *Finnegans Wake* are works of the yea-sayer. One must be tone-deaf indeed not to hear the notes of an Irish resurrection of mankind in *Finnegans Wake*.

1960, 1961, 1971

THE DYING GLADIATORS OF SAMUEL BECKETT

The first thing to be said about Samuel Beckett—and I suspect it will be the last—is that he is essentially a poet. This statement may seem illogical because the general public knows him as the author of a play, *Waiting for Godot*, written in prose, and is beginning to know him as the author of a trilogy, *Molloy* (1955), *Malone Dies* (1956), and *The Unnamable* (1958). In Beckett's case, unlike that of many others who begin a literary career by writing a slender book of poems (Beckett's was *Whoroscope*, 1930), the fact retains its importance in his later prose. It is reinforced by a second volume of verse, *Echo's Bones*, which was published in Paris by George Reavey under the imprint of the Europa Press (1935).

Beckett's prose comes from the same imaginative fount that his early poems do; the later prose is far better than the poems, but it is prose written as poems are written, conveying emotion directly to the reader. His stories and his play have the structure of poems rather than strictly narrative and dramatic forms. That is one reason out of many why audiences were first disquieted then moved by *Waiting for Godot:* they came to see a play; what they heard was something that did not imitate poetry as they knew it, but was the economical, sometimes ambiguous language of a poetic imagination.

The second thing to be said is that Beckett is a comic writer of the first order, one who has profound understanding of human destiny. At the highest moments of Beckett's farcical situations, he is most serious, most revealing and in a certain sense (of which there is more to say) *religious* in his view of the human comedy. In his writings, the emotions caused by terror, pity, despair, the death-wish, and love are purged by laughter. Beckett achieves a nearly classical distinction, ancient enough, but he has renewed it in twentieth-century terms, of what comedy should be; his heroes are mock tragic heroes—his "Dying Gladiators"—yet never attaining respect among living creatures around them, or a desired funereal dignity. They are never completely damned or blessed. They inhabit purgatory.

In speaking of Beckett's "Dying Gladiators" I use the phrase advisedly. A gladiator's martyrdom was not that of a kinglike tragic hero. The tragic fall was not his; death was for the amusement of those who witnessed his fall in a Roman circus. However skillful, however brave he might be, whatever immortality he achieved was an anonymous one. The gladiator was outside the orbit of Roman society, or rather he was in it only on the level of being an entertainer. The Christians saw his death as an incident in the martyrdom of man. Beckett's heroes also exist, or try to, outside the conventions of a society as complex as any in the ancient world.

But how did Beckett find such creatures, one might ask. In himself? Of course. Yet the question demands a far more objective answer. Beckett's emotional and intellectual heritage is in evidence here; it includes the peculiarities of Protestant Anglo-Irish, south Irish parentage, education at Dublin's Trinity College, Beckett's interest in the German philosophers, his probable reading of Bergson's essay on laughter. Beckett's early surroundings, clearly shown in his first book of stories, *More Pricks Than Kicks* (1934), are of the Protestant in a Roman Catholic country, a place that is "out of the world" in one sense, and deeply heretical in another; it is a condition of exile at home. Even when the Anglo-Irishman leaves Ireland his tendency is to become more Irish than the actual Irish, to be haunted by a few drops of Irish blood in his veins. It is characteristic of him to turn to Europe, not England, as his intellectual home.

The Catholic Church in Ireland has always taken pride in being more Catholic than the Pope at Rome; its effect on the Protestant living in south Ireland is to infuse, if only by osmosis, a daily conviction of living, either well, or more frequently poorly, within the orbit of a Christian world. The Protestant position in Ireland is one fork of a three-pronged theological agony, of which the other two are the established order of the Church at Rome and the provincial bigotry of the Irish Catholic. In Ireland the most extreme Calvinist cannot equal the passionate bigotry of the Irish Catholic; in Ireland the most sincere atheist finds his position belittled by the sneaking conviction that he is committing blasphemy by existing at all; even he cannot escape an unheroic damnation. When Yeats wrote ". . . Because this country has a pious mind . . ." he thought of Ireland and not less of Colonus; it was also a country in which "a man can be so crossed;/Can be so battered, badgered and destroyed/That he's a loveless man . . ." and though Yeats was constantly forced into a heretical position, he was also forced into an admiration for Von Hügel. A gifted Protestant in south Ireland always feels the prodding of the triple-pronged fork. Even if he leaves Ireland as Beckett did (he lives in Paris and has written novels and short stories, plays, poetry, and criticism in French),[1] the conflicts of theological doubt and faith pursue him. His ragged soul still walks in purgatory.

[1] As of 1961, Beckett had written the following in French: *Mercier et Camier, Molloy, Malone Meurt, L'Innommable, Comment c'est, Nouvelles et textes pour rien; Eleuthéria, En attendant Godot, Fin de partie, Acte sans paroles I; Poèmes 38–39, Trois poèmes; Barm Van Velde.*

In his prose Beckett has sustained the ancient, sometimes parallel, association of religion with poetry; and if at times they seem to vanish, they are just around the corner. Scratch an Irish poet, and if the scratch is deep enough to draw blood, the result, however heretical it may be, will be a religious poem.

From the publication dates of Beckett's books we know that the earliest of them appeared when critical attention had been turned to writing of "social content." This partly explains why *More Pricks Than Kicks* and *Murphy*, both published in London, were ignored. The effort to read immediate "social consciousness" into Beckett's writings is a waste of time; Beckett's concerns are with the conflicts of flesh and spirit, of mind and soul; one has to strain to read superficial political meanings into them. Other reasons why the books were ignored are also clear. *More Pricks Than Kicks* is a collection of stories, all Irish, which, put together, almost make a novel; they are uneven, and to their credit today, nonprofessional, their brilliance untarnished, the work of a "divine amateur." Among the stories, *Dante and the Lobster* and *Love and Lethe* await rediscovery; reread today they both absorb and transcend the Irish city and landscapes around them. At the time of their first publication the young Beckett could be dismissed as a charming writer whose direction was unknown; today we recognize in *Love and Lethe* a better version of Graham Greene's short storty, *A Drive in the Country*.

It makes little difference which story was written first (I suspect Beckett's was); the point is that if one is writing about a dangerous young man who takes a girl for a drive in the country with the intention (unknown to her) of forcing her into a suicide pact, it is better to give it a comic turn as Beckett does than to make it vulgar by converting it into a slick magazine story melodrama. In Greene's story, the girl escapes the clutches of the young man and leaves him to put a bullet through his silly self-destructive head, then returns home, virtue triumphant, her lesson learned, to her dear dull parents. It is very like a Hollywood script and unconvincing. In Beckett's story the girl forces Irish whiskey down the young man's throat (drinking half the bottle herself) until he is too drunk to aim a gun at anything, and then instructs him in the pleasures of making love. There is a ring of truth in all the stories of *More Pricks Than Kicks*, and it is he, young Belacqua, who gives the book an air of being the first draft of a novel, and he is also the first of Beckett's "Dying Gladiators."

2

". . . and they drew all manner of things—everything that begins with an M—"

"Why with an M?" said Alice.
"Why not?" said the March Hare.
Alice was silent.
The Dormouse had closed its eyes by this time, and was going off into a doze; but, on being pinched by the Hatter, it woke up again with a little shriek, and went on: "—that begins with an M, such as mousetraps, and the moon, and memory, and madness . . ."

—Lewis Carroll, *Alice in Wonderland*

After *More Pricks Than Kicks* Beckett's settings leave provincial Ireland unnamed; *Murphy* is a stop off in London, South Kensington —and memorably, Kensington Gardens, a place made famous by two visitors before Beckett, J. M. Barrie and Henry James. I am aware that many readers of Beckett's writings will think first of Joyce, then Kafka; they are not wrong in doing so; Beckett has obvious debts to both, but the point is that he has taken his own direction, and in that way he is playing another tune than theirs. The direct influence of Joyce (master that he is and will remain) has probably sterilized more young writers than reinspired them; of those who felt his dominance only a few and Beckett is one, have had enough strength of character, and enough to say in their own right, to survive. The Beckett who holds attention is the Beckett who has absorbed the teachings of a master and has walked in a road of his own making. A primary reason why Beckett's later writings strike beneath the surface of entertainment is, of course, the emotional charge of their religious associations. Another reason, scarcely less important, is that Beckett's comedy has behind it certain truths of philosophic origin. Those who complain that Beckett is so "negative" in his views, should remember Nietzsche's "yeas" and "nays"—and finally that two negatives can produce an affirmative. In Beckett's *Molloy* and *Malone Dies* there are several excellent parodies on the subject of education; to the reader of German philosophy these seem to stem from Schopenhauer's remarks on education in his essay *The Art of Literature.* I quote from Schopenhauer on men of learning, a passage which may be read as a comment on Beckett's wit in his parodies on education. Murphy refuses to read books; Moran attempts to instruct his son: these scenes seem to have behind them touches of the same quality of wit that is in the following:

The wig is the appropriate symbol of the man of learning, pure and simple. It adorns the head with a copious quantity of false hair, in lack of one's own: just as erudition means endowing it with a great mass of alien thought. This, to be sure, does not clothe the head so well and naturally, nor is it so generally useful, nor so suited for all purposes, nor so firmly rooted; nor when alien thought is used up can it be immediately replaced by more from the same source, as is the case with that which springs from soil of one's own. So we find Sterne, in his *Tristram Shandy*, boldly asserting *an ounce of a man's own wit is worth a ton of other people's.*

Beckett's wit is supremely his own; if at times his technique resembles Joyce's, his application of it is in terms of his own imagination. Consciously or not, though I suspect consciously, for Beckett's heroes carry with them a conflict between mind and body, Beckett sounds the depths of a truth concerning education; to say the least, the farcical situation he presents has intellectual tension behind it, and because Beckett is a poet, the intellectual paradox is stated in terms that evoke the emotional response of laughter.

In the same way, one of the roots of Beckett's comedy may be discovered in Bergson's essay, *Laughter*. All the flaws in the Broadway production of *Waiting for Godot* may be traced to "slickness" of presentation, which allows for "nice-nellying" a statement, and therefore vulgarizes it. The original depth is covered over, if not lost. Small and vulgar clichés creep in, such as Bert Lahr's famous "Billy Watson's sliding-act" repeated at least once too often. Beckett's detailed parodies of clothing, his descriptions of what his heroes wear, are related, if anywhere, to Bergson's remarks in *Laughter* on dress:

> This vision of the mechanical and living superimposed one upon the other leads us to consider a yet vaguer image, that of some sort of rigidity clamped to the mobility of life, trying ungracefully to follow life's lines and to imitate its fluidity. One can then see how easy it is for an article of clothing to be ridiculous. One can almost say that any fashion of dress has its laughable side. Only, when it is a question of current modes we are so used to the garments that we tend to accept them as an integral part of the body that they adorn. Our imagination fails to separate the two. The idea no longer occurs to us to oppose the inert rigidity of the envelope to the supple activity of the object enveloped. Here the comic element rests in a latent state. It will immediately break out when the natural incompatibility between the envelope and the enveloped will be so striking that even the traditional reconcilement will not succeed in consolidating their union: such is the case of the top hat, for example. Imagine the case of an eccentric who walks the streets in fashions of bygone days; our attention is then called to the clothing, we distinguish it completely from the wearer, we say that the wearer is *disguising* himself (as if every form of dress was not a disguise), and the laughable side of the fashion passes from the shade into the sunlight.[2]

[2] *Laughter: The Meaning of the Comic*, by Henri Bergson; translated by C. Brereton and F. Rothwell. New York: The Macmillan Company, New Eversley Series 35, 1935. (Subsequent quotations are also from this edition.)

Beckett also follows certain Bergsonian laws for the logic of imagination as opposed to those of the conscious mind, that is, of organized, mechanical, and "conforming" society. Beckett strikes beneath "the logic of mind" to "a dream dreamed by the whole of society," which is why Beckett has never had the least concern for immediate political and social movements.[3] As artist he is at an opposite extreme from those who have yielded to the fantasies of social science, Again, Bergson is relevant.

> A proposition like this one: "my everyday clothing forms a part of my body" is absurd in the eyes of reason. Nevertheless the imagination holds it as a truth. "A red nose is a painted nose," "a Negro is a white man in disguise," yet more absurdities for the reason, but elemental truths for the simple imagination. There is thus a logic for the imagination which is not the logic of the mind, which sometimes opposes it. . . . It is something like the logic of the dream, but of a dream that will not let itself be abandoned to the caprice of individual fantasy, since it is a dream dreamed by the whole society. . . . It obeys certain laws, or rather, certain customs, which are to the imagination that which logic is to the mind.

From these associations we may turn to the sleepy Dormouse's remarks on M; the Dormouse has fallen into a dream within a dream (since Alice's *Wonderland* is itself a dream) and speaks from it. The conversation took place at a "mad tea-party" which exists within the logic of imagination. The institution-sanitarium scenes in *Murphy* and *Malone Dies* are at the same dream-within-dream levels. Murphy yields to the social need of taking a job, which may be equated with entering an institution—the institution is a mental hospital, and Murphy, as a male nurse, the lowest, most nearly radical position in it, encounters the castrating results of holding a job at all. He is also being prepared for death by fire, a pagan death, a loss of Christian identity. In *Malone Dies* the institution scenes blend from a dingy rooming house to dream-within-dream settings of a mental hospital-*cum* monastery—and "why not" as the March Hare would say, why should not Beckett's "Dying Gladiators'" names begin with an M? They find themselves in places that are like ill-lighted interiors of old-fashioned cheesecake-shaped mousetraps, lunacy from the moon invades their quarters, they are much concerned with memory and philosophic muchness—they have come a long way from provincial Ireland, and yet certain dimmed, hilly, raining, half-pastoral mel-

[3] It is true that Beckett has not been involved in sectarian arguments, but that did not prevent him from active participation in the French Resistance. At the German occupation of Paris in 1940, Beckett said "I couldn't stand with my arms folded."

ancholy images persist. *Alice in Wonderland* may not be Beckett's source for his use of M: but his use of it is as valid as the Dormouse's defense of drawing things from a well; and the most important thing drawn from a well has been truth.

Beckett's writings are centrifugal, not linear in movement; they are coneshaped, very like the spiral described in Yeats's *A Vision*, and the last scenes in *Murphy* and *Malone Dies*, though they seem to be dislocated from what has gone before, are visionary "summings up," the moments of a "showing-forth" that Joyce wrote of in *Stephen Hero*. The flying kite scene over Kensington Gardens in *Murphy* is one of the finest passages in twentieth-century prose. The choice of a garden for the scene has a classical precedent in French literature which extends from *The Princess of Cleves* to *Strait Is the the Gate*. Beckett has done many things at once with that scene; he has "summed up" Murphy's impotence, since he is now heroically dead by pagan fire, by having his mistress, a mock-widow, nurse an impotent old man flying a kite from his wheelchair. Yet the kite for him is a nearest approach to heaven, the nearest approach to control of a visible universe. Kensington Gardens and the large sky above them may also represent nature surrounded by the most impressive of man-made things, the largest of modern cities. A half ironic balance is struck to close a hilarious, lightly written comic novel.

In respect to the texture of their prose *Molloy* and *Malone Dies* are far more closely woven than Beckett's earlier writings; certain scenes are reworked, reinforced and given accumulative meaning. A scene in the rain is reset from *A Wet Night*—one of the less successful stories in *More Pricks Than Kicks*—in a memorable passage in *Malone Dies*, and the parodies on education through the early stories are renewed, intensified, and given in greater variation in *Murphy*, *Molloy*, and *Malone Dies*. Though in purgatory, Beckett's heroes move toward a state of becoming; the passion, the agony of purgatory is theirs, they must still wait for the epiphany, "the showing-forth," something beyond their trials, their errors, which cannot be named.

Malone Dies is filled with references to the Gospel of John, negatively said because Malone, always in a state of becoming, never achieves a place in the true light, "the true light, which lighteth every man that cometh into the world." The epiphany at the end of *Malone Dies* is a casting off into the grey light of the sea, and the scene recalls "Except a man be born again, he cannot see the Kingdom of God. Nicodemus saith unto him, How can a man be born when he is old? Can he enter a second time into his mother's womb, and be born? Jesus answered, Amen, Amen, I say unto thee, Except a man be born of water and the Holy Spirit, he cannot enter into the Kingdom of God." Malone has not stepped beyond purgatory for the rebirth of his spirit, but has reached water. This passage from the Gospel of John also gives pertinent meaning to the first page of *Molloy:* "I am in my mother's room. [the effort to enter a second time into his mother's womb] It's I who live there now. I don't know how I got there."

The crutches, the sticks, the hats, the shoes are erroneous, ridiculous, unnatural projections of the body as Beckett's characters wear them; one guide to their origins may be found in Diderot's speculations on a blindfolded man's use of two sticks for eyes. Malone, since he lives or dies in semidarkness, is half-blind; it is his stick that makes him sure of possessing things on earth. Molloy is dependent upon his crutches and a bicycle; that error frustrates the nature of the body; the inanimate projections deform growth. If Diderot's blindfolded man represents the life of reason, then that life in semidarkness becomes deformed, is a kind of death. So much for the substrata of Beckett's mock-tragic and wholly farcical situations; the point is that they stir emotions which lie beneath them. The last turn that Beckett makes concerns memory.

Beckett's mock heroes have defective memories—which is a deeply human, often ridiculous limitation of the mind. In *Waiting for Godot,* Gogo insists "I either forget things immediately, or I remember them forever." Truly enough, he forgets what happened yesterday or the day before, or the day before that. His memory, defective, fractional, has hold only on the fact that he *is* waiting; he remembers a continuity of waiting and becoming, a nearly instinctive process, something like (but in him translated into human terms) the abstract life force, constantly becoming that which Bergson described in his *Creative Evolution.* What he is waiting for is called "Godot"; but Gogo can make an error, if only for a moment, that Pozzo (another character in the play) is "Godot." Godot remains ambiguous and not of this earth; he is left open for the reader or audience to fill in his name. Gogo's one positive gesture out of the "nays" that surround him is the strength to wait, Gogo and Vladimir may be regarded as two human negatives, two errors that together, as they touch hands, create the "yea." They reject suicide; the power to wait preserves them. The other pair of friends, Pozzo and Lucky, destroy each other; they may read as destructive elements of friendship on earth, the master-slave complex of violent feeling; they ride on the stage and off; they lack the unworldly strength to wait.

No paraphrases of Beckett's writings can hope to equal the actual performance of what he says. The best one can do is realize that his prose, like poetry, has its own shades of meaning and association. Today, and at a moment when most writers have become willing to conform to whatever demands society makes upon them, Beckett stands almost alone. He too is becoming, and I strongly suspect that although he is as invisible as Godot (except in Paris) he has come to stay.

1956, 1961

WEST
OF SATURN

POET WITHOUT CRITICS: ROBINSON JEFFERS

At the moment there are good reasons for rereading the poetry of Robinson Jeffers. First of all, the poet himself is a singular figure in American letters and he occupies the rare position in this country of being a "poet" in the European sense of the word. He insists upon holding to a world view as well as his own handful of currently unpopular opinions. He has become a master of a style without nervous reference to recent fashions in literary criticism. "I can tell lies in prose," he once wrote, which means that his primary concern is with the statement of a few essential poetic truths. Today it is obvious that he is willing to leave a final judgment of what he has written to the decision of posterity.

To reread him is to step aside from the classroom discussions and shoptalk of poetry that flood the rear sections of literary quarterlies where his name is seldom mentioned at all. He is well removed from the kind of company where poetry is "taught" so as to be understood, where critics and reviewers are known to be instructors of literature in colleges and universities. But he is also at some distance from the time when his Californian narratives in verse, *Roan Stallion* and *Tamar*, swept through the furnished rooms and studios of Greenwich Village with the force of an unpredicted hurricane. That was thirty years ago. Today as Jeffers is reread there is no danger of being smothered by the heavily breathing presence of a deep-throated, bare-thighed-and-breasted Jeffers–D. H. Lawrence cult, who had read Freud not wisely but with artless ardor and spent vacations in New Mexico.

Writers like Lawrence and Jeffers who are worshiped by cults, frequently inspire the more violent forms of academic snobbery. Neither came from the "right" prep school, college, or university; neither Oxford or Cambridge could claim Lawrence, nor could the Ivy League universities and colleges in the United States gather their share of glory from Jeffers's reputation. Both Lawrence and Jeffers have outlived their cults; and Lawrence, safely dead and of British origin, no longer irritates the thin, tightly stretched surface of academic temper in the United States. This phenomenon, which is not without its trace of envy, partly explains the neglect, in quarterly reviews, of Jeffers's later writings. It can be said that in recent years

Jeffers has been a poet without critics, but this does not mean that his name has been forgotten, his books unread, or his plays in verse neglected on the stage. A few years ago his *Medea* had a respectable run on Broadway, and an off-Broadway theater in New York found audiences for his new play, *The Cretan Woman.*

The initial advantage of rereading Jeffers's poetry now is that it can be approached without the formulas of critical fashions ringing in one's ears. Since 1925 he has published more than fifteen books of verse—a quantity of poetry which resembles the production of his ancestors, the romantic poets of nineteenth-century Britain. Rereading his poems, one finds them falling into three divisions: the Southwestern narratives with their richness of California sea-sky-and-landscape; the shorter poems which are largely conversation pieces—for Jeffers is not a lyric poet—and a fine group of elegies, his *Descent to the Dead,* the result of a visit in 1929 to the British Isles; and the semidramatic poems inspired by Greek themes and overlaid with Nietzschean and twentieth-century philosophies.

2

It is best to begin when and where Jeffers's earlier reputation began; the time was 1925 and the place was New York; and credit for the publication of *Roan Stallion, Tamar, and Other Poems* should be given James Rorty, a writer who met Jeffers during a stay in California and with selfless enthusiasm persuaded New York friends to read *Tamar,* to write about it, to make the presence of Jeffers known to New York publishers. Although Jeffers never shared the excitements and diversions of literary circles on the Atlantic Coast, the moment was prepared to receive his semi-Biblical, semi-Sophoclean American Southwestern narratives. Discussions of Steinach operations for restoring sexual vitality were in the air, and so were questions from Krafft-Ebing, Freud, and Jung; D. H. Lawrence's *The Rainbow* was in print as well as Sherwood Anderson's *Dark Laughter.* If a post-World War I urban generation had not discovered sex, it had learned to talk loudly and almost endlessly about it. Nothing was easier than to apply cocktail conversations to Jeffers's *Tamar* and *Roan Stallion,* which at first reading—and particularly to those who lived in cities—held the same attractions as an invitation to a nudist colony on the Pacific Coast.

Yet it was not without self-critical discernment that Jeffers gave first place to *Tamar* when he prepared his *Selected Poetry* in 1935. For whatever reasons his public had accepted it twelve years earlier, at a time when he had passed the age of thirty-five, the poem has all the merits of a style that he had made his own. As early as 1912 he had paid for the printing of a first book, *Flagons and Apples;* in

1916 a second book, *Californians*, had been published by Macmillan; and neither, aside from the praise of a small group of friends, had received encouragement. His friendships, which included the long-sustained devotion of his wife, Una Call, also embraced the good will of George Sterling, who had known Ambrose Bierce, Joaquin Miller, and Jack London, and who was one of the few to see promise in Jeffers's early books of poems. Like Jeffers, who had been born in Pittsburgh in 1887, Sterling, a native of New York State, had become a converted Californian. Sterling's own verse had been inspired by the pages of *The Savoy* and *The Yellow Book* as well as by readings in Oscar Wilde and Ernest Dowson. "Poetry . . . ," he said, "must . . . cherish all the past embodiments of visionary beauty, such as the beings of classical mythology." Sterling's last work, shortly before his suicide in 1926, was a pamphlet written in praise of Jeffers. No doubt Jeffers had been made aware of the presence of evil through his wide readings, but it was through the loyal patronage of Sterling that he became an heir of "Bitter" Bierce. To the general reader, however, Jeffers's first two books offered little more than glimpses of a belated debt to Dante Gabriel Rossetti in *Flagons and Apples*, and a Wordsworthian manner, which included hints of pantheism, in *Californians*.

Before Jeffers met his wife and Sterling he had had an unusual education. He was the precocious son of a teacher of theology at Western Theological Seminary in Pittsburgh. His father taught him Greek, Latin and Hebrew; and when the boy was five and six, took him on trips to Europe. For three years, between the ages of twelve and fifteen, his father sent him to boarding schools in Switzerland and Germany; and at fifteen, Jeffers entered the University of Western Pennsylvania. The next four years were spent in Occidental College and the Universities of Zurich and Southern California, and these years included studies in medicine and forestry. All this would be of no importance if it did not throw light on the individual ranges of Jeffers's poetry, his familiarity with Greek and Roman and Biblical themes, with German philosophy, with medical terms and semi-scientific details, and—since he read French with facility—his possible knowledge of the writings of Sade. Certainly his education provided reasons for an affinity with Sterling, whose ideas of poetry embraces, however vaguely, "beings of classical mythology." At the very least, Jeffers is a writer whose early years had prepared him for more than a regional view of the world and its affairs.[1]

[1] Jeffers's education was of a kind familiar to well-to-do European gentry of the nineteenth century, but considerably less so to young Americans of the same period. Exceptions in the United States were Henry James's early travels with his father, and the continued educations after

A second reading of *Tamar* reveals it as a Biblical story in Californian undress. Characters in Jeffers's Southwestern narratives, from *Tamar* to *The Loving Shepherdess*, from *Give Your Heart to the Hawks* to *Hungerfield*, are often lightly clothed and are subject to the wind, sun, and rain of Californian climate. Chapter 13 of 2 Samuel is one source of Jeffers's parable, which contains the story of Amnon's love for his sister Tamar.[2] Other associations taken from the two books of Samuel permeate the poem, for the sons of Samuel "walked not in his ways, but turned aside after lucre and took bribes, and perverted judgment," a statement which is appropriate to Jeffers's view of America and Western civilization. As a parable the poem acquires the force of a Calvinist sermon from an American pulpit, yet it also carries within it echoes of Nietzsche's speech of Silenus, "What is best of all is beyond your reach forever: not to be born, not to *be*, to be *nothing*," and behind these words Sophocles' remark, "Not to be born is best for man." In Tamar's words the echoes are clearly heard: "O God, I wish / I too had been born too soon and died with the eyes unopened. . . ." Jeffers also puts into the mouth of Tamar a remark which has its origins in the doctrines of Sade "we must keep sin pure / or it will poison us, the grain of goodness in a sin is poison. / Old man, you have no conception / Of the freedom of purity." And as Tamar speaks she has given herself over to unchecked forces of evil. In Sade's novel *Justine*, his heroine is tortured because she fails to purge her taint of goodness; as the poem nears its end, the whipping of Tamar by her brother is the last love scene between them.

This is not to say that Jeffers by voicing echoes of Sade's doctrines had advanced them as examples for Californians to follow; it is rather that he has given the forces of evil a well-established voice of authority, but in doing so he has succeeded with such vehemence that he might be misunderstood by a careless reader. Even at this risk, he has also succeeded in giving the unleashed forces of hell refreshed reality. In his poem the house of David, Tamar's father—and Tamar is the daughter of King David in 2 Samuel—is destroyed by fire which in its first association creates a literal image of hell and, in its second, of the funeral pyres of the Romans.

So far I have mentioned only the principal elements of *Tamar*, its

---

college of Longfellow, Trumbull Stickney, George Cabot Lodge, and Henry Adams. Jeffers's development as a narrative poet also follows the precedent of many major nineteenth-century poets; Jeffers and his writings are "in the tradition."

2 For biographical information concerning Jeffers, as well as the fact that one of the sources of *Tamar* may be found in 2 Samuel, I am indebted to Lawrence Clark Powell's *Robinson Jeffers: The Man and His Work*.

Californian setting, one of the sources of its story, and a few of the concepts which are made relevant to the retelling of the story—but these do not complete the list of associations that the poem brings to mind, for *Tamar*, beneath the surface of a swiftly moving plot, has a richness of detail which rivals the complex fabric of Elizabethan dramatic verse. In the Biblical story the seduction of Tamar by Amnon is scarcely more than an invitation to come to bed; in Jeffers's version the seduction scene has an Ovidian ring: a hidden stream, a pool tempts brother and sister; naked, they enter it and one recalls Ovid's stories of Narcissus and Echo, Hermaphroditus and Salmacis, and by association there is a particularly Roman touch, a glimpse of Phoebus' chariot wheel, from a window of David's house overlooking the Pacific:

It was twilight in the
room, the shiny side of the wheel
Dipping toward Asia; and the year dipping toward
winter encrimsoned the grave spokes of sundown. . . .

It is this kind of richness that places *Tamar* among the major accomplishments in twentieth-century poetry. And what of the ghosts that haunt the house of David in *Tamar*? They are very like the images of guilt that invade the darkened walls of Macbeth's castle. An idiot sets fire to David's house, and one thinks of the line ". . . a tale told by an idiot, full of sound and fury." [3]

How deliberate Jeffers was in making a highly individual combination of Californian locale, Biblical and Greco-Roman themes, Elizabethan richness of detail, plus Nietzschean ethics and Calvinist denouements, it is impossible to say. The great probability is that, having

[3] In Jeffers's short poem *Self-Criticism in February*, there are the following lines which describe the nature of his ghosts, his romanticism, his unchurched belief in God:

It is certain you have loved the beauty of storm, disproportionately.
But the present time is not pastoral, but founded
Of violence, pointed for more massive violence: perhaps it is not
Perversity but need that perceives the storm-beauty.
Well, bite on this: your poems are too full of ghosts and demons,
And people like phantoms—how often life's are—
. . . .
you have never mistaken
Demon nor passion nor idealism for the real God.
Then what is most disliked in those verses
Remains most true.

With the exception of *The Cretan Woman*, this and subsequent quotations are from *The Selected Poetry of Robinson Jeffers*. New York: Random House, 1935.

a deeply felt desire to warn the world of the dangers of its involvements in world wars, Jeffers brought all the resources, conscious or hidden, of his imagination into play. To Jeffers, World War I was a warning of weaknesses inherent in a civilization that permitted mass murders and a situation that approached total war. War, by example, creates a precedent for violent action; and in *Tamar* that conclusion is shown by the desire of Tamar's brother to leave his father's house to go to war, not merely to escape the consequences of evil at home, but to plunge himself into scenes of mass destruction. Private violence and public warfare are mutually influential—and the essential sin was not to walk in the ways of Samuel.

Whatever else may be said of Jeffers's beliefs and opinions as they appear with marked consistency throughout the various poems he has written, he has gone to war in the cause of peace; and it should also be said that Jeffers's emotional fervor, his honesty, and his lack of personal vanity strongly resemble the evangelical passion of his Protestant heritage: his image of Christ is always divine. His poem to America, his *Shine, Perishing Republic*, has that fervor, its eloquence, its nobility, its protest against earthly tyrants:

> And boys, be in nothing so moderate as in love of man, a
> clever servant, insufferable master.
> There is in the trap that catches noblest spirits, that caught—
> they say—God, when he walked on earth.

But before one considers the merits of Jeffers's best writings, one should spare breath for certain of their failures, for Jeffers is a poet of large flaws and no weaknesses—and the flaws are often easier to see than his larger merits. In the great army of characters that his poems present to us, one has yet to discover a wholly admirable or completely rounded human being—a nearest approach, and her virtue is one of courage, is the heroine of *Give Your Heart to the Hawks*, a woman who attempts to save her husband from suicide and fails. An impatient reader of Jeffers, overwhelmed, yet half attracted, and then repelled by the scenes of overt Lesbianism in *The Women at Point Sur* and by the sight of a mother offering herself, half naked, to her son in *Such Counsels You Gave to Me* would conclude that the same poet kept bad company and was himself "immoral." The same reader would also find difficulties in fully accepting Jeffers's beautiful pastoral, *The Loving Shepherdess*, which may have been written with a memory of the Elizabethan John Fletcher's *The Faithful Shepherdess* in mind.[4] The witless little shepherdess, dressed in the fewest of rags,

[4] This supposition is not so fantastic as it may seem: John Fletcher's lyrical *The Faithful Shepherdess* was far too static in movement to be a successful play; it is, however, an excellent poem. Its plot closely resembles

is open to all men, young and old; and it is as though she had obeyed Sade's instructions to little girls. Whenever in Jeffers's poetry one finds a possible echo of Sade's doctrines, the mind, if not the blood, runs cooler. Even Robespierre and Bonaparte, worldly men enough at the sight of blood, and who welcomed Sade as a forthright critic of elder institutions, were shocked and grew chilled when they read Sade's manifestoes in the cause of sexual freedom; they were not prudes, but they concluded that Sade's remarks were too much deliberation in the pursuits of his particular happiness; his logic created a law for sexual lawlessness that all institutions, ancient or modern, have been forced to reject. Jeffers's desire to deal solely with elemental passions tends to mislead the reader into the colder regions of hell which are a paradox of romantic agony: the reader is repelled.[5]

Another reader, equally impatient, finds something ridiculous in Jeffers's scenes of sexual violence; since no comic relief is given to the reader in Jeffers's Californian narratives, the reader is forced to supply that missing element in the progress of the story—and sex viewed from a point outside the scene itself always has a touch of the ridiculous in it; if it did not there would be no moments of relaxation in the stories that used to be told in smoking cars. It is almost gratuitous to say that Jeffers's characters lack humor, which is a flaw that Jeffers shares with Wordsworth; and in the progress of his more violent scenes of action, a need is felt for a drunken porter to cross the stage in *Macbeth*. This does not mean, however, that Jeffers lacks ability to write of drunkenness; few scenes in contemporary fiction can equal the vividness of the drunken party which is prelude to the story of *Give Your Heart to the Hawks;* in poetry, and in its own grim fashion, its veracity equals the mild, half melancholy scene of E. A. Robinson's *Mr. Flood's Party*. (Robinson, by the way, is one of the few elder American poets for whom Jeffers has expressed firm admiration.) *Such Counsels You Gave to Me* must be counted as one of Jeffers's more conspicuous failures: the bare bones of the Oedipus complex shine too brightly through it. As the story opens one knows only too well that the weak son is fated to poison his red-faced, hard-drinking father; since 1900 this situation has been the stock property of countless novels and plays; a sinister yet charming hero-villain

---

Jeffers's poem with this difference: Fletcher's shepherdess is deceived into being promiscuous through magic worked by a sullen shepherd and she is at last rescued and absolved by a river god.

[5] In a footnote to the pamphlet called "Frenchmen! A further effort is needed if you would be republicans!" in his *La Philosophie dans le Boudoir* (1795), Sade wrote: "The first stirring of desire that a girl feels is the moment that Nature means her to prostitute herself, and with no other consideration in mind, she should obey Nature's voice; she outrages Her laws if she resists them."

disposes of a father who is overweight or a rich aunt who spikes her tea with whisky. But in Jeffers's case these flaws are not those of a small-minded writer or a minor poet.

3

Jeffers's merits as a poet are less well known than the flaws which I have just enumerated. From *Roan Stallion* and *Tamar* onward, Jeffers's technical contribution to twentieth-century poetry has been the mastery of alternate ten and five stress lines in narrative verse; in some of his shorter poems and in passages of some of his dramatic sequences, he employs a five and three stress variation of his narrative line. In this particular art no living poet has equaled him, and no other poet in America, from Philip Freneau to E. A. Robinson, has developed a narrative style of greater force, brilliance, and variety than his. While reading one of Jeffers's poems one never falls asleep; although there are times when his moral fervor is overweighted and has results which seem far from his stated intentions, he has never committed the greatest of all literary crimes—dullness. Among his shorter poems, his conversation pieces have contained prophecies which at the moment of publication seemed wrongheaded, probably mad, or willfully truculent. Time has proved Jeffers right more frequently than his adverse readers had thought possible; although the poem is too long for quotation here, the thoughtful cannot fail to be impressed by his *Woodrow Wilson* (*February 1924*) today. Wilson, the nearly tragic American hero, has been and still is the most difficult of all public figures to write about, yet Jeffers has succeeded in doing so. The poem's last lines, words spoken as if from Wilson's lips, indicate, however briefly, the nature of Wilson's failure:

> "This is my last
> Worst pain, the bitter enlightenment that buys peace."

Jeffers's opinions (which are less political than colored by his hatred of war, his adaptation of Nietzschean ethics, and nonchurchgoing Christianity) occasioned his publishers, in a recent book of his poems, *The Double Axe*, to disclaim responsibility for them. Jeffers had strange things to say of World War II and its aftermath, which he had predicted long before they arrived; he was much too familiar with the scene to be tactful; in another ten years he will probably be found less far from the truth than the majority of his contemporaries. There has been considerable misunderstanding of Jeffers's portrait of Hitler which he included in *Be Angry at the Sun* in 1941; his Hitler was a figure not unlike Macbeth, a Macbeth who could be imagined as the hero of a Wagnerian opera; his doom was accurately foretold; yet at the time Jeffers's poem appeared many thought that Jeffers had praised Hitler, or at least had made him seem too powerful. There is less doubt today that Jeffers's portrait needs no retouching to give it greater veracity.

Of the shorter poems, his volume *Descent to the Dead* is among his masterpieces; it includes his lines on *Shakespeare's Grave*, *In the Hill at New Grange*, *Ghosts in England* and *Iona: The Graves of the Kings*—all memorable poems. It is impossible for an anthologist to make a neat selection of Jeffers's poems and then bind them shrewdly between the poems written by his contemporaries. It so happens that Jeffers has never written an "anthology poem"; [6] he is best represented by his *Selected Poetry* which shows the range of his narratives tempered by his elegies, self-critical comments, and occasional observations; many of them may be read as footnotes to his longer poems. Selections of his shorter poems by anthologists distort the essential qualities of his poetry.

A few quotations from Jeffers's shorter poems do show, however, how he has shocked people of rigidly fixed political opinions; from *Blind Horses* one may take the lines:

> Lenin has served the revolution,
> Stalin presently begins to betray it. Why? For the sake of
> power, the Party's power, the state's
> Power, armed power, Stalin's power, Caesarean power.

And these were printed in 1937 when many people throughout Europe and some in the United States thought differently or would have feared to make their opinions known at all. And from *Thebaid* the observation:

> How many turn back toward dreams and magic, how many
> children
> Run home to Mother Church, Father State.

This is a statement which, like other elements in Jeffers's poetry, many may find easy to read but difficult to take; and yet it defines with Jeffers's insight and discernment a symptom of the times through which he has lived. Of the same temper are these lines from *Ave Caesar:*

[6] The perfect "anthology poem" is a showpiece of which Poe's *The Raven* and Tennyson's *May Queen* and *Crossing the Bar* were valiant examples; many minor poets seem to write for anthologies alone; and indeed, some poets like A. E. Housman are at their best when a small selection of their poems are reprinted in anthologies. With more wit and, incidentally, more truth than tact, Laura Riding and Robert Graves reviewed the practice of editing anthologies in their book, *A Pamphlet Against Anthologies.*

We are easy to manage, a gregarious people,
Full of sentiment, clever at mechanics, and we love our
luxuries.

Something of the force of Jeffers's sense of the past may be glimpsed at in these lines from *Ghosts in England:*

There was also a
ghost of a king, his cheeks hollow as the brows
Of an old horse, was paddling his hands in the reeds of Dozmare
Pool, in the shallow, in the rainy twilight,
Feeling for the hilt of a ruinous and rusted sword. But they said
"Be patient a little, you king of shadows,
But only wait, they will waste like snow." Then Arthur left
hunting for the lost sword, he grinned and stood up
Gaunt as a wolf; but soon resumed the old labor, shaking the
reeds with his hands.

It is scarcely necessary to add that this image of King Arthur searching for Excalibur and his early moment of glory has the character of major verse. And the style in which it is written also reveals Jeffers's interlinear art of writing verse.

4

Jeffers's success in reviving Greek themes through Nietzschean and even Wagnerian interpretation has also been a source of annoyance to those who hope to read their classics in "pure" translations. The "pure" translation of Greco-Roman classics do not and cannot exist in English; and it is a truism that absolute translations of poetry from one language into another cannot be made. The best that can be hoped for is that the translator has a more than literal understanding of the poetry he translates and that he has the genius to convert his original sources into poetry in English. Jeffers's recreations of ancient stories, particularly the plays of Euripides into English dramatic verse, have never pretended to be more than adaptations of situations, scenes, and characters. Actually, his performances are as far removed from their original sources as Shakespeare's adaptations from Plutarch's *Lives* in *Julius Caesar* and *Antony and Cleopatra*, as far as Jeffers's *Tamar* is from 2 Samuel in the Old Testament. In his own way he has applied to ancient writings Ezra Pound's rule, "make it new." Like W. B. Yeats, Jeffers was not "a born dramatist"; as Yeats was essentially a lyric poet, so Jeffers has been a distinguished writer of contemplative and narrative verse. As Yeats's adaptation of *Oedipus at Colonus* reflects Irish seascape in a Dublin accent, so Jeffers's adaptations from the Greek are never far from the climate of the California Pacific Coast.

If Jeffers, even more than Yeats, is not a professional dramatist and is far removed from those who can be called "men of the theater," there are times when his poetry reaches high levels of dramatic power. This has long been evident in his variation of the Orestes cycle in *The Tower Beyond Tragedy;* and its concluding statement of how Orestes "climbed the tower beyond time, consciously, and cast humanity, entered the earlier fountain" (walked then, as Nietzsche would say, beyond good and evil) places the poem among the major accomplishments of our time. The same power enters his poem *At the Fall of an Age,* with its story of the death of Helen on the island of Rhodes where she was worshiped as a tree goddess, twenty years after the fall of Troy. The two speeches of Achilles' Myrmidons, risen from the dead, have all the accents of living yet timeless verse; the second speech runs as follows:

> Is there any stir in the house?
> Listen: or a cry?
> Farm-boys with spears, you sparrows
> Playing hawk, be silent.
> Splendid was life
> In the time of the heroes, the sun went helmeted,
>   the moon was maiden,
> When glory gathered on Troy, the picketed horses
> Neighed in the morning, and long live ships
> Ran on the wave like eagle-shadows on the slopes of
>   mountains.
> Then men were equal to things, the earth was beautiful,
>   the crests of heroes
> Waved as tall as the trees.
> Now all is decayed, all corrupted, all gone down,
> Men move like mice under the shadows of the trees,
> And the shadows of the tall dead.
> The brightness of fire is dulled,
> The heroes are gone.
> In naked shame Agamemnon
> Died of a woman.
> The sun is crusted and the moon tarnished,
> And Achilles has chosen peace.
> Tell me, you island spearmen, you plowboy warriors,
> Has anyone cried out in the dark door?
> Not yet. The earth darkens.

There is nothing in poetry written during the twentieth century that is quite like this speech; few poets have written as well and the authority of the speech is unmistakable. Jean Cocteau once wrote that a true poet writes to be believed, not praised, and in these lines Jeffers's art of persuading the reader is unquestionable. Nor is he less convincing in the writing of Aphrodite's speech in his play, *The Cretan Woman*, a play inspired by and not a translation of Euripides:

> . . . So I have come down to this place,
> And will work my will. I am not the least clever of
> powers of heaven . . .
> I am the goddess
> the Greeks call Aphrodite; and the Romans will call me
> Venus; the Goddess of Love. I make the orchard-trees
> Flower, and bear their sweet fruit. I make the joyful
> birds to mate in the branches, I make the man
> Lean to the woman. I make the huge blue tides of the
> ocean follow the moon; I make the multitude
> Of the stars in the sky to love each other, and love
> the earth.
> Without my saving power
> They would fly apart into the horror of the night. And
> even the atoms of things, the hot whirling atoms,
> Would split apart: the whole world would burst apart
> into smoking dust, chaos and darkness; all life
> Would gasp and perish. But love supports and preserves
> them: *my saving power.*
> This is my altar,
> Where men worship me. Sometimes I grant the prayers
> of those that worship me: but those who reject me
> I will certainly punish.[7]

The quality of this speech equals the speeches in the plays of the Greek dramatists, but it is also singularly modern poetry; the quality of its language is direct and unstrained—no irrelevant effort at meaning is forced into it: the poetic nature of the speech is *there*, and for its purpose cannot be said in any other way; it is evidence enough of the genius of the man who wrote it. *The Cretan Woman* is a far more successful play to read than Jeffers's *Medea;* for his *Medea* opens with a flood of emotional speeches that cannot be sustained throughout the first act, therefore the play is topheavy, and his readers as well as his audiences are likely to be exhausted long before the final curtain falls. Jeffers's version of Euripides' *Hippolytus* reserves its strength for the last scene and agony of Theseus; and at this conclusion, one believes that Jeffers has lost none of the mastery that he acquired thirty years ago, rather he has set himself the further task of transforming his narrative genius into writing verse for the stage, or perhaps television.

Robinson Jeffers's accomplishments and the modesty of his private life, now saddened by the death of his wife, should serve as an

[7] *Hungerfield and Other Poems*, by Robinson Jeffers. New York: Random House, 1954.

example to the present as well as the next generation of writers. Within the last thirty years he has made no compromise with the changing fashions of the day. For some readers Jeffers's attitude, which is not unlike the positions held by William Faulkner and W. B. Yeats, has always seemed too aristocratic. Even now I can hear someone saying, "Jeffers loves nothing but rocks and stones; I love mankind." But those who love abstract mankind too feverishly deny the rights of individual distinction and all the choices between men of good and bad, and by implication they also deny the right of the artist to be himself. Jeffers has reestablished the position of the poet as one of singular dignity and courage. He is neither voiceless nor without his readers; and he is not without wisdom in seeming to await the verdict of posterity.

1955, 1961

HISTORY AND THE PROSE OF WILLIAM CARLOS WILLIAMS

"History, history!" says Dr. William Carlos Williams, and then with brilliant asperity continues, "We fools, what do we know or care?" [1]

The quantum of irony in Williams's remark, though clear enough, should be carefully considered, and in the way I read it, it might well be taken as a warning. History is a humiliating subject for any man to think of knowing: and however much, however little we know of it, we always care, and that is where the trouble is likely to begin. The desire to know history is a near relative of the desire to know truth, and that is where, for most of us, a pit lies waiting. It is a deep pit, overlaid with an innocent branch or two, cut down from a near-by tree, and among a scattering of wilted leaves, there are easily plucked twigs and tamed, resistant grasses. At its sides and at an attractive distance, one also finds rare specimens of jungle flora. It is a pretty place and only a very few of the so-called professional historians come back from it alive. For the moment I can remember the names of only three who came back whole: Herodotus, Edward Gibbon, and Henry Adams, and of these, Herodotus, being the eldest and most respectable, is best known as "the father of lies."

Perhaps there has always been a great number of different kinds of people who were eager to think of themselves as historians. Perhaps this was always so, but during the past few years, there seems to have been an increase of their published work; they seem to have become more vocal, more insistent that the field of history is theirs to have and to hold, and is in itself a proof of their authority to speak aloud. There it is, that deep pit, growing more inviting every day: and to it come engineers, and social workers, members of the D.A.R.; psychiatrists, economists, and students of anthropology, newspaper men, and politicians by the hundreds, research workers in the sciences, and, no doubt, an aviator or two. Executives of all kinds have come to it, from insurance company offices, from the Stock Exchange, from banks to overawe club banquets or trustee meetings or to deliver commencement day addresses at schools and colleges. And in addition to all these, there are those many talkative members of a generation (of whom some write novels) who have a strong memory of what

[1] *In the American Grain*, by William Carlos Williams; with an Introduction by Horace Gregory. Norfolk, Conn.: New Directions, 1939.

their grandfathers told them about the Civil War. The clearing in the jungle shines before them and they walk into it.

Of course, we have always known that history, like poetry, is an ancient trap laid for the credulous and literal minded. This common knowledge has been abroad so long that we are apt to forget the obvious hint that only those who have imagination survive their fall from unhappy innocence. Many, and I would say, far, far too many, are still victims of that fall: good, earnest people who are maimed and battered, who are forced to carry on a half-existence, distrusted by their fellows and of continual embarrassment to their friends.

Nor is it enough to have convictions and a powerful will to interpret them. Here history most resembles truth, and however violent its events have been and however lively they still appear, its exterior seems almost passive, and certainly tempting, if not altogether calm. Here, it seems to be waiting for the strong man to claim it, to do whatever he pleases with it and to make it his own forever. To use history for their purposes alone is the common ambition of the politician and the political journalist, and some have done so, and have made that great pit yield great profits for them. But even here imgination has been translated into action; and when that happens, politicians become statesmen and mere corporals become heroes—and here it is not what they do to history that matters, but what history does to them.

There must be imagination at work to discern the fables of history, to know their mutable faces, to know their language. Those who ignore them are sure to be lost at the deepest level of the pit. Their shrewdness is then known for the true stupidity that it is and always has been. They are the lost, the very lost, who are forgotten with remarkable ease and are unearthed only by industrious persons in libaries for whom the discovery of an unknown name may score a one-hundredth of a point toward a Ph.D.

It is in this relationship, between what is sometimes called fable what is sometimes called fact, that the "historical imagination" plays its part. And here there has always been a long established kinship between the historical imagination and poetry. The serious historian of the ancient world is careful never to forget his Homer. He may discriminate among the fables that Homer has set before him, and in the course of his researches, he may reject a number of them. But there they are; and they happen to remain in a better state of preservation than the buried cities unearthed by archeologists. There is a particular kind of reality alive within them that will permit neither neglect nor violation: and in the reading and interpretation of history everything falls dead unless that reality is perceived. The truth of events as a cautious historian may come to know it, and the meaning of that same truth to a people who have converted it into a common heritage demand a living, active synthesis. This is as true today as it always was, and the fables of American history, youthful and knowingly familiar as they may seem to some of us, are no exception to the rule.

One might almost say that the active fables of a human culture are the means through which it lives and grows. They enter deeply into the very idiom of national speech; their meanings shift as the spoken language changes. On this continent, they are "in the American grain" and it is humanly impossible to adopt an impartial, or what was once called a "scientific," attitude toward them. Science, as we have come to know it, is none too quiet in making its own discriminations, and shall we say it has its own signs, its own language by which its own truths are tested and modified? Shall we say that the imagination of a Willard Gibbs, whose language is abstract only to those who do not understand it, has its own nucleus of fables—or shall we call them the mathematical symbols of reality?

Our nationality which answers to the name, American, is neither at the center of a huge continent nor is it floating loosely around its East, West, and tropical coast lines and harbors. It is a language, and it requires a particularly active and discerning imagination to keep pace with it and to speak it truly. Without knowing that language as well as the signs and symbols it employs, the would-be historian is almost helpless. Lacking that particular insight, the professional historian is in the same unfortunate position as that of the nonprofessionals who cross his field. He may contribute a formula or a theory toward a revaluation of history in general, but he will need someone at his side to translate it, some one to make it intelligible to Americans.

It is at this point that Williams's discovery of an American heritage becomes important. His manner is almost aggressively nonprofessional and rightly so, for he is not here to record American history nor to give us a new sequence of events. He is here to present its signs and signatures, its backward glances, and by implication, its meanings for the future.

If I have misled some readers into thinking that *In the American Grain* is a historical textbook, or a book of essays in history, or a series of historical narratives, I wish to correct that impression before I go one word further. It is none of these. It is a source book of highly individual and radical discoveries, a book of sources, as one might say a river is a source of health to the fields and orchards through which it runs. And like that river in its uneven course, now quick in sunlight and now flowing to hidden roots of trees and flowers, the book has subterranean depths and turnings. I think it is not too much to say that this analogy also resembles its early reputation.

In the American Grain was first published in 1925 and before that date an early chapter appeared in *Broom.* I have no way of knowing how many people saw a few of its chapters in magazines or read the book, but I do know that as it fell slowly out of print, its reputation grew. I suspect that several other writers came upon it and kept the memory of its insights and the quality of its prose within the hidden chambers of their own knowledge and imagination. My immediate example is Hart Crane's *The Bridge* which was published five years later and which carried within it traces of the impression left upon those who first read *In the American Grain.* These traces are to be found throughout the poem: a fragment of Williams's quotation from Thomas Morton's *The New England Canaan* is reproduced on the half-title page of *Powhatan's Daughter* and like selections may be quickly recognized in the concluding pages of Williams's chapter on Columbus and in the closing stanzas of *Ave Maria.* Even the quotation from Edgar Allan Poe's *The City in the Sea* (whose original title was significantly written as *The Doomed City*), "Death looks gigantically down," smolders in a half-line of *The Tunnel* and also appears in Williams's book, placed over "a dead world, peopled by shadows and silence, and despair. . . ." These similarities should not of course be read as plagiarisms, nor should we exaggerate their obvious claims to a relationship that exists between them and the publication of *In the American Grain.* The point is that Williams's book exerted an influence that rose from the subsoil of the time in which it was written, and like all work of highly original temper and spirit and clarity it survives the moment of its conception. In this respect the book has something of the same force that generates the work of others, the same brilliance, the same power to shed light in darkened places that we have learned to respect in Marianne Moore's poetry and Gertrude Stein's *Three Lives.*

Another association that *In the American Grain* brings forcefully to mind is the period of critical impressionism in America, that hour in the 1920s when Sherwood Anderson published his notebooks and D. H. Lawrence's *Studies in Classic American Literature* were read. *In the American Grain*, though not resembling either, is of the same moment that lies behind a barrier of critical controversy in American letters dividing this moment from an hour when certain strength was derived from highly individual insights and convictions. A reaction against mere self-expression, mere sensitivity and feeling, came in with the disciples of what was then called humanism. And against this movement came those who sought to clarify the direction that Vernon Louis Parrington had already taken. At this distance the quarrel which now seems older than its years, now also seems to have been one in which its two opposing factors united against a common enemy. The enemy was impressionistic thinking and activity, and in the heat of the moment, all work of personal identity and imagination became suspect. Without entering into the merits and abuses of the controversy, it should now be possible to look behind the dust raised in that hour. During the time of the rising quarrel, everything that had a personal exterior aroused fears and distrust of heresy and was therefore publicly ignored or attacked as the true heresy it was supposed to signify. Through these brief years *In the American Grain* shared something of the public obscurity that was intended to cover the remains of personal heresy and choice. Meanwhile, the book was kept intact for the discerning reader and as it may be read today, it retains its original coloring and a great measure of its purity.

What I have just said is another way of saying that certain recent beliefs and attitudes in criticism have begun to reverse themselves: although the mannerisms of impressionistic criticism have been properly discredited and should not be revived, it is now admitted that the writer cannot shift the very foundations of his beliefs without endangering the verbal truth of what he has to say. It had also been discovered that the raptures and ardors of sudden conversion to any cause, however valid the cause itself may be, seldom, if ever, revive the dying powers of imaginative insight and creation. Human growth is far too slow to admit violent denials of its immediate past, and writers, quite like other human beings, become inept and voiceless should they attempt to deny the continuity of their heritage.

Anyone who has read all of William Carlos Williams's prose and verse becomes aware of its great ability to grow at its own pace. And if anyone is looking for the secret of its good health and the freedom it exerts within an individual speech and manner, it may be found in its determination to "stay at home," to accept the roots of its being and to grow slowly to its full maturity. This radical willingness to accept the limitations of normal growth has given Williams's work a quality that resembles an aspect of life itself; it is a kind of reality that absorbs its own mistakes and shortcomings and should be cited as an example of true well-being.

William Carlos Williams has been referred to as being "sincere," but the difficult question of sincerity in art, which is too often confused with gossip or speculation concerning the personal or public behavior of the man who happens to be a writer, should be referred to the continuity of his imagination and the speech that gives it meaning. We cannot expect to answer so large a question to the satisfaction of everyone, and Paul Valéry has devoted no small degree of his fine intelligence to warn us of the dangers of considering it with any seriousness at all. Yet I believe that the more important difficulties of the question may arrive at a fruitful, if partial solution, by observing the triple unities of speech and imagination and emotion, and of their relationship to each other within a book.

One of the peculiarities of this question is its seeming lack of relevance to classical literatures: that is, it seems absurd to question the sincerity of Homer, of Sophocles, or of Aeschylus, or the authors of *The Palatine Anthology*. In these cases the relevance of the question seems all too clear and certainly naive. What we have learned to respect in the remains of an ancient literature—and these however dimly they may be interpreted and translated—are its elements of unity. In instances where the authorship is obscure, we can at least distinguish between the language of one period and that of another until at last we enter the world of the Middle Ages by way of Rome. The unities of time and of place in the poetic drama tended to strengthen the unities of speech and tradition—and a discernable continuity of ritual and moral attitude answers the question of sincerity before it rises to the surface of the reader's mind.

As we approach the writing of our own time, the question re-emerges in many forms, and however we try to dismiss or slide beyond it, it remains to stir our sense of guilt and to evaluate the writer's integrity. One hears the world "sincerity" used as a term of polite abuse as well as dubious praise: and to us its implications may mean no more than the writer is a good fellow of admirable intentions—give the poor dog the merits of sincerity and let his work be damned. It is sometimes futile to reply that the unintelligent, the insensible, the undiscerning, the unimaginative (if they are writers), are incapable of sincerity in what they write; their relationship to what they say is already compromised before they start; at best they are merely writing with half a voice and half an ear, and their beliefs rest upon such shallow ground that they are meaningless almost before we discover what they are. I suspect that the clear evidence of sincerity in Williams's work is no mere illusion created by his literary personality, nor do I believe that verbal continuity of *In the American Grain* is a fortunate accident. One cannot divorce its theme from the voice that speaks it; and even its lengthy quotations from *Poor Richard* and John Paul Jones derive their pertinence from Williams's entire scheme of presentation.

I also believe that Williams's theme, though for a separate reason, is no less dangerous than the desire to know history or a definition of sincerity which seems so necessary in describing the nature of his work. The old theme of America as a new world to be rediscovered at every turn has rather more than its full share of contradictions. The impulse to make all things new, to build new cities in a clearing of the forest, to abandon projects with the scaffolding in air, to move onward to another El Dorado is a familiar complex of the American tradition. It contains within it the sources of our wealth and poverty, our despair and hopefulness, and it is something that Herman Melville saw before him as he wrote:

> The Ancient of Days forever is young,
> Forever the scheme of Nature thrives;
> I know a wind in purpose strong—
> It spins *against* the way it drives.
> What if the gulfs their slimed foundations bare?
> So deep must stones be hurled
> Whereon the throes of ages rear
> The final empire and the happier world.

It is the "happier world" that seems so often to elude us and is the world Williams so frequently discovers on earth and not in heaven. To make these discoveries seem alive and new also implies the cheerful will to outface the dangers of a theme that grows too large for habitation, and too many writers have already lost themselves in that blue vault in which the images of rebirth and the sensations of becoming are reiterated with alarming regularity. One might almost say that our long continued faith in "the American renaissance" is a habitual response to living on this continent, as though we waked each morning to find a new world stillborn at our door. The faith contains so many apparitions of a dead new world that one is now tempted to respond to them with the same gesture which was implied as John Webster's Duke of Calabria looked down at his dead sister:

> Cover her face; mine eyes dazzle: she died young.

But Williams makes this discovery of his tradition with the insight of a man who walks into a brightly lighted room and there, for the first time, actually sees the things he has lived with all his life. He then makes his selection of what truly belongs to him and discards others; he repairs some pieces that have become chipped or broken, some he adapts to his immediate needs and some he leaves untouched —but all are endowed from this moment onward with the same qualities of suspense and animation that seem to enter an old house as it waits for the arrival of an heir or a new master.

As Williams wrote in his note on poetry which appeared in *The Oxford Anthology of American Literature:*

> In my own work it has always sufficed that the object of my attention be presented without further comment. This in general might be termed the objective method . . . since the senses did not exist without an object for their employment all art is necessarily objective. It doesn't declaim or explain; it presents . . . Times change and forms and their meaning alter. . . . Their forms must be discovered in the spoken, the living language of their day.

Therefore, the earlier chapters of *In the American Grain* are rich in selection from original documents and the continuity of their separate statements is preserved by Williams's quickened adjustment of his own prose to their cadence and imagery.

Within this pattern of selection and commentary I find but one example that seems to betray the moment of time in which the book was written. During the 1920s the general feeling against Puritanism slipped into third gear and ran beyond control. The reasons for it are so well known that they deserve no further defense or contradiction. It is true that one whole side of Puritan culture represents a destructive element in the American tradition and something of its decadence was felt and recognized in Eugene O'Neill's *The Great God Brown.* In itself it contains the ambiguity of Melville's wind that "spins *against* the way it drives" and like the image of that wind it seems to stir hatreds and admirations that are both too vague and too large for hasty discrimination. I would say that Williams's choice of quotation from Cotton Mather echoes the usual cry against the Puritain without revealing the full character of Mather's genius. It contains too little hint of Mather's wit and administrative abilities, and scarcely anything at all of the imagination that created political parables with such memorable skill. Williams is on firmer ground when he writes of the Puritan "spirit" and its meaning:

> And so they stressed the "spirit"—for what else could they do?—and this spirit *is* an earthly pride which they, prideless referred to heaven and the next world. And for *this* we praise them, instead of for the one thing in them that was valuable: their tough littleness and the weight of many to carry through the cold; not their brokenness but their project of the great flower of which they were the seed.

So with an eye that is aware of the reality existing in the fables of history, even to the recording of Washington's famous "reputation for truthfulness," and with a fine perception of the hidden values of sincerity, that kind of truth that is best described in the qualities he attributes to Aaron Burr, Williams creates an atmosphere that many Americans should recognize as home.

I leave the discovery of William Carlos Williams's prose to his readers, yet I cannot resist the temptation to quote the two closing paragraphs of his chapter on Sir Walter Raleigh, for there are few examples in twentieth-century writing equal to its lyricism:

> Sing, O Muse and say, there is spirit that is seeking through America for Raleigh: in the earth, the air, the waters, up and down, for Raleigh that lost man: seer who failed, planter who never planted, poet whose works are questioned, leader without command, favorite deposed—but one who yet gave title for his Queen, his England, to a coast he never saw but grazed alone with genius.

Question him in hell, O Muse, where he has gone, and when there is an answer, sing and make clear the reasons that he gave for that last blow. Why did he send his son into that tropic jungle and not go himself, upon so dangerous an errand? And when the boy had died why not die too. Why England again and force the new King to keep his promise and behead him?

And there is no writer who has perceived the complex figure of Lincoln—whose very name seems always to evoke the worst of histrionic rhetoric and hackneyed gesture—with greater boldness:

It is Lincoln pardoning the fellow who slept on sentry duty. It is the grace of the Bixby letter. The least private would find a woman to caress him, a woman in an old shawl—with a great bearded face and a towering black hat above it, to give unearthly reality.

Since the writing of Walt Whitman's elegy, *When Lilacs Last in the Dooryard Bloom'd*, Williams is, I think, the first American to give the huge, unwieldy myth of Lincoln a new and vivid semblance of reality. A literal reading of Williams's image is, of course, the false one, and the pit of history waits for those unhappy creatures who attempt it.

If, as I believe, *In the American Grain* contained the proofs of a living heritage in American prose some fifteen years ago, it should be said again that it seems even more alive today. And unless I am very much mistaken, that quality of freshness which few poems and fewer works of prose possess will endure within it for many years to come.

1939

GUNS OF THE ROARING WEST: A NOTE ON COWBOY CULTURE IN THE UNITED STATES

As all the world knows well there is a huge, brightly colored plastic figure, large as the Thanksgiving Day puppets in a department-store street parade, which answers to the name of "American Culture." It is a cowboy: it wears a ten-gallon Stetson, a red bandana around its neck, grey fox-haired chaps,[1] a checkered shirt, and five-inch heeled boots with iron spurs, around its waist a holster dangles; it carries guns, two horn-handled, silver-mounted, six-shooters, and slung across its back a Spanish guitar; it drinks and dances, fires its guns and shouts and sings; it never copulates and seldom feeds upon its diet of griddle cakes, salt pork, and beans.

In cinema theaters all over Europe the cowboy is known. Even in Venice, the most singular of southern European cities, and at a hundred paces from Piazza di San Marco, one sees an image of the cowboy on cinema posters bleaching between instructions to vote Communist or anti-Communist or Social Democratic—or in the image of a small boy offering his withered, crushed, yet still green fifty-lire note to a black-shrouded old woman in exchange for a bottle of Coca-Cola. On closer view the child may not be the son of an American tourist, but one of those blue eyed, fair haired Venetian children who under a broadbrimmed Stetson hat and behind simulated fur chaps and plastic water pistols wears a white lace collar and a clean linen Fauntleroy suit of a cut that was worn by his father forty years ago. If Venetian, the child's mature little face, which so strongly resembles the faces of children in Tiepolo's street scenes, makes his outer costume look all the more incongruous and perishable.

If one journeys farther southward to Rome the image of the cowboy costume still persists, and takes on, as all things do in Rome, a golden afternoon glow of historical perspective. In the Via Condotti, in Greco's, a café once visited by Keats and Leopardi and Mark Twain, there is a faded photograph of Buffalo Bill with his ten-gallon Stetson set upon his curls. An elderly Italian nobleman whom I met

[1] The American cowboy is an heir of the Mexican *vaquero* who wore leather *chaparrejos* to protect his legs against the hazards of brush and thorns. See Louis C. Kleber, "The Era of the American Cowboy" in *History Today* (London), May 1972, vol. XXII, no. 5, pp. 338–345.

remembers him, remembers his fine horses, his bareback riding. The Prince, a judge of brilliant horsemanship, holds in his memory of Buffalo Bill a vision of an America he has never visited; the vision squares with frequent views of the Wild West on Roman cinema posters.

The European image of cowboy culture in the United States is logical enough; well-read Europeans of earlier generations found the Leatherstocking tales of Cooper as remote and as romantic as Scott's re-creation of the Middle Ages in *The Talisman* and *Ivanhoe*. To the European the American Indian fighter, the Indian, the cowboy, the two-gun shooting gamblers and sheriffs—all scenes of the American Wild West—held the charms of being barbaric, and of existing outside the laws of everyday behavior. As for scenes that were less romantic, Europe could supply them; and the European vision of cowboys and Indians also served to keep aggressive America itself at a safe distance across the Atlantic; it was more pleasant to think of American cowboys, childlike and active as they always seemed to be, than to reflect on the American as he actually was and is today.

As we come closer to American shores the cowboy is less sharp in outline, less well-formed in his associations than he is abroad. Fifty years ago in the Middle West he existed between the covers of paper-bound books for boys that were sold across the counters of dingy toy and candy shops for a dime. These were shops in "foreign" neighborhoods of the city, in warehouse districts where Poles and Italians seemed to appear on the streets out of nowhere; actually they came from tenements above the shops where goods were sold at wholesale, from cold-water lofts over machine shops, from clapboard shanties near railroad tracks and coal- and lumber-yards. Between the covers of these books the cowboy's adventures were seen in their brightest colors by the foreign-born—to the American child the cowboy's true glory shone only in Wild West shows. The star performer in these was Buffalo Bill himself, and the Wild West show was never literature, but something seen and heard under a canvas top, not quite a rodeo, not quite a circus, yet the excitement of seeing live Indians on horseback and the prospect of shaking hands with Buffalo Bill made the Wild West show a more memorable event than other entertainments on a summer afternoon.

Further Midwestern associations with herds of cattle and the men who corraled and drove them were far less glamorous: the scene was of stockyard squalor, of dust, penned animals, and blood—and a distant cousin of the cowboy (a heavy-shouldered, thick-armed fellow he often was) drove his plunging, bewildered herd from mud-caked pens into the slaughterhouse. The sights, the smells of the stockyards in the valley were enough to make one lose one's taste for beef.

As the Wild West shows declined, the vaudeville stage, the "musical comedy," the newly founded motion picture industries in California revived the image of the cowboy. On the stage in the persons of Fred Stone, a singing acrobat who migrated from playing the "Straw Man" in *The Wizard of Oz* to a lariat-swinging dancing-cowboy show, and of Will Rogers, a specialist in cracker-barrel comment on the news, the cowboy image took on a reputation for double-jointed tap dancing and shrewdly native philosophy. On the stage his guns were no more than props, to be fired off only in moments of extreme hilarity, and in this interval of his mutation the cowboy merged with the figures of Harlequin and the Tramp, the rejected suitor of society, its outcast as well as its genial critic, news commentator, and wit. It remained for the movies to mount him on his horse again, to provide him with a locale of sagebrush, a few miles of desert, and a place where strong drinks were served across the bar.

A timely variation of the cowboy proper came with the figure of the Western bandit, the "bad cowboy" who frequently held up stagecoaches and on rare occasions lived in sin with women. The latter image of Western freedom as opposed to the conventions of Eastern, even Puritanical morality arrived on Broadway in 1906: this melodramatic war of the moralities book place in William Vaughn Moody's play *The Great Divide*, where the heroine represented New England's repressed emotions, and the hero, an Arizona outlaw, signified far Western paganism. It was the first commercial success on Broadway made by an American poet, but it advanced neither his poetry nor his wit; the play was a milestone in the further decline of Moody's poetic sensibilities. Four years later and with less success than Moody's play, Puccini's opera *The Girl of the Golden West*, starring Caruso as a California bandit, had its first night at the Metropolitan Opera House in New York. Neither the genius of Toscanini who conducted the score nor Caruso's phenomenal popularity could save the opera from immediate disaster. Caruso's bulky presence was genially Neapolitan and his voice was far too soulfully near-falsetto to make the image of a Western "bad man" plausible in the public mind, nor did the golden girl, clattering across the stage on horseback in the last act to rescue Caruso from hanging, help the situation. The roaring cowgirl, Puccini learned unhappily, was not another Madame Butterfly.

The failure of the opera did not however retard the success of the "Westerns" in movie theaters. As early as 1914 the long lean features of William S. Hart were magnified upon the silent screen: he brought an image of earnest sadness to the role of the lonely cowboy or reformed "bad man"; the face he wore resembled that of a Methodist preacher at a revival meeting, and like Tennyson's Sir Galahad, "his strength was as the strength of ten because his heart was pure."

The West reflected in the silent films had had its sentimental origins in the verses and stories of Bret Harte, and the world of Bret Harte held at its center the pre-bellum days of the California gold rush. The cowboy migrations westward were a post-bellum phenomenon, but on the screen the two eras were telescoped into a single panorama of Western romance; scenes of barroom fights, of chivalry to girls and women, of campfire loyalties among men, of fear and contempt for the foreigner, the "Heathen Chinee"—all these were the elements, rapidly tossed together, in a Western film. The early days of the movies coincided with the popularity of Zane Grey's Western romances, which sold into the millions in reprint editons.

At the farthest remove from the West itself, in New York, the image of the cowboy acquired at a certain moment something of the simplicity and vividness it has today in Europe, and shorn of its contradictions, its distinctions of being a sheriff or an outlaw, it was an image of being irrevocably American. The moment I speak of was thirty years ago; the scene was a very small, triangular clothing-repair shop fitted into the corner of a decaying building near the waterfront of New York's Chelsea. The tailor was unmistakably Russian Jewish, a pale, clean-shaven little man bent over a sewing machine; he seemed ageless, or rather one of those who reach a meridian of middle age at twenty-five, prematurely bent and shriveled, and who until they arrive at ninety show no further signs of age. Between the racks of clothing against the wall and above his head was a large framed and glazed full-length photograph, retouched with crayon, of himself in cowboy costume. It had probably hung above his head for at least ten years: from the photograph and under the broadbrimmed Stetson, deep, mournful eyes stared at me, but a hint of levity close to a swagger showed in the angle of the thin narrow shoulders, and the fur-chapped legs looked as though they were going to break into a movement of the Cossack dance. Where had the original snapshot been taken? Had it been at Coney Island or on the beach at Far Rockaway? Had a print of it been sent back home to Russia, the visible proof that at last the man beneath the Stetson hat was an American? These were questions I did not care to, did not dare to ask. Something of the madness, the rightness, the irony of Kafka's *Amerika* and of Rimbaud's *Le Bateau Ivre* were in that photograph.

2

The Western trail did not come to an end in 1924; it grew broader, more sinuous, and spread like a multicolored sheet of cellophane across the American continent. One of its colors was rose-pink. The end of the 1920s brought with it the Great Depression as well as the political left-wing policy of the United Front, a front that included young intellectuals of all degrees, novelists, poets, magazine editors, composers, painters, and schoolteachers, down to those who gloried in having no brains at all. The test of one's loyalty to the general cause was sympathy with the vast unemployed, with the underprivileged, and the hope was to achieve a contact, however tenuous, with the people, the mass, the American folk. Such terms as "bourgeoisie" for the businessman, and "kulak" for the American farmer or provincial landowner, were too foreign for general understanding, or, for that matter, political propaganda. The popularity of the Western films offered a possibility; it was quickly assumed that a short cut to the psyche of America could be channeled by re-creating, reinterpreting life on the American frontier. It was argued that the Closing of Frontiers had been followed by the Rise of Capitalism; and of course the frontiersmen, including the cowboy, having been dead for seventy years, had been disenfranchized; these fine, reckless fellows could be looked upon as true Americans, forefathers of a shifting, migrating westward "proletariat." These, then, were the spiritual ancestors of the recently unemployed factory workers, the true folk who made up songs, who had a literature of "proletarian" origin and intention.

I may seem to have oversimplified the left-wing political aspect of the cowboy cult as it appeared in the darkest days of the 1930s, but the left's political directors, since their reasoning emanated from offices in New York, vastly oversimplified whatever they regarded as American history. It was true, too, that the far Southwest with its army of migrant day-laborers, its own contributions to the cause of the I.W.W., its socialist literary heroes, Jack London and Upton Sinclair, was drawn at that time into the left-wing would-be cultural orbit as part of the national United Front. And as if to give half-humorous authority to a left-wing interpretation of American frontier life, its lawlessness as well as its "proletarian" heroism, President Roosevelt's favorite song was *Home on the Range;* it was then convenient to ignore Roosevelt's gift for worldly showmanship and irony. It was forgotten, also, that an earlier, and Republican, President Roosevelt had written a book called *The Winning of the West,* and that during the Spanish-American War Theodore Roosevelt had commanded a troop of cavalry known as the Rough Riders.

But of more importance to the cowboy cult of the present mid-century were school textbooks for children, many of which were written under the influence of a left United Front in education, W.P.A. projects, and expressions of liberal opinion then prevailing. The teaching of American history in grammar schools merged with and shaded into scenarios of Western films and of Lone Ranger programs on the radio; American history was presented as a series of continual migrations across the continent. In a popular illustrated textbook of the 1930s more than one-third of the pictures were scenes of frontier life; it was as though American life from 1492 to 1930 consisted of scripts for fantasies issuing from Hollywood and from broadcasting studios in New York. From these pages one would gather that the imaginative literature of the nation had reached its apotheosis in the songs of Stephen Foster, cowboy ballads, and Negro work songs, and that intellectual progress was to be seen only in terms of building railroads, vulcanizing rubber, the invention of the Morse code, and the successful flight of an airplane at Kitty Hawk; added glories were Whitney's cotton gin, and the Ford car.

It is impossible to say how deeply children responded to textbooks of this kind, for culture on the level of a vigorously promoted cult is so easily acquired that it quickly fades; this view of history was more like a Saturday-night shampoo than an actual penetration of images upon the brain. Rather than a bold misrepresentation of historical facts, the picture these books gave was a blurred, cheerfully vague, swiftly moving panorama of ships and Indians, raccoon-capped pioneers, "underground railroads" for escaping Negro slaves, covered wagons and gold rushes, stagecoach robberies and singing cowboys. It supplemented the more exciting scenes of violent action in movie theaters and the noise of pistol shots and hoofbeats from the Lone Ranger on the radio. Whatever the political intention which came to light in this parade of the American psyche out-of-doors, the faceless heroes depicted were only figures in a migrating army of swarming, antlike pioneers, all members of an imaginary American "proletariat," spontaneous in speech and song and action, and distinguished only by the colorful trappings that they wore. This hero's properties—a horse, a tumbler filled with whisky, a gun, a broadbrimmed hat, or a cap of raccoon skins—were of more importance than the man inside the clothes. In the events through which this hero moved violent action took the place of thoughts and motives, and was a substitute for inner conflicts and moral choices.

The textbook view of history I have just described created a tendency toward a complete cultural vacuum in the American grammar school; the history it portrayed was certainly without depth, without perspective, without individual distinction, without religion, and since the folk hero of the plains lacked human personality, he was as valid between the covers of a "comic book" as he was on the screen or over the radio, which meant that the kind of truth his image contained had little more than the technicolor brilliance of costume melodrama.

3

But what, one may reasonably ask, of the songs that the folk hero sang? And what was their composition? Was the mixture entirely false and meaningless? Through the 1930s textbooks of cowboy songs were published and the burden of their worth was that they proved the existence of an American folk literature; these, so the legend ran, were "the songs that people loved," the hillbilly songs, the work songs, the songs of the mountains and plains. The legend seemed plausible enough: at the full tide of a cocktail party and with the aid of a guitar, the cowboy song was often the prelude for collecting funds to be sent off in the direction of the Loyalist, antifascist cause in Spain, or to Germany, France, or China or wherever a left-wing drive was in the air. The more drinks served, the more authentic, the more appropriate Southwestern songs and music seemed. The music was easy to play and the songs were easy to sing; and the work songs were especially exotic to those who earned their living sitting at typewriters in urban office buildings; the company usually included a few stray academicians, schoolteachers, politicians, newspaper columnists, magazine editors, their wives or their stenographers, a night-club singer, an anthropologist, and a popular writer on Indian folklore.

Such occasions were not merely "democratic" but were conducted with the determination that everything said and done should be exclusively American. Any suggestion that certain foreign elements might be contained within a cowboy ballad or hillbilly song aroused alcoholic anger; one was considered not only disloyal to humanitarian causes, but dangerously unpatriotic. The recent textbooks were sufficient evidence to prove how down-to-earth, how valiantly American, how "proletarian" the singing cowboys were.

But behind the 1930 textbook façade of the Southwestern ballad and the cowboy song, a few trails lead back into historical truth. The first is that the Kentucky mountain melodies have their origin in sixteenth- and seventeenth-century music: some of them echoed from Hampton Court, Woodstock, and Whitehall and some of them in French and Italian strains from the Scottish Queen Mary's Holyrood. This was remembered music from Court festivals in the British Isles, and was carried west and south to what later became American poor white settlements in the Southern hills. The late seventeenth and early eighteenth centuries brought revivals of old Border ballads, and during the latter half of the eighteenth century older songs and ballads were systematically collected along with a few songs of less authentic heritage; some became nursery rhymes, some were reset and almost polished out of existence, and many floated with corruptions of court dances into square dance across the Atlantic to regions which social scientists call "the depressed areas" of the South. The zither took the place of the spinet and the clavichord, and as the music moved westward the Spanish guitar replaced the lute. The flute, and later the mouth organ instead of the Scots' bagpipe, were heard—and the nostalgic, wailing notes of music had within them a memory of a soil that was neither the hills of Kentucky or of Virginia, but of the Scottish highlands and Loch Lomond.

And who was the cowboy? Often enough, since he increased in prominence and in number during the decade following the Civil War, the cowboy was the dispossessed, displaced Southerner, the younger son of an old plantation family or of smaller gentry from farms and hill villages that had slipped downward into ruin; but he could handle a rifle and ride a horse, and he carried with him a long-inherited dream of chivalry. He also took with him still another strain of remembered music which was less pure than the earlier songs and ballads, and this was of the *Irish Melodies* of Thomas Moore whose drawing-room concert tour of the South (he sang his songs prettily to Southern ladies) was not forgotten. The *Irish Melodies* of Moore, all too tactfully reset from earlier Irish music by Moore's friend, Sir John Stevenson, were refined versions of the sentimental ballad sung in London's concert halls; they probably inspired a few of Stephen Foster's airs. But whether they did or not, the songs and ballads that cowboys remembered had three mainstreams of earlier origin: the Scottish Border, the sentimental, latter-day Irish ballad, and English music echoed from the Court as well as from the popular ballads pouring from London's nineteenth-century beer and music halls. One need not stress the point at great length that the cowboy song is not, was not, as "purely American" as it seemed to be, nor was it the original, spontaneous production of Southwestern folk life. The nearest approach to a regional literature in the cowboy's music were a few of his work songs, his cattle calls to herd the beasts, his crooning variations of old songs to soothe them, his snatches of melody sung while guarding camp at night to keep untamed animals away and to keep himself awake.

Claims for a "pure" folk literature have often been exaggerated; the theory that it springs spontaneously from the people is a dream too often held in the minds of politicians who seldom read a book. In the 1930s Communist-fed critics and lesser literati shared that dream. Deeper research into and closer reading of folk songs always points to an elite which originates the songs and inspires variations. The elite may be composed of court poets and composers; it may be the priests or doctors of a tribe; in the civilization that we know, the so-called folk song usually has its source in the commercially inspired music hall and, in the twentieth century, the tin-pan alleys behind Broadway, Sunset Boulevard, and Shaftesbury Avenue, the elite which creates the musical revues, the vendors of synthetic folk-song wares.

The real cowboy had his "sing downs": those who remembered the greatest number of airs, who added words to them or misremembered them at length, became members of an elite at his campfire. After the campfires disappeared, and the cowboy himself, like the cigar-store Indian, vanished, his round-up calls and ballads drifted into the studios of Hollywood and the tin-pan alleys of Broadway; this was a natural course for cowboy songs and ballads to take, and some few of their melodies came home to the sources of their being—came back to the places where folk music is manufactured as the "best loved" songs of the Nation and each lyric is written to "soothe the lonely heart."

Even at best, the cowboy song as it came to the cowboy, and passed through his vocal chords and the strings of his guitar, was a diluted strain of sentiment and longing for a girl and for a place he never saw; the charm of the song was in the Southwestern drawl that accented it, but this was the singer's gift and not the quality of its words and music. One tires quickly of such cultural fare, which is more than half synthetic and too often pale and thin. In such collections the humorous ballads with their rough edges and their crude glimpses of frontier life have the curiosity value of Currier and Ives prints—but all lack the depth of ancient origins. It is foolish to demand greater authenticity for art that was bastard art at the time of its revival in the Southwest and hopeless to build a sense of cultural heritage upon it. Yet it is not without its moments of amusement: I remember hearing from a red-lighted juke box the voice of a Negro night-club singer, singing a version of *Loch Lomond*, a Jacobean song of the same family to which some few of the cowboy ballads originally belonged.[2]

4

Not the least interesting property of the cowboy cult is the aura of chivalry that drapes its shoulders. If the cowboy's memories of songs and dances had been crossbred by transient strains of music-hall origins, his ideals of chivalry were of a distinctly higher order; these ideals however remote they were from his immediate situation

[2] In Sarah Orne Jewett's *The Country of the Pointed Firs* a sane, intelligent, and lightly sentimental description of American "folk songs" may be found: "William mastered his timidity and began to sing. His voice was a little faint and frail, like the family daguerreotypes, but it was a tenor voice, and perfectly true and sweet. I have never heard 'Home, Sweet Home' sung as touchingly and seriously as he sang it; he seemed to make it quite new. . . . It was the silent man's real and only means of expression, and one could have listened forever, and have asked for more and more songs of old Scotch and English inheritance and the best that have lived from the ballad music of the war." Although Miss Jewett's "William" was a New Englander, he accurately reflected the taste in music of his fellow countrymen, and he lived in the decade of the 1870s.

as the shepherd-swain on horseback—and poorly paid—combined the manners of Spanish heritage below the Mexican border and of the plantation families in the American South. He was Don Quixote *in petto* with a drop of Aztec blood plus the image of elder cotton and tobacco gentry before the Civil War; nor was the chivalry of West Point forgotten; in the 1830s and the 1840s, Southern families had been in the saddle at West Point and that memory lent a heritage that was both pious and military.

In gaming, horse trading, and drinking at the bar the ideals of this peculiar set of chivalrous origins persisted; in the person of the unshaven, unschooled herder of wild cattle the ideals may have seemed imaginary, or at the very least innocent enough, but in drink, in barroom scenes, in brawls, affairs of honor mounted to the head, quickened the draw of guns from holsters, and in fistfights and floggings released in the cause of defending the name of a fair, but usually absent lady, the passions and ardors of the Marquis de Sade.

In reality the duties of being a cattleman's wife were stern to the point of exhaustion as well as to the loss of good looks at the age of twenty; abnormally early marriage, frequent childbearing, and the job of housekeeping in a hut or shanty made the prospect of being a cowboy's or even a small ranchman's wife decidedly less lovely than ideal—and since in the face of this prospect women and girls on the frontier were few, the need of keeping the taboos against adultery strong and a girl's name "pure" was proportionally great.[3] Therefore the ideal of a chivalrous attitude toward women flourished. Only in moments of "badness" and on semiannual occasions of receiving pay and drinking in town was the cowboy guilty of permitting "scarlet women" to rob his pockets; in these affairs he was more frequently the victim than the aggressor; his heart and mind were fixed on "the girl back home." In matters of sex the cowboy façade had all the innocence, the "purity," the unworldliness of Don Quixote's crusade. In maintaining that façade, sex was obviously and readily sublimated in the firing of guns and defending cowboy codes of honor by beating an enemy to a pulp on the barroom floor.

As the cowboy image was transformed to the novel of Zane Grey, the movie screen, the semipolitical beer and cocktail parties of the 1930s, the radio, and latterly TV, the cowboy codes of chivalry were strictly upheld; they became accepted as a standard of morality for children. Good cowboys loved their horses and their mothers; they befriended women and children and were kind to their friend and servant who was once their enemy, the Indian (in the Lone Ranger series the Indian was a crude revival of Sancho Panza com-

[3] I am indebted to the researches of Miss Nina Lane for these remarks on the plight of those who married cowboys.

bined with the Noble Savage); they never stole; they spoke truthfully and to the point and were often silent; they were *beaux idéals* of healthy living in the open air; they enjoyed simple food and ate it without undue delay or comment. The image of the remembered and desired girl vanished into an almost abstract and general politeness toward all womankind.

Although sex vanished almost altogether from the cowboy legend, parents of Freudian persuasion encouraged rather than disciplined small boys who in imitation of cowboy habits bought and fired toy pistols at fathers and small girls. The guns, were, of course, instruments of symbolic action: a two-gun child by directing the fire of one gun at an erring parent and the other at a little girl could accomplish the rituals of love and of death (including the mysteries of the Oedipus complex) with the greatest efficiency. Some parents claimed that the dual action introduced young sons to profound understanding of how life begins and ends. Such action it was believed had more directness and deeper meaning than the breaking of furniture, the ineffectual stoning of cats and dogs, the drowning of kittens and the killing of insects. In this fashion the cowboy cult with its violent contradiction in the firing of guns and loud threats of instant death as opposed to long-sustained verbal silences and politeness to women satisfied two extremes of theory in the raising of children.

Advertising agencies which served the manufacturers of patented breakfast food and bread were not slow in grasping the possibility of using the cowboy cult in actually selling their products to children. In addition to sponsoring radio programs which included cowboy scenarios, packaged cereals were sold with Indian and cowboy pictures either concealed within the package or boldly traced outside, of Indian children being shown devouring huge bowls of cereal in perpetuity.

The TV phenomenon of Hopalong Cassidy is of the same genre that produced the Lone Ranger of twenty years ago, and on TV the cowboy image has multiplied; in Eastern cities like New York, retail stores outfitting children feature cowboy and cowgirl clothing in extravagant (and expensive) detail; miniature chaps, Stetsons, boots, belts, leather jackets are in high fashion; and it is obvious today that toy manufacturers make the larger share of their goods in the image of cowboy chivalry.

The commercial support and wide distribution of products adapted to the cowboy cult among children are not surprising to those familiar with the world in which we live. Nor is industrial and commercial adaptability to demands for colorful, and often perishable goods peculiarly American; we inherit from Europe the larger pattern of stimulating, if not always inventing, a popular demand for things that appeal to the naive, the innocent, the immature. It is only in our enormous production and distribution of popular goods to gratify the taste of whatever is called "the common man," his wife and his progeny, even to the third generation, that we seem to excel, and that is why the child-tailored version of the cowboy cult gives the illusion of having attained gigantic proportions.

After all it is not the American child but rather his parents, educators, psychologists, physicians, and entertainers who create his transient and worldly desires for things to see and hear, to know, to buy, to cherish. It is but a short step from presenting education as a form of play to education in the form of shallow, vivid, commercially inspired entertainments. The true importance of the cowboy cult among children and its variations on movie screens and radio and TV programs as well as in children's books and toys is the mirrored reflection of what the middle-aged American wants his children to believe and know.

At the moment the cowboy cult casts its reflections on many aspects of urban and semirural American life. It demonstrates its color and vigor in Western "dude ranches" for the furthering of better mental health and outdoor exercise, where patients are dressed like heroes and heroines of Western films. At the other extreme from cures for arthritis and mild cases of schizophrenia, homosexuals of both sexes wear cowboy dungarees in lower New York's bars and restaurants. And between these extremes, even the most "well adjusted" of unimaginative, lower-middle-class husbands and wives dress in modified cowboy costume on Saturday afternoons. In Midwestern cities and towns on the fringes of the Southwest border motorcar salesmen and politicians pose before newsreel cameras in cowboy regalia. Their stenographers, stenographic pads in hand, are shown in cowgirl costumes, in fringed leather shirts and boots, taking dictation at glass-covered desks. At civic and Rotary Club cocktail and dinner parties the cowboy–cowgirl dress prevails, and it shields from nakedness the robust wives of business executives as well as nightclub dancing girls who have been imported from Hollywood or Newark or New York.

5

It is possible that the thirty-five-year-old cult of cowboy habit, literature, and drama has reached its apotheosis in the United States. Meanwhile the cult offers a wide range of interpretation: in the 1930s it served the purpose of the left-wing cause with the same enthusiasm that it now supports grass-rooted republicanism. Its latest variation among children evokes an earlier pioneer image—the Daniel Boone coonskin cap, so recently worn by a crusading and fatuously smiling politician. Another variant could be the Indian poncho, which for the moment seems to be neglected. The cult may be read as a persistent nostalgia for an American past of open frontiers—the feeling expressed in Cole Porter's song, *Don't Fence Me In.* But even in this interpretation, the meaning is ambiguous; it could be a prelude to spaceship internationalism as well as an extreme of insular national feeling. More than anything the cult expresses the desire to dramatize a brightly surfaced and thin layer of American history, one that can be read at a glance with the mind untroubled by the need of serious understanding or research. It is a pictoral short cut back to the illusion of feeling very much at home in the United States.

As for the cowboy cult in action on the TV screen, it falls into the pattern of TV versions of the Lincoln legend, with the image of the boy Lincoln building wooden w.c.'s in virgin forest clearings. It is of the same genre as that which superimposes F. D. Roosevelt's smile over the grim features of Andrew Jackson and calls this collation of images a portrait of Thomas Jefferson. Beneath the reflected glare and heat of TV spotlights, all thoughts of historical relevance vanish, for history as it is conveyed to us in the cult of the cowboy is strenuously unmemorable, and it usually calls for the aid of alcohol to give it authority and conviction.

In the environs where the cowboy cult has flourished the names of Motley, Prescott, Parkman, and Henry Adams are unknown, even Freeman's mastery of military detail in reconstructing the battles of the Civil War is foreign to the kind of entertainment that the cowboy cult provides. It is probable that the cowboy cult will dwindle in favor of another plastic, easily malleable symbol of American hopes, hilarities, and fears, and within another decade the noise of jet-propelled space rockets on TV sets will drown out, tune out the explosions sounding from the guns of the roaring West.

1954

INDEX